Husbands, Wives, and Lovers

Husbands, Wives, and Lovers

Marriage and Its Discontents in Nineteenth-Century France

Patricia Mainardi

Yale University Press
New Haven & London

Designed by Gillian Malpass

Printed in China

Library of Congress Cataloging-in-Publication Data

Mainardi, Patricia.
Husbands, wives, and lovers : marriage and its discontents in
nineteenth-century France / Patricia Mainardi
p. cm.
Includes bibliographical references and index.
ISBN 0-300-10104-X
1. Marriage in art. 2. Family in art. 3. Arts, French–19th century.
4. Marriage--France–History–19th century. 5.
Divorce–France–History–19th century. I. Title.
NX650.M29M35 2003
700'.4543'094409034–dc21
2003002426

A catalogue record for this book is available from
The British Library

frontispiece
Philibert-Louis Debucourt, "The Casement Window 1" (detail), 1791.
First state, handcolored aquatint with etching and engraving.
Bibliothèque nationale de France, Paris.

endpapers
"In mariage today, why blindfold the eyes? / Even if they were open,
he wouldn't see any better," *Le Colin Maillard*, 1816. Handcolored etching.
Dist. Martinet. Bibliothèque nationale de France, Paris.

Contents

Les Contraires, Nº 4

Ce qu'on voit et qu'on ne devine pas.   *Ce qu'on ne voit pas et qu'on devine*

1   Frédéric Bouchot, "What one sees but doesn't know / What one knows but doesn't see," *Les Contraires*, 4. Lithograph from *Lithographies d'après les dessins de Gaillot*, 1829. Dist. Gobert. Bibliothèque nationale de France, Paris. ("Ce qu'on voit et qu'on ne devine pas / Ce qu'on ne voit pas et qu'on devine")

Preface

It is absurd to say to a young woman: "You shall be faithful to the husband you have chosen," and then to force her to marry a boring old man.

Stendhal, *On Love*[1]

A RECURRENT THEME OF EIGHTEENTH-CENTURY ETCHING and engraving, later transposed into nineteenth-century lithography, concerns "seeing" with titles such as "What one sees but doesn't know" and "What one knows but doesn't see" (Figure 1). The conundrum aptly describes the problems in relating cultural production to social history, my long-term project as an art historian. I start from two premises: that cultural studies must be historically grounded and that the arts represent an important aspect of the study of history. My project is thus always twofold, to show the various ways in which cultural production and historical conditions can inform each other, and, at the same time, to illuminate a particular historical period and specific works of art.[2]

In this study, I focus on the widespread obsession with adultery that characterized the decades following the 1789 Revolution and the revision of family law established by the 1804 Napoleonic Code. This corpus of French law, now called simply the Civil Code, was one of the major accomplishments of the Revolution, replacing numerous regional codes, written and customary, royal and canon. While it represented an advance in governance, subjecting all citizens, at least in principle, to the written, uniform, rule of law, it also preserved and universalized some of the less desirable laws and practices of the Old Regime that defined women's legal status as inferior to men.

The family, as conservative and revolutionary thinkers wrote (and still write), is the basis of the State, and power relations within the family echo those of the polis as a whole. In the late eighteenth century and the early nineteenth, the family as an institution was the site of multiple and highly contested issues, including women's roles, primogeniture inheritance, paternal authority and the establishment of public and private spheres. During these decades, the traditional practice of arranged marriage was slowly giving way to the modern concept of companionate marriage. Despite the perceived advantages of arranged marriages, however, one unwelcome byproduct, as Stendhal pointed out, was adultery, although social concern for this offense did not extend to the behavior of husbands who, traditionally, were free to philander. The disorder represented by female adultery, however, functioned as a lightning rod for many conflicts resulting from the confrontation of Revolutionary ideals with traditional values. Under the new laws of inheritance and paternity, primogeniture was outlawed and all children born into a marriage inherited equally. As a result, adulterine children, another not uncommon and equally unwelcome byproduct of arranged marriages, now represented a real economic threat to the financial stability of families.

Once private morality had become a public issue, relations between husbands, wives, and lovers assumed societal and political significance and provoked impassioned debate, in the cultural arenas of visual and literary production as well as on the floor of the National Assembly. The widespread perception of adultery as a major social problem is, then, a particularly appropriate subject for a study of the ways in which art mediates social experience, rapidly transforming an historical social issue into a cultural theme. The highly contested cultural arena is the crucible in which this transgression assumed complex and contradictory significance. From that fray emerged modern bourgeois family values.

Although my study extends from the late eighteenth century to the mid-nineteenth, its central focus is on Restoration France (1815–30), Waterloo to the July Revolution. Because its dynamic was that of political reaction following revolutionary change, the period offers an ideal moment for a study of cultural transformation, the formulation of new cultural tropes and the revision of older ones. Under the repressive politics of the Restoration, the arts had either to transform their ideological underpinnings quickly or to become overtly oppositional. Antagonisms developed between an official culture, sponsored and subsidized by the State, and its various challengers: the remnants of aristocratic culture, the emergent bourgeois culture, and what would become the oppositional culture of the avant-garde at its moment of genesis in Romanticism. These antagonisms persisted, became endemic, and are still operative today.

The study is organized as a series of monographs, each exploring a different medium, its practitioners, audiences, reception, and themes. In the introduction, I set the scene for this moment of history with its rapidly changing jurisprudence in the decades from the Old Regime to the Restoration. Without this background, one cannot distinguish either the players or, finally, what is at stake in the aesthetic realm. In chapter 1, I move to actual legal cases and introduce some of the men and women whose lives were dramatically altered by the new laws of the Civil Code. The transvaluations quickly called forth a multitude of conduct and advice manuals to assist readers in their attempts to come to terms with the new family values; chapter 2 explores this *littérature conjugale*, as contemporaries called it. With chapter 3, I begin a survey of the changing visual tropes of graphic imagery, from eighteenth-century etching and engraving to nineteenth-century lithography. The point of view of the younger generation of men who saw themselves targeted by the new legislation is important here, as they retaliated with often hilarious caricatures of their elders. Chapter 4 is set in the theater, where the didactic messages emanating from each camp are transformed into the characters of husband, wife, and lover who play out on-stage scenarios fraught with meaning for their audiences. Chapter 5 reverts to home, to the solitary reading of contemporary novels that present more developed characters and plots revolving around issues of marriage and conjugal fidelity. Finally, in chapter 6, I explore the adultery motif in its most abstract form, in paintings whose subjects are from history and literature, but that are, nonetheless, charged with contemporaneous attitudes towards this theme.

As I move from the historical narrative through its transmutation into the highest realms of art, the thread that runs through the plot, as it were, is the attempt to find personal happiness and to define what ideal relations between men and women should be in the modern world. In the ensuing two hundred years, the question has not yet been resolved.

This study began almost three decades ago when, as a graduate student, I saw the exhibition *French Painting 1774–1830: The Age of Revolution* and was astonished by Horace Vernet's painting *Mazeppa and the Wolves* (Figure 91). It was the most bizarre image I had ever seen, and the interpretation presented by the catalogue entry left me unconvinced. The painting became the subject of my research paper in Professor Jack Spector's Romanticism seminar at the Graduate Center of the City University of New York, and, remaining unsatisfied even with my own interpretations, I returned to the theme regularly over the years. The breakthrough came when, in one of those serendipitous events that scholars have come to expect, an erroneous book delivery at the New York Public Library resulted in my receiving Alexandre Dumas's *Mes Mémoires*, wherein I discovered his essay "Cuckoldry, Adultery and the Civil Code."[3] *Husband, Wives, and Lovers: Marriage and Its Discontents in Nineteenth-Century France* is the result of that happy accident, with my original *Mazeppa* study, now greatly revised and expanded, forming chapter 6.

As the project developed, it broadened from art history into related fields. As a result, my debts to friends and colleagues are immense. Many read all or parts of the manuscript at various stages, and much of what is valuable in this study I owe to them; my heart-felt appreciation and gratitude go to Iska Alter, Stephen Edidin, Beatrice Farwell, Jan Goldstein, Sarah Hanley, Herman Lebovics, Catherine Nesci, and Abigail Solomon-Godeau. In my first formulation of the subject, many years ago, Jack Spector and the late Louis Finkelstein offered encouragement and valuable advice, and so I owe them special thanks; they were there at the beginning.

Keeping up with relevant bibliography in several fields would have been impossible were it not for the generosity of many scholars. In addition to those cited above, I warmly thank, in the field of literature, Rachel Brownstein, Wendy

Fairey, Priscilla Clark Ferguson, Joan Ungersma Halperin, John Isbell, Marie-Pierre Le Hir, William B. Long, and Jann Matlock. In jurisprudence, Amira Zahid helped with translations, and the late Bernard Silve not only clarified innumerable points of French law, but presented me with a nineteenth-century copy of the Civil Code that I will always cherish. My colleagues in art history helped in many ways over the years: thank you to Marek Bartelik, Veronique Clagnon-Burke, Marie-Claude Chaudonneret, Elizabeth Childs, William Clark, Madeleine Fidell-Beaufort, Danielle Johnson, Diane Kelder, Dale Kinney, Christine Kondoleon, Susan Koslow, Heather Lemonedes, Régis Michel, Helene Roberts, and Leonard Slatkes. Several historians helped me to clarify and articulate the issues: Leora Auslander, Suzanne DeSan, Rachel Fuchs, Ann Ilan-Alter, Sheryl Kroen, Darline Gay Levy, Gary Marker, Karen Offen, Bryant Ragan, and William Reddy; all deserve some of the praise and none of the blame.

Manuscripts do not become books of their own accord. My happy experience with Yale University Press can be attributed to my editor, Gillian Malpass, her assistant, Sandy Chapman, and to Ruth Thackeray who is the kind of copy editor about whom authors fantasize but are rarely fortunate enough to encounter. Working with them was a pleasure; my heartfelt gratitude to all three.

The project could not have been completed without the ongoing support of the CUNY Research Foundation, whose repeated PSC-CUNY grants enabled me to spend several summers doing research in France. I am grateful also to Irving Lavin for the semester I spent at the Institute for Advanced Study, where I wrote the first drafts of several of the chapters. Thanks to Robert Viscusi and Ethyl R. Wolfe, a year-long appointment as Wolfe Institute Fellow at Brooklyn College, CUNY, allowed me to complete a draft of the entire book.

Over the years, as the project developed, I tried out my ideas in numerous venues, and received valuable feedback and criticism in all of them. Most valuable were my experiences at the University of Chicago History Workshop, the New York Area French History Seminar, and the Columbia University Seminar on Women and Society, whose members read various drafts and offered critiques that ultimately made it a better book. Keynote addresses at the Nineteenth-Century Studies Association Annual Conference, the Middle Atlantic Symposium in the History of Art, and the Interdisciplinary Nineteenth-Century Studies Association Annual Conference provided ideal opportunities for feedback from specialists in the field. I have also had the advantage of conference audiences at the Barnard Feminist Art History Conference and the annual conferences of the College Art Association, the Society for French Historical Studies, and the Colloquium in Nineteenth-Century French Studies. Talks at the Art Institute of Chicago, Alfred University, University College London, the University of Hong Kong, the Santa Barbara Museum of Art, East Carolina University, Smith College, the Sterling and Francine Clark Art Institute, and the University of Michigan, among others, always resulted in suggestions that eventually found their way into the text.

Several of the chapters have been published in various forms. An early draft of part of chapter 3 was published as "Why is Caricature Funny?" in the journal *Persistence of Vision*, having been presented at the 1995 "Humor in the Visual Arts Symposium" sponsored by the Ethyle R. Wolfe Institute for the Humanities at Brooklyn College, CUNY; a thank you to Elizabeth Weis who organized the symposium and edited the journal issue.[4] Some ideas developed at the 1994 "Working on France" Twenty-Fifth Anniversary Symposium of the Maison Française of New York University were published as "Impertinent Questions" in *French Historical Studies*; my thanks to Herrick Chapman who organized the symposium and edited the journal issue.[5] Chapter 6 was published in an earlier version as "Husbands, Wives and Lovers: *Mazeppa*, or Marriage and Its Discontents in Nineteenth-Century France" in Régis Michel's *Géricault*, after being presented at the 1991 Géricault Colloquium at the Musée du Louvre; I thank Régis Michel, who organized the colloquium and edited the anthology.[6] A later version was published as "Mazeppa" in *Word & Image*; thanks to John Dixon Hunt.[7]

Interdisciplinary scholarship is always a collaborative effort. Without these friends and colleagues, this book could never have been written. I hope that this result is in some way commensurate with their generosity.

Since that day when I first saw Vernet's *Mazeppa and the Wolves*, this text has grown in unexpected ways. If I have learned anything in the process, it is how malleable themes are, and how infinitely resourceful human beings can be in the face of adversity. The men and women who laughed and cried over unjust laws almost two hundred years ago still have the power to move us, while the laws themselves are a bare memory.

Patricia Mainardi
Brooklyn, New York
September 2002

Note

I have translated *mariage de raison* throughout as "marriage of reason" instead of "marriage of convenience" to avoid the pejorative sense of the latter; in traditional bourgeois families, a *mariage de raison* was considered a desirable objective. The French word *femme* means both "woman" and "wife"; I have translated it according to context. Where English translations exist I have cited them, although I have often made minor revisions to the texts. All titles and quotations are given in English in the text and in the original language in the notes. Ellipses in square brackets indicate that a word or phrase has been omitted; all other ellipses are as in the original text. Laws are cited by article in the Civil Code or its corollary the Penal Code; since all such texts are identical, I do not cite specific editions, although I include several in the bibliography.

Measurements are given in centimeters for paintings but, following standard convention, are omitted for prints.

In the late eighteenth century and the early nineteenth, French spelling and accents had not been standardized. While the current practice is to modernize older texts, I am not a specialist in the French language, so I have transcribed the texts as I found them, retaining, for example, *enfans* for *enfants*, *aisné* for *aîné*, and *-oient* for *-aient* (as in *seroit* for *serait* or *connoître* for *connaître*).

Introduction:
To Laugh or To Weep

ALEXANDRE DUMAS (1802–70) IN HIS *Mémoires* dated the French obsession with adultery from the promulgation of the Napoleonic Civil Code in 1804. Looking back nostalgically at the Old Regime, he wrote:

> It is true that, in the time of Molière, this was called cuckoldry and everyone laughed about it; in our time it is called adultery and everyone weeps over it.

> Why then is what was called cuckoldry in the seventeenth century called adultery in the nineteenth?

> I am going to tell you.

> It is because in the seventeenth century the Civil Code had not yet been invented.

> The Civil Code? And what on earth does the Civil Code have to do with it?

> What it has to do with it you are about to see.

> In the seventeenth century there were rights of primogeniture, inalienable property rights attached to titles, trusts, and entails. In the seventeenth century, the eldest son inherited a father's name, his title and his fortune; his other sons became knights, soldiers, or priests.

> To these other sons, he gave to the first a Maltese Cross, to the second a leather helmet, and to the third an ecclesiastical collar.

> As for the girls, he didn't even bother with them; they married whomever they wanted if they were pretty, whomever they could if they were ugly. For those who didn't marry either whom they would or whom they could, there remained the convent, that great burial ground of hearts.

> At that time, although three-fourths of marriages were marriages of convenience and were arranged between people who scarcely knew each other, the husband was nearly always certain that his first male child was his own.

> This first male child, that is to say this son, inheritor of his name, his title and his fortune, once he had sired it, what did he care who sired the knight, the soldier or the priest? It was all the same to him, by God; often he didn't even ask. [. . .]

> Things have certainly changed now, damn it all.

The law has abolished primogeniture, and the Code prohibits inalienable property rights attached to titles, trusts, and entails.

The division of the fortune is equal among the children. There isn't even any longer the exclusion of the girls: the girls, like the boys, have the right to inherit from their father.

Then, from the moment when this law established that all children born in a marriage would share its inheritance in equal portions, he cared very much whether these children were really his, because the child who is not at all his, but shares his fortune with those who are, is, plainly speaking, a thief.

And that is why adultery is a crime in the nineteenth century and why cuckoldry was a joke in the seventeenth century.[1]

Dumas's witty essay oversimplifies the issue, as there were marked regional differences in French inheritance law before the Civil Code, the first unified national code of jurisprudence in France.[2] Nonetheless he did identify a phenomenon – the obsession with adultery – that was very real for his contemporaries. During the Revolutionary period the French legal system had been transformed, and throughout the later decades of the eighteenth century an upheaval in family values was indeed taking place.[3] In the decades following the Revolution, cultural production at all levels engaged with these new ideas, upholding, critiquing, or rejecting them. From the cheap lithographs that adorned the open-air stalls along the Seine to the paintings exhibited in the hallowed galleries of the Louvre, from boulevard melodrama to the haughty Théâtre-Français, cultural production both led and followed the social transformations in family structure. If one were to examine post-Revolutionary cultural production in the light of Dumas's analysis, many familiar works would emerge in a new perspective. One would be able to see more clearly their ideological thrust and one could uncover, like archeologists, hitherto unknown strata of the *mentalité* of the epoch. That is what this study proposes to do.

Marriage itself had long been a metaphor for the State, with the husband as king ruling over his wife and children ("the people") or, in a related metaphor, the husband as the head, the intellect, ruling over the wife as the body.[4] In this analogy, adultery was not just an act of disloyalty to one's spouse, but treason, an attack on the social order. As Natalie Zemon Davis wrote in her classic article "Women on Top," female disorder traditionally equaled social disorder – with the adulterous woman one of its prime emblems.[5] When, after the 1789 Revolution, adultery assumed the additional significance of being identified with the life-style of the aristocracy, it played an even more important symbolic role in political discourse.

The place that adultery occupied in the *mentalité* of early nineteenth-century France parallels that played by prostitution in the later decades.[6] The two aspects of female sexuality were often considered interrelated and were sometimes conflated. While "public women" (*femmes publiques*) constituted the lowest levels of prostitution, its upper reaches included the mistresses of the rich and powerful, and even, according to one contemporary, respectably married bourgeois women with lovers.[7] During this earlier period, however, it was adultery, not prostitution, that seared its way into the national consciousness as a major moral problem.

Adultery cannot be understood in isolation, however, for as an issue it goes to the crux of the legal problems surrounding marriage during this period. As the bourgeois marriage based on the nuclear family gained currency during the late eighteenth century and the early nineteenth, the open marriage favored by the aristocracy became increasingly identified with immorality.[8] The immorality of the ruling classes was, in fact, widely identified as one of the causes of the French Revolution, leading to the rigid moral standards (some might say the hypocrisy) of the Restoration period. At the same time, the new emphasis on the companionate marriage in France, which most historians date to the late eighteenth century, encouraged higher expectations of the married state.[9] These expectations clashed with the traditional system of arranged marriages attacked by Enlightenment reformers such as Antoine Caritat, marquis de Condorcet (1743–94), who believed that the inevitable result of such marriages was adultery because, in the absence of divorce, such marriages, although often unhappy, were indissoluble.[10]

After Waterloo (1815) and the return of the Bourbon monarchy, France entered into a period of political reaction when the governing alliance of "Throne and Altar" attempted to reverse many of the reforms of the Revolution.[11] As a result of the ensuing debates and the rapid shifts in law, the transparency of the "natural" was lost, and everything became open to question. When laws change repeatedly within a lifetime, reversing themselves several times, the result is often widespread insecurity and cynicism: once the guise of "normalcy" has fallen away and all theoretical positions must be argued, ideology is revealed in all its nakedness.

During these years, marriage was being culturally redefined: arranged marriages were increasingly perceived as inconsistent with the rights of individuals in the modern world and were gradually replaced by marriages based on mutual attraction. This was not a smooth transition, however, for partisans on both sides of the debate argued continuously over the relative chances of disaster embodied in each marital arrangement. In the cultural warfare that ensued, the arts played an important role and cultural production became blatantly ideological.[12]

This book examines the cultural warfare over the issue of marriage as it progressed from the most literal representations of, or challenges to, the new social order to the most allusive. It looks at the art and literature of the post-Revolutionary period, but first I offer a brief survey (although in greater depth than Dumas) of the legal changes that took place between the Old Regime and Dumas's cynical lament over what he and his contemporaries perceived as the unfortunate results. For whether the legal changes initiated or followed the new values, the fact remains that cultural production of the period was inextricably bound up with the new system of values articulated by the Civil Code and dependent on it for meaning.

Old Regime

> Every man is king in his home.
> Old French proverb[13]

In every political system there is a delicate ecology of social interrelationships enabling the system to function as a whole. While this study focuses on the obsession with adultery that developed in the early nineteenth century, this issue cannot and should not be considered in isolation from the rest of family law, including codes governing marriage, children, inheritance, separation, and divorce. Before the 1789 Revolution, French law consisted of different regional codes and common-law traditions. Family law was a combination of royal law, canon law, and local custom, with the customary laws of each region differing widely and a gradual erosion of Church jurisdiction in favor of the State.[14] The one point of convergence of all the legal codes was that marriage was indissoluble and that, in keeping with Catholic religious doctrine, there could be no divorce, although separations were allowed in certain extreme cases. Dumas's insouciant depiction of life in the Old Regime did have some validity for the propertied classes, where the sole purpose of arranged marriages was to produce a male heir, after which the spouses often led separate lives.[15] Regardless of class, however, whatever personal freedom a woman enjoyed was held on sufferance and not on legal rights. A woman remained under the legal authority of her father or husband, or even her brother or uncle if they were her closest male relatives.

Under the Old Regime, children did not reach the legal age of majority until they were twenty-five (women) or thirty (men). Until that age they could not marry without parental consent, and their wages and property were held in usufruct by their father. He could betroth them from the age of seven, although the legal age of marriage was twelve for girls and fourteen for boys. Marriage was a union of two families as much as of two individuals.[16] Although women and children were severely disadvantaged in the legal system, in the upper classes family disputes could bypass the legal system altogether through the use of *lettres de cachet*. Originally a royal prerogative intended to place the king above the law, this privilege had been extended gradually to the family head, usually the father. Such documents, ordering imprisonment for arbitrary periods of time, could be obtained without a hearing or showing cause; adulterous or spendthrift wives and disobedient children were the usual victims. *Lettres de cachet*, intended to avoid the scandal of court procedures, were denounced throughout the eighteenth century, and, like the Bastille, became an important symbol of arbitrary and unjust power.[17]

Marriage was the institution that most defined women's lives. In his *Marriage and the Family in Eighteenth-Century France*, James Traer traced the conception of marriage in France from the "traditional" or "patriarchal" family, where the power resided with the husband/father, through its challenges by Enlightenment philosophers and their heirs, the revolutionaries. Sarah

Hanley has defined the "marital-regime" analogy at the basis of French family law as "a system of governance coupling husband and king, dowry and domain, household and state, on parallel governing tracks."[18] The authority of kings was thus extended to husbands and fathers.

During the Enlightenment, new ideas of the value of the individual arose, leading to a call for egalitarian relationships within the family, for companionate marriage, the freedom to choose one's spouse, and for the right to personal happiness, even if that meant divorce. The idea of marriage based on romantic love instead of familial ambition, what was called *mariage d'inclination* as opposed to *mariage d'intérêt* or *mariage de raison* was new in France, for the courtly love tradition had always regarded love and marriage as mutually exclusive.[19] Enlightenment philosophers proposed the novel idea that bonds of affection and not duty should hold the family together.[20] While reformers felt that the marriage for love, being freely chosen, would eliminate adultery, such *mariages d'inclination* were nonetheless viewed with suspicion by all classes.[21] From the aristocracy to the bourgeoisie, among artisans and peasantry alike, arranged marriages (Figure 2) were an accepted family strategy for amalgamating wealth, whether that wealth was defined as land, titles, businesses, or simply cash. In addition to these material benefits, tradition held that

2   Grandville, "A Marriage of Reason," *Les Métamorphoses du jour*, 28, 1828–29. Handcolored lithograph. Lith. Langlumé, Dist. Bulla. Bibliothèque nationale de France, Paris. ("Un mariage de raison")

Les Métamorphoses du Jour.   n.º 37.

J. Grandville del.   Lith. de Langlumé.

Et dans cette demande en séparation, Messieurs, observez bien deux choses.

3   Grandville, "And in this plea for separation, sirs, observe well two things," *Les Métamorphoses du jour*, 37, 1828–29. Handcolored lithograph. Lith. Langlumé, Dist. Bulla. Bibliothèque nationale de France, Paris. ("Et dans cette demande de séparation, Messieurs, observer bien deux choses")

the mutual esteem and respect said to result from these "marriages of reason" was a more solid foundation for a lifetime union than was passionate love, always considered fleeting and unstable. Marriage for love was simply not part of this equation.

This rationally conceived universe could not prevent human beings from seeking love, so adultery was a constant concern (Figure 3). While canon law recognized adultery as equally offensive to marriage whether committed by husband or wife, and allowed either spouse to sue for separation on such grounds, civil case-law favored the husband.[22] In the mid-eighteenth century, the renowned French jurist Robert-Joseph Pothier (1699–1792) compiled and systematized French laws, legal decisions, canon and Roman law into a series of treatises that later served as model for the Civil Code.[23] Pothier's influential *Treatise on the Power of Husbands over the Person and Property of Their Wives* (1768) discusses marriage, separation, and adultery. His first sentence is: "Marriage, by establishing a community of husband and wife, where the husband is the head, gives to the husband, in his role as head of this community, a right of domination over the body of his wife that extends to her property as well."[24] The first article of this treatise states: "The dominance of the husband over his wife consists, by natural law, in the husband's right to exact from her all the duties of obedience due to a superior."[25] Pothier invoked early Roman law, where the power of the paterfamilias over his wife, children, and household was so immense that it extended even to the power of life and death. Although classical Roman law provided more equality between spouses, and even allowed divorce, Pothier and other legal authorities preferred to cite as antecedents the earlier codes where women had virtually no legal rights, were unable to enter into contracts, sue in courts, bequeath property, or exercise the rights of citizens.[26] Pothier's apology for the unequal application of law to husband and wife (although he stopped short of advocating the power of life and death) is worth citing in its entirety because it emerged time and again in French jurisprudence, and was eventually canonized in the Civil Code:

> Adultery committed by the wife is infinitely more injurious to the proper organization of civil society since it tends to plunder the family and result in the transference of property to adulterine children who are alien to it. Adultery committed by the husband, however, although extremely criminal in itself, is, in this regard, without consequence. Furthermore the wife, who is an inferior, does not have the right to police the conduct of her husband, who is her superior. She must assume that he is faithful, and jealousy must not lead her to investigate his conduct.[27]

A decade later Jean-François Fournel (1745–1820) compiled a *Treatise on Adultery in Jurisprudence* (1778) consisting of excerpts from Pothier, who had, in turn, adapted Justinian's Novelle 134.[28] Justinian's law was observed in France from 1523 to the 1789 Revolution (minus the provision on flogging errant wives). Fournel set forth what had become the standard provisions of case-law practice:

(1) A woman convicted of adultery is relegated to a convent;
(2) Her husband takes her property and dowry;
(3) For two years (or whatever the court decides) her husband can visit her and take her back, and during this time she wears secular dress;
(4) After two years, if her husband does not take her back, her head is shaved, she is veiled, forced to don a religious habit, and must live in the convent for the rest of her life;
(5) Even in this case, however, her husband can take her back at any time;
(6) Her accomplice will be fined, banished, or even sent to the galleys, according to the gravity of the crime.[29]

Justinian's draconian punishment for a wife's adultery had been somewhat mitigated by his approval of divorce, but it should be noted that French legal scholars, while invoking the authority of Roman law for accreditation, freely omitted any provisions with which they disagreed.

During the Old Regime, punishment for the wife's adulterous "accomplice" was arbitrary, depending on his age and class. The lower his status *vis-à-vis* hers, the more severe his punishment. The most severe punishment, even death, was reserved for male household members convicted of a liaison with their master's wife; this class included clerks, secretaries, and tutors, as well as music, dance, and drawing teachers, and, of course, domestic servants.[30] While extreme punishment was rare, it nonetheless existed as a powerful deterrent in the cultural *imaginaire* of several centuries. In marital matters, a husband enjoyed royal prerogatives in that only he could pardon his wife, while his adultery was not even a punishable crime. Voltaire (1694–1778) ridiculed this moral inequality in his *Questions on the Encyclopedia* (1772) by imagining a wife turning the tables on her adulterous husband and threatening to have him condemned, his head shaved, and his property seized.[31]

In the Old Regime, the resolution of family and marriage disputes was divided between religious and civil courts, but adultery cases went to civil courts alone. While husbands and fathers could take the public route through the court system, it was often fraught with scandal: *lettres de cachet* provided simpler solutions, allowing the offender to be quietly incarcerated without either legal proceedings or public scandal. Convents were the usual depots for cast-off wives, but for those in the lower strata, hospices such as Bicêtre or Salpêtrière became prisons for misbehaving wives as well as for invalids, the insane, and the homeless. A pension to cover room and board had to be paid while a wife was imprisoned but, in recompense, the husband retained control of his wife's dowry.[32] In light of this, Pothier made very clear in his *Treatise on the Contract of Marriage* (1768) that husbands benefited far more from a wife's imprisonment than from a suit for separation, for a wife granted separation regained control over her own property, albeit only through the proxy of a judge, lawyer, or male relative.[33] Adultery suits were, in fact, often the vehicle used by a husband to stop his wife's suit for separation, as discussed in chapter 1.[34]

Despite these severe laws, by the late eighteenth century prosecutions of wives for adultery, while still legal, had come to seem like bizarre symbols of injustice. Voltaire wrote that a husband who instituted a criminal process against his wife on these grounds would be accused of barbarity.[35] Sarah Maza has pointed out that, in the years leading up to the 1789 Revolution, familial and matrimonial cases repeatedly called into question the nature of the social contract, their notoriety as *causes célèbres* helping to undermine the Old Regime.[36]

This was the legal reality in Old Regime France. Since statistics are incomplete and fragmentary, there is no way of ascertaining how often its laws were invoked or applied.[37] Nonetheless, as can be seen by the storming of the Bastille, the hated symbol of injustice that by 1789 stood virtually empty and unused, symbolic value often outweighs statistical reality. What is certain is that adultery in France was legally a private matter, to be negotiated by husbands with the authority of the judicial system, but, in the face of increasing public notoriety, disapproval of the punishments meted out to wives had become more and more vocal.

The Revolutionary Period

The Revolutionary program of reform arose directly from the writings of the Enlightenment philosophers. Since the late seventeenth century and through the eighteenth, the power of husbands had been increasingly equated with tyranny, despotism, and even slavery. In the decades leading up to the 1789 Revolution, the power of husbands and fathers was also associated with the monarchy, and, as a result, many of the Revolutionary reforms of family law were designed to curtail their authority.[38] Indeed Lynn Hunt has even proposed that one could view the entire Revolutionary episode as a "family romance" in the Oedipal sense of the sons attempting to eliminate and replace their fathers.[39] The Revolutionary project of family reform emphasized individualism and egalitarianism, with the replacement of duty by affection. Revolutionaries wanted to abolish *lettres de cachet*, secularize marriage, legalize divorce, lower the age of majority, and establish equal inheritance among children by abolishing primogeniture and ending distinctions between legitimate and illegitimate children. Overall, their intention was to diminish the power of fathers over family members, as well as the power of the Church over every aspect of life. If the family was now to be a site of greater equality, so too would be the new State; the marital-regime analogy would continue to function, but both entities would now be transformed into more egalitarian social units.

Perhaps the most glaring inequality in need of reform was the inheritance laws. Before 1789 France had numerous regional customs and laws. Primogeniture was customary both for the aristocracy and the peasantry because both classes wanted to preserve their lands undivided, and aristocratic titles were attached to estates. Daughters often received a dowry instead of an inheritance, but in some regions of France they might receive nothing at all. In many regions parents could legally favor one child over another. As a result, after the Revolution the attack on primogeniture came from all classes, and, as Suzanne Desan has noted, the issue of inheritance received more attention than any other.[40] The *cahiers des doléances* vociferously demanded equal inheritance rights, and so the revolutionary legislation guaranteeing equality of inheritance, still in effect today, was established by law on March 15, 1790.[41] At first this was only among the former nobility whose titles had been abolished shortly after the Revolution, but on April 8, 1791 equality of inheritance was decreed for all intestate cases.[42] This was a clear departure from past practice. By March 7, 1793 equal inheritance had become law throughout France, was extended to all offspring including illegitimate ones, and was made retroactive to July 1789.[43] Even adulterine children were entitled to inherit one-third of the legal share they would have received had they issued from a legal marriage.[44] Although the law's primary intention was to break up large estates and spread wealth more equitably, nonetheless daughters benefited. Other Revolutionary legislation allowed women to maintain control over their dowries and to enter into contracts without their husband's consent. The inheritance rights of the surviving spouse, male or female, were diminished, however. During the Old

Regime, the surviving spouse was usually guaranteed *jouissance* or usufruct of community property during his or her own lifetime, but by the rules of 1793 and 1794, half the deceased's estate, at most, could go to the surviving spouse, with the rest going directly to the children.[45] The surviving spouse had usufruct only if it was specified in the marriage contract. Widows were the primary losers under this law, still in effect today, since they could be obliged even to vacate the communal dwelling.

Lettres de cachet were another popular target for reform. Their use had already been limited in 1784, but abolishing them altogether was one of the first projects of the National Assembly, which began studying the question in the fall of 1789 and outlawed them on March 26, 1790.[46] Shortly thereafter, family courts, the *tribunaux de famille* were established to settle disputes privately within families.[47] These family courts functioned fully, arbitrating disputes between husbands and wives, fathers and children, only between August 16, 1790 and February 28, 1796. After 1796 their functions were limited to divorce cases and those involving orphans and minors, and they were abolished altogether in 1804 when the Civil Code was promulgated.[48] The idealistic concept of creating a court based on the new non-hierarchical family, united by bonds of love and not of authority, had lasted less than six years.

The contradictions of a Revolutionary program that espoused conflicting conceptions of women's rights manifested themselves from the beginning. The Constitution of 1791 proclaimed that "the law considers marriage only as a civil contract," and, of course, all civil contracts could be dissolved by mutual consent.[49] The same Constitution of 1791 was the site of a major controversy over adultery. Its proposed article 13, "On the Municipal Police," attempted to reinstate Old Regime laws on adultery, but was even more draconian.[50] The proposed article retained the Old Regime principle that only husbands would be empowered to bring a charge of adultery while being themselves exempt from any such charge, but it appended the provision that on conviction there would be a minimum one-year prison sentence for the wife and three months for her accomplice, and to that added a financial bonus, unparalleled even in the Old Regime: the husband could now seize not only his wife's dowry, but one-eighth of her accomplice's fortune as well. In Old Regime France, the husband had been entitled to seize only his wife's dowry. In her address to the National Assembly in the summer of 1791, Etta Palm d'Aelders (1743–99) called it "the most unjust thing done in barbarous centuries."[51] Even men agreed with her. Louis-Jean-Henri Darnaudat, the deputy from Béarn, demanded its withdrawal, stating "The penalties proposed by the committee are unquestionably much milder than those decreed by the former laws, but I still find them unjust because, from what we know of society, it would most certainly be true to state that men are often much more guilty than women."[52] Adrien-Jean-François Duport, the deputy from Paris, added "injustice would persist if, after we have so well established the rights of men in this social contract, we were to forget or neglect the rights of women."[53] After these speeches, to applause great enough to be noted in the official record, the Assembly voted to send the offensive article 13 back to committee, where it quietly expired.

Revolutionary sentiment followed that of the Enlightenment in questioning the unequal application of law to men and women. Louis de Saint-Just (1767–94) challenged the traditional arguments for unequal punishment expounded from Justinian through Pothier and Fournel, when he wrote: "I would like someone to explain to me once and for all why a husband who deposits adulterine children in someone else's family, or in several other families, is less criminal than a wife who places only one such child in her own family."[54] While Revolutionary idealism pushed forward towards equality of rights for women, centuries of tradition simultaneously pulled back, towards the preservation of male privilege and the reinstatement of women's inferior legal status. It is a dialectic that has been repeated often subsequent revolutions. In the 1790s the result was that, in the face of conflicting demands, the Revolutionary laws maintained a discreet silence on the subject of adultery.

On September 20, 1792 the National Constituent Assembly took an unprecedented step, by voting a law authorizing divorce.[55] It specified numerous grounds for the dissolution of marriage, including mutual consent, incompatibility, mental illness, cruelty, abandonment, moral depravity, or emigration, and at the same time it abolished separations. It did not mention adultery. Although this move was progressive, as the case-law practice of the Old Regime with its severe punishments for a wife's infidelity was thus eliminated, Sarah Hanley has argued that this silence actually protected male interests since it eliminated one of the major grounds on which wives could bring a divorce suit "for cause" and thus ensure a division of community property.[56] The economic results of divorce were extremely negative for women, but, even so, women formed the primary constituency for the new divorce law. Statistics are fragmentary, but there were an estimated 30,000 divorces in France from 1792, when the law was instituted, to 1803 when it was changed (Figure 4).[57] Although many divorces were no doubt formalizations of long-standing separations or abandonment, nonetheless it is striking that divorce seekers were predom-

4 Pierre-François Legrand, "Republican Divorce," 1793. Etching in wash technique. Bibliothèque nationale de France, Paris. ("Le Divorce républicain")

inantly women. In urban centers, where single women could more easily find
lodging and employment, women comprised over 70 per cent of divorce plaintiffs. Something was obviously very wrong with the institution of
marriage.

The Civil Code

> Fathers and grandfathers are always magistrates in their families.
> Portalis, "Discussion of Issues in the Bill on Marriage, Forming
> Title v of the Civil Code, Presented on 16 ventôse, an xi"[58]

The project of reforming and systematizing all the laws of France into a national
code was begun immediately after the 1789 Revolution, but the Civil Code was
not completed until the early years of the nineteenth century, and was not promulgated until 30 ventôse, an xii (March 1, 1804).[59] Its name was changed to
the Napoleonic Code (Code Napoléon) in 1807, but this honorific was eliminated at the Restoration. Its corollary, the Penal Code establishing punishments
and penalties in accordance with the provisions of the Civil Code, became law
on January 1, 1811. The Civil Code was largely the work of four men, François-
Denis Tronchet (1726–1806), Jacques de Maleville (1741–1824), Félix-Julien-
Jean Bigot de Préameneu (1747–1825), and Jean-Etienne-Marie Portalis
(1746–1807), all trained in the law, all appointed by First Consul Napoléon
Bonaparte.

The Code they produced reversed many of the reforms of the Revolutionary
period.[60] From a combination of new statutes and the most restrictive regional
laws and customs, they generalized and standardized the incapacity of married
women. Pothier's *Treatise on the Power of Husbands over the Person and Property of Their Wives* was incorporated into the Civil Code virtually unchanged.[61]
Why this happened has been one of the most difficult questions of the period
and one that was largely ignored until female historians took it up. Sarah
Hanley has described this period as a complex one during which continued
adherence to male right and "presumptive female blame" finally caused the
radical social and political promises of the French Revolution to "stagger off
course."[62] Lynn Hunt sees the progress of the Revolution as a logical development, pointing out that, while early Revolutionaries had been opposed to the
rule of fathers (paternalism), they were not necessarily opposed to the rule of
husbands or of men in general (patriarchy).[63] In this light it is not surprising
that when the time came to consolidate and rationalize the various laws that
had been enacted piecemeal during the tumultuous Revolutionary decade, the
resultant Civil Code preserved the principle of male rule. James Traer has interpreted this by emphasizing instead the continuities of the Civil Code with Old
Regime legal codes, pointing out that, despite the preservation of male rule,

there were some areas of improvement in women's civil status.[64] What is generally accepted in all these readings is that women's rights were rarely a matter of conviction followed by the Revolutionaries who seized power. The rights of women were proclaimed when necessary, abandoned when convenient, a cynical strategy that has been followed in revolutions ever since the eighteenth century.

The Civil Code suppressed women's rights that had barely become established during the preceding decade. A woman could no longer enter into contracts, plead in court, or control her own property. She was legally obliged to live wherever her husband chose, and divorce was further constricted. Children fared little better. The age of majority, thirty for men and twenty-five for women during the Old Regime, had been reduced during the Revolutionary decade to a uniform twenty-one, with children no longer needing parental consent for marriage.[65] The Civil Code, while keeping the female age of majority at twenty-one, raised it for men to twenty-five. No one could marry without parental permission before the age of majority, and until then the father controlled property and income in usufruct. The Code also reinstated a limited form of *lettre de cachet*: fathers could have their children confined for up to six months without having to justify their reasons.

The Revolutionary laws had established equality among all children, legitimate and illegitimate, but, under Civil Code article 312, marriage became the only legal source of paternity, harking back to the Roman principle *Pater is est quem nuptiae demonstrant* (the father is the one indicated by the marriage). The Code retained the Revolutionary laws establishing equal inheritance among children, but now limited that right only to legitimate children. A married man was now forbidden to recognize his adulterine child legally. Such children would have no inheritance rights whatsoever and would be forced to bear throughout life the shameful civil status of "adulterine child," more humiliating than the "natural child" status of illegitimate children. During the Old Regime, a married man had been permitted to recognize an adulterine child, and a single woman could use the legal concept of *recherche en paternité* to bring a paternity suit forcing the father to pay child-rearing costs. Under the Civil Code all paternity investigations within or without marriage were forbidden (Figure 5). Within marriage, as Dumas noted, a husband was legally the father of whatever children his wife bore. While this benefited married women, both because the paternity of their own children could not be questioned, and because a husband's assets could no longer be requisitioned to pay for the maintenance of his illegitimate children, unmarried women had no legal recourse at all for child support. Unmarried men, however, were permitted to recognize their "natural" children, should they wish to do so.

The liberalism of the divorce law of 1792 had been challenged from its inception by royalists and social conservatives who saw in it the potential for family breakdown that would lead, they were convinced, directly to social breakdown.[66] In 1803 this divorce law was repealed and replaced by the more restric-

Les Métamorphoses du Jour.   *N̶49.*

Oh ! c'est positif, ma chère, la recherche de la paternité est interdite.

(Code Civil, art 341)

5   Grandville, "Oh, it's certain, my dear, paternity investigations are outlawed. (Civil Code, art. 341)," *Les Métamorphoses du jour*, 49, 1828–29. Handcolored lithograph. Lith. Langlumé, Dist. Bulla. Bibliothèque nationale de France, Paris. ("Oh! C'est positif, ma chère, la recherche de la paternité est interdite. [Code civil, art. 341]")

tive one of the Civil Code, greatly limiting the grounds for divorce and, for the first time, writing an adultery law into French jurisprudence.[67] The husband could now divorce his wife for adultery, but the wife's options in similar circumstances were limited to one extreme case: she could divorce her husband for adultery only if he maintained his "concubine" (as the law termed her) in their conjugal dwelling. Women had earlier been the principal plaintiffs in divorce but, after these changes, the numbers dropped from an estimated 30,000 in the decade 1792–1803 to 2500 in the period 1803–16.[68]

On November 15, 1808 the Conseil d'état discussed the important project of bringing the Penal Code into alignment with the Civil Code. The problem of adultery prosecutions posed many difficulties, as comte Regnaud de Saint-Jean-d'Angely (1762–1819) pointed out:

> In this bill, we, in effect, return to the system of ancient law. In former times divorce was not allowed. In consequence, the law permitted the husband to prosecute his adulterous wife without breaking the ties that unite them. He could even take her back, and by so doing abrogate her punishment.

The Napoleonic Code, on the other hand, supposes that the punishment for adultery would be decreed against the wife only after her husband has obtained a divorce and that the evidence of her crime would have been gathered during the divorce procedures.

It is to this principle that we ought to restrict our discussion: prosecution for adultery ought to be permitted only as part of a divorce action. It would be scandalous if a husband had his wife condemned as unfaithful, but nonetheless did not want to break with her.[69]

In the discussion that ensued, comte Jean-Baptiste Treilhard (1742–1810) disagreed with this sentiment, insisting that "We must leave the husband free to chastise her without either divorcing her or separating from her."[70] No one present questioned the harsh punishments proposed for women; on the contrary, the presiding member of the committee, "His Royal Highness the Prince Archchancellor of the Empire" (Eugène de Beauharnais, 1781–1824), considered the proposed penalties too lenient: "It seems also to His Royal Highness that a crime which has consequences as disastrous as does adultery ought to be punished with a sentence more severe than imprisonment from three months to two years."[71]

As these men drafted the Code, their concerns were twofold. Insofar as they were husbands, they wanted to punish adulterous wives and their lovers, but they also wanted to maintain their own freedom to indulge in extramarital affairs with impunity. While there was general agreement on the necessity of severely punishing guilty wives, what if the husband himself committed adultery with a married woman? His Royal Highness the Prince Archchancellor of the Empire worried that "This referral [to the criminal courts] would be all the more inappropriate if the accomplice accused of adultery held a distinguished State position."[72] A wife's adultery had traditionally been seen as a crime against her husband, with prosecution left to his discretion. Because the Conseil d'état wanted the most stringent legislation possible, however, it even entertained a proviso that a husband who ignored his wife's adultery could then be accused of collusion in the crime. At issue here was the legal question of whether adultery was a private crime only against the husband, which he alone had the right to prosecute, or whether it was a crime against the State, which then had the obligation to prosecute the wife, her lover, and even her husband if he neglected his duty to maintain order in his household. Assigning the problem to the husband's discretion gave him infinitely more power, truly making him a magistrate in his own household, but it also weakened society's justification for prosecuting this "private" offense. Defining a wife's adultery as a crime against the State, which had an overriding interest in preserving family order, strengthened the jurisprudential basis for legislation but weakened the husband's authority, and might even leave him open to prosecution for complicity. As the Prince Archchancellor said: "It would be most unfortunate if a senator, a State councilor, a judge, could be summoned before the tribunals on a mere suspicion of collusion."[73]

On February 10, 1810 Louis-Joseph Faure (1760–1837) presented the conclusions of this Conseil d'état to the Corps législatif, summing up the arguments and reaching conclusions that often reiterated those of Pothier half a
century earlier:

> Among the offenses to morality is included the violation of the marriage
> pact, whether this offense be committed by the wife or by the husband. The
> adultery of the wife is a much greater offense because it leads to graver con-
> sequences and could bring a child into a legitimate family who is not in any
> way the offspring of the man who is its legal father. The Penal Code, in spec-
> ifying the punishment that should be decreed against the wife, has only made
> it conform to article 298 of the Napoleonic Code, this Code that is praised
> everywhere for its most religious respect for morality: it carries an impri-
> sonment handed down by the correctional police of three months minimum
> to two years maximum.
>
> It will be recalled that in the bill, in article 309 of this same Code, the
> husband is given the authority to suspend this sentence by consenting to take
> back his wife. In effect, the wife is guilty only towards her husband; he ought
> then to have the right to pardon her.
>
> If the wife is guilty only towards her husband, then only he has the right
> to prosecute her; these charges ought then to be prohibited to anyone else,
> because no one else has any standing or concern in this matter.
>
> Furthermore, the husband would be barred from initiating this procedure
> if he himself has been condemned for adultery. In this case the law would
> reject him as unworthy of trust because, since he can be convicted of adul-
> tery only on the complaint of his wife, as we have seen, it is very much to
> be feared that he might seek revenge.
>
> The accomplice of the wife will be condemned to the same penalty, and,
> in addition, to a fine.
>
> With regard to the prosecution of the husband for adultery, it can take
> place only on the charge by the wife, because she alone is concerned with
> the infidelity of her spouse. The wife can enter this complaint only when he
> has maintained his concubine in their conjugal dwelling. In all other cases,
> the investigation would often degenerate into an inquisition: but in this one
> allowed by the law, the offense is common knowledge. This is in the same
> spirit as the Napoleonic Code, which allows the wife to demand divorce for
> the adultery of her husband only by presenting the same evidence with regard
> to the concubine. As for the offense, it will be punished by a fine.
>
> The law of 1791 was silent on the violation of the marriage pact by the
> husband or the wife. The provisions of the new Code will correct this
> omission.[74]

And thus the Civil Code reversed the silence of the Revolutionary period. For
women, the Civil Code represented an even further retreat from the Revolutionary ideals of equality. It re-established the case-law practice of the Old

Regime, now canonized into law, punishing the adulterous wife and once again designating the husband as the ultimate arbiter. Sentences were now limited, however, to fixed terms; the husband could no longer leave his wife imprisoned in a convent for the rest of her life, but merely for two years for the first offense, with the sentence doubled for each new instance of recidivism.[75] The Penal Code also established – for the first time – a new privilege for husbands. Its article 324 stated: "Murder committed by the husband of his wife, as well as of her accomplice, at the moment when he catches them *in flagrante delicto* in their conjugal dwelling, is excusable."[76] Under Old Regime law, he did not have this right, and, although the courts might well have shown leniency towards such a crime, the murder would at the least lose him the right to inherit her property. The Napoleonic Code eliminated this safeguard, judging that such a murder was "excusable violence" and leaving open the possibility that the murderer could inherit from his victim.[77] It also established standard punishments for the wife's lover for whom, in the Old Regime, punishment had varied according to his social status. In the past he had rarely been prosecuted, at most merely fined. The provisions punishing the wife's lover fell heaviest on young men of good family, who were traditionally initiated into the rites of love and advanced in their careers by older married women.[78] Now they would lose their special privilege under the law, and would be treated as common criminals.

In the case of divorce for adultery, a judgment that fell almost exclusively on the wife (since the husband was virtually exempt from prosecution), the Code prohibited the guilty party from ever marrying the accomplice.[79] The proviso barring the husband from prosecuting his wife for adultery if he himself had been condemned for the offense was new, but since it was virtually impossible for the wife to win such a suit, it was insignificant. One improvement under the Code was that the adulterous wife did not lose her dowry upon conviction, as had been the case under the Old Regime.[80] Her husband did, however, maintain control of it, whether she was convicted, in prison, or happily married and living at home.[81]

The real winners under the new Code were fathers and husbands: one might even say that *puissance paternelle* and *puissance maritale* were re-established once husbands were allowed to "execute" wives caught *in flagrante delicto*.[82] In some ways the Civil Code was even more harsh towards women than the Old Regime had been, for it not only re-established the power of fathers and husbands over them, but it also closed off whatever loopholes and compensations the former legal codes and systems had offered. There were, however, a few areas in which women's lot was improved by the Civil Code: *lettres de cachet* were abolished, as was primogeniture. Daughters now had the right to inherit equally with sons, and wives could henceforth make their own last will and testament, a right that had not been universally recognized under regional customary laws. Within their own nuclear families, however, wives were now placed at the far end of the inheritance chain. Unless a marriage contract recognized their prior claims, they could (and often were) left destitute at the death of their spouse. Under the Civil Code, even illegitimate, although not adulterine, children had greater statutory claims on an estate than did wives.

The Restoration

With the Restoration of the Legitimist Monarchy in 1815, the alliance of "Throne and Altar" was reinstated, and all provisions of the Civil Code contradictory to Catholic dogma were suppressed. That year vicomte Louis de Bonald (1754–1840), a returned émigré and leading conservative spokesman, told the Chamber of Deputies that "to tolerate divorce is to legislate adultery, it is to conspire with man's passions against his reason, and with man himself against society."[83] By decree of May 8, 1816 Louis XVIII (1755–1824) abol-

ished divorce "in the interest of religion, of morality, of the monarchy, of families."[84] Divorce remained illegal in France until the Naquet Law of 1884.[85] During the intervening decades, the only solution to an unhappy marriage would be, as it had been under the Old Regime, a separation agreement, either a *séparation de corps*, a residential separation that allowed a wife legally to live apart from her husband, or a *séparation de biens* that separated their finances (Figure 6).

The result of these changes in law was a legal morass. The jurist Merlin de Douai (1758–1838) proved to be prescient when he warned the committee drafting the Penal Code: "Never in France has the charge of adultery been admitted unless the husband wanted a legal separation at the same time."[86] Under the Revolutionary legal codes the charge of adultery had been admissible only as part of a divorce suit. The Civil Code departed from this tradition by separating the two legal procedures, but continuing to allow divorce. After 1816, however, divorce was suppressed while adultery remained criminal. Many legal scholars had noted this as a potential problem in framing the divorce laws, and over the next decades they would have ample cause to remember the prophecy of comte Regnaud de Saint-Jean-d'Angely, noted earlier: "It would be scandalous if a husband had his wife condemned as unfaithful, but nonetheless did not want to break with her."[87]

Under the new laws, a wife granted a separation was still subject to prosecution under the adultery laws. A separated husband, however, was freed of even the minor proscription against maintaining a concubine in their conjugal dwelling, since after a residential separation there no longer was a conjugal dwelling. All children born in a marriage were now entitled to equal inheritance, paternity investigations were outlawed, and there was no longer the possibility of either recognizing or, except under extreme circumstances, repudiating adulterine children. While this last was of potential benefit to women and their children within marriage, nonetheless, the potential for marital unhappiness was vast. As Dumas pointed out, it was something to weep over.

6 Vatier [Emile Wattier?], "Conjugal Ladder. Last Step Downward: Separation," 1824. Lithograph. Lith. G. Engelmann, Dist. Sazerac et Duval. Bibliothèque nationale de France, Paris. ("Echelle conjugale. Dernier échelon descendant: La Séparation.")

I

Unhappy Families:
Courtroom Dramas

A husband would have to be really stupid to be afraid of his wife; but
for a wife not to fear her husband, she would have to be a hundred
thousand times more stupid.

> Horace Raisson, *The Conjugal Code*[1]

TOLSTOY WROTE THAT HAPPY FAMILIES were all alike but that each one was
unhappy in its own way.[2] Perhaps that is true for the novelist, but historians sometimes find that even unhappy families are all alike and often for
much the same reasons. In this chapter I describe some of the men and women
for whom the provisions of the Civil Code were more than mere judicial
abstractions. They are known through their representations, either the ones
they constructed for themselves in the legal briefs with which they sought to
influence the judges and the larger public, or through their representations in
the journals of the day that reported and debated their cases. Sometimes the
images were contradictory; often they were surprisingly consistent. Either way
they illustrate the *mentalité* of the period.

Since the court records no longer exist, the major source for case studies of
the period is the *Gazette des tribunaux*, a journal that began publication in the
late eighteenth century, ceasing publication during the Revolutionary period
but resuming in 1825.[3] It appeared several times a week, chronicling current
judicial proceedings in Paris, with columns also devoted to provincial and
foreign courts. The attention devoted to any single case varied, however, not
only according to its jurisprudential importance, but also according to its public
interest, for the *Gazette* had a large non-professional audience as well. It was
read for its lurid tales of human drama, few of which could have found their
way past official government censors had they been presented as fiction. Stendhal, in fact, took his plot for *The Red and the Black* from one of these cases.[4]
The *Gazette* published court testimony, the oratorical *tours de force* of competing lawyers, legal briefs, narrative summaries of cases, and its own commentary on any and all judicial matters. It was, as one lawyer said, "a journal
that is in every hand, that everyone reads."[5]

facing page Pierre-François Legrand, "Republican Divorce," 1793 (detail of Figure 4).

The question of whether the cultural focus on adultery had any basis in social history can be resolved easily, for police blotters, court records, and the *Gazette* all demonstrate that these laws were duly enforced. Paris police bulletins show one to six cases monthly, about equal in incidence to other crimes of a "private" nature such as attempted suicide, abortion, and infanticide, although all, no doubt, occurred more frequently.[6] Adultery differed from these other crimes in that, while they were considered crimes against the state, adultery could be prosecuted only on the complaint of one of the spouses. Because it was virtually impossible to convict a married man of adultery, cases that came to court were almost invariably against married women and their (usually bachelor) lovers. Not every husband who filed charges of adultery against his wife followed through on his complaint: the criminal justice statistics for the 1820s show a pattern throughout France of many more arrests than prosecutions.[7] Since the standards of proof were minimal, and a husband had the right to have the case dismissed at any time, the disparity in numbers between arrests and prosecutions seems to imply that husbands were often satisfied with merely having their wives arrested and imprisoned but not actually tried and sentenced. Wives whose cases went to prosecution usually spent at least a month in jail before their trial, as is demonstrated by a comparison of the *Gazette des tribunaux* with Paris police records. Such cases rarely ended in acquittal.[8] Even in the most extenuating circumstances, wives received at least the minimum sentence of three months in jail.

While the cases that ended up in court constituted only a small percentage of those arrested, the number of arrests themselves no doubt represented an even more minuscule proportion of the incidence of this offense, which the *Gazette des tribunaux* called "this affront that betrayed husbands so rarely decide to prosecute in the criminal courts."[9] Nonetheless, if court records are any indication, adultery represented a major theme in the *mentalité* of the period. The *Gazette des tribunaux* commented in 1826: "either the ladies of Paris are becoming more unfaithful than ever before, or Parisian husbands are becoming greater enemies of adultery and greater friends of scandal. What is certain is that, for some time now, we have been seeing in the courts a mass of infractions of the conjugal pact."[10]

The literature of the day provides an accurate, if somewhat sanitized, depiction of this social phenomenon. In fact, the cases recounted in the *Gazette des tribunaux* are melodramatic to an extent that even Balzac would find extreme. Consider, for example, the case of the twenty-five-year-old Madame Descharmes. In 1826 her aging husband charged her with committing adultery with a handsome shopkeeper's assistant named Beauval. To entrap them, Descharmes followed them in disguise: "He shaved off his black mutton-chop whiskers," the *Gazette* reports from the court record, "replacing them with enormous mustachios, large eyeglasses covered his eyes, and green Polish-style trousers were substituted for his usual overalls. To complete his disguise, a half-opened sleeve with his arm in a sling made from a black scarf gave him the air of a recently wounded soldier."[11] Despite what seems a disguise straight out of vaudeville, Monsieur Descharmes managed to entrap the young lovers *in flagrante delicto*, and each was sentenced to three months in jail. After Madame Descharmes had served half her sentence in the Madelonnettes prison, where female offenders were customarily incarcerated, Descharmes relented and took her back, invoking article 337 of the Penal Code which stipulated: "The husband has the right to annul this judgment by consenting to take back his wife."[12] Beauval, however, was left in jail to finish out his term, for the courts had never managed to work out the accomplice's fate in these circumstances.[13]

Legally, *flagrante delicto* was the most convincing proof, even excusing murder under Penal Code article 324, which stated: "The murder committed by the husband of his wife, as well as of her accomplice, at the moment when he catches them *in flagrante delicto* in the conjugal dwelling is excusable."[14] Needless to say, husbands went to extremes to procure this type of proof. Monsieur Chatard, for example, who ran the baths in the rue des Bourdonnais, suspected that his wife was having an affair with a young man named Péchet, and so he, along with a friend and two gendarmes, hid in a closet in his house until the two "had attained the highest degree of criminality possible in such a situation," as the *Gazette des tribunaux* tactfully put it, whereupon they leaped out and arrested the guilty pair. Each was sentenced to a year in prison.[15] Less successful was the miller Etienne Génicis of Montpellier who, suspecting that his wife was carrying on with his assistant Poly, pretended that he was leaving on a trip. He returned secretly, however, and followed them to his mill; on confronting them there, he knocked down his wife and proceeded to chase Poly, who jumped from a window and broke his leg. Unfortunately for Génicis, the court ruled that since the entrapment had taken place away from his home and he had not waited for them to attain "the highest degree of criminality" before confronting them, the *flagrante delicto* provision of the law was inapplicable. His violence against Poly was thus illegal, although the violence against his wife was considered excusable. For "aggravated assault" against Poly, Génicis was condemned to four months in jail.[16]

The standard of proof for convicting wives was so low as to be virtually nonexistent. In one of the spectacular adultery trials for which Rouen was becoming notorious (not for nothing did Flaubert situate *Madame Bovary* there), the lawyer Senard explained:

Proof is not needed against the guilty wife. It is different for the accomplice, but for the wife the offense of adultery can be proven in every possible way. It is enough that the magistrates have a strong conviction of her guilt. [. . .] It must be like this, for these cases would present enormous difficulties if it were always necessary to obtain proof of *flagrante delicto*. Often it would be impossible. Immorality would be the consequence with the result that they could lead scandalous lives with impunity.[17]

This striking disparity in the standards of proof required for conviction – for her merely "a strong conviction of guilt" on the part of the judges, for him nothing less than *flagrante delicto* or incriminating correspondence, led to the peculiar result that at times only the wife, but not her lover, was convicted of this crime that, by definition, necessitates an accomplice. One Dame Nocus was among these unfortunates, receiving a sentence of six months in prison. The *Gazette des tribunaux* commented: "This trial shows a situation that is remarkable, although fairly common, that the said Lejeune, her accomplice, was not prosecuted along with her because the lawyers did not find in the evidence the requisite proof to charge a man with adultery, that is to say, either *flagrante delicto* or correspondence."[18]

The dependence on written evidence or *flagrante delicto* for a male conviction was a result of the reluctance of the authors of the Penal Code to admit the testimony of witnesses who could so easily be suborned. This problem was demonstrated by the case of Monsieur Dufriche, who married an heiress and then attempted to frame her for adultery; if his attempt were successful, she would be imprisoned and he would gain full control over her fortune. Dufriche produced four witnesses who claimed that from a ladder placed against her bedroom window they had seen Madame Dufriche in bed with his former valet Puchot. When it was proven that the bed could not even be seen from the window, the four were given jail sentences for perjury, but Dufriche was excused, "acquitted, being as he is her husband." He was fined, however, and she was granted a financial and residential separation because an unproven denunciation was legally a "grievous insult," and, as such, constituted one of the few legally acceptable grounds for a wife's suit for separation.[19]

Because a husband's adultery was in most cases considered excusable, the cases that came to court usually involved adultery between a married woman and an unmarried man, often precipitated by the woman's pregnancy. Since the Civil Code did not allow paternity investigations, but provided instead that all children born of a marriage were legally the husband's (article 312), even a husband who was willing to turn a blind eye to his wife's affairs would fear the inheritance complications resulting from the birth of an adulterine child. Such was the case, for example of a Madame P. from Rouen, thirty-four years old, who was charged with adultery with an eighteen-year-old named Léon, the son of a family friend. Monsieur P. charged that his wife was a spendthrift, but she said that he beat her and was bringing charges only to gain control over her dowry. The case was complicated and contradictory and dragged through the lower courts for months, with seventy witnesses being heard, before it eventually arrived at the Cour royale de Rouen, the highest level of regional court. The one uncontested fact in the case was that the affair had been going on for some time, but that P. had charged his wife with adultery only after she had become pregnant. The fact that Madame P. received the minimum sentence of only three months, while Léon was acquitted, no doubt reflects the court's displeasure that what had obviously become a public scandal was so long tolerated by the husband.[20] There was a similar case in Nîmes: Monsieur Ponton married Henriette Jalatte but they never lived together. Eventually she took up with Monsieur Firmat, moved in with him and bore two children by him, children who, according to the laws on paternity, had to be registered under the name Ponton, her legal husband. At this point Ponton went to court in an attempt to repudiate these children, but the Cour royale de Nîmes denied his petition on the grounds that, although Mme Ponton had been living openly with Firmat, Ponton had not charged her with adultery immediately after each child's birth as the law stipulated (article 316). In the court's ruling that the children were legally Ponton's, despite all evidence to the contrary, there was once again the sense of the court's displeasure at the husband's forbearance.[21]

In the rare case of a prosecution for "double adultery" (meaning that both parties were married), only the husband of the female offender was allowed to bring charges. One such case was that of Madame B., a dry-goods merchant, and Monsieur D., a music teacher, both from Autun. It is interesting because of the exemption tradeswomen enjoyed from the strictures of the Civil Code barring women from all commercial activities. The two were arrested after having spent three days together in a hotel in Lyons where, Madame B.'s husband testified, he had thought she had gone to attend the fair of Luzy. They both received four-month jail terms.[22] Examples such as this served to demonstrate to husbands that they were better off dallying with unmarried women, where they could not be prosecuted for adultery.

Among the petite bourgeoisie, shopkeeper's assistants seemed the most common "accomplices." Perhaps this was because they were young, single, and available, and because madame tended to work in the shop alongside her spouse and his assistant, providing ample opportunity for intimacy to develop. Monsieur Amelle, for example, an old soldier in his forties who, the *Gazette* reported, had lost both his nose and his cheek in the Revolutionary Wars and was now a wigmaker, had the police arrest and charge with adultery his young wife of barely twenty and his young assistant Theuriet.[23]

Abandonment by her husband was the standard defense put forth by the wife against this charge; although never accepted, it sometimes mitigated the punishment. Monsieur Demigueux of Bercy, a café-keeper, lived far above his means and, when ruined, abandoned his wife and children to escape his creditors. A carter named Guillaume offered his protection to Madame Demigueux, who testified, as her defense, that need and hunger had forced her to accept his kindness. Eventually Demigueux returned and charged them both with adultery and theft of the possessions he had left behind. The courts were not terribly sympathetic, and so gave Madame Demigueux the minimum sentence of three months in jail, and let Guillaume off completely.[24]

Most of the adultery cases came from the artisanal and petit-bourgeois classes, with a smattering of aristocrats whose domestic disputes always received inordinate attention in the liberal press. Members of the bourgeoisie, however, so detested public scandal that they rarely attempted to resolve this problem in court. As an oft-cited French verse stated: "Complaints are for the fop, scandal is for the fool; The respectable man betrayed withdraws and says not a word."[25]

Members of the urban lower classes rarely took their domestic disputes to court for a different reason: they rarely married.[26] Legal marriages were expensive and were necessary chiefly to secure the orderly transfer of property, of which they had little. Adeline Daumard has noted that, in 1820, 68.1 per cent of Parisian adults left no estate at all.[27] Although common-law husbands might have been just as indignant over real or perceived affronts to their honor, the law offered them no assistance. For women, on the other hand, common-law marriages were in many ways more advantageous than legal ones and even provided them with a modicum of rights. The children of such unions were considered to "belong" to the wife, just as the children of legal marriages "belonged" to the husband. Should a common-law marriage break up, the wife could enter into another such union without fear of prosecution for adultery, and she could keep her children. If the common-law husband recognized the children, however, he then shared equal rights over them; in practice this meant that his rights had priority over hers. In compensation, however, such recognized "natural" children could inherit, while adulterine children could not. Madame Bidault, a textile worker from Lyons, for example, lived with Monsieur Richard, a retired lieutenant colonel; she bore a child whom he recognized legally as his daughter. When the couple split up, he abducted the child and, despite Madame Bidault's plea to the court pointing out that "natural children" legally belong to the mother, the court awarded the child to him on the grounds that he was better able to provide for the child's future.[28]

On occasion a husband from the lower classes availed himself of the protection of the law against his wife's adultery. This was unusual enough for the *Gazette* to comment that "prosecutions for these offenses brought before the criminal courts are very rare in the working class."[29] The case, that of Jean-Denis Guichard against his wife and Monsieur Tendre, came to court in May 1827. The *Gazette* stated:

> Two poor workers were brought before the court today on this charge. From the looks of the two defendants before the trial, gloomily seated one next to the other, you would never guess that these two were being tried for this offense. Monsieur Tendre (he's the defendant) is 41 years old. There is nothing good-looking or seductive about him except his name. Mme Guichard, his accomplice, passed the age of illusions at least 20 years ago. Her flushed and bloodshot face, her irritation when she was interrogated, formed a striking contrast to the extreme pallor and apathy of her accomplice.[30]

The *Gazette* found the proceedings droll enough to publish the court transcript, commenting "Let's listen to Jean-Denis Guichard set forth his accusation, interrupted at each word by the sarcastic remarks of the female defendant."[31]

> *Guichard*: I have been married to Madame for ten years . . .
>
> *The Wife, angrily*: Yes, and so much the worse for me.
>
> *The Judge*: Don't interrupt. Plaintiff, are you legally married?
>
> *Guichard*: Yes, your honor, in a civil ceremony and in the holy Catholic Church.
>
> *The Wife*: Yes, that's true, and I'll say it again, so much the worse for me.[32]

As neither of the accused could afford to be represented by a lawyer, the judge questioned them himself. When asked "What do you have to say for yourself?," Madame Guichard answered: "What I have to say, by God, is that he beat me more than I deserved. He left me with nothing, me and three poor little children. When I asked him for money, he beat me and said: 'Go out tonight and earn it.'"[33] The interrogation continued:

> *The Judge*: You fled the conjugal domicile and took the furniture with you.
>
> *The Wife*: Some furniture! I demand a week's recess to bring in witnesses. He sold everything, piece by piece. I walked out in broad daylight with a child in my arms and ten sous in my pocket.
>
> *The Judge*: You had an illicit relationship with Tendre.
>
> *The Wife*: I didn't even know him before I left that scoundrel. I met him when I was working as a street-vendor. He saved me from destitution and we lived together.[34]

They each got the minimum, three months in jail. Tendre received, in addition, a fine of 1000 francs, a vast sum for a working-class person. On hearing this, Madame Guichard shouted: "Much obliged to you! And for this gentleman who beat me so much, you haven't given anything to him?"[35] But her husband had committed no offense under the Civil Code.

The three-month minimum sentence seems to have been standard punishment for a wife's first offence; acquittals were extremely rare, although the wife's accomplice often escaped punishment altogether, either because there were no incriminating documents or because he insisted that he did not know she was married. It is worth noting that the practice often described in novels, of lovers having pet names for each other, had a serious legal motive in that such pseudonyms protected the male partner from prosecution. The standards of proof for convicting the wife were so low, however, that such a ploy afforded her little protection.

Since the Civil Code specified that a wife was obligated to live with her husband wherever he chose (article 214), it was virtually impossible to prove that she had been abandoned. Even if he had moved out of their conjugal home, this signified merely that their communal dwelling was elsewhere, namely wherever he now resided. If he disappeared, therefore, and she subsequently took up with someone else, that became *prima facie* evidence of her adultery. In a case billed as "adultery among the honest artisans," the *Gazette des tribunaux* related the story of Monsieur and Madame Violat, poodle groomers on the Pont Neuf.[36] Monsieur Violat gave up poodle grooming to set himself up as a veterinarian on the boulevard Montparnasse, abandoning his wife and child in the process. Madame Violat eventually took up with a young man, her neighboring dog groomer on the Pont Neuf. Monsieur Violat found out about it and returned to charge her with adultery. The case is typical in that no explanation is offered as to why Monsieur Violat would want to bring charges against a wife whom he had obviously abandoned. Perhaps William Reddy is correct in stating that the husband's "honor" demanded it, but it should also be noted that, under the law, should an abandoned wife bear an adulterine child, this child would be her husband's legal heir.[37] Money is an incentive at least as strong as honor. In any case, Monsieur Violat produced witnesses who swore that her husband had mistreated her, had thrown her out of their conjugal dwelling shortly after their marriage, and had left her in "the most complete destitution." Neighbors testified that she was forced to beg for food in the dead of winter, and that they gave her lentils when she came to them with her baby in her arms. Her accomplice produced the standard excuse that he did not know she was married, ineffective in this case, as they were neighbors. They were each sentenced to three months in jail, the lenient punishment implying that the court believed that Violat really had abandoned his family.

The law of residence was invoked again when an imprisoned wife completed her sentence, or when her husband pardoned her at some anterior point. She was then legally obliged to return to the husband's domicile. Imagine for a moment that homecoming, of which no novelist has left a description, no artist an image. . . .

Why would a husband want his wife to return in these circumstances when there was obviously no love between them? Perhaps because a residential separation automatically carried with it a financial separation. When a man maintained his wife in his household, he retained control over her dowry and her earnings, from which she was supposed to receive an allowance in keeping with their station; if she was imprisoned, however, he would be obliged to pay only a pension towards her expenses. The advantage of maintaining one's wife at home can be seen in the case of one Madame Naylies. With 150,000 francs of capital, she was rich. She had obtained a residential and financial separation (*séparation de corps et de biens*) because of her husband's violence. He appealed the case and the judgment was overturned, so she was forced to return to him. In her subsequent petition to the court, she charged that he had locked her up in a miserable bedroom with barred windows and forced her to eat alone, cheap meals that he had engaged a local restaurant to supply for no more than 60 francs monthly. While she slept on a straw pallet, he enjoyed the magnificent bed she had brought as part of her dowry.[38] In this case, the wife received a modicum of justice in that the court ordered Monsieur Naylies to treat her *maritalement*, that is, appropriate to her status as his wife. He was ordered to remove the locks and to allow his wife the freedom of their communal dwelling, to give her an allowance from her dowry income, to furnish for her a separate apartment suitable to her station, to receive her at meals and to instruct the domestic servants to treat her with respect. But Madame Naylies was wealthy; one can imagine what the lives of less fortunate women were like. In these circumstances, it is understandable that wives did not want to return to their husbands after they had petitioned unsuccessfully for a legal separation or had completed prison sentences for adultery.

In 1826 the Paris Cour de cassation, the supreme court of France, took up a knotty question, never before decided: "When a wife has been directed by court order to return to the conjugal domicile, can she be compelled to go there by the use of official force?" In front-page articles, the *Gazette des tribunaux* reported on what was described as a landmark decision. Madame Liegey de Lunéville of Nancy had petitioned the courts for a residential separation. It was granted, but her husband had appealed and the judgment had been overturned. She was therefore required to return to their communal dwelling. She refused, and so the courts allowed her husband to seize her revenues; she continued to refuse, and so the court was asked: "Can police force be used to return the wife to the home and to the conjugal bed?"[39] The judicial decision was "yes" because otherwise the wife would have obtained *de facto* the separation that the courts had refused to grant her.

Trapped in an unhappy marriage, the best a woman could hope for was a *séparation de corps et de biens*. A *séparation de corps*, a separation of domicile, was the closest to divorce that a woman could get between 1816, when divorce was suppressed, and 1884 when it was reinstated. Even with a separation, however, she was still considered married, and so remained subject to adultery laws; this meant that until her husband died she could never enter into another relationship without fear of prosecution and imprisonment. The *séparation de corps* automatically carried with it a *séparation de biens*, a financial separation, although a financial separation could be obtained without a residential separation. A financial separation was requested most often to protect a wife's property, as, for example, when the husband had already exhausted his own assets; Civil Code article 1443 specified that "the wife can obtain a financial separation when her dowry is imperiled." This could even be a family strategy to protect assets during bankruptcy, but it did not mean that the wife was now in control of her own finances. Even with a financial separation she continued to have the same legal status as a minor whose assets were held in trust. She could neither lend, borrow, buy, nor sell without the authorization of her husband or, if they were legally separated, a judge.[40]

The misogyny of the law was extreme. In Rouen, for example, a Madame C. had already obtained a financial separation from her husband, a businessman who had declared bankruptcy. She then moved out and took up residence with her mother in a house that she (Madame C.) legally owned. After C. had lost everything, however, she allowed him to move into that dwelling, but because of his "abuse of power and ill-treatment," she petitioned for a residential separation, asking the court to make him leave her house while the case was being tried. Instead the court ruled that, if she wanted to live apart from her husband, she would have to enter a convent, but that, despite the financial separation, her husband was legally entitled to remain in what had now become their communal dwelling.[41]

Even a separation of domicile did not free the wife from the draconian laws. The Cour royale d'Aix decided in the case of "the wife L." that "Several judicial decrees have confirmed that a separation of domicile does not prevent the wife from being prosecuted for having committed adultery."[42] Madame L.'s attempt to invoke articles 336 and 339 of the Penal Code, which stated that if the husband kept a concubine in their communal dwelling he would be barred from charging her with adultery, was dismissed on the grounds that, because their legal separation had nullified any "communal dwelling," he was henceforth exempt from that provision of the law. The fact that he was was legally separated from his wife and was living openly with another woman did not, however, prevent him from charging his wife with adultery. She received the maximum penalty, a two-year sentence, with the added provision that, as with any other crime, she would be under police supervision, i.e. probation, for five years after that, with the sentence doubled should she repeat the offense.[43] An unintended consequence of the fear of paternity investigations that the formulators of the Civil Code had enshrined in the laws forbidding this activity was that men such as Monsieur L. were now forced to choose between prosecuting an ex-wife or possibly being obliged to support adulterine children who were not their own but would become their heirs. It was Hobbes's choice.

When separations of domicile were granted, it was usually because of the husband's excessive violence. In fact, the charge of "abuse of power, excessive physical violence and grievous insult" had been invoked for centuries by wives seeking separations.[44] One successful plaintiff was Madame Perrier. "One of the witnesses at the hearing swore, among other things, that when he tried to separate the two spouses during one of their fights, the said Perrier seized his hand violently: 'You're breaking my hand!' cried the witness. 'Oh, excuse me,' said Perrier, 'I thought that was my wife's hand.'"[45]

Women were powerless to change the law, but on occasion they did manage to demonstrate their dissatisfaction with the workings of "justice." In a case among florists, for example, a Monsieur Letarouilly charged his wife with adultery, producing as evidence incriminating letters that he had seized in her quarters; a husband was legally entitled to seize his wife's correspondence but not vice versa.[46] Madame Letarouilly was sentenced to three months, but her accomplice was acquitted. Letarouilly was not satisfied, however, and the *Gazette des tribunaux* reported:

> The husband, upon leaving the hearing, complained of the leniency of the court. When some of his neighbors advised him to go back and reclaim his wife, he responded *that he would rather pay to keep her in prison*. This remark nearly caused an unpleasant incident in the waiting-room, where a

great number of women attacked him. He would not have escaped from them had his lawyer not protected him.[47]

Clearly the law was not perceived as operating in the interests of all its citizens. One could argue that it was gradually undermined by public incidents such as these, which, in the course of subsequent decades, eventually led to permanent reform.

These cases were all duly reported in the *Gazette*, most receiving a single laconic article reporting the circumstances and the court's decision. There was one case, however, that continued for almost ten years and became a national *cause célèbre*, fought up from the local courts of Rouen to the Paris Cour de cassation. This case merits extended attention here, for it encompasses many of the issues that have already been introduced in these other less sensational court battles.

The Cairon Affair

In the first issue of the *Gazette des tribunaux*, there was the announcement: "We have learned that the marquis de Cairon has filed a complaint with the office of the King's Prosecutor, charging his wife with adultery."[48] What had been a steamy local scandal in Rouen thus broke into the national consciousness. The scandal had been titillating Rouen for as long as ten years, but, through the *Gazette des tribunaux*, it would become a daily staple of national life. Its notoriety was not, however, limited to the *Gazette*, for virtually every Parisian newspaper reported on the trial, prefiguring the sensational journalism that would characterize the later decades of the nineteenth century.[49]

The catalyst for the marquis's complaint was that he had lost his case in the Rouen Cour royale. After this court decreed that his wife was entitled to a financial and residential separation, he had then decided to continue his campaign at the national level. The battle was waged through public opinion as much as through the courts, with each side producing *mémoires judiciaires*, the legal briefs originally known as *factum*, that, in the course of several centuries, had been transformed from dry legal documents presenting a case to the judiciary into sensational literary works directed to the larger public and intended to influence the "court of public opinion" as much as the judges.

The adultery and separation trials of the marquis and marquise de Cairon were distinguished from hundreds of other such cases that wended their way through the legal system principally because of the aristocracy of its principal parties. This alone would ensure that it remain for months on the front page of journals as disparate as the *Gazette des tribunaux* and the official government newspaper *Le Moniteur universel*. Even more unusual, all the parties to the dispute published judicial memoirs. In the pre-Revolutionary period such memoirs often exposed the scandalous underside of upper-class life, condemning aristocratic power and undercutting the monarchy. Sarah Maza has portrayed them as a powerful force in spreading the political ideas that led to the 1789 Revolution. She has analyzed their melodramatic narratives and stereotyped characters as those "that peopled the collective imagination of French men and women at the end of the Old Regime, the stock characters of what French scholars call *l'imaginaire social*," and she has described their central villains as corrupt grandees whose wishes were carried out by brutal underlings, their central scenario as the struggle of the little man against his betters.[50] They often culminated in a denunciation of power based on wealth and lineage, ultimately leading to an attack on aristocratic power.[51] In Maza's analysis, the archetypal narratives of a wife's infidelity and insubordination were laden with connotations of political chaos and change, resonant in the decades leading up to the 1789 Revolution.[52] In the same manner, the Cairon case with its multiple memoirs by the husband, the wife, and the lover, provides valuable insights into the new post-Revolutionary laws, their application and their consequences, thereby also exposing the changed and charged political landscape of the post-Revolutionary period.

Such publications were exempt from censorship insofar as they were intended (at least in principle) for the usage only of the judiciary, to whom all the lurid details of a case were considered necessary to work out adequate proofs and punishments. Wealthy litigants such as the marquis de Cairon could, however, simply print up large editions and give them away in order to gain the widest possible publicity and support.[53] "The city of Rouen, the countryside, Paris, all are inundated with them," the marquise's lawyer protested to the court; "Public transport, cafés, reading-rooms are overflowing with these publications signed Augustin de Cairon."[54] The marquise had her defenders as well, however. Two memoirs plus numerous letters to Parisian newspapers carried her name as author, although, as was also possible with her husband's memoirs, they may have been ghostwritten by lawyers.

The judicial memoirs of the marquise de Cairon were the most important of the case because she initiated their publication with a separation suit in 1823 in Rouen. In her memoir, she laid out all the facts, both those accepted by all parties and those that were disputed by her husband; his memoir was primarily a defensive response to her allegations. Writing in the first person, in an emotional style appealing directly to the reader, the marquise began her tale thus:

> Suppose someone dared to write to the magistrates whose duty it is to offer equal protection to all: "Magistrates, a woman who was born into a respectable family, possessor of a great fortune, mother of five children, was suddenly, without trial, without charges, without an arrest warrant, and merely on the orders of her husband, thrown into a prison intended for hardened criminals. After eight days of detention, each circumstance of which was another crime, she was abducted in the middle of the night and taken violently to another prison forty leagues from her home. There she was thrown in with condemned and convicted prostitutes. Deprived of her name

and her clothing, she was compelled to wear burlap, forced into the harshest labor, and fed during the first months on the black bread usually given to domestic animals. She was kept there for three entire years, until the moment when a belated protection was granted to her by the superior authorities. Other outrages even more odious were committed. Of the five children that she bore, two disappeared at the same time as their mother. At the moment when she was abducted, she was pregnant. While it is true that this last child did not perish in her womb as a result of the horrible treatment that she received during this time, he had scarcely come into this world when he was torn from his mother's arms and thrown into a foundling hospital as though he had been born of unknown parentage."

    After hearing such a tale, wouldn't anyone be inclined to think that it was the product of a deranged imagination that attributes to our century, with its protective government, events that would dishonor even periods of disorder and barbarism? Nonetheless, this story contains only the truth. These outrages, these criminal intrigues, happened several years ago, and they are continuing today. This woman, so cruelly treated, thrown for more than three years into prison, without a trial, without even being charged, this mother whose child, despite her tears, was torn away from her, that woman is I, the wife of Monsieur de Cairon, who now controls my fortune.[55]

Her married life began ordinarily enough. The wealthy young heiress Adélaïde Hays-Delamotte entered into an arranged marriage with Augustin de Cairon in November 1804. She was seventeen, he was twenty-nine; both families were from the vicinity of Rouen.[56] The Cairon family was one of the oldest in Normandy: Guillaume de Cairon had accompanied the Duke of Normandy in the Norman conquest of England in 1066.[57] "My parents wanted this union, and I gave my consent to it," she wrote simply.[58] For wealthy and ambitious bourgeois families such as hers, marriage into the nobility, even the impoverished nobility, offered social status in exchange for the wealth they brought to such a union. Her considerable wealth was estimated at 20,000–30,000 francs annual income. Under the law, her husband would control it after their marriage. "He saw me only as a rich heiress," she later wrote, "he married me for money. He had no affection to offer me."[59] Nonetheless, although their marriage was clearly not a happy one, she bore five children in eleven years. The marriage deteriorated rapidly, however, after the birth of their fourth child, Gabriel-Augustin, in 1814; her husband suspected that the child was not his. Her story is the usual one of blows and insults, of being locked in and locked out, of deprivation and penury – ironic in her case since she had a personal fortune although no control over it. After Gabriel's birth, she rented quarters elsewhere in Rouen because, she claimed, her husband's valet often refused to give her the keys to her own apartments. She claimed that on one occasion she was forced to sleep on the kitchen floor until her father-in-law intervened. Nonetheless, the marriage continued for another two years, until 1816.

    On the evening of June 18, 1816, six weeks after the returning monarch

Louis XVIII had abolished divorce "in the interest of religion, of morality, of the monarchy, of families," the Rouen police commissioner Rollet knocked on the door of Madame de Cairon's apartment, asked her name, and arrested her.[60] Cairon and his valet Martel were waiting outside; the three men took her to the prison of Saint-Lô, where she was incarcerated for "debauchery and missing papers."[61] The timing was important because only a few weeks earlier the legal solution to these events would have been divorce, with Madame de Cairon's sizeable fortune and personal liberty returned to her.[62] Once divorce was abolished, however, and she no longer had the option of escaping the marriage, the marquis no longer had any incentive to accept what had clearly become a marital détente. A week after Madame Cairon's arrest, Rollet arrived at the prison of Saint-Lô at one o'clock in the morning in the marquis's carriage, ordered her to get into it, and escorted her to the Refuge Saint-Michel on the rue Saint-Jacques in Paris.[63] There she was registered under the name "Victoire."

There were three classes in the Refuge. The first class served as a retreat for well-to-do women who wished to withdraw from the world and were lodged as first-class pensionnaires. The second class was made up of women who, although convicted of crimes, nonetheless had the means of nourishing themselves at their own expense or whose relatives paid for their board. The third-class prisoners, however, called "penitents," were destitute convicts who were obliged to work for their daily bread.[64]

Madame de Cairon was forced to spend twenty months among the penitents.[65] As penniless women incarcerated in such places were usually from the lowest social classes, it is rare to have a description of their lives. Her own account of her imprisonment was published in the Rouen court decision as well as in the *Gazette des tribunaux*, and probably presents a fairly accurate description of prison life.[66] The marquis denied only that she had ever been forced into the class of penitents, but, based on the evidence, the Rouen court ruled that he was indeed responsible for her commitment there. Madame de Cairon wrote:

> I was stripped of my clothes and given a dress of black burlap. On my head was placed the round cap meant for women convicts. So dressed, I was led into the class of penitents.
>
> In the Refuge Saint-Michel, the class of penitents is intended for women convicts, for prostitutes and hardened criminals, and for those who haven't the means of buying off the work that the State imposes on them. How hard they are forced to work to pay for their black bread! . . . In brief, here is their life.
>
> In winter, they rise at six in the morning and attend religious services until daybreak. At dawn, the penitents, numb with cold, descend to their workroom where, in the most profound silence, they are put to work on soldier's overshirts, or on some other work of this kind. At nine, they are given brown bread that is often so hard that even animals would reject it. Only the most

pressing hunger would force anyone to eat it. At eleven, they have permission to talk while they are working, but they are not allowed to show any preference and must speak without preference to everyone, regardless of the crime each has committed. The refectory to which they descend for dinner has no fire, it is humid and very cold, and the meal they receive consists of boiled vegetables or salted herring.

Such is the life to which the marquis de Cairon, on his own authority and by abusing the influence that he could obtain from his name and from my fortune, condemned his unfortunate spouse. Yes, of three years and one month that I spent in this prison, I lived twenty-two months under the regime of penitents, with women convicts and condemned prostitutes whom the State maintained at its own expense. I wore their clothing, I lived on the same brown bread that they were given, I worked with them despite my weakness and my condition, and sometimes I saw them, in the midst of their labors and despite their own depravity, give me a pitying look and try to offer me some consolation. [. . .] The marquis de Cairon alone was unmoved. He demonstrated a degree of barbarism unknown in our times. After having obtained against his spouse a *lettre de cachet*, how had he carried it out? While he was enjoying her entire fortune, while he was depriving her of her children, he was spending money not to spare her from an unhealthy milieu, nor from the harshest work and the coarsest food, but in order that she be punished again each day with severity.[67]

Eight months after her arrival, on February 16, 1817, "Victoire" gave birth to a son who was named Pierre-Marie Victoire. The marquis was convinced that this child was not his, and so, in violation of Civil Code article 312, stating that the husband is legally the father of every child born within a marriage, the newborn was taken away, registered as of unknown parentage, and sent to a foundling home, the Hospice des enfants trouvés. From there the child was transported 40 leagues in midwinter (perhaps back to Rouen), arriving, as was no doubt expected, dead.[68]

From June 25, 1816 to the end of February 1818, Madame de Cairon remained in the class of penitents, after which she was allowed to reclaim her own clothing and was relieved from hard labor. The *Code d'instruction criminelle*, the code of investigative procedures within the Civil Code, set the statute of limitations on crimes at three years (article 638), and so, after this period had elapsed, the marquise filed a complaint with Bellart, the Chief Prosecutor (*Procureur-général*) of the Cour royale de Paris. He visited her in prison and, through the Prefect of Police Anglès, ordered her released.[69] She emerged from prison in July 1819, one month after the three-year statute of limitations specified by the Civil Code had expired; her husband could no longer prosecute her.[70]

This was by no means an unusual strategy. A similar case occurred when a Monsieur N., having spent several years in the French colonies on business, returned to France to find that his wife had had an affair during his absence.[71]

To avoid prosecution she went into a convent for three years. During her absence her husband had obtained a separation of domicile, but when she emerged from the convent, he could no longer prosecute her for adultery because the statute of limitations had expired. In reporting this, the *Gazette des tribunaux* commented that this was an important and controversial point of law.

The marquise de Cairon recalled that when she was released from prison, "The first thing I did with my liberty, so long overdue, was to file a petition against my spouse asking for a residential separation." She added: "Who couldn't understand that communal life would henceforth be impossible between this man and me?"[72] Nonetheless, in June 1821, her request was denied by the Tribunal de première instance, the lower court of Rouen, and she was ordered to return to her husband.[73] She appealed, however, and three years later the Cour royale de Rouen overturned the lower court's decision and granted her a *séparation de corps et de biens* that entitled her to separate her residence and her finances from the marquis. The marquis was forced to pay all the expenses for both the original case and the appeal, and police commissioner Rollet, who had carried out the original arrest and incarceration, was condemned for arbitrary arrest and for falsifying official documents.[74]

The court ruled that the marquis, who was not only a local aristocrat but the mayor of his commune, had arranged the entire abduction and imprisonment with Rollet.[75] He had never filed formal charges against his wife, the only circumstance under the Civil Code that could justify police involvement. During Madame de Cairon's week-long imprisonment in Saint-Lô, Rollet had never informed the proper authorities, neither the King's Prosecutor (*procureur du roi*) nor the Examining Magistrate (*juge d'instruction*), as he was required to do. Without either an arrest warrant (*mandat d'arrêt*) or a warrant of commitment (*mandat de dépôt*), the entire procedure was not only illegal, but, as the lawyers for the marquise pointed out, it was uncomfortably reminiscent of the pre-Revolutionary *lettres de cachet* by which the head of a family could have his wife or child imprisoned indefinitely without either charges or legal recourse.[76]

Because the Civil Code specified that the father had primary custody of his children (articles 373–80), the Rouen Cour royale awarded the five Cairon children to the marquis. The court also decreed, however, that Madame de Cairon could institute legal proceedings to give her deceased son the posthumous civil status that would declare him the marquis's legitimate son. The law was extremely clear on this point: regardless of the marquis's suspicions, his wife's child was his child (article 312). The marquis's response was to appeal the separation decision still again, now bringing the civil case to the Cour de cassation in Paris, the supreme court of France. At the same time, as the *Gazette des tribunaux* had noted in its first issue, he charged his wife with adultery in the criminal branch of the court system.[77] This put him in the untenable position foreseen by the framers of the Civil Code, who insisted that adultery and divorce prosecutions should be indivisible. With the abolition of divorce, their foresight was undone, so the marquis was allowed to argue simultaneously in one court that he loved his wife too much ever to be separated from her, and, in another court, that she was a common criminal who should be imprisoned.

The justification for the new charges, he said, was that his wife had been living with a young medical student named François Soubiranne ever since she had left the convent, and that she had even borne two children by him. Since Madame de Cairon remained subject to adultery laws although legally separated from her husband, the lovers lived under assumed names in Paris or its environs, being known as Monsieur and Madame Lecomte.[78] Their eldest child, Eugène-Polidore, had been born on January 19, 1821 and registered as of unknown parentage, although two months later Soubiranne legally acknowledged paternity. He insisted that the mother was unknown, however; to do otherwise would risk adultery charges. Their second child, Frédéric-François, was born in July 1823, with Soubiranne acknowledging him at birth, although he also was registered as of an unknown mother. And so these two children had a most unusual civil status in that they had an acknowledged father but an unknown mother.

Why did the marquis wait several years to take action against the couple? He had begun the first round of legal (or, to be precise, illegal) activity by imprisoning Madame de Cairon, but he did so, as already noted, only after the new Restoration laws had abolished divorce and had thus freed him from the possibility of losing her fortune. In this new round of proceedings, Madame de Cairon's lawyer, Barthe, noted that Cairon had protested his love for his wife while she was asking for a separation, but as soon as she had obtained it he published a memoir ruining her reputation, claiming to have caught her *in flagrante delicto* with a coachman. Only then did he begin prosecution against her for adultery.[79] By the marquis's own admission, it was not the birth of these children that had provoked him, although to meet the requirements of the law he insisted that he had just discovered their existence. The precipitating factor, he acknowledged, was that on July 21, 1823 the marquise made a new will that gave part of her fortune to her two sons by Soubiranne.[80] French inheritance law under the Civil Code abolished primogeniture and decreed that legitimate children should inherit equally (article 745). A woman was obliged to leave her dowry to her children in equal portions, but the law also specified that the inheritance should be divided into two to four portions depending on the number of children, with one of the shares always being discretionary (article 913). Although adulterine children had no legal right to inherit, the marquise was within her legal rights in deciding to will the discretionary quarter of her fortune to her two youngest sons (or to whomever she chose) – but it was this gesture that precipitated the marquis's prosecution for adultery.

The marquis's appeal of the separation decree to the Paris Cour de cassation was a civil matter; the supreme court did not actually rehear cases but reviewed them only to ensure that all points of law had been correctly interpreted. It took only two sessions to reconfirm the Rouen verdict, finding the marquis guilty of "abuse of power and extreme physical violence" against his wife, confirming her right to a legal separation, both residential and financial, and condemning him to pay "indemnity, fine and expenses."[81] The essential legal question was whether this ruling could set aside the concurrent adultery proceeding in the criminal courts.

The marquise's criminal trial for adultery became a *cause célèbre* which rivalled the great scandals of the pre-Revolutionary decades. The *Gazette des tribunaux* gave it the coverage of a major event. It began a few days before the civil case, but continued for many months afterwards, with witnesses, testimony, oratory, and appeals. While the earlier court proceedings in Rouen had been confined to a local audience, thanks to the *Gazette des tribunaux* all of France was party to this later case. "For a long time, scandal-lovers have been waiting impatiently for the opening of this trial," the *Gazette* reported, "the rank of the plaintiff and the deplorable notoriety of the earlier proceedings before the provincial court, which they hoped would be repeated today, attracted to the courtoom a considerable crowd of curiosity-seekers."[82]

Eighteen witnesses were called, a social spectrum of early nineteenth-century France. The wetnurse Aumont testified that the couple lived together at Antony, outside Paris, under the name Lecomte and that their children called them "mama" and "papa." The innkeeper Barrier said that they had lodged with her, sharing a room together under the name Lecomte. The housemaid Françoise testified that she thought they were married. The upholsterer Hubert found them an apartment in Paris. The porter Branche ran errands for them and remembered that she was pregnant. The widow Pilon did housekeeping for them and testified that there was only one bed in their bedroom. And so it went. The deliberations took only thirty minutes and they were both convicted. They each received the maximum penalty, two years in prison with an additional fine of 100 francs for Soubiranne.[83]

The case hung in this limbo for almost two months, with the civil case of separation decided for Madame de Cairon, but the criminal case of adultery decided for the marquis. Madame de Cairon and Soubiranne appealed their criminal convictions and the case was argued again, this time before even larger crowds than before, "among whom one noticed several elegantly dressed ladies. All the benches were occupied by lawyers in their robes," reported the *Gazette des tribunaux*.[84] The case had become an entertainment spectacle: "A large audience filled the room when the defendants entered. They were given chairs to spare them the embarrassment of sitting in the dock where thieves and swindlers usually appeared. Madame de Cairon's appearance was extremely elegant. The lady wore a dress of violet velour, half covered by a white cashmere shawl. Her black velour hat was ornamented with white maribou feathers, and a large black veil descended, as is the custom, down to her knees." Soubiranne was described as "a very attractive young man," while the marquis met with less approval: "he's already an old man, with gray hair, red face and green eyeglasses."[85]

Under discussion was the thorny legal issue that Madame de Cairon had been awarded a separation because of the marquis's ill-treatment of her, and yet at the same time she had been convicted of adultery. When the Cour royale of Rouen had ruled that "the said Cairon was guilty of abuse of power and excessive physical violence against his wife, and, in these circumstances, left to her own conscience, she cannot be judged to have violated any law," it had based its decision on the Enlightenment principle of the individual right to liberty and happiness, as well as on the secular definition of marriage as a legal contract.[86] The Prosecuting Attorney (*avocat du roi*) of the Paris adultery trial, however, employed the marital/regime analogy of the pre-Revolutionary period that traced an absolute and hierarchical authority from God through Kings to Husbands:

> It is, gentlemen, the family that is the basis of society: it is through the respect that we owe to family bonds that this great chain is maintained that binds man to all his obligations. When this first link is broken, there is nothing but anarchy. The state is shaken by the blow that strikes at family obligations, and in these proceedings where liberty is so often mentioned, we would like to conclude by repeating that true liberty can be based only on good morals.[87]

The poles of the debate were thus clear, as they had been throughout the trial. On the one side, the law, represented by the Prosecuting Attorney, proposed *puissance maritale*, in the form of male right, as the cornerstone of the State. Against that was the decree of the Cour royale of Rouen supporting the inherent rights of the individual, even a female individual, to liberty and happiness. Which would prevail? A *cause célèbre* of pre-Revolutionary France might well have been resolved with a ruling similar to that of the Rouen court. This was the Restoration, however, and so the Paris court's final decision held that: ". . . abuse of power, excessive physical violence and grievous insult, even though they have been accepted as grounds for a residential separation on the petition of the wife, do not qualify as the grounds specified in article 339, and do not deprive the husband of the right to bring a charge of adultery."[88] Article 339 of the Penal Code specified that only if the husband kept a concubine in their communal dwelling would he be deprived of his right to prosecute for adultery.

Nonetheless, this court did seem slightly more sympathetic to the lovers, and so it lowered their sentences to eighteen months imprisonment for her, eight for him. In France, however, the prosecution can also appeal a verdict, and it did. As a result, the case was reviewed a third time: the two-year sentences were reinstituted, and an additional fine of 2000 francs, the maximum allowable by law, was levied on Soubiranne. The court explained that it had reached this verdict "Considering that the sentence decreed by the previous judges is inadequate to the gravity of the offense."[89]

Almost as an aftermath, a short notice appeared in the *Gazette des tribunaux* several weeks later, announcing that the marquis had been granted a repudiation of paternity for Soubiranne's two sons. One of them had died, and the other would now have his civil status changed to "adulterine child" (*enfant adultérin*), a more shameful title than the euphemistic "natural child" (*enfant naturel*) that most illegitimate children carried.[90] As the marquis was clearly out of compliance with the provisions of the law, as specified in Civil Code articles 312–18, in that he had waited several years before attempting to repudiate these children, it can be assumed that he (unlike the unfortunate Monsieur Ponton) was allowed to do so only because of his aristocratic status. The story disappeared from the press after that. The *Journal de Rouen*, however, which had been following the case from the beginning, concluded its summary of the final judgment with the news that "It is definite that Mme de Cairon has fled to Belgium."[91]

Despite the high melodrama and notoriety of the case, what is of concern here is its dynamics, so very different from the *causes célèbres* of the eighteenth century. So I now focus on the strategies of self-representation, to see what was effective and what was not in the social milieu of Restoration France.

The Husband

Augustin, marquis de Cairon, began his memoir with a quotation from the Bible: "Such is the way of an adulterous woman: she eateth, and wipeth her mouth, and saith, I have done no wickedness (Proverbs 30: 20)."[92] While presenting himself as the guardian of morality, within the first page he had already acknowledged another reason for his action:

> Suddenly new facts were revealed to me. I had thought that the hatred of my spouse was entirely exhausted on me when I learned that she planned to turn it against my children as well. I learned that it wasn't enough for Madame de Cairon to have sullied their name, but that she wanted to avenge herself on them for the tears that they mingled with those of their father. I learned that she wanted to dispossess them when I am no longer alive, in favor of the adulterine bastards whose existence she shrouds in shameful secrecy, for fear that there might remain in me enough fortitude to protest, in the name of the sacred laws of nature, against the outrage she was contemplating.[93]

In brief, he claimed that he had just learned that his wife had made a new will on July 21, 1823, granting the disposable quarter of her estate to her two children by Soubiranne. For more than twenty pages, the marquis harped on this fact without acknowledging that only one-fourth of her estate was in question, or that, in fact, she had the legal right to dispose of this portion however she wished. He claimed that he was acting from fear that, since the Civil Code provided that all children born within a marriage were legally the husband's (article 312), her two adulterine children by Soubiranne might someday prove that the marquise was their mother, and thus be legally entitled to claim him as their father, and thereby a share of his patrimony equal to that of his own children.[94] The marquise, in her memoir, ridiculed this as absurd, pointing out that he already had 400,000 francs of debt and therefore had no patrimony to share even with his own children. She insisted that it was *her* money he was worried about, not his own.[95] In any case, since the Civil Code specifically forbade any investigation of either maternity or paternity in the case of adultery (articles 334–42), the marquis's supposed fears were spurious.[96] He concluded his memoir as he had begun it, with the accusation that his wife had "dispossessed five legitimate children in favor of her two adulterine bastards."[97] In his memoir's "Consultation," where lawyers customarily discussed the fine points of law bearing on their client's case, the marquis's lawyers discussed, not the adultery charge that was the actual subject of the legal proceeding, but the possibilities and ramifications of the marquis's repudiation of these two children. This was a separate legal case, but one dependent on the success of the adultery proceedings, as he could not repudiate the children until they were proven to be his wife's – and therefore legally his.

Apart from these financial concerns, the marquis showed himself to be extremely aware that "our proceedings must be retried before the grand court of public opinion," as he put it, and, more important yet, that he was losing in that arena: "Madame de Cairon will no longer succeed in stirring up against me a powerful public opinion that she has misled, just as she has misled Justice right in its own temple."[98] As befitted his lofty class position, he repeatedly expressed contempt for this public arena in phrases that echoed the class warfare of the 1789 Revolution, albeit now mixed with some apprehension:

> She portrays herself in the eyes of all France as an unfortunate victim who has smashed her chains and who demands justice against her oppressors. Just because she has trampled underfoot everything that is most sacred, she thinks she has the right to invoke the cause of liberty. Seduced by this word, even men of talent come to her assistance, and to the aid of this all-powerful cause. She has succeeded in stirring up in her favor the spirit of partisanship that clamors for me as its victim.[99]

Apparently the legal proceedings were not following the path he had first envisioned when he had appealed the Rouen decision several months earlier. Then he had charged that those proceedings had been conducted in closed court, and had therefore deprived him of the broadest possible publicity necessary for a fair decision on his marital problems.[100] Now that all of France was party to these problems, he was on the defensive. He was determined to prove that he had not had her confined to the class of penitents at the Refuge Saint-Michel, that he was unaware of the birth of her child there as well as the births of her two children by Soubiranne, and that, ultimately, he was acting, not for himself, but only for the benefit of their other children who were being deprived of their inheritance.

Legally speaking, he had three imperatives. He had to somehow disengage himself (against overwhelming evidence to the contrary) from the illegalities

committed by Police Commissioner Rollet in the arbitrary arrest and imprisonment of his wife. He had to demonstrate total ignorance (again against overwhelming evidence to the contrary) that Madame de Cairon had given birth to
a son in the Refuge, because otherwise he would have violated the Civil Code
by suppressing the infant's civil status as his son. And finally he had to prove
that, until the moment when he filed suit for adultery, he had been unaware
that his wife had given birth to two children by Soubiranne several years earlier;
otherwise he would have exceeded the time limits for repudiation of paternity.
Since, in fact, he had waited to file adultery and repudiation charges until after
she had obtained a residential and financial separation, he was not in a strong
position to argue any of these cases. It was undoubtedly on the advice of his
lawyers that he focused on the repudiation case, which went to the heart of
a property-oriented judiciary. This gave him a rationale for belatedly filing
criminal adultery charges against his wife, since only if she were found guilty
of adultery with Soubiranne could he then prove that the two children were
her adulterous offspring; hence the importance of testimony alleging that the
children called them "mama" and "papa." With this legal strategy, he could
resolve both problems at once: he could have his wife imprisoned for adultery
(and regain control over her fortune) and he could disown the two children.
Since the criminal adultery case would take precedence over the civil separation case, this was the only way that he could evade the consequences of her
winning a legal separation.

The Wife

The marquise did claim for herself, as her husband charged, the role of innocent victim, but it was more than that. Her repeated reference to "arbitrary
arrest" touched a raw nerve, not just among the liberal opposition, but even
within the aristocracy itself, for that class was disadvantaged by the memory
of the pre-Revolutionary *lettres de cachet*, a symbol as potent as the Bastille of
the injustices of the Old Regime. In her memoir, Madame de Cairon attempted
to drive this point home:

> The Marquis de Cairon has pretended ignorance of what the whole world
> knows today. In his eyes *lettres de cachet* still exist. He had me detained for
> three entire years with no formal proceedings, and he thinks he had the right
> to tell me that my *detention would be permanent*. This is how he speaks: *the
> minister AND WE, WE have absolute power to do as we wish*. If the Marquis
> de Cairon had pronounced these words in good faith, if he had confused the
> regimes in his own mind, then he might be able to think that a husband today
> could have his wife abducted because he claimed to have a grievance against
> her, or that he could throw her *for ever* into prison, while he could quietly
> take possession of her fortune. But such an error, even if it were possible,
> certainly does not excuse the ill-treatment that I received. The regime of the

class of penitents that the Marquis de Cairon imposed on me would always be considered barbaric, even at the time when *lettres de cachet* were in force. He, however, states that *these rights have been reclaimed by me*. What odious hypocrisy![101]

While the marquis focused his case on his repudiation of the adulterine children, Madame de Cairon focused hers on his illegal treatment of her. Her lawyers' main legal argument was based on article 4 of the 1814 Constitutional Charter which repeated the provisions of the *Declaration of the Rights of Man* (1789): "The individual liberty of French citizens is guaranteed. No one may be arrested or prosecuted except under the provisions of the law and according to its established procedures."[102] Both her memoirs emphasized her husband's repeated violation of her individual rights under the law. In these ways, both spouses sidestepped the adultery issue, he because it cast him in an unflattering light, she because she could not hope to deny it.

While focusing on the violation of her individual rights was a clever strategy, and perhaps the only one possible in the circumstances, Madame de Cairon's charges of religious hypocrisy were perhaps less advisable, given the climate of the Restoration. She charged that the marquis's appeal to morality masked his real desire to obtain her fortune:

Oh you [. . .], you who offered, scarcely a few days ago to receive me in your home, where I would find love and happiness, but who today, throwing off the masks of hypocrisy, bring charges against me with the most revolting cynicism because I have refused to leave my fortune in your hands, something you find necessary because of the disorder of your finances. Who cannot see into your soul? Cease to speak of morality and religion. Greed dictates your false promises, so refuted by your behaviour, and greed dictates today your accusations![103]

During the pre-Revolutionary decades, Madame de Cairon's plea would no doubt have found a receptive audience, and her case would have become a *cause célèbre* symbolic of the abuse of power by the aristocracy. The Cour royale of Rouen clearly saw it in this light, for the "Observations" section of the final published decision concludes with this statement:

To the applause of all France the Court of Rouen has condemned certain *corrupt* police acts invoked by the aforesaid Cairon, and has declared *that such acts cannot be upheld by magistrates who acknowledge only the law and its established procedures, procedures stated and confirmed by article 4 of the Charter which guarantees to all French citizens that the regime of lettres de cachet is forever outlawed.*[104]

Nonetheless, the court seems to have been uneasy about the political ramifications of its decision, for the concluding sentence asks: "Would it be possible that this monument erected by the Court of Rouen to natural law, to justice, might be struck down by censorship and overturned by the Supreme Court?

We can scarcely believe it."[105] The separation decision was upheld by the Cour de cassation, but by filing the criminal suit for adultery, the marquis accomplished his purpose nonetheless.

The Lover

François Soubiranne, the young medical student with whom the marquise shared her life for several years, seems to have been much more than just a handsome young lover. What was unusual in comparison with other cases of the period was both his willingness to assume responsibility for his children and his refusal to avail himself of the standard defense: "I didn't know the lady was married." Soubiranne was twenty-seven at the time of the trial, eleven years younger than the marquise and a student of the famous surgeon Baron Dupuytren at the Hôtel-Dieu, the finest hospital in Paris; he would have had an excellent future in medicine. The medical profession as a whole was a hotbed of liberalism, so it is not surprising that this young man attacked the marquis in class-conscious terms, presenting himself as the product of a poor but respectable milieu, raised by an aunt and devoting himself to the care of the unfortunates in the Hôtel-Dieu. Of himself and his sons he wrote:

> This name, although unknown, will be enough to honor them, and, make no mistake, if there exist in France titled families, there exist as well common people who would not exchange their virtue and respectability for *a nobility* that is sometimes merited but which is also sometimes merely *inherited*.[106]

Addressing the marquis directly, he presented himself as a young man who "dedicated [himself] completely to the duties of his profession, spent many hours each day at the leading hospital of Paris at the sickbeds of the downtrodden [. . .] while you were rich and lazy."[107]

In the world of the restored monarchy, this was not a propitious strategy. The student Soubiranne presented his judicial memoir himself, and no doubt wrote it himself as well. It lacks the judicial review (*consultation*) that would have placed his case in the best light, emphasizing its legal strengths, glossing over its weaknesses. That is what the lawyers for both the marquis and Madame de Cairon had done. Instead, the young and idealistic medical student tried to make his case by citing his own industrious dedication, contrasting that with the dishonesty and corruption of the marquis who, he charged, had suborned witnesses and employed police agents "who went so far as to offer money and protection in order to obtain testimony that they had the effrontery to dictate in advance."[108] Times had changed, however, and a plea of solidarity with the oppressed could no longer make the mighty tremble. The final verdict reasserted the primacy of morality, even hypocritical morality, in the law. One could not expect otherwise in Restoration France.

A Happy Ending . . .

In fact, the tale continues well beyond the Restoration regime. Ten years after his flight with Madame de Cairon to avoid imprisonment, Soubiranne became involved in a libel suit that was clearly related to their trials of the 1820s.[109] A second libel suit took place in the 1850s.[110] In the judicial memoirs for these two cases, he related the story of their subsequent life together, supported by transcriptions of many related documents. The marquis had died in 1826, after the couple's prosecution and flight from France. As the Rouen newspaper had reported, Soubiranne and Madame de Cairon had indeed gone into exile in Belgium. They apparently lived on borrowed money, for in her will she mentioned "debts contracted during the worst days of my life, in France and abroad."[111] Five years later, after the "Three Glorious Days" of 1830 had toppled the harsh legitimist regime of the Restoration and replaced it with the more liberal July Monarchy, they returned to France and married.[112] Although she was now a widow, the Civil Code specifically prohibited those convicted of adultery from ever marrying their accomplice (article 298). Somehow, however, under the more lenient regime of the Orleanist King Louis-Philippe, these two managed to do so.[113] They settled in Quévreville-la-Poterie, outside Rouen, the marquis's ancestral commune, where Soubiranne assumed the marquis's position as mayor. Nominated to the Légion d'honneur for his military service in 1833, he was dismissed from his post as leader of the local National Guard after the 1851 *coup d'état* that established the Second Empire and retitled Louis-Napoléon as Napoléon III. Soubiranne gave up medicine and became a littérateur, serving as editor for the journals *L'Indiscret* and *La Pénélope*, writing a long polemic in verse entitled *Le Chaos*, surveying the politics of his age, and becoming director of the Théâtre-Italien, the Italian opera house in Paris that Rossini had directed earlier.[114] The only reminiscences of his former life were the recurrent duels and libel suits that continally raked up his and Madame de Cairon's scandalous love affair. She died in 1850 at the age of sixty-three, leaving her wealth to her five children by the marquis, to her husband François Soubiranne, and to their surviving son, Eugène-Polidore Soubiranne. The following generation seems to have returned the family to the dull respectability of its ancestors, for the Bibliothèque nationale de France contains a tract on banking published in 1882 by P. Soubiranne de La Motte, who would have to be either their son Eugène-Polidore (who would have been sixty-one), or perhaps Eugène's son.[115]

This tale of husband, wife, and lover, in all its melodrama, extending through four regimes and as many revolutions, is, in its own way, as typical of nineteenth-century France as the more familiar image of conventional bourgeois respectability. The story of *l'affaire Cairon* would never have been allowed on stage during the nineteenth century because it flouted conventional morality. Its plot of aristocratic imprisonment, illegitimacy, repudiation, culminating in the triumph of personal happiness over moral strictures, might well have proved too racy even for a novel. Madame Bovary, after all, never bore an adulterine child and punished herself for her transgressions with suicide, yet the publication of Flaubert's novel caused its author to be prosecuted. Not even George Sand dared invent a tale to match that of *l'affaire Cairon*. In the tumultous period of the late eighteenth century and the early nineteenth, the dramatic extremes of melodrama did not, perhaps, represent such flights of imagination as one has been led to believe.

2

The Art of Keeping Wives Faithful: (Mis)Conduct Manuals

Men who have lost their wives are sad; widows, however, are merry and gay. Women even have a saying about the joys of widowhood. There is, therefore, no equality in the marriage contract.
Horace Raisson, *Code of Gallantry*[1]

DEBATES OVER THE PROPER NATURE and conduct of marriage provoked a whole body of literature during the Restoration, ranging from serious essays on the marriage question to conduct manuals and books of advice directed to men, to women, to those married, and to those still single. If serious philosophical and legal tomes constituted one end of this spectrum, then witty and cynical satires on the current state of morality were at the other; the best known of these was the *Physiology of Marriage* (1829) by Honoré de Balzac (1799–1850).[2] In all their variety, these publications formed what was called *littérature conjugale*, a broad category of works attempting, in one way or another, to make sense of the rapid shifts in marriage law and custom that had taken place over the preceding decades. No one, during this period, could be overly confident in the "naturalness" of his or her views on the marriage question. Arranged marriage or marriage for love – each had its partisans, its critics, and its *littérature conjugale*. That there was a ready audience for these publications is evident from both their number and their variety. What better way to introduce the cultural tropes of the period than by surveying the advice and counsel available to a population trying to make its way in a rapidly changing world?

One of the popular marriage manuals was written by the "vicomte de S***," a pseudonym of J.-P.-R. Cuisin, who, like many other writers, adopted an aristocratic identity in order to give his works an elegant cachet. His book, like many of its genre, was simultaneously serious and satirical, as can be seen from its title: *Conjugalism, or The Art of Marrying Well: Advice to Young Men to Marry a Beautiful and Rich Young Woman, and to Young Ladies to Be United with a Handsome, Well-Built and Wealthy Man: Code of Matrimonial Lessons Based on Moral Precepts with Some Very Curious Anecdotes about This Very*

Important Relationship of Marriage (1823).[3] On the first page the author
quoted the renowned wit Sophie Arnould (1744–1802) who "compared marriage to a sack of dangerous serpents, among which one could scarcely find one
or two good eels. 'Blindfolded, one puts one's hand in the sack,' she said, 'and
one would have to be born under a very lucky star to evade some cruel serpent
and find only the *good eel.*'"[4]

This anguish had become much worse since the abolition of divorce, which
had been legalized in 1792 only to be suppressed at the return of the monarchy
in 1816. Once established, the right to divorce was sorely missed. As the
vicomte de S*** put it: "No more divorce to separate two human beings for
both of whom 'until the last breath' [. . .] seems like a bad smell."[5] He wrote
movingly of the loveless marriage: "the hatred, the loathing, the infidelities, the
quarrels, the belated recriminations, the tearful reproaches,"[6] concluding "Now
these two spouses have to bear indefinitely the yoke of a double chain of hope-
less bondage, riveted by the laws."[7] As a result of this situation, there was a
burgeoning audience for the new marital literature.

The ongoing debates over the nature of marriage resulted in advice books
and conduct manuals being organized according to the types of marriage. For
example, the vicomte de S*** had a chapter entitled "Concerning Marriages
of Affection, of Love, for Money, of Convenience and Parentally Forced Marriages. – Recommended Behavior in All These Situations."[8] Received wisdom
believed that love matches were based on fleeting superficial attractions that
could never endure; only parents could choose an appropriate spouse for their
children. As the vicomte de S*** explained: "It is truly fatal for the cause of
sentiment, for the credit of love, that *marriages of inclination* are nearly always
unhappy. These overwhelming grand passions, which claim to be nourished
only on the charms of pure platonic raptures, to subsist on sighs, on meta-
physics, on rolling eyes, on spasms and sugar water, can scarcely ever survive
the trials of marriage without suffering an abrupt demise."[9] Marriages based
on financial gain were equally condemned as having little chance of success.
Happiness could never be part of such marriages: "it flees such a house whose
atmosphere of cold calculation, of selfishness, of sordid opportunism, has, from
the first day, installed Avarice in its bedroom, scales in hand, to ward off for
ever, laughter, playfulness and love."[10] And finally, for a generation raised on
Goethe's *Werther* (1774) and Chateaubriand's *Atala* (1801), the viscount
warned that marriages arranged by parents against the wishes of their children
would lead inevitably to the most tragic results of all, their children's madness
or suicide.[11] Thereby lay the essential contradiction: marriages of affection were
certainly doomed to failure, but unless the parties were well matched in social
class, wealth, character, even personal attractiveness, most arranged marriages
were also doomed to failure. No wonder Sophie Arnould compared the conjugal union to a sack of serpents!

The vicomte de S***, as well as all the other marital-advice writers, well
understood that marriages arranged without the consent of those involved had

one infallible consequence: "In coercing a young woman into a union that she abhors, you free her for ever from the demands of her conscience that, from the moment she is at the altar, cannot accept a forced vow of fidelity and virtue. After barely a month of marriage, I already see *cuckold's horns* overshadowing the entrance to the marital bedchamber."[12] Despite these sentiments, few commentators would go so far as Stendhal (1783–1842), who wrote in his *On Love* (1822) that "there is only one way of obtaining greater fidelity from women in marriage, and that is to give freedom to young girls and the right to divorce to married couples."[13] Most writers contented themselves with observing that arranged marriages were unjust – and then focusing on methods of coercing women to remain faithful to husbands they had not chosen.

A major component of the marital literature concerned advice to betrayed husbands. Balzac began his *Physiology of Marriage* by asking: "Is it not a novel enterprise to which any philosopher might devote himself, of showing how a woman may be prevented from deceiving her husband?"[14] While all agreed that infidelity was the inevitable result of forced marriages, there were those who supported such marriages anyway. Traditionalists held forth the hope that arranged marriages would not necessarily be forced marriages because, although lacking in passion at the beginning, they would eventually result in lasting love. For traditionalists, it was love matches that were problematic. Etienne de Senancour (1770–1846), for example, in his often reprinted book *On Love: From the Earliest Laws to the Conventions of Modern Societies* predicted nothing but disaster for marriages of inclination:

> For this union to be bitterly troubled, all that is necessary is for one of the spouses to be seized by a new and uncontrollable passion. [. . .] The probabilities of a happy marriage are much stronger for those who have only an attachment reconciled with prudence. An affection that is justified predominantly by moral qualities, a mild affection that is nonetheless restrained, will be able to survive until that moment when the spouses don't even want to replace it. Youth in its first flush usually has too high hopes and too much impetuosity to consider all the proprieties of marriage.[15]

But there were many who did not distinguish among the fine points of coercion in arranged marriages, finding them all equally loathsome, mercenary, and doomed to infidelity, as the pendants of Figures 7 and 8 demonstrate.[16] The vicomtesse de G***, at the very beginning of *The Art of Being Loved by One's Husband: A Collection of Precepts for the Use of Women Who Have Tied the Conjugal Knot, and Very Useful for Young Ladies Desirous of Submitting to the Laws of Hymen*, explained her objections to marriage as it was then defined:

> In our times, marriage, this institution so noble that it seems to have come from God, is no longer anything but a purely commercial transaction, where the participants calculate coldly, scales in hand, a union that is mercenary and opportunist. Unhappy marriages are the results of this ridiculous mania of marrying people who don't know each other, and of subordinating marital

7 Charles-Joseph Traviès, "The Marriage of Reason. Poor child! ...," 1830.
Lithograph. Lith. V. Ratier, Dist. Aubert. Bibliothèque nationale de France, Paris.
("Mariage de raison. Pauvre petite! ...")

fidelity to the sacks of gold that the future wife will bring to the marriage.
It is therefore necessary to attempt to lessen the problems of these inappropriate marriages if they can't be entirely eliminated, and that is my intention
in this work.[17]

The Civil Code was the fulcrum of this situation. Its provisions spelled out
the new order of things, and, as discussed in the previous chapter, its strictures
were well enforced. But the law can be seen in two ways, either as the creator
of social mores, or as the final act in a social drama, as the ultimate reification
of mores already sufficiently accepted to support the enactment of those laws,
but still sufficiently contested to necessitate those laws in order to ensure compliance. Laws, then, point in two directions, both to the ideal and to the real.

Suites d'un Mariage de raison.

A qui la faute?...

8   Charles-Joseph Traviès, "The Results of a Marriage of Reason. Whose fault is this? . . . ," 1830. Lithograph. Lith V. Ratier, Dist. Aubert. Bibliothèque nationale de France, Paris. ("Suites d'un mariage de raison. A qui la faute? . . .")

The major beneficiaries of the post-Revolutionary marriage laws, were, of course, the married men who wrote them in order to ensure that their wives would remain faithful while they themselves could sow their wild oats without fear of consequences. The primary class of the disenfranchised was women, both the married women who faced draconian punishments for transgressions, and the unmarried women who were no longer allowed to sue for paternity should they bear a child.[18] Women had limited options for protest, however, since they did not enjoy the rights of citizenship. The most vocal of the dis-empowered classes was that of unmarried men who, in previous centuries, had been allowed a certain degree of freedom in their relations with married women of their own or lower social classes. It was the educated segment of this class of young bachelors that was most stung by the new regulations and most active in expressing disapproval. One of the striking ways in which that disapproval manifested itself was in the *littérature conjugale*, which took as its subject the state of contemporary morals. This fashion was at its height in the 1820s when it spawned hundreds of publications, including satiric studies of marriage and parodies of the Civil Code. By the end of the decade it had given way to the novels of manners and morals, the *roman de moeurs*, of which Balzac became the best-known author.[19]

This "marital literature" can be divided broadly into two categories, one directed to women and the other to men. In general, the literature directed to women was didactic, moralizing, and utterly humorless, while that directed to men was cynical, sardonic, witty, and amoral. The most representative type of women's marital literature was the manual for the young wife, which taught her how to run a household properly. A popular example, often reprinted, was Madame Pariset's *Manual for the Mistress of the Household*, written in the form of letters to a young woman on her marriage and followed by recipes.[20] Clearly addressing herself to young women of means, Madame Pariset counseled separate bedrooms (or at the very least separate beds) and separate sitting-rooms for each of the spouses. "Trust in my experience," she wrote, "no sentiment can protect you from the embarrassment of too great a familiarity with certain details of everyday life."[21] Her conviction that too much intimacy would be detrimental to marriage was widely shared, although male writers were often opposed to separate bedrooms on the grounds that this arrangement facilitated a wife's infidelity.[22] The popular novelist Caroline-Stéphanie-Félicité Du Crest, comtesse de Genlis (1746–1830) also wrote a *Manual for the Young Wife* giving much the same advice about leading separate lives, and offering recipes and household cleaning tips. Genlis concluded with the advice that the wife's primary duty should be: "Anticipate the desires of your family and satisfy them."[23]

Many essayists criticized women's education or lack thereof, as did Claire-Elisabeth-Jeanne Rémusat (1780–1821) in her influential *Essay on the Education of Women* (1824); Genlis, in addition to her novels, published *Adèle and Théodore, or Letters on Education* (1782); and Pauline Guizot (1773–1827) wrote *Domestic Education, or Family Letters on Education* (1826).[24] These women all saw a young girl's education as doing nothing to prepare her for marriage, keeping her ignorant and inexperienced, an idea often expounded by earlier Enlightenment thinkers such as Voltaire and Condorcet.[25] Although at times they were social critics, these authors rarely challenged the underlying assumptions about women's role in society. Rémusat, for example, devoted her *Essay on the Education of Women* to an exploration of "the three states of girl, wife and mother that constitute the existence of women," concluding that "Men should be trained for the institutions of their country; women for men."[26]

Besides stressing the domestic virtues of economy and cleanliness, the manuals' standard advice to women was to fulfill their husband's every whim, to be, as Virginia Woolf described in her classic study *A Room of One's Own*, a mirror doubling his size.[27] The vicomtesse de G***, in *The Art of Being Loved by One's Husband*, even provided specific advice to women based on their husband's station in life. The wife of "a man of rank," for example, must "lighten the cares, which his concerns cause him"; the wife of a merchant must learn all the details of commerce so that she can run his business during his absence. The wife of an artisan must become "a gentle virtuous companion who, through her affectionate care and devotion, makes him forget his weariness, and she should especially console him for the injustice of fate."[28] In this latter case, the viscountess suggested: "He arrives, his wife runs to greet him carrying in her arms their child, the fruit of their love. She wipes the sweat from his brow, embraces him, and all his troubles are forgotten."[29]

The dramatic scenarios proposed by these writers extended even to a wife's correspondence with her husband, and to this end model letters were often included. They present a striking example of the complex interrelationship between art and life, fiction and history. Variations of these letters were common in the epistolary novels of the eighteenth and nineteenth centuries, such as Rousseau's *Julie, or the New Héloïse* (1761), Laclos's *Dangerous Liaisons* (1782), or Balzac's *Lily of the Valley* (1835–36). They were also published in letter-writing manuals such as *The New Universal Secretary, or The Epistolary Code, Presenting Models of Letters of Love, Marriage, Business, and Commerce*.[30] Stendhal mocked such conventions in *The Red and the Black* where his protagonist, Julien Sorel, borrows a set of conventional love letters and dutifully copies them out one by one to send to the woman he is pretending to court, so bored with the process that he even forgets to change the names.[31] Presumably the vicomtesse de G*** was entirely serious, however, in the model letter that she proposed a woman send to her husband during his absence on business affairs. It begins:

My dear Adolphe,

Only three days have passed since your departure, and each day seems like a year to me. Everything around me has lost its charm. Only those objects that remind me of you have the power to interest me. Nothing can distract me from the cruel sorrow that our separation is causing me, and if it must continue any longer, I do not know what will become of me. Never before have I realized so vividly how much I love you as I have since the moment when I was deprived of your presence. Finish as quickly as you can with the accursed business that keeps you so far from your Eléonore, and as soon as it is completed, return as quickly as possible.[32]

A more sinister aspect of such model letters was presented in the marital separation suit brought by the marquise de Cairon in 1825, as described in the previous chapter. When her husband produced her letters to him written during her imprisonment in the Refuge Saint-Michel, acknowledging her transgressions and begging his forgiveness, she counter-charged that in order to obtain news of her children she had been forced to copy such letters from models given to her – and she introduced the model letters into the court proceedings as evidence.[33] Even the choreographed scenario of delight at one's husband's return proposed by the vicomtesse de G*** had its negative parallel in the suggestion by the director of the Refuge Saint-Michel that, on the rare occasions when the marquis visited, Madame de Cairon should throw herself on her knees before him and beg for mercy.[34]

Because conduct manuals for women were resolutely idealistic and ignored the seamier side of life, they made dull reading. As a result, other genres of advice book, intended only for men, filled the vacuum. The shift from idealism to realism, from the determined focus on the positive to the gleeful exploitation of the negative, is the subject to be explored here. There is a fine line dividing the didactic works from the satirical ones, however, with many attempting to have it both ways, parodying the standard forms of advice-giving while at the same time offering advice.

The skewed nature of advice literature can be illustrated by comparing the conduct manuals intended for women, such as the vicomtesse de G***'s *The Art of Being Loved by One's Husband*, which counseled the virtues of simplicity, honesty, and fulfillment of a husband's every desire, with those directed to men, which assumed a man's desire to seduce many different women and advised duplicity and manipulation as basic techniques.[35] There is an implicit misogyny in the publications directed towards men, which take the position, half seriously, half in jest, that women are an irrational, strange, and alien species. The subtitle of Charles Chabot's *Conjugal Grammar*, for example, is *General Principles through which Wives can be Trained to be at Your Beck and Call and Rendered as Gentle as Lambs*.[36] Its first chapter is titled "Concerning the Defects of Women" and lists, among female shortcomings, jealousy, anger, insubordination – and "the love of liberty."[37] The ambivalence implicit in the last "defect" undermines the rest and, as usual, puts the misogyny on a shaky foundation. Is it being asserted? Is it being satirized? This strategy of having it both ways does not result in a neutral stance, however, but in one that simultaneously mocks and affirms dominant male attitudes, co-opting criticism and reinforcing stereotypes.

Many publications appeared with the word "code" in the title, parodies of the high seriousness of the Civil Code, but now applied to intimate, even trivial, matters. The *Conjugal Code*, the *Code of the Boudoir*, even the *Code of the Cravat*, all functioned by paying homage to the Civil Code, the great code of the century, while at the same time critiquing the new sociological tendency to classify systematically all human behavior by parodying it to an extreme.[38]

Although works parodying legal codes had also been produced during the eighteenth century, they had then comprised only a small percentage of the huge market for "light literature," which also included manuals, almanacs, treatises, and anthologies. The transition of "codes" from a minor eighteenth-century genre to the major literary trend of the 1820s can be attributed to one event, the promulgation of the Civil Code (1804–11), and to one individual, Horace-Napoléon Raisson (1798–1854). Raisson thought up the subjects and directed a stable of writers who actually wrote them, whereupon he published them, either anonymously, under pseudonyms, or under his own name.[39] The codes were profitable and were usually reprinted several times, often given new titles and authors for each edition; they each sold around twelve thousand copies.[40] Although the attribution of authorship is complicated because of the vagaries of their production, Balzac is the best known of Raisson's writers. He wrote several of the most popular codes, either in whole or in part, and eventually produced the one example that outlived the fashion that inspired them, the *Physiology of Marriage*.

The first of the literary codes is usually identified as the *Code of Honorable Men, or The Art of Not Being Taken in by Scoundrels*, written by Balzac and Raisson and published anonymously in 1825; by its third edition in 1829 its title had been changed to the *Penal Code: A Complete Manual for Honorable Men* and it carried Raisson's name as author.[41] The shift in title attests to the looming importance of the Civil Code during the period. By 1829, when Raisson published his *Conjugal Code, Containing Laws, Rules, Applications and Examples of the Art of Marrying Well and Being Happy at Home*, the long shadow of the Civil Code was such that it functioned almost as a parallel text, with each section of Raisson's parody footnoted to the appropriate legal article.[42]

Occasionally in the literary codes there are flashes of sympathy for women. In his *Conjugal Code*, for example, Raisson quoted three articles from the Civil Code:

Art. 212: Spouses owe each other mutual fidelity, sustenance, support.
Art. 213: The husband owes protection to his wife, the wife owes obedience to her husband.
Art. 214: The wife is obliged to live with the husband and to follow him wherever he chooses to live.[43]

In his critical commentary, Raisson's response to these laws was:

That the wife ought to be faithful to her husband, nothing is more just; by a legitimate reciprocity he also swore before the mayor to remain faithful to her. But that she should *follow* her husband like his shadow, that she owes him *obedience*, that's enough to make all the young wives of the world revolt. They would certainly be justified in crying out against this tyranny and in complaining that 'the men make the laws.'[44]

The "misconduct manuals" almost invariably reversed the traditional comparison of the relative gravity of the husband's and wife's infidelities. The great eighteenth-century jurist Jean-Etienne-Marie Portalis (1746–1807) had written:

It is incontestable that husbands and wives ought to be faithful to their promised vows, but the infidelity of the wife entails more corruption and has more dangerous results than the infidelity of her husband. Therefore men have always been judged less severely than women. All enlightened nations, through experience and a kind of instinct, are in agreement that the more lovable sex ought to be more virtuous for the good of humanity.[45]

In nineteenth-century marital literature, however, this hierarchy of guilt was usually subverted. Etienne Senancour, for example, wrote: "In general, a man is much more guilty in his licentiousness, because his infidelity is more voluntary than that of his wife, whose behavior is nearly always in response to his."[46] To be sure, such sentiments were not consistent with the rest of the texts within which they appeared; they correspond, in fact, to an historical moment in which few men could take a political position entirely consistent with all their conflicting sympathies. With regard to attitudes towards women and marriage, the most characteristic aspects of the period are ruptures, disjunctions, contradictions.

A complication of the dialectic between the serio-comic codes and the great Civil Code is presented by the entirely serious books of legal advice with titles so similar to those of the satirical codes that they inadvertently became part of the same phenomenon. The lawyer Narcisse-Epaminondas Carré wrote a popular *Code for Women*, for example, that had no humorous intention whatsoever.[47] With the Civil Code making so many major changes in women's legal rights and responsibilities, Carré's book was intended to provide the information that a woman would otherwise have to visit a lawyer to obtain. In its preface he stated:

> We then resolved to provide a genuine service to women by choosing, among the numerous provisions of our legislation, those which specifically apply to women, by presenting them in a clear and methodical fashion stripped of all legalistic terminology in order to render them intelligible, and by explaining them with regard to the considerations of utility or justice that informed them.[48]

Auguste-Charles Guichard's two-volume *Code for Women* (1823) was even more popular.[49] His book, more engaging than Carré's business-like alphabetical listing of topics, is subtitled *Stories and Conversations through which a Simple Reading Will Teach, in a Short Time and without Fatigue, What Is Most Important for Them to Know in Order to Be Able to Direct Their Own Affairs, to Recognize and Defend Their Interests in All Circumstances of Life*. Guichard used the device of fictional discussions with the family lawyer to convey information in a less formal way. He recounts, for example, the story of the unhappy Monsieur Dumont who came to him after seizing his wife's letters to her lover. Dumont told the lawyer: "It's especially her loathsome accomplice whom I would like to see convicted; as for her, although she might be equally guilty, I am nonetheless inclined to pardon her."[50] Guichard responded:

> Yes, but you can do nothing whatsoever to have him punished without having your wife condemned at the same time. Before you embark on such

a course of legal action, I am asking you to think clearly about its consequences, about the deplorable sensation it will cause, about the scandal that
nearly always surrounds such cases. I urge you to consider the deleterious
effect that it would produce on public opinion, harming even the husband
who brings the charges! Moreover, the wife's defense lawyer nearly always
brings counter-charges that are often damaging to the plaintiff!"[51]

Guichard's narrative style served to blur the distinctions between fact and
fiction further, bringing his legal manual even closer to the novels that would
later incorporate similar conversations, and to the *Gazette des tribunaux* whose
columns confirmed the wisdom of his advice.

In addition to these "Codes," there were also numerous books offering advice
under the title of *The Art of....* Many of these had their origins in the eighteenth century, for example *The Art of Knowing Women* or *The Art of Keeping
Wives Faithful*.[52] Such books had a renewed vogue in the 1820s, often revised
and embellished with additional prefaces and chapters to bring them up to date.
This makes them extremely valuable in establishing the differences in attitudes
between the two eras. Emile Marco de Saint-Hilaire (1796–1887) directed this
competing group of publications in much the same way as Horace Raisson produced the literary codes; they had titles such as *The Art of Tying One's Cravat*
(1827) and *The Art of Paying One's Debts* (1827).[53] In *The Art of...* literature, the same fine line divided serious books from those with a satirical intention. As with the Codes, works that addressed themselves to women were
straightforward conduct manuals, while those directed at men were sardonic
and satirical manuals of, if anything, misconduct. *The Art of Being Loved by
One's Husband*, for example, attributed to the vicomtesse de G***, had solemn
advice for young brides on everything from the necessity of keeping kitchen
utensils spotlessly clean to offering models of dutifully affectionate letters to
send during a husband's absence, like the one quoted above. *The Art of Keeping
Wives Faithful*, on the other hand, offered men witty and outrageous suggestions for ensuring a wife's fidelity.

The best known type of this proto-sociological, proto-self-help literature is
the "physiology," a literary genre inaugurated in 1825 with the *Physiology of
Taste* by Anthelme Brillat-Savarin (1755–1826), and culminating four years
later with Balzac's *Physiology of Marriage*; books of these types continued to
be published well into the 1840s when they enjoyed a renewed vogue.[54] The
term "physiology" came originally from biology, where it denoted the study of
the functions and organs of living creatures. By the eighteenth century, its
meaning had been extended to human behavior, principally through the influential study by the Swiss naturalist Johann Kaspar Lavater (1741–1801), whose
study *Physiognomony, or The Art of Knowing Men from the Features of Their
Physiognomy* (1775–78) was published repeatedly over the next half century
in many translations, abridgments, and popularizations.[55] By the early nineteenth century, his theories emphasizing the importance of physiology on psychology were so well known that they were widely used by *littérateurs*, who,

in a lighter vein, applied the same classificatory methodology to contemporary manners and mores. This literature corresponds to the moment in the development of Western thought when the "social sciences" were invented and when even history began to proclaim itself an exact science.[56] The literary codes and physiologies satirized the positivism of this new methodology by purporting to describe and classify all human experience objectively. Their pseudo-scientific tone resonated in the early nineteenth century through association with this major current of contemporary philosophical inquiry. This, no doubt, accounted for the transformation of what had been a minor genre into a flourishing publishing phenomenon, eventually taken up by novelists and caricaturists as well. Balzac, for example, owned the 1820 edition of Lavater's *Physiognomy*, and Daumier's cartoons drew upon Lavater's theories.[57]

The codes and physiologies offered witty pseudo-scientific reportage of the contemporary social universe while also claiming to advise readers (with a greater or lesser degree of plausibility) on how to avoid the dangerous situations so entertainingly described. The French public, it seemed, had a limitless appetite for such works which, if nothing else, offered realistic descriptions of the contemporary social milieu. In a period of rapid social change, such literature could perform a valuable social function by validating contemporaneous lived experience, often disjunctive with current literary idealism. The codes and physiologies were the avant-garde of this phenomenon, to the extent that Maurice Bardèche has credited their success in the 1820s with the birth of the *roman de moeurs*, the novel of social observation that soon replaced them in popularity.[58] They constituted an ephemeral phenomenon, but one that defined a period and pollinated the literary efforts of subsequent decades.

If one were to establish a continuity of marital literature, it would range from the didactic idealism of works by Genlis and Rémusat, at one pole, to the didactic realism of the lawyer-counselors on the other. The works in between aimed more at entertainment than didacticism, but their satire was nuanced enough that they often seemed to veer close to one or the other of these poles.

How should this literature be evaluated, insofar as much of it was continuous from an earlier period? One way is to look closely at how it changed over time, to attempt to understand what new exigencies were driving it. As an example, take *The Art of Keeping Wives Faithful*, which was first published in 1713, republished in a revised third edition in 1783, and revised again in 1828. In its earliest incarnation, it was a straightforward little book, organized according to types of women (Wealthy Women, Beauties, Coquettes, etc.), offering strategies for controlling each of them.[59] By 1783 it had expanded into two volumes, with additional anecdotes and a commentary which, on occasion, was surprisingly feminist. Its introductory pages set the tone of a delightful romp on an amusing subject. The new edition was attributed to a duchess who said "This book should be republished, first of all because wives would buy it for their own amusement," to which an abbé, party to the discussion, commented "Jealous husbands would buy it too, so they could learn its lessons," and an

Englishman present added: "And gallant lovers would buy it so they could outwit the jealous husbands."[60] The 1783 edition presented a hodgepodge of contradictory points of view, combining the seriousness of the earlier work with the worldliness, wit, and Enlightenment principles of the later decades. Its text was ornamented with sparkling anecdotes of fickle lovers and cuckolded husbands, making the subject seem like a parlor game, or more accurately a game of musical boudoirs. At times it provided an almost camp commentary on the serious precepts of the earlier work. For example, it reprinted these pompous sentiments of 1713: "Since it is to marriage that man owes his existence, he is therefore obliged to marry in turn in order to restore to the world what the world will lose on the day of his death." This is followed by the wry commentary: "I know a Parisian family where there are six uninterrupted generations of bastards, and a lot of people feel that the world will not lose anything when they die."[61] At other times the 1783 edition countered the earlier misogyny with social criticism from an Enlightenment point of view. In a section labeled "Commentary," added in 1783, there was a passage entitled "The Law's Injustice towards Women," in which the author stated:

> Isn't it foolish to insist that women be beautiful, passionate, and desirable, not only chaste but even faithful to husbands who aren't faithful to them? If we want them to do their duty, then we have to obey the laws as well, not the laws that our injustice and our tyranny have imposed on this charming sex, but those that the wisest women would make had they the power to do so.[62]

Another commentary, entitled "Miseducation of Young Ladies," stated:

> Because women are trained from infancy in the art of pleasing and in the conduct of love, their grace, their appearance, their language, everything that surrounds them, their whole life and all their education is directed only to this end. [. . .] If we then marry them off to men whom they do not love, do we think that they will accept never experiencing love, when they have never thought of anything else?[63]

By the 1828 printing, these passages sympathetic to women had been excised, and the book was given a new subtitle; it was now called *The Art of Keeping Wives Faithful and Not Being Cuckolded by Them: Intended for Husbands and Lovers. Taught in Five Lessons*. On the cover page there was now an epigraph: "Oh Janus, how fortunate you were to have eyes in front and in back! You didn't have to worry about being cuckolded, nor of being ridiculed whenever you appeared. – Persius."[64] The duchess's remark, that women would find the book vastly amusing and would be its prime audience, was replaced with a frontispiece, "Very Important Notice," obviously directed at an exclusively male audience:

> The dangers to which husbands and lovers are continuously exposed have manifested themselves in more and more frightening ways during the publi-

cation of this book. As a result we recommend to those at risk the immediate purchase of this little book regardless of price. Only it can protect them from what I would not wish to happen to them.[65]

Satiric though it might be, this "Notice" acknowledges that the contemporary situation had become more frightening to men. The cheerfully disorganized quality of the eighteenth-century work, with anecdotes, asides, and commentary sprinkled throughout a text that was itself presented in no particular order, was replaced in 1828 with a strict and stern organization akin to that of the legal codes. Each of its five lessons was now clearly organized and numbered, with the material taken from the earlier editions sorted into categories. The five lesson titles give a clear idea of the book's intention, which had become more didactic than amusing: "Different Types of Behavior of Married Women," "Precautions to Take and Dangers to Avoid with Regard to One's Wife," "Methods of Taking Advantage of the Virtues and Failings of One's Wife," "A Short Course on Morals and Hygiene Indispensable to Every Husband Who Wants to Keep His Wife Faithful," and, lastly, "Recommended Techniques for Lovers to Keep Their Mistresses Faithful."[66]

If one can learn from the book's omissions something of the *mentalité* of this later period, one can learn equally well from its additions. A commentary entitled "Errors of Modern Philosophers" was added in 1783, stating "It is not true that a wife's infidelity is meaningless from the political point of view, for it saps the strength and virtue of the human race."[67] This sentiment was completely in accord with the marital/regime concept that the family mirrored the State, but when this passage was reprinted in the 1828 edition, there was a significant addition to it: "A wife's infidelity is even more consequential for her children than for her husband because they are cheated out of their paternal inheritance. In states where children were raised at public expense and where all property was held in common, at Sparta for example, infidelity did not cause the same kinds of problem."[68] The earlier concern for a moral society has now been replaced by an anxiety over inheritance, an issue that, as Alexandre Dumas pointed out (in the passage quoted in my Introduction), had gained new importance since the abolition of primogeniture and establishment of equal inheritance among all children born into a marriage.[69]

In comparing the different editions, one can learn equally well from what was retained. It is incorrect to assume that because themes are continuous, they have no significance. Adeline Daumard, in her classic study of the French bourgeoisie, wrote: "The theme of adultery in literature or in theater is too old to have the slightest historical significance."[70] On the contrary, one must assume that the continuation of literary themes represents a continuation of those concerns, just as their alteration or disappearance represents a shift to new issues or the rejection of older attitudes. And so, in looking at the reprints of *The Art of Keeping Wives Faithful*, one should be as attentive to the material that remained constant as to that which changed. In this regard, several of the "lessons" were not only retained from edition to edition, but were included in later similar books.

Chief among these is a warning to keep wives away from female friends, among whom widows were considered the most dangerous: "too free in discussions of gallantry and too knowledgeable of the intricacies of amorous intrigues. They quickly offer themselves as confidantes, and all too often give a wife lessons which lead only to deceiving her husband."[71] Another recurrent piece of advice, aimed at the upper classes, was on buying the loyalty of servants, presented under the heading "What a husband should do to find out what is going on in his household when he is absent." As some of these strategies have been noted in the context of the criminal courts, the passage is worth citing *in toto*:

> Other than these various precautions, do not forget to make use of the valets and servants for your advantage: it is through them that nearly all the intrigues of wives are conducted, or at least they always know about them. A wife will never dare to embark on any amorous liaison when she knows she is being watched. There is nothing easier for a husband than making them allies: some bonuses in recognition of their zeal, giving notice of dismissal if they hesitate, and forcing them to accept that dismissal if it happens again. This will make him loved and feared. Let your wife know that you have confidence in them, let her know that they are in your pay, and let her believe, if possible, that you are giving them more than you are admitting so that she despairs of any hope of winning them over.[72]

The 1828 edition of *The Art of Keeping Wives Faithful* was not the only one of these publications to be directed to an exclusively male readership. The preface of Chabot's *Conjugal Grammar* announces: "In conclusion, I will teach husbands how to be masters of their households, how to rule and how to enjoy themselves."[73] Balzac began his *Physiology of Marriage* with a prohibition on women's reading it: "He has, so to speak, engraved on the frontispiece of his book the wise inscription placed on the door of some institutions: *Women May Not Enter.*"[74] The growing separation of gender roles characteristic of bourgeois society had by the 1820s produced a schism even in light literature.[75] Suspicion, even paranoia, towards women was now considered "normal" – even while it was being parodied.

Virtually all the works discussed here acknowledged the Civil Code as their generating principle. Many of them reprinted all or many of its laws pertaining to women, or cited it like the Bible. Often the format of the Code was borrowed, with the text organized into a facsimile of titles, chapters, and articles.[76] The authors of both the light literature and the serious manuals of jurisprudence gave as their *raison d'être* women's supposed incapacity to read and to understand the Civil Code; both classes of author then took it upon themselves to explain its provisions, the lawyers to her directly, the *littérateurs* to her husband in order that he might better control her. Whether acknowledged or not, all this literature was responding to the obsession with adultery that had gripped the nation. Raisson's *Conjugal Code*, for example, never explicitly broached the subject, and yet on its cover, beneath the title and author's name, there appeared a familiar quotation from *Hamlet* used in a new and surprising context: "To be or not to be, that is the question."[77] At the end of the book's two hundred pages, Raisson clarified the significance of this quotation:

> This little book would seem incomplete to us, unless we added some words on a grave and delicate subject, one that more than one reader should have been astonished not to see mentioned in this conjugal code. *To be or not to be*, for many husbands that is the major question. The depressing columns of the *Gazette des tribunaux* bear witness every day that the anxieties that are striking so many level-headed people at the same time are not altogether imaginary.[78]

Perhaps the notoriety that Balzac's *Physiology of Marriage* achieved was because he dared to speak the word, to name the terror that beset so many husbands. In the introduction to this work he wrote:

> As a matter of fact, at the time when, much younger, he studied French law, the word ADULTERY caused him unusual reactions. Of vast importance in the Civil Code, never did this word appear in his imagination without dragging in its train a dismal retinue: Tears, Shame, Hatred, Terror, Secret Crimes, Bloody Wars, Fatherless Families, Unhappiness, all were personified before him and rose up suddenly when he read the cursed word: – ADULTERY![79]

To avoid being cuckolded, husbands were advised to take extreme measures. Much of the seemingly bizarre behavior seen in court cases of the period was actually counseled in the marital literature, which often advised husbands to use against their wives "deceit, punishment, or house arrest."[80] Wife-beating was condemned by all the writers, chiefly because, although legal, it was counter-productive, leading to antagonism, resentment, and, eventually, to more marital infidelity. Chabot's *Conjugal Grammar* was the wittiest on the subject:

> Once the quarrel has begun and the husband has used force to reduce his wife to silence, can he hope to live with her from then on in harmony? – No. – Can he hope that she will remain faithful to him? – No. – Can he hope that she will not betray him again? – No. – Let him remember that vengeance is the pleasure of the Gods, and may he say *to himself* '*I've been done!* . . . I've been done!' And once he has indeed been done, may he remember not to become jealous! . . . That would accomplish nothing at all.[81]

Chabot suggested instead that, as punishment for a wife's disobedience, the husband should say "*Madame, you cannot leave the house for two weeks*, and I forbid you to have visitors." He then advises the husband: "Lock her up in your bedroom; take the key and put it in your pocket under your handkerchief, and you can rest assured that, unless her heart is altogether hardened, this dreaded punishment will bring about a favorable change for you and for her."[82]

All authors agreed that a wife's reading matter had to be supervised. Many gave lists of books either to be recommended or to be avoided. High on all the lists of forbidden books were Laclos's *Dangerous Liaisons* (1782), Voltaire's *Candide* (1759), and Rousseau's *Julie, or The New Héloïse* (1761). Among the few acceptable books, Chabot listed the novels of Genlis and the moral treatises of the legitimist vicomte de Bonald.[83] Genlis was herself too modest to recommend her own books, but she suggested Rousseau's *Emile* (1762), Bernardin de Saint-Pierre's *Paul and Virginia* (1787), and the letters of Marie de Rabutin-Chantal, marquise de Sévigné (1626–96), and Françoise d'Aubigné, marquise de Maintenon (1635–1719).[84] Balzac claimed to approve only of fables, fairy tales, and geography.[85]

The corrupting power of a wife's friends was a continual subject of concern. The various editions of *The Art of Keeping Wives Faithful* had been warning of the danger of widows for over a century, but there were other categories to avoid as well. Cousins were a cause of constant anxiety. In the large families that were common in France, cousins were ubiquitous, and the normal constraints against too much familiarity with the opposite sex could not be adequately enforced within a family. Cousins were distant enough for the incest taboo to be inoperative, yet close enough to enjoy a degree of intimacy otherwise prohibited. The relationship between first cousins (*cousins germains*) was, in fact, a problematic one, prohibited in marriage by canon law under the Old Regime on the grounds that, since extended families lived together, cousins were more like siblings and marriage would be a form of incest.[86] Although the Civil Code legalized such marriages, some uneasiness seems to have remained.[87] Raisson, in his *Conjugal Code*, laid out the pitfalls in his "Fifth Section: Dangers. Chapter One. The Young Cousin."[88] He warned: "The young cousin is the same age as the wife; they were raised together. In their childhood games they were always in perfect accord. They said 'tu' to each other."[89] The alternatives? "There are no half-measures possible with the young cousin; you must either shut him out completely or receive him cordially like a friend or a relative. The first solution is rude, the second is dangerous."[90] The vicomte de S*** advised mothers "to be constantly on the alert for signs of intimacy with the young cousin."[91] Balzac noted that the wife's lover "is seldom one of the family, unless he is a cousin."[92] The vast number of contemporaneous prints featuring cousins (Figures 9 and 10) attest to this fear by showing what was obviously intended to be interpreted as an adulterous relationship.

Schoolfriends were another source of worry. "Schoolfriends cause more dissension in households than gallants," Raisson wrote, "A young wife cannot be forbidden to see her schoolfriends: all that a husband can do is to be absent as little as possible during their visits, which soon will become less frequent."[93] Even mothers were suspected of being too indulgent.[94] The logical end of this, absurd as it might seem, was Raisson's judgment that "A young wife can have

9   Edme-Jean Pigal, "This is my cousin," *Scènes populaires*, 42, 1823. Handcolored lithograph. Lith. Langlumé, Dist. Gihaut et Martinet. Bibliothèque nationale de France, Paris. ("C'est mon cousin")

10   Charles Philipon, "It's always 'My cousin this, my cousin that!,'" *Amourettes*, 15, 1827. Lithograph. Lith. Ducarme, Dist. Ostervald l'aîné et Hautecoeur-Martinet. Bibliothèque nationale de France, Paris. ("Toujours: mon cousin par ci, mon cousin par là!")

no friends safely other than her father and her husband."[95] While Raisson was doubtless being satirical, the vicomtesse de G*** repeated the standard advice: "At best a young wife ought to have the fewest number of friends possible." She concluded by stating: "Anything is preferable to the society of women, and I agree with one husband who said, with unusual candor, 'I would rather find my wife with a grenadier than with someone of her own sex.'"[96] The reason for all this anxiety about women talking among themselves? "They discuss everything and everyone."[97] In other words, women talking together were likely to pool their information, thus making the deceit counseled to husbands by the misconduct manuals that much more difficult to sustain.

    Although the *Gazette des tribunaux* made everyone aware of the problem of adultery through the numerous prosecutions of wives reported in its pages, the manuals were unanimous in counseling husbands to avoid legal action. The verses of Gresset were often cited, both in the courts, as noted in the previous chapter, and in the advice manuals: "Complaints are for the fop, scandal is for the fool; / The respectable man betrayed withdraws and says not a word."[98] Less poetically, Raisson advised: "A wise husband ought to applaud these words of Montaigne: 'It's folly to want to publicize a misfortune for which there is no remedy, that shame exacerbates and rapidly spreads through jealousy, and for which vengeance harms our children much more than it heals us.' "[99] This advice, while facetiously given, is the same as that noted above, where the lawyer Guichard, in his fictionalized discussion with an outraged husband, in all seriousness counseled him to think about the scandal that always follows adultery charges.[100]

A husband's best method of ensuring a virtuous wife, the experts advised, was to be faithful himself. The most impassioned plea for this came from the vicomte de S***:

> Believe me, despite the satires of Boileau and all the detractors of the fair sex, most wives who misbehave, who yield to lovers, have long suffered in silence with lonely tears, have long deplored the infidelity of a husband who is fickle, who gambles, who is a wastrel, who is the scandalous lover of some shameful courtesan. He has deserted the marriage bed and crushed her with silence and contempt, and he plays no role for her other than that of a vile eunuch who, like a tyrant, guards a treasure, which he permits no one to touch. Yes, be faithful, tender, devoted, give the first example of order and of virtue, and your wives will be virtuous. Vice is contagious; it is difficult for a woman, no matter how well born she may be, to preserve her innocence, her modesty, with a husband who returns home every night stinking with the contagious odors of debauchery.[101]

Balzac, always the realist about his contemporaries, did not share this standard opinion that men should set a good example. He stated frankly "for a man, at any rate, fidelity is impossible."[102]

As the conduct manuals that dealt realistically with marital problems were directed at men, women rarely learned (at least from books) how to deal with what seems to have been a common occurrence, namely the infidelity of husbands. To the extent that husbands followed the advice to limit or closely monitor their wife's intimacy with other women, even their mothers, most avenues of information (except novels) would be closed to them. The vicomtesse de G*** was one of the few to broach the taboo subject openly:

> Often a man becomes unfaithful, and the bizarreness of the human spirit is such that a young spouse, lovely and endowed with all the qualities that make life worth living, is abandoned for someone else worth far less. That, however, is the nature of infidelity, we should not be surprised by it.
>
> The wife's position then becomes difficult; she must be especially careful not to anger her husband by ill-mannered behavior. She will succeed only in exasperating him. On the contrary, she should increase her care and consideration; she should feign complete ignorance of his infidelities. She should let a tear furtively escape her eye, and when her husband draws near, she should

quickly wipe it away. No matter how callous a man might be, he can't resist this spectacle, and soon, returning to his better nature, he will know how to atone for the grave wrong he has committed, by increasing his kindness and consideration. I know how difficult it is to suffer one's sorrows in silence, but what good is scandal? A prudent woman ought, above all, to avoid compromising the name that she bears by parading the errors of an unfaithful spouse before a public that is always malevolent and cruel.[103]

The viscountess summed up her position by stating: "Indulgence, I repeat, is the only means to employ to bring back an unfaithful husband."[104]

The vicomte de S*** shared her opinion, counseling women to "Vary your appearance as well, for the human spirit loves variety. Be in turn animated, pensive, melancholy and capricious. Do not neglect to cultivate your mind, to enrich it with reading. Learn how to play a musical instrument. Be a captivating chameleon."[105] If these masquerades don't work, why then "His infidelity can't be blamed on your lack of effort."[106]

Considering women's legal powerlessness, these approaches combining resignation and passive aggression might well have been the best options available. Whether effective or not is impossible to know, but the advice given in Raisson's *Conjugal Code* was a good deal more brutal and probably a good deal more realistic as well:

Wives who are no longer loved, hide your tears. They will never bring a husband back to your side. Do not increase your efforts to please him, do not try to dazzle him with your talents or acquire new ones. Do not try to show off your intelligence, your charm! All these efforts will be useless! [...] Once love has died it cannot be rekindled, and if, on occasion, an inconstant love returns to the one betrayed, it is more likely because she seems happy that he is gone rather than that she is lamenting his cruel abandonment.[107]

Raisson here abandoned his occasional sympathy for women by offering a final indignity to the betrayed wife: "There is one point in marriage that cannot be emphasized enough, and that is that the infidelity of husbands, this constant source of discord, of quarrels, of recriminations, is for the most part the result of the inadequate efforts that their wives make to please them."[108]

While forming the principal subject of marital literature addressed to men, the subject of a wife's adultery was rarely mentioned in the literature addressed to women. On occasion, however, there were depictions of the horrible consequences of such a crime. The vicomtesse de G*** was most effective in recounting the dreadful results of what she called "The dangers of affairs and the disastrous and irreparable consequences of marital infidelity."[109]

There is no solace for the adulterous wife, she finds herself condemned by a kind of censure. He whom she preferred to her husband soon abandons her for another and repays her with contempt for the sacrifice of her honor that she made for him. A miserable fate awaits her; she wanders through life consumed with regret. There is no one to whom she can confide her sorrows, the confession of which covers her with shame. The terrible consequence of a single error is that death alone can end her sufferings.[110]

To underscore this terrible fate, the viscountess relates the sad story of Adèle, the daughter of the honorable widower Monsieur de Florville. When she turned seventeen, he married her off to an older man, the rich merchant Dupont. She was virtuous and happy until he left on a business trip and her friend Madame de Mont-Désir, the widow of a military contractor, invited her to her country estate at Montmorency, where the widow's lover the comte de Resembert and his friend Valbonne schemed to seduce her. Fortunately, one of Dupont's servants warned him of this dangerous situation – Dupont had obviously read the conduct manuals' sections on "What a husband should do to find out what is going on in his household when he is absent."[111] He rushed home, arriving just in time. His servants beat up Valbonne and threw him out. "The unfortunate Adèle threw herself at his feet, he regarded her with contempt and walked out without saying a word."[112] Adèle fell ill with a high fever and, in her delirium, the only word she could say was her husband's name. Her father was summoned to visit his dying daughter one last time. Adèle survived, however, and was reconciled with her husband. "'All is forgotten,' Dupont said, embracing her. 'You were weak rather than guilty, but one minute later. . . . Remember, my Adèle, that society is full of vicious creatures for whom the sight of virtue is a continual reproof, and whose sole occupation is to lay traps for those of either sex weak enough to be influenced by their wicked advice."[113] Adèle had a long convalescence, but she recovered fully and eventually produced a large family to whom she was an example of virtue. And when her own daughters came of age, "she never forgot, in all the advice her maternal wisdom gave them, to lay out before their eyes the disastrous consequences of dangerous liaisons."[114]

In this moralized revision of Laclos's *Dangerous Liaisons*, the notorious eighteenth-century tale of depravity was "corrected" to correspond to the new bourgeois morality. In the nineteenth century, this story of Adèle and Dupont became a stock situation in bourgeois theatre, as described in chapter 4. Through it, authors could explore a taboo subject while escaping censorship, because the evil deed was prevented at the last minute, and because the near-disaster could purport to function as a morality tale.

Chabot's *Conjugal Grammar* concludes with a series of twelve maxims headed "What a Wife Ought to Know":

1. We recommend that she should always be modest;
2. That she promptly obey her husband;
3. That she love him for ever;
4. That she remain faithful to him;
5. That she observe the principles of honesty;

6. That she shun coquetry and affectation;
7. That she be sweet, lovable and kind;
8. That she dress with decency;
9. That she take good care of her household;
10. That she raise her children with proper values;
11. That she study the *Conjugal Grammar*;
12. And finally that she remember always to remain virtuous.[115]

There was no corresponding list of twelve commandments for husbands.

Balzac's Physiology of Marriage

Balzac's *Physiology of Marriage* was the culmination of the *littérature conjugale* of the 1820s. While physiologies continued to be written on a wide variety of subjects for several decades, after 1830 Balzac and others transferred their close observation of social customs to the novel as a form of literary expression that was gaining in importance during these years. Balzac's *Physiology of Marriage, or Meditations of Eclectic Philosophy on Conjugal Happiness and Misery* is the only one of these codes and physiologies to receive major critical attention. Scholars have noted that it occupies a key position in Balzac's oeuvre. It has been linked in theme to such later novels as *The Duchess of Langeais* (1834), *The Lily of the Valley* (1836), *The Woman of Thirty* (1842), and *The Muse of the Department* (1843), many of which borrowed whole sections from his *Physiology*. By virtue of its early date it marks the beginning of his *Human Comedy*, that series of novels through which he attempted to depict his entire epoch; despite its chronological precedence, Balzac placed it in the final volume of the *Human Comedy*, thereby marking its conclusion.[116]

When published in late 1829, it created a scandal. The liberal press applauded it because it exposed the hypocrisy that marked the regime of Charles X (reg. 1824–30), while the bourgeoisie and conservatives in general criticized its cynical attitude toward marriage.[117] Balzac himself reviewed it twice, lavishly praising its anonymous author.[118] He announced at the outset that, under the Restoration, morality and religion have now triumphed and so virtuous women may indeed remain virtuous.[119] He then devoted the next several hundred pages to demonstrating that such women do not exist: Balzac was, in effect, challenging one of the Restoration's key claims, that it represented a chastened and sanitized monarchy and aristocracy that had no relation to the former profligacy of the upper classes, a profligacy that had been accused of precipitating the 1789 Revolution.

Balzac's Physiology of Marriage has been thoroughly analyzed by Catherine Nesci and others in relation to sources such as the novels of Laurence Sterne or contemporaneous medical literature, as well as in its relation to Balzac's own later novels.[120] It has been less adequately studied in the context of other works in the same class of literature, and not at all in relation to the shifting legal sands of his period.[121] Studies of French literature have, until recently, focused on canonical authors and have neglected popular literature; so much of this marital literature came from Raisson's group that it might easily seem that Balzac wrote it all. Nonetheless, worthy as it may be to focus attention on the precedents and influence of the *Physiology of Marriage*, if one disregards the numerous earlier and contemporaneous codes, physiologies, and conduct manuals that shared the same attitudes, and often the same anecdotes, Balzac's work will seem more original than it is. For the purposes of this book, it is more important to point out the similarities than the differences, to show that Balzac's work, as well as others of the same genre, all participated in the construction of the *mentalité* of the period.

Balzac claimed that he began working on his text in 1820, although most Balzac scholars agree that it was written between 1824 and 1826. It was published first in 1826, then expanded and published in its definitive version at the end of 1829. Because Balzac borrowed the components of earlier satirical marital literature, it can be viewed as the culmination of the genre. In many ways it is more reminiscent of droll eighteenth-century compilations than of the harsher contemporaneous moralities. In sheer outrageousness it often declares itself frankly as satire, whereas the others teeter on the brink of realism. For example, as part of his "matrimonial catechism," Balzac stated "A man cannot marry before he has studied anatomy and has dissected at the least one woman."[122] The husband who is afraid of being "minotaurized" (i.e. cuckolded) is counseled never to permit his wife to go for a walk without him, to undermine her health so that she is too weak to betray him, even to forbid her to pray to any but the female saints of heaven.[123] She should be kept sick, pregnant, and illiterate, for "By ignorance alone is despotism maintained."[124]

The obvious conclusion to be drawn from these extreme measures is, as Balzac himself repeatedly stated, that adultery is the inevitable outcome of marriage. His conclusion is all the more strengthened by his claim "to gather together those things that everyone knows and no one says."[125] While the stated purpose of his book, expressed in its "First Meditation," is to prevent wives from deceiving their husbands, it is clear that its true purpose is to demonstrate that such an undertaking is impossible. Like the eighteenth-century engravings of "The Useless Precaution," examined in chapter 3, it seems that no matter what a husband might do, he will inevitably be outwitted. If Balzac presents his readers with the inescapable contradiction of love (usually illicit) vs. duty (usually marital), it is love that always triumphs. This alone should identify Balzac's camp, for in the bourgeois theater, as discussed in chapter 4, it was quite the reverse, with duty always triumphant. And yet the satirical codes and physiologies were directed to the same audience as the bourgeois theater; in the lengthy pseudo-sociological "First Meditation: The Subject," Balzac explicitly defined his audience as the well-to-do, the "leisured rich," the same audience that attended the plays of Eugène Scribe; he specifically excluded the working classes and tradesmen. This audience accounts for the book's notoriety, for the

bourgeoisie was a class noted for hypocrisy, to whom Balzac had the effrontery to say "those things that everyone knows and no one says."

Balzac was born in 1799, and his membership in the "French generation of
1820" placed him squarely in a cohort that Alan Spitzer has described movingly as being disenfranchised by the gerontocracy of the Restoration regime.[126]
In the early editions of the *Physiology of Marriage*, its author was identified as
"a young bachelor," and it is in this persona that he "counsels" aging
husbands throughout his book: "The conspiracy that over one million hungry
bachelors are plotting against you creeps upon you slowly, but it is nonetheless sure."[127] He assures husbands that not only are bachelors plotting to seduce
their wives, but that "it is impossible for them not to win the struggle in the
end!"[128]

Critical attention has been focused on Balzac's attitude toward women,
attempting to determine whether he was sympathetic or misogynist, and yet it
is obvious that he vacillated between the two positions. Even more striking is
his provocative attitude toward married men, who are "foreordained," as he
put it, to be "minotaurized" by their wives regardless of the lengths to which
they go to avoid this fate. Anecdote after anecdote demonstrates that no husband is safe, that the enemy is everywhere. His aphorisms underscore this:
"Marriage is a duel, in which, if you would triumph over your adversary, you
must watch the passing of every hour of the day and night, for if you so much
as turn your head, the lover's sword will pierce you to the heart."[129] Listed as
worthy of suspicion are a wife's mother, cousins, maid, doctor, schoolfriends,
and intimate friends in general: "A husband should mistrust every single friend
his wife may have."[130] Despite these many and varied precautions, the husband
consistently loses; many of Balzac's anecdotes focus on such a husband who,
despite a perfect system of vigilance, is, nonetheless, cuckolded.

What does this mean? Eve Kosofsky Sedgwick's *Between Men* offers one possible explanation for such a triangulated relationship between husband, wife,
and lover, proposing that these relationships are ultimately between the two
men with the woman being merely a pawn.[131] This certainly seems to be the
case of the marital literature written by young bachelors such as Raisson and
Balzac. In the *Physiology of Marriage*, Balzac's married elders are mercilessly
tormented. His sympathy is clearly with the young bachelors, whose dilemma
is "as wearying to themselves as it is dangerous to society":[132]

> The average age at which a man marries is thirty; the average age at which
> his passions, his most violent desires and longings are fully developed, is
> twenty. Hence, during the best ten years of his life, that springtime, as it were,
> when his beauty, his youth, and his inclinations render him most formidable
> to husbands, he has to remain without the possibility of finding any *legal*
> satisfaction for the irresistible longing for love that agitates his whole
> being.[133]

As women of his own age and class will be either carefully guarded virgins or
already married, Balzac concluded that bachelors are forced to choose between

three kinds of crime: if they remain chaste their health will be impaired; if they succumb to temptation either they will degrade themselves by having intercourse with women of the lower classes, who will no doubt give them a venereal disease, causing their health to be impaired anyway; or they will be obliged to compromise virtuous married women of their own class.[134] Bachelors must make cuckolds of married men merely in order to survive.

The wealth of anecdote and opinion making up the *Physiology of Marriage* casts an interesting sidelight on the Penal Code's article 339, which specifies that a husband can be convicted of adultery only if he keeps a concubine in the communal dwelling. While this case might seem so extreme as to be rarely invoked, Balzac revealed that it often meant seducing a servant, a state of affairs the wife might even have engineered in order to gain her own freedom: "A husband who is fairly caught in this trap must remember that he will never be able to reproach his wife for her conduct when she eventually charges him with being too intimate with her maid and packs her off with her child and a pension."[135] The Penal Code (articles 336–39) specified that should the husband be found guilty of this transgression, he would lose the right to charge his wife with infidelity; for Balzac, this would be a wife's "insurance policy" against the harsh measures of the Penal Code. These would be the cases that never came to court because the husband and wife had reached a détente of mutual blackmail that precluded legal prosecution by either of them.

The ambivalence towards women demonstrated by the authors of conduct manuals directed at men, alternately sympathetic and critical, occasionally veering into outright feminism or misogyny, has often been noted in the case of Balzac. His attitudes were simply those of his class, caste, and cohort, the young men of the French generation of 1820. Their misogyny was shared with their contemporaries, even with the hated legitimists of the older generation and with the returning émigrés. In fact they shared it with virtually the entire political spectrum except the Saint-Simonians. Their occasional sympathy with women's plight was just as natural, however, for they constituted a generation seeking its own freedoms. They could not completely avoid recognizing that women as a class were oppressed and denied the basic rights of citizenship, and yet neither could they quite bring themselves to include women in their own libertarian ideals. The result was an often-incoherent blend of competing and conflicting self-interests, conspicuously expressed in the marital literature discussed here.

There is a touch of admiration that often creeps into this literature's discussion of the wife's refusal to give up her liberty. Chabot, for example, after quoting article 213 of the Civil Code that decrees that "the wife owes obedience to her husband," added: "In vain does one place the Civil Code in the hands of the fair sex. In vain does one force them to study it. Nothing can induce them to follow this article to the letter."[136] Is that admiration or condemnation? When Balzac compared the husband with a king and the wife with the unruly people whose insurrection must be prevented or quelled, where are his sympathies? Extreme conservatives had traditionally invoked the marital/regime analogy, but Balzac was evidently satirizing their politics at the same time as proclaiming them. His sympathies, as were those of his cohort, were divided. The literary critic Sharon Marcus has asked whether Balzac's *Physiology of Marriage* is a commentary on misogyny or an enactment of it.[137] It is simultaneously both.

The fact that husbands did indeed resort to many of the harsh measures suggested in these satires, as court records show, only demonstrates that this marital literature, despite its extremism, was more realistic than fanciful. Satire is a fragile endeavor accomplished by trespassing only a hair's breadth over the line of reality. As all the satirical marital literature, the Codes and Arts and Physiologies, had the hidden agenda of demonstrating that it was really impossible to control one's wife and to force her to remain faithful, its authors were proposing that adultery was inevitable. Considering that these authors were, for the most part, unmarried and in their twenties, and that the literature was clearly directed to older married men, the witty observations on the inevitability of wives' infidelity can be read as an implicit threat. The generational conflict, well described by Alan Spitzer, was, however, inextricably interwoven with the gender conflict identified by Eve Kosofsky Sedgwick.[138] Adultery may well have become "something to weep over" as Dumas said, but, in contrast to the real-life courtroom dramas where women were clearly the victims, the weeping in the light-hearted and contemporaneous *littérature conjugale* seems to have been done principally by the older generation of married men.

3

When Seeing Is Believing:
The Graphic Image

FROM THE SATIRIC (mis)conduct manuals, discussed in the preceding chapter, to their visual counterparts in caricature is but a short distance. Visual imagery, however, presents different questions of interpretation. When one grasps the meaning of something, one says, "I see," for seeing connotes both intellectual and visual comprehension. This chapter is structured around "seeing" in both senses of the word, as I explore both what is seen and how it is seen. The double meaning of "seeing" is well demonstrated by a print of 1814, "Three Ways of Seeing" (Figure 11), showing the different ways in which French, English, and Mediterranean husbands "see" a wife's infidelity. The French husband pretends he sees nothing ("It would upset me if everyone laughed at me. The wisest course is to take heart and to resign myself"); the English husband "sees" an opportunity to win a financial settlement for damages ("Let's figure out how to turn a profit from each act of infidelity. Let's go to court and demand a huge compensation"); while the Mediterranean husband "sees" his honor insulted and so seeks vengeance ("Oh, you monsters, fear my avenging fury! You will both perish, traitor and betrayer alike").[1] And what did the caricaturists "see"? Absurd laws and customs, made by their elders, deserving of merciless ridicule, and providing the fodder for a century of memorable images.

Although caricature had been widely practiced in Europe for centuries, it did not flourish in France until the Revolutionary period.[2] Michel Melot has attributed this lag to the power of French censorship, always vigilant in suppressing indecent as well as political images, to the absence of the bourgeois culture that generally provided the audience for caricature, and to the cruel exaggerations and distortions of this art, the antithesis of the classical ideal that traditionally ruled over French aesthetics.[3] Nonetheless, caricature arrived in force after 1789, supported by even the Committee of Public Safety, which tried to harness it as a weapon in the Revolutionary cause.[4] As a result, caricature in France always carried with it the odor of subversion, even when its subjects were seemingly harmless. Early printed caricatures were either etched or engraved (or a combination of both), but the new medium of lithography,

11 "Three Ways of Seeing: Parisian Manner; English Manner; Mediterranean Manner," 1814. Handcolored etching. Bibliothèque nationale de France, Paris. ("Les Trois Manières de voir: Manière parisienne; Manière anglaise; Manière méridionale")

invented in the closing years of the eighteenth century, soon provided a cheaper and easier way of producing images: lithographs, involving drawing on stone and then treatment with a chemical solution, could be reproduced in thousands, whereas a print-run for etchings or engravings numbered, at most, hundreds. After an artist provided the drawing, the lithographer would supervise the technical processes. The engraver or etcher, on the other hand, was the artist, even when the work was reproductive. Their talent was so respected that, from the founding of the Académie des beaux-arts in 1648, a separate section was devoted to *gravure*, a category that included both etching and engraving. Even today, the Cabinet des estampes of the Bibliothèque nationale de France catalogues these prints by the name of the etcher or engraver, not that of the artist who provided the original drawing, while lithographs are catalogued only by the name of the original artist and not that of the lithographer. From the beginning, the implication was clear: intaglio was a form of high art, while lithography was not.

In the early nineteenth century, the most prevalent visual images treating the theme of "seeing" were lithographic caricatures showing an old husband, his young wife, and her young lover. A typical example is "(After the Ball) Tomorrow!" of 1824 (Figure 12) by Charles Philipon (1806–62). Such imagery had long been a staple in the print trade, as can be seen in the etching "The Eyeglass Merchant" of 1776 (Figure 13) by Jean-Baptiste Le Prince (1734–81).[5] One should note that the presence of spectacles (or, by extension, telescopes) in Western art traditionally signified that their user could not see, in the sense of "comprehend." Because of the continuity of this theme of husband, wife, and lover, commentary has tended to identify such subjects as traditional and thus to dismiss them from serious investigation.[6] If one were to take a more anthropologically informed view of the subject, however, one could not accept that the imagery produced in such quantities over long periods of time could be meaningless and socially functionless. Instead one would accept the premise that all visual imagery has meaning and function within a culture, that although these meanings may be complex and contested, varying according to audience and circumstance, nonetheless it is possible to hypothesize a relationship between cultural production and lived experience. That is my intention here.

The interpretation of visual imagery is as delicate a task as steering past the twin perils of Scylla and Charybdis: on the one side, problems of privileging innovation; on the other, those of an over-emphasis on tradition. Modernist art historians have tended to privilege innovation and the creativity of individual artists by assuming that the work of art under consideration is so exclusively the product of individual genius and imagination that it bears little relationship to societal forces. When tradition is privileged over innovation, however, and a theme can be traced over long periods of time, historians of all stripes have often assumed it to be, for that very reason, without any *specific* history or social function. The theme is then viewed much like a planet that remains in orbit from its own velocity, outside history, timeless and eternal. Social historians have their own ways of misreading imagery, with a tendency to regard visual images as direct illustrations of lived experience. Focusing less on individual artists, stylistic movements, and iconographic traditions, social historians often assume that a work of art is an unmediated window to the world, its meaning transparently obvious. Without the study of visual traditions, however, the end-result is similar to that of the individual-genius reading, an image isolated from its interpretative context.

On seeing an image for the first time, a social historian might begin by asking, "what does it mean?" as though it comes into the world *sui generis*, without antecedents, without context. An art historian, however, is more likely to look *through* the image to ask first "where does it come from?" Where it comes from includes the producers of the imagery as individuals (feminists would add as *gendered* individuals), but also as members of a nation, a period, and a class. Equally part of "where it comes from" are the medium and the stylistic move-

ment within which the image appears, each with its own formal traditions and iconography. Throughout the history of art, different media have been addressed to different constituencies of viewers and have served functions as different as those for paintings and cartoons. Even within media there are sub-categories: within contemporary photography, for example, there exist news photography, art photography, and family snapshots, to name just a few, each with its own function and audience.

While eighteenth-century painters and engravers produced themes similar to that of "The Eyeglass Merchant," those artists also produced a variety of other themes, from religious and moral to the licentious works widely attributed to upper-class taste.[7] As a result, these earlier themes come from a different source, and occupy a different strategic position in the visual spectrum of the period. Lithography, on the other hand, the medium of the Philipon image, was invented in the 1790s and was never quite respectable in France because of its early use in political caricature and its association with industry. From its beginnings it was associated with radical and oppositional politics, an identification underscored by the fact that its early practitioners tended to be young men from the liberal opposition.[8]

12 (*facing page*) Charles Philipon, "(After the Ball) Tomorrow!," *Les Amours du bon ton*, 5, 1824. Lithograph. Lith. Villain. Bibliothèque nationale de France, Paris. ("La Sortie du bal) Demain!")

13 Jean-Baptiste Le Prince, gr. Isidore-Stanislas Helman, "The Eyeglass Merchant," 1776. Etching after painting of 1773. Bibliothèque nationale de France, Paris. ("Le Marchand de lunettes")

Lithography represented modernity, creeping industrialization, and opposition politics, while etching and engraving signaled tradition, the high standards of artisanal craftsmanship, and respectable upper-class taste. As the nineteenth century progressed, engraving became increasingly identified with aesthetic and political conservatism, lithography with aesthetic and political dissent. An illustration of the low status of lithography was given in an essay published in 1828, "Observations on the Morals and Customs of Parisians at the Beginning of the Nineteenth Century." Its authors, Joseph-Marie Pain and C. de Beauregard, described the home of a man infatuated with modernity, the sure sign of a political liberal: "His salon is decorated with lithographs, on the mantelpiece there is a large clock whose face, hands, and frame are made of cardboard; on each side is a vase made of fake marble."[9] Here the lithographs are also considered fake, ersatz engravings. So even if exactly the same image were produced in these two media, they would be as different as silver from plastic or, as noted here, as marble from cardboard.

Because of their huge print-runs, lithographs were cheap, and this gave them a popular urban audience, but there were even cheaper prints, the crude woodcut *images d'Épinal* destined for the rural lower classes. The function of

LA JEUNE MARIÉE.

14   François Georgin, "The Young Bride," 1828. Handcolored woodcut. Dist. Pellerin, Epinal. Musée national des arts et traditions populaires, Paris. ("La Jeune Mariée")

prints was a major determinant of the types of image produced for each audience. Since works of art, even cheap prints, were less a part of rural culture, the subjects of *Épinal* prints differed, tending towards images of piety and patriotism.[10] Marriage scenes, when represented, were idealized, as in *The Young Bride* (Figure 14) by François Georgin (1801–63), an oft-repeated image. As poorer households displayed the few prints they owned, while wealthier collectors kept most of their numerous prints in portfolios for private delectation, a parallel can here be drawn of public vs. private discourse.[11]

Although the sophisticated cynicism intrinsic to urban culture (apparent in Figure 12) was absent in prints intended for rural audiences, one cannot conclude that this implies the absence of the behavior depicted, no more than one can assume that its presence proves that such behavior was common. Works of art played a more idealistic role in the countryside, almost as ambassadors from an alien culture, and, as they were on continuous public display, they showed a public face. Other cultural practices such as the rural custom of *charivari* ("shivaree" or "rough music" in English) carried out the parallel task of negative commentary on moral transgression.[12] This should be seen as a change in medium, from graphic design to performance art, for charivari, the noisy clanging of pots and pans under the windows of a moral offender, was a highly ritualized and theatrical form of expression.

A second major methodological concern should be the destination of the imagery: "Who is it for?" This is as important as its source. Visual imagery does not exist in a vacuum, but always within a social matrix, somewhat like an arrow shot into the air whose trajectory can be traced both forward and backward: where it comes from and where it is going. In the early nineteenth century, the medium of lithography itself signaled its audience, namely the liberal and politically oppositional classes, as well as the lower urban economic strata that could not afford engravings. Lithographs were published as single sheets, in albums, and in the new illustrated journals of the liberal opposition whose caricaturists and publishers were often arrested for violation of the strict censorship laws.[13] These journals began to appear with *Le Nain jaune* in 1814, and their numbers grew throughout the century.[14] *Le Charivari*, established in 1832, was the best known of them, its very title signaling its intention of social criticism. The noisy rural ritual of social censure was replaced in this sophisticated urban journal by wickedly funny satires, both visual and literary, relentlessly ridiculing every foible of the ruling classes.

In the lithographs of husband, wife, and lover, the generational warfare between old men and young men is foregrounded in a way that is absent in earlier prints; it is notable in Philipon's "(After the Ball)" (Figure 12). The young men in these later prints are invariably represented as handsome and elegant, while their elders are shown as cloddish, unattractive, and stupid, unable to "see" what their wives are up to, even with the aid of thick eyeglasses. They do not "see" in either sense of the word. In earlier prints on similar themes, generational warfare is less graphically inscribed on the face and figure of the old husband. The viewer is meant to notice, for example, the cruel caricature present in the lithograph "The Useless Precaution" of 1819 (Figure 15). The husband is depicted as short, fat, and ugly, in comparison with the handsome lover who helps the old man's lovely young wife escape from his locked house; on the old man's forehead the bumps of the cuckold's horns are already beginning to sprout. Neither cruelty nor caricature feature in an earlier etched version by Le Prince (Figure 16). The old man dozes, ineffectual against his wife's flirtation, but he is in no way vilified. The transformation of this trope must be read as a metaphor for all the other types of generational warfare that were rampant during these post-Revolutionary years, when the Restoration monarchy reinstated a ruling gerontocracy and effectively disenfranchised the younger generation of men. This competition and animosity between generations of men, as described in Lynn Hunt's *The Family Romance of the French Revolution* and in Alan Spitzer's *The French Generation of 1820*, was summed up succinctly by Balzac: France had "only two ages, youth and senility."[15] And it was most definitely youth that produced these caricatures: the principal artists working in this medium during the Restoration, Edme-Jean Pigal (1798–1873), Grandville (pseudonym of Jean-Ignace-Isidore Gérard, 1803–47), and Philipon, were all under thirty, as were the authors of the satirical marital literature discussed in the previous chapter.[16] These artists established the tropes made famous later in the century by artists such as Honoré Daumier (1808–79) and Paul Gavarni (Guillaume-Sulpice Chevalier, 1804–66).[17] Philipon went on to

15 (*right*) "The Useless Precaution," 1819. Handcolored lithograph. Dist. Martinet. Bibliothèque nationale de France, Paris. ("La Précaution inutile")

La Précaution inutile —

16 (*below*) Jean-Baptiste Le Prince, gr. Isidore-Stanislas Helman, "The Useless Precaution," 1779. Etching after painting of 1774. Bibliothèque nationale de France, Paris. ("La Précaution inutile")

17   Charles Philipon, "Madame's Friend," *Epoux parisiens*, 2, 1825. Lithograph. Lith. Langlumé, Dist. Martinet et Frérot. Bibliothèque nationale de France, Paris. ("Un Ami de madame")

establish the publishing house La Maison Aubert (1829) and the journals *La Caricature* (1830), *La Charivari* (1832), *Le Journal pour rire* (1849), and *Le Journal amusant* (1850), all of which published the work of the major nineteenth-century caricaturists.[18] Many of them incurred numerous fines and prison sentences from a variety of political regimes throughout the century, thus reinforcing the "credentials" of the medium as determinedly oppositional.

In these images of husband, wife, and lover, the female is presented as "between men," to use Eve Kosofsky Sedgwick's term.[19] The female here is the trophy in the competition between two generations of men. She is often depicted quite literally "between men," standing between her husband and her lover, as in Philipon's "Madame's Friend" (Figure 17). In this caricature, even the men's costumes are clearly coded in order to differentiate the two generations. The old husband wears outmoded knee britches, while the young lover is dressed as a fashionable dandy. Through his greater attractiveness, the young lover visually articulates the threat and the taunt that Balzac made in his *Physiology of Marriage* (discussed in chapter 2 above), that young men would inevitably steal their elders' wives.

So for whom is this print intended? It is unlikely that the old gents shown here would be flattered at their depiction, but it is equally unlikely that such men would be patronizing the journals and publishers responsible for the production of these prints.[20] Would women dare to own such images, at a time when such transgressions were severely punished? Whether they owned them or not, young women married off to unattractive old husbands might well form an appreciative audience for such images. In any case, in the early nineteenth century the young male artists, who greatly resembled the heroes of the prints they created, were in the camp of the political opposition: they churned out caricatures ridiculing the older entrenched generation of men, in the suspect medium of lithography, and published these prints either in opposition journals or through publishers who themselves were often imprisoned for political offenses. It is remarkable, not that I am reading these genre images as politically charged, but that no one else has previously done so.

An essential part of the social meaning of any image is bound up with the breadth of its distribution, how loudly it speaks its message. Prints, by their very nature, are multiples and are the result of collaboration among several individuals – the artist, the engraver or lithographer, the printer, the colorist, the publisher, the printseller, the purchaser. Lithographic equipment was expensive, workshops and salesrooms had to be maintained. By their nature, then, prints represent a more socially ratified imagery than unique works of art, such as paintings, that can be produced by individual artists with a minimum investment. This observation is underscored by the fact that, when a painting did achieve widespread fame, engravings or lithographs of it were immediately produced to bring that image within the sphere of a larger public. Since the concept of limited and numbered print editions was unknown before the late nineteenth century, plates or stones were printed until either they or the demand wore out. Lithographic stones could produce thousands of prints, but even intaglio plates could be recut and reprinted.[21] The existence of dozens of variations on a theme, or numerous re-editions, bespeaks a compelling social resonance. The message is then echoed, repeated, and ratified by thousands of voices. In the same way that reprises of successful films show that a responsive chord has been struck in the public consciousness, the existence of numerous variations on a theme, even plagiarism, indicates continued audience demand, and allows a kind of hierarchy of importance for individual themes to be established. In this way prints serve as more accurate indices of cultural values than do paintings, which by their nature are unique objects and thus are more likely to represent an individual point of view. For this reason, art historians are interested in the unique image, the work of one individual, while social and cultural historians are more interested in common images widely diffused throughout a culture from high to low.

While country folk bought whatever images they owned from travelling peddlers (*colporteurs*), urban dwellers bought individual prints from a wide spectrum of printshops. Henri Monnier (1799–1877) shows a fashionable boutique selling framed etchings and engravings (Figure 18), while Nicolas-

Toussaint Charlet (1792–1845) represents the opposite extreme (Figure 19), a stall along the embankments of the Seine with lithographs pinned up for passers-by to see. Somewhere in the middle were shops like the Delpech establishment (Figure 20) depicted by Carle Vernet (1758–1836). As can be seen in these images, an audience for prints of all kinds is no more limited to collectors than a television audience is limited to those who buy videotapes. Robert Goldstein, in his *Censorship of Political Caricature in Nineteenth-Century France*, has shown that lithographic imagery throughout the nineteenth century was more rigidly censored than text, on the grounds that it was cheap, readily available, and appealed to those who could not read.[22] Governmental concerns about the effects of lithography can be readily understood in the light of the means of distribution here, for cheap lithographs were more likely to be displayed outdoors, pinned up for passers-by, while expensive engravings were sold in elegant boutiques inaccessible to the poor and illiterate.

   Although the label of "tradition" has often been attached to visual tropes, they all have histories. Like Heraclitus' river, each occurrence is different even when seemingly the same. This becomes evident when one locates the ends of a tradition, when it began, when it mutated, when it disappeared. The title of Renate Bridenthal's and Claudia Koonz's valuable study of women's history, *Becoming Visible*, is a good parallel here for, in art as well as in social history, themes become visible at certain moments.[23] Even themes continuous over centuries had to have been sustained by ongoing social conditions or they would have disappeared – as many did. Before the eighteenth century, for example, "The Amorous Old Man" (Figure 21) was a common theme, showing an old man attempting to seduce a young woman through an offer of money.[24] The issue of marriage never complicated this trope, however, and it was not until the mid-eighteenth century that the old man's competition, in the person of the young lover, became "visible." Images of adultery existed, to be sure, in both secular and in religious contexts. A familiar secular image is that of the "guild of cuckolds," as seen in Figure 22; if anything, such images "normalize" adultery by presenting it, not only as inevitable, but even as something of a joke. The most prevalent religious image was the biblical lesson of Christ's forgiveness of the woman taken in adultery, but such images customarily depicted her in social isolation, without either lover or husband. Not until the mid-eighteenth century was the entire cast of characters revised and united in a single image, with adultery represented as a generational problem. It might, in fact, be an aspect of modernity that allowed young men to displace their elders in an "open market" competition, for love as well as for other "commodities"; note also that the eighteenth century is usually identified as the origin of both economic and philosophical modernism.

   Some themes lasted for centuries. The earliest examples of "The Battle for the Culotte," for instance, date from the fifteenth century, showing a husband and wife, each wanting "to wear the pants in the family" (Figure 23).[25] Natalie

18 (*above*) Henry Monnier, "The Merchant of Prints," *Boutiques de Paris*, 4, 1827. Handcolored lithograph. Lith. & Dist. Delpech. Bibliothèque nationale de France, Paris. ("Le Marchand d'estampes")

19 (*facing page top*) Nicolas-Toussaint Charlet, "The Merchant of Lithographs," *c*. 1819. Lithograph. Lith. & Dist. Delpech. Bibliothèque nationale de France, Paris. ("Le Marchand de dessins lithographiques")

20 (*facing page bottom*) Carle Vernet, "F. Delpech Lithographic Publisher," 1818. Lithograph. Lith. & Dist. Delpech. Bibliothèque nationale de France, Paris. ("Imprimerie lithographique de F. Delpech")

Zemon Davis's "Women on Top" offers valuable possibilities for interpreting such long-term themes.[26] Her article proposes that the persistence of such themes of "unruly women" tacitly acknowledges the norm (wives are supposed to be submissive, obedient, and faithful), by ridiculing its transgressors. At the same time, however, such themes keep resistance alive by proposing, articulating, and thereby normalizing an alternative vision of the world. In the "Battle for the Culotte," the proposed reality is that both spouses are actually equal in strength and independence, while in the multitudinous "Husband, Wife, and Lover" images, the proposed reality seems to be that, if spouses are unsuitably

Le Marchand de Dessins Lithographiques.

Imp. Lithog. de F. Delpech

Imprimerie Lithographique de F. Delpech.

21 (*above*) "The Amorous Old Man," early eighteenth century. Etching. Dist. Landry. Bibliothèque nationale de France, Paris. ("L'Amoureux Vieillard")

22 "Your guild meets at the sign of the horns. You should go there to enroll yourself in the book of martyrs; and if anger makes you sad, why then console yourself with a drink," *c.* 1660. Engraving. Dist. Jacques Lagniet. Bibliothèque nationale de France, Paris. ("A la corne jenins, c'est vostre confrairie / Vous y devez venir pour vous faire enroller / Au livre des martyrs; et si la fascherie / Vous attriste, en buvant allez vous consoler")

A la corne jenins, c'est vostre confrairie
Vous y devez venir pour vous faire enroller
Au livre des martyrs, et si la fascherie
Vous attriste, en buvant allez vous consoler

23 François Guérard, "The Battle for the Culotte," *c.* 1690. Etching. Bibliothèque nationale de France, Paris. ("Le Débat pour la culotte")

matched, then women owe no loyalty to husbands they have not chosen. The message of the imagery actually cuts in both directions. Despite all the varying interpretations of visual imagery, it is rarely acknowledged that images are often not just multivalent, but are even able to present contradictory readings simultaneously.

These images of old men with unfaithful young wives and their young lovers did not, then, have such a long history in Western art. Such images appeared in the mid-eighteenth century and disappeared in the course of the nineteenth. They flourished, in fact, during the same period that marked the struggle for hegemony of the concept of marriage for love. The tradition of arranged marriages in France was both long established and long contested, as is clear in the many novels and plays dealing with this conflict from the seventeenth century onwards.[27] The persistence of the theme might not, then, be a sign of its *lack* of specific historical significance, but an indication of its *long-term* historical significance. The "proof" of this is that the theme has gradually disappeared during the modern period as spouses have become more evenly matched in age, and as the custom of arranged marriages itself has gradually diminished in the Western world.

The question of reading these particular images in the light of social history remains. Is seeing believing? This question can be answered in two ways, either symbolically or literally. The sudden arrival of the young lover into the earlier trope of old man and young woman, and the transformation into a *ménage à trois* could be interpreted as corresponding to a symbolized social reality, in which the specter of the marriage for love has begun to intrude on the tradition of the arranged marriage. The generational rivalry foregrounded in these revised images can be read as corresponding also to the transformation in social relationships during the period, when respect for figures of paternal authority – principally fathers but, by extension, old husbands as well – was greatly diminished.[28] In that sense, these images "envision" new social roles and attitudes.

The question "How widespread were these May–December marriages?" is more difficult to answer. As accurate statistics before the late nineteenth century are available for only small self-enclosed communities, not for large urban centers, a definitive answer is impossible.[29] Nonetheless, while it is certain that first marriages in rural areas were usually between spouses in their twenties, urban and upper-class families – the ones targeted by these images – seem to have preferred a wider disparity in age.[30] It was, in fact, commonly accepted among the propertied classes that men should not marry before age twenty-five to thirty, while women were usually married before twenty.[31] The Cairon marriage, discussed in chapter 1, was typical in that she was seventeen, he twenty-nine. In any case, second marriages in all regions, the obvious targets of these images, were most often between a widower and a much younger, previously unmarried, female. Because of high childbirth mortality, there were many widowers, and population studies are unanimous in confirming that they remarried more often than widows, usually within a year.[32]

Such marriages were as controversial in cities as they were in the countryside. Whether urban or rural, they were fiercely resented by young men who were forced to remain celibate while their elders depleted the pool of nubile young females, and since the older men could offer more in the way of worldly goods (and the bride had little say in the matter), the older men would almost always have priority in their choice of wives, even second wives. The contemporary reformers Guillaume-Tell Doin and Edouard Charton wrote that since young men could not even consider marriage before age thirty, the result was that they became sexually frustrated and were forced to develop depraved morals, a rationale that Balzac slyly offered as an apology for young men's seducing older men's wives.[33]

In the countryside this resentment and frustration often resulted in a charivari carried out by young men at the remarriage of a widower to a young woman; in the cities, lithographs, often published in such journals as *Le Charivari*, served much the same function of ridicule. Besides remembering that the primary impetus behind this social criticism had more to do with the infringement of male prerogatives than with the advocacy of women's rights, one must also remember that the statistical occurrence of a perceived transgression is not the crucial determinant of its social meaning. Often the specter of a perceived abuse takes on a significance seemingly out of all proportion to its statistical occurrence and becomes invested with symbolic value in contingent fields. And so, although it is unlikely that May–December marriages were all that numerous, the fact that they occurred at all was perceived as an affront to the property rights of young men over "their" women and thus, symbolically, became charged with all the injustices of a gerontocracy. Similarly, while it is highly unlikely that so many young wives married to old husbands sought young lovers for solace, at least some did – as is evidenced by the court cases discussed in chapter 1.

If one thinks of visual production as a field of social discourse, one can understand immediately that at any moment some subjects have resonance and others do not. Visual imagery does not then correspond simply to the existence of any social condition, but to its position within this field of discourse; not to its statistical probability, but to its symbolic value.

The trope of the old husband, young wife, and her young lover continued unabated from the eighteenth century into the nineteenth, from the respectable medium of engraving into the politically suspect medium of lithography. There was, however, a rupture in the continuity of the theme, marked by the husband's sudden self-awareness and anger: he suddenly opened his eyes and began to "see." Images of stalking and catching appeared suddenly in France after the Revolution, replacing the blissfully unaware spouse of earlier decades. This new situation can be seen in a lithograph by Louis-Léopold Boilly (1761–1845), "Oh, what a fool he is!" (Figure 24), and in Pigal's later version "That's my wife, damn it! It's impossible!" (Figure 25). This new awareness can best be illustrated by comparison with earlier images of inadvertent catching and "seeing." In the eighteenth-century etching "What! My son-in-law! It's you!" (Figure 26), the situation seems more comical than dangerous, with the lover, hiding under a dress form, exposed by a husband who seems more startled than angry. In "Love on Trial" (Figure 27) by Pierre-Antoine Baudouin (1723–69) the situation is described thus: "in returning from court, the magistrate Siguret finds his wife sleeping in the arms of the abbé de Bois-Robert."[34] Siguret seems neither surprised nor enraged at discovering, not only his wife's adultery, but a man of the cloth as her lover.

How can these images be interpreted? Can it be assumed that eighteenth-century husbands didn't care? No, but it is known that what was formerly an individual husband's problem, which he could deal with as he chose, either with a *lettre de cachet* ordering his wife's imprisonment without trial or simply by ignoring the situation, refusing to "see," took on, after 1789, the resonance of a social problem – at least in part as a reaction against the profligacy of the upper-classes in Old Regime France.[35]

The next stage after stalking is armed intervention, a theme that was non-existent in the eighteenth century. Although Boilly does show the cuckolded old

Ah! ah! qui est là?

C'est ma femme parbleu! Pas-possible!

26   "What! My son-in-law! It's you!" Eigh-teenth century. Etching. Bibliothèque nationale de France, Paris. ("Quoi! mon gendre! C'est vous!")

27   Pierre-Antoine Baudouin, gr. Beauvarlet, "Love on Trial," c. 1777. Etching. Bibliothèque nationale de France, Paris. ("L'amour à l'épreuve")

24   (*facing page top*)   Louis-Léopold Boilly, gr. Simon Petit, "Oh, what a fool he is!" Etching after painting from Salon of 1791. Bibliothèque nationale de France, Paris. ("Ah! Ah! Qu'il est sot!")

25   (*facing page bottom*)   Edme-Jean Pigal, "That's my wife, damn it! It's impossible!" 1822. Handcolored lithograph. Lith. Langlumé, Dist. Gihaut et Martinet. Bibliothèque nationale de France, Paris. ("C'est ma femme parbleu! Pas-possible!")

28   Grandville, "The Hare Taken in His Den," *Les Métamorphoses du jour*, 3, 1828–29. Handcolored lithograph. Lith. Lespirant, Dist. Bulla. Bibliothèque nationale de France, Paris. ("Le Lièvre pris au gîte")

husband shaking his fist at his rival (Figure 24), weapons do not begin to appear until much later, in prints such as Grandville's "The Hare Taken in His Den" (Figure 28), and the later, even more menacing image by Jules-Joseph Bourdet (1799–1869), captioned "So, I'm a stupid old man, am I! So, I'm an old fool, am I! So, I'm obsolete, oh, handsome cousin of my oh-so-guilty wife! It's time to end all that. You will die, both of you, by God!!!" (Figure 29). Bourdet has confined himself to the standard features of the trope, a handsome, dandyish young lover contrasted with an ugly, bespectacled old husband in old-fashioned attire who, although now armed and dangerous, is nonetheless adorned with the cuckold's horns in the form of his headscarf. Grandville wittily complicates this still further with multiple layers of symbolism, transforming the husband into an old hunting dog, the lover into a fashionable young hare, and the wife into a lascivious monkey, while decorating the wall behind the lovers with a hunting scene showing the hound attacking the hare. The room is decorated with an antlered stag head, the traditional sign of a cuckold, but there is now

29 Jules-Joseph Bourdet, "So, I'm a stupid old man, am I! So, I'm an old fool, am I! So, I'm obsolete, oh, handsome cousin of my oh-so-guilty wife! It's time to end all that. You will die, both of you, by God!!!" *Les Liaisons dangereuses*, 9, 1838. Lithograph. Lith. Caboche. Bibliothèque nationale de France, Paris. ("Ah! Je suis un vieux stupide, ah! Je suis une vieille ganache, ah! Je suis rococo, joli cousin de ma trop coupable épouse, il est temps que tout cela finisse; vous périrez tous deux! Sacristi!!!")

a rifle slung beneath the horns: this cuckold is armed and dangerous! No wonder the monkey-wife is wringing her hands in anticipation of the confrontation.

In the course of a few decades, the husband's militant response to his wife's adultery has become socially condoned and "visible." These images of a husband who does "see" comprised the fastest growing body of imagery of the period, bolstered, no doubt, by the new laws which gave husbands the right to murder wives caught *in flagrante delicto*, a right they did not have under the Old Regime. As a result, these images present simultaneous and contradictory readings: while ridiculing the betrayed husband, they also demonstrate the very real dangers of adultery. After the Revolution these prints were so numerous that representations of the husband who does not "see" became increasingly rare.

One of the few eighteenth-century French "catching" images is the painting *Mars and Venus Surprised by Vulcan* (Figure 30) by François Boucher

Mars et Venus, dont Apollon decouvre le
coñierce et en inftruit Vulcain.

30   François Boucher, *Mars and Venus Surprised by Vulcan*, 1754. Oil on canvas, 166 × 85 cm. Wallace Collection, London.

31   Noël Le Mire, "Mars and Venus, whose liaison was discovered by Apollo who then told Vulcan," 1765. Etching after Boucher from *Les Métamorphoses d'Ovide gravées sur les dessins des meilleurs peintres français par les soins des Sr Le Mire et Basan graveurs* (Paris: Basan & Le Mire, [1770]). Bibliothèque nationale de France, Paris. ("Mars et Vénus, dont Apollon découvre le commerce et en instruit Vulcain")

(1703–70). It has a murky provenance, but the one clear fact is that it was not highly sought after in France and ended up in England where such images were more acceptable.[36] When Noël Le Mire (1724–1800) engraved this subject for Ovid's *Metamorphosis* (Figure 31), he kept Boucher's theme, titling his work "Mars and Venus, whose liaison was discovered by Apollo who then told Vulcan," but in his image angry Vulcan is nowhere in sight.[37] While the

32 Grandville, "Mars and Venus Surprised by Vulcan: Caught . . . ," *Galerie mythologique*, 3, 1830. Handcolored lithograph. Lith. Langlumé, Dist. Bulla. Bibliothèque nationale de France, Paris. ("Mars et Vénus surpris par Vulcain: Enfoncé . . .")

eighteenth-century aristocracy that formed Boucher's audience seem to have had an insatiable appetite for depictions of Venus' amorous exploits, the situation of her cuckolded husband was not resonant in social discourse and so remained invisible. Vulcan as outraged husband made a return appearance only in the following century, when Grandville brought him back in his "Mars and Venus Surprised by Vulcan: Caught . . ." (Figure 32). Here, Grandville underscores the difference between the aristocratic tradition of the amorous exploits of the gods and the new bourgeois morality. For Grandville, Vulcan is just another outraged plebeian husband demanding his rights in the face of his pretty young wife's adultery with an aristocratic and handsome military officer. Again the traditional image of the stag/cuckold adorns the wall, but Grandville has added other witty and original touches. Mars is disarmed, his sword and helmet discarded during his lovemaking, but Vulcan, a brawny blacksmith in leather apron, is accompanied by several workmen, one of whom menacingly grips a hammer, visually juxtaposed to Mars's now-useless sword. The weapon is crude and working class, but it will prevail. The net result is a confrontation

33   Pierre-Antoine
Baudouin, gr. Nicolas
de Launay, "The Sentinel
Off-Guard," 1771. Etching.
Bibliothèque nationale de
France, Paris. ("La Sen-
tinelle en défaut")

34 (*facing page*)   Honoré
Fragonard, "The Armoire,"
1778. Etching. Bibliothèque
nationale de France, Paris.
("L'Armoire")

of class overlaying and underscoring the ostensible conflict of class-defined
moral codes.

   In any era, images with little resonance in social discourse exist in vastly
reduced numbers, if at all. In eighteenth-century culture, adultery played a
relatively minor role in visual imagery, while fornication not only provided the
plot for numerous novels, but inspired quantities of visual imagery as well. To
judge by the quantities of what we might call "fornicatory" imagery, protect-
ing a daughter's virginity seems to have been much more important at the time
than safeguarding a wife's virtue. Often quite droll, this "fornicatory" imagery
seems to fall into two major categories: either the young lovers successfully
evade her guardians, as in Baudouin's "The Sentinel Off-Guard" (Figure 33),
or they get caught, as in the sly etching "The Armoire" (Figure 34) by Jean-
Honoré Fragonard (1732–1806), in which the young swain's hat seems to stand
up with no visible means of support.

   The visual codes were quite clear and legible to their audiences. The presence of both parents, or at least the mother, in these prints gives an infallible
indication the image concerns the sexual transgression of a daughter and not

L'ARMOIRE

a wife. In adultery tropes, the "seeing" (or not seeing), the spying, and the catching are always done by a single male figure who, in context, can represent only the husband.

By the nineteenth century, the relative popularity of the themes of fornication and adultery were reversed in visual imagery: for every fornication image, there were now dozens of adultery images. This finding parallels the thesis of Tony Tanner in his study *Adultery in the Novel*, which proposes that seduction and fornication were the primary eighteenth-century literary themes, replaced in the nineteenth century by adultery.[38] In terms of resonance, it might also be noted that, in the nineteenth century, the myriad images of the husband catching his wife and her lover were not paralleled by images of the wife catching her husband, a subject that might have had more significance for female viewers. I have found only two such images, one before and one after the period of this study. An eighteenth-century etching by Baudouin, "The Indiscreet Wife" (Figure 35), shows a boudoir scene between the husband and an unidentified female, probably a servant, while the "indiscreet wife" of the title crouches behind a pile of bedding to spy on them. The nineteenth-century

35   Pierre-Antoine
Baudouin, gr. Nicolas de
Launay, "The Indiscreet
Wife," 1771. Etching.
Bibliothèque nationale de
France, Paris. ("L'Epouse
indiscrète")

36 *(facing page top)* Jules
David, "The Wife Who
Sees Too Much," 1834.
Lithograph. Lith. Lemercier,
Dist. Jeannin, Paris, &
Ch. Tilt, London.
Bibliothèque nationale de
France, Paris. ("La Femme
y voit trop.")

37 *(facing page bottom)*
Jules David, "The Husband
Who Doesn't See," *c.* 1834.
Lithograph. Lith. Lemercier,
Dist. Jeannin, Paris, &
Ch. Tilt, London.
Bibliothèque nationale de
France, Paris. ("Le Mari
n'y voit pas")

lithograph is by Jules David (1808–92), "The Wife Who Sees Too Much"
(Figure 36), his pendant to "The Husband Who Doesn't See" (Figure 37). These
images are constructed as cautionary tales, announcing that the wife should *not*
see precisely what her husband, on pain of ridicule, *ought* to see. When one
reflects that her adultery was legally defined as a crime while his was considered normal, and that legally she had few rights under the law, one can understand that the social discourse that would have made such events visible was
absent.

The asymmetry of the marriage contract is illustrated by the pendants "The
Faithless Man" (Figure 38) and "Oh, the Faithless Woman!" (Figure 39) that
present male and female versions of betrayal. Even the titles convey a greater
degree of outrage at the female's offense whose title is exclamatory, not simply
declarative. The faithless female, from the propertied classes judging by her
dress and the interior décor of the scene, is shown cheating on her husband,
who is spying on them from beneath a table; one might well call this image
"The Indiscreet Husband." In the pendant, her male counterpart's offense is
not adultery, but impregnating and then abandoning a poor, unmarried woman,
a milliner, judging by the mannequin on the floor. Her unmarried status is con-

LA FEMME
Y VOIT TROP.

Paris, Imprimé rue du Croissant, N°16.

Lith. de Lemercier

London by Ch. Tilt, 86 Fleet Street.

1834 - 359

LE MARI
N'Y VOIT PAS.

Paris, Imprimé rue du Croissant, N°16.

Lith. de Lemercier

London Ch. Tilt, 86 Fleet Street.

1834 - 404

Le Perfide.

veyed by the salutation "Mademoiselle" on the letter she holds, her poverty by
the splintered and worn floor of the room, bereft of furniture other than the
baby's cradle and the chest on which she sits. The faithless man of the title is
invisible, both in this image and in the legal codes.

Another example of a discourse gaining or losing visibility is the eighteenth-
century campaign for a redefinition of fatherhood that ran parallel to the contemporaneous campaign to elevate motherhood.[39] The fatherhood campaign
attempted to reform the traditional authoritarian father into a friendly and
affectionate family member. Beginning in mid-century, this new paternal ideal
was noticeable in all domains, social, philosophical, political, and cultural.[40]
Numerous engravings appeared during these years depicting the pleasures of
paternity. Etienne Aubry (1745–81) in "Paternal Love," Jean-Michel Moreau le
jeune (1774–1814) in "True Happiness," and Philibert-Louis Debucourt
(1755–1832) in "Paternal Pleasures" (Figures 40–42), all show fathers, ranging
from the rural to the well-to-do, in affectionate loving relationships with their
children. Previously these kinds of image were most familiar in Western art as
part of the "world upside-down" trope that demonstrated only the absurdity of
the behavior depicted. Beginning in the eighteenth century, the nurturing father

38 (facing page)
A. M., "The Faithless
Man," 1823. Litho-
graph. Lith. Langlumé,
Dist. Cornillon.
Bibliothèque nationale
de France, Paris.
("Le Perfide")

39 S. C., "Oh, the
Faithless Woman! . .
.," 1824. Lithograph.
Lith. & Dist.
Langlumé.
Bibliothèque nationale
de France, Paris.
("Oh la perfide! . . .")

was contrasted with the rifle-toting mother, as can be seen in an image from *Men's Folly, or the World Upside-Down* (Figure 43).[41] It carries a legend that left no doubt whatsoever about the perceived folly of a nurturing father: "The wife has the musket, she the female. Even worse, the husband dandles the infant on his knees."

World Upside-Down prints were prevalent throughout Europe from at least the seventeenth century, freely plagiarized from one country to another. Single-leaf sheets, usually crudely printed and colored woodblock prints, these customarily combined gender-bender images with more obvious "upside-down" tropes such as horses riding men, masters attending servants, trees growing upside-down. Seen together, they served to underscore the absurdity of any reversal of gender roles. The images featuring women are now especially interesting, as they show women drinking and smoking, preaching in church, fighting duels, serving in the civil guard, hunting and shooting – a virtual catalogue of what was considered absurd and ridiculous female behavior in previous centuries but what has since (except dueling) become familiar. As Natalie Zemon Davis would point out, at the same time that these prints mocked the behavior depicted, they nonetheless envisioned its possibility.

40 Etienne Aubry, gr. Jean-Charles Levasseur, "Paternal Love." Etching
after painting from Salon of 1775. Bibliothèque nationale de France,
Paris. ("L'Amour paternel")

At least one of these "world upside-down" images, that of the nurturing
father, was transformed from absurd to ideal and back again in the course of
a century. The eighteenth-century etchings of paternal bliss obviously share a
visual genealogy with the crude popular woodcuts shown here, and perhaps in
a very real way the etchings were consciously intended to represent the "world
upside-down." Since Enlightenment reformers did intend to remake contemporary mores as part of a new vision that they "saw" as diametrically opposed
to their contemporaneous reality, the result would indeed be a "world upside-
down" – but much improved because of that.

Unfortunately, the campaign for nurturing fatherhood lasted only a few
decades and was ultimately unsuccessful, swiftly collapsing during the Revolutionary period when the image of the father became too closely identified with
the repressive monarchy.[42] By the nineteenth century the ideal of the nurturing
father had become *in*visible and, thereafter, insofar as fatherhood images
existed at all, they were produced in the service of anti-feminism. A lithograph
from *The Vicissitudes of Paternity* (Figure 44) is probably one of the first such
images, with its anti-feminism inscribed on the father's angry features. This is

41 Jean-Michel Moreau le jeune, gr. Jean-Baptiste Simonet, "True Happiness." Etching with engraving from *Troisième Suite d'estampes pour servir à l'histoire des modes et du costume en France dans le dix-huitième siècle. Année 1783* (Paris: Prault, 1783). Bibliothèque nationale de France, Paris. ("Le Vrai Bonheur")

42 Philibert-Louis Debucourt, "Paternal Pleasures," *c.* 1790. Color etching. Bibliothèque nationale de France, Paris. ("Les plaisirs paternels")

indeed a "world upside-down" in that the wife reads, an intellectual activity considered more fitting for a man, while her husband attempts (unsuccessfully it appears) to nurture his child, an activity that, by the nineteenth century, was considered exclusively a woman's role. By the early nineteenth century, paternal love, so eulogized by Enlightenment philosophers, had in fact disappeared from the public discourse on family roles, and, by the Restoration, fathers and husbands had regained much of their former authority. Gender roles had become so rigidly codified that soon only women would be identified with family values. Later in the century, Daumier produced several series of lithographs caricaturing any departure from these newly defined gender roles. In *The Blue-Stockings* (1844) and *Socialist Women* (1849), he often made an explicit connection between the wife's reading (or, even worse, writing) and the husband's child-nurturing in order to underscore, still again, the absurdity of any reversal of "natural" gender roles.[43] Daumier's lithograph "Farewell my dear, I'm going to my publishers" (Figure 45) is a typical example of the equation of female literacy and independence with "the world upside-down."

The campaign for motherhood was a good deal more successful than that for fatherhood, and its effects are, in fact, still apparent in Western culture. Many scholars have discussed this campaign, which had, as one of its principal motivations, a desire to limit the high infant-mortality rate resulting from the prevalence of wetnursing. Before this, children, except among the poorest classes, were rarely reared at home. Anyone who could afford it shipped them off to wetnurses soon after they were born, and there they spent the first several years of their lives, returning, if they survived, to families where they barely knew their own parents.[44] All this was of great concern to the social reformers of the Enlightenment, who mounted a major campaign in the cause of marriage, motherhood, and the nuclear family – indeed *invented* childhood as a separate and special period of life. Children previously had been considered miniature adults with no special rights or privileges; now great care was taken

43   "The wife has the musket, she the female. Even worse, the husband dandles the baby on his knees," *La Folie des hommes, ou Le Monde à rebours*, 1719. Woodcut. Musée national des arts et traditions populaires, Paris. ("La Femme a le mousquet la quenouille. L'Epoux et berce pour surcroît l'enfant sur ses genoux")

*La femme a le mousquet la quenoüille, L'Epoux
Et berce pour surcroît l'Enfant Sur Ses genoux .*

44 B. [Frédéric Bouchot?], "Marie! Victoire!! the milk! the baby! everything . . . ," *Les Vicissitudes de la paternité*, 1824. Lithograph. Lith. Langlumé. Bibliothèque nationale de France, Paris. ("Marie! Victoire!! le lait! l'enfant! tout . . .")

45 Honoré Daumier, "Farewell my dear, I'm going to my publishers . . . I probably won't be back until very late . . . don't forget to feed Dodore twice more . . . if he needs . . . something else . . . you'll find it under the bed . . ." *Les Bas Bleus*, in *Le Charivari*, 8 Feb. 1844. Lithograph. Lith. & Dist. Aubert. ("Adieu mon cher, je vais chez mes éditeurs . . . je ne rentrerai probablement que fort tard . . . ne manquez pas de donner encore deux fois la bouillie à Dodore . . . s'il a besoin . . . d'autre chose . . . vous trouverez ça sous le lit . . .")

to set forth a program of child-rearing and education that would make them into happy, healthy, and productive citizens.

The key to this shift was the role of women who were now called upon to nurse their children at home, to educate them, and to set a good example as both wife and mother. As Carol Duncan observed in her article "Happy Mothers and Other New Ideas in French Art," the campaign for motherhood was carried out in all areas of French culture.[45] The joys of maternity became

46 Jean-Michel
Moreau le jeune,
"The Delights of
Motherhood,"
gr. Isidore-Stanislas
Helman, 1777. Etching
with engraving from
*Seconde Suite
d'estampes pour servir
à l'histoire des modes
et du costume en
France dans le dix-
huitième siècle. Année
1776* (Paris: Prault,
1777). Bibliothèque
nationale de France,
Paris. ("Les Délices de
la maternité")

a popular theme in art as well as in literature, in poetry, and in prose, and especially in the expository writing of the philosophers. "Keep your family comfortable," Diderot advised husbands, "give your wife children; give her as many as you can; give them only to her and be assured of being happy at home."[46]

Myriad images were produced in the service of this motherhood campaign. Moreau le jeune's "The Delights of Motherhood" (Figure 46) should be seen as the pendant to the idealized fatherhood depicted in his "True Happiness" (Figure 41). Not surprisingly, however, the female version of idyllic parenthood is much better known as it has had continued social resonance. The trope of the "Happy Mother" continued from the eighteenth century, through the Revolutionary period, and well into the nineteenth century with no rupture. If anything, "The Happy Mother" (Figure 47) of the 1790s by Augustin Saint-Aubin (1736–1806) is even more delirious than Moreau le jeune's earlier version. In the early decades of the nineteenth century, however, the image, although itself relatively unchanged, was now given a new title. No longer called "The Happy Mother" or some variation thereof, it was now titled simply

47 Augustin Saint-Aubin, gr. Antoine-François Sergent and Gautier l'aîné, "The Happy Mother," c. 1793. Colored stipple engraving. Bibliothèque nationale de France, Paris. ("L'Heureuse Mère")

48 Alexandre-Evariste Fragonard, "The Good Mother," 1826. Lithograph. Lith. Delpech. Bibliothèque nationale de France, Paris. ("La Bonne Mère")

"The Good Mother." A lithograph of 1826 by Alexandre-Evariste Fragonard (1780–1850, the son of Honoré Fragonard) (Figure 48) shows the familiar maternal image, now retitled and transformed by lithography. By this time it seems no longer to have mattered whether a woman was happy, it was now sufficient merely if she behaved herself. At the same time, the two pendants, "The Happy Mother" and "The Happy Father," were transformed, with "The Good Mother" now contrasted only with "The Bad Mother." "The Happy Father" simultaneously disappeared from the fields of both social discourse and visual imagery. The new frame of reference can be seen in "Contrasts," two pendants by Achille Devéria (1800–57). "The Good Mother" (Figure 49) is united with her husband and children as a happy family unit, but "The Bad Mother" (Figure 50) tells her maid "Get rid of these children, they are annoying me," while her lover lurks behind a half-opened door awaiting their departure. In the visual

49   Achille Devéria, "The Good Mother. 'How happy I am, my dear!',"*Les Contrastes*, 1834. Lithograph. Lith. Delaunois, Dist. Neuhaus. Bibliothèque nationale de France, Paris. ("La Bonne Mère. 'Mon ami, que je suis heureuse!'")

50   Achille Devéria, "The Bad Mother. Get rid of these children, they are annoying me,"*Les Contrastes*, 1834. Lith. Delaunois, Dist. Neuhaus. Lithograph. Bibliothèque nationale de France, Paris. ("La Mauvaise Mère. Débar-rassez-moi de ces enfans, ils me gênent")

culture of the early nineteenth century, "The Bad Mother" gradually replaced "The Good Mother," and her offense was always the same – adultery.[47]

The new public morality that followed the 1789 Revolution caused a graphic illustration of what can happen when social discourses abruptly collide.[48] In the early 1790s Boilly published two engravings as variations on the "Before" and "After" images popularized by Hogarth; they were originally titled "What Will Happen" (Figure 51) and "What Has Happened" (Figure 52). In 1794 the Société républicaine des arts denounced Boilly for producing immoral engrav-ings, and although there is no conclusive evidence, these may well have been among the prints at issue.[49] The French for "What Will Happen" is "Ça ira," the title of a famous revolutionary song, and Boilly may well have over-estimated the revolutionaries' sense of humor. He escaped the guillotine only by publicly repenting and producing *The Triumph of Marat* for the inspection

51 Louis-Léopold Boilly, gr. Mathias, "What Will Happen," 1790s. Stipple engraving. Bibliothèque nationale de France, Paris. ("Ça ira")

52 Louis-Léopold Boilly, gr. Victor Texier, "What Has Happened," 1790s. Stipple engraving. Bibliothèque nationale de France, Paris. ("Ça a été")

of the Committee of Public Safety. He reissued these prints with chastened titles: "What Will Happen" became "The Dangers of Experience," and "What Has Happened" became "The Married Couple on Rising."[50] At the Salon of 1795 he further repented, showing a painting entitled *A Holy Family*.[51]

A similar phenomenon can be observed in the work of the engraver Philibert-Louis Debucourt, who, also in the 1790s, began a typical Old Regime theme, an old husband who doesn't "see" what is going on between his wife and her young lover.[52] The first state of "The Casement Window" (Figure 53) depicts a sleepy old husband whose young wife, under his tutelage, is reading *The Art of Keeping Wives Faithful*, the conduct manual discussed in chapter 2. Meanwhile, unnoticed by him, she slips a note to her lover who has climbed up an exterior ladder to receive it. Before the engraving went on sale, however, Debucourt abruptly sanitized it (Figure 54), bringing it into alignment with the new Revolutionary family values. The adulterous tryst has now become a charming family scene, with innocent children replacing the guilty lover. In its

53 Philibert-Louis Debucourt, "The Casement Window I," 1791. First state, handcolored aquatint with etching and engraving. Bibliothèque nationale de France, Paris. ("La Croisée")

54 Philibert-Louis Debucourt, "The Casement Window II," 1791. Second state, handcolored aquatint with etching and engraving. Bibliothèque nationale de France, Paris. ("La Croisée")

revised second state, the print has, in fact, become a "Happy Mother" image, with the benevolent old husband now safely awake and alert.

The rupture during the Revolutionary period in the continuity of the Old Regime theme of husband, wife, and lover, and its subsequent reappearance in the new medium of lithography, cannot then be interpreted simply as a reinstatement of a traditional theme. Restoration morality was notoriously straitlaced, with a good dose of hypocrisy as well. Joseph-Alexandre de Ségur (1756–1805), in his multi-volume and often-reprinted work *Women: Their Condition and Their Influence on the Social Order among Different Peoples Ancient and Modern*, commented on the Restoration court of Louis XVIII: "This stringent morality that was the rule of conduct, in the days of prosperity as well as in those of disgrace, was, no doubt, a strange novelty."[53] The chastened aristocracy was ostentatiously demonstrating that it had reformed its morality

55 Charles Philipon, "For Marriage: 1. A young orphan of 18 with a dowry of 80,000 francs. 2. A middle-aged widow with an income of 10,000 livres. These ladies are guaranteed to be without flaws or faults. Interested parties can view them at the establishment of Monsieur Procurer for a modest fee (50 francs)," *Les Annonces: Petites-affiches parisiennes*, 5, 1829. Lithograph. Lith. V. Ratier, Dist. Hautecoeur-Martinet, Gihaut, Violet. Bibliothèque nationale de France, Paris. ("A marier 1. Une jeune Orpheline de 18 ans, dotée de 80 mille francs. 2. Une Veuve d'un âge mur, ayant 10 mille livres de rentes. Ces Dames sont garanties sans tare ni défauts; Les Amateurs peuvent les voir chez M. Procure, moyennant la modique rétribution d'usage [50 francs].")

and again deserved to rule, and the bourgeoisie was equally determined to present a public image of even greater probity. George Sand's novel *Indiana* (1832) and Stendhal's *The Red and the Black* (1830), discussed in chapter 5, present devastating portrayals of the hypocrisy of both classes, and, of course, that was the whole point of Balzac's *Physiology of Marriage* (1829). So the gleeful production of quantities of "Husband, Wife, and Lover" images in lithography, the very medium of dissent, by the young men of the liberal opposition would invest these images with a content such that, even if they were identical with those produced during the Old Regime, their meanings would now be different. In the Old Regime such prints winked slyly at shared peccadilloes; now they had become transgressive, abrading a stern public morality.

Now, for a moment, I would like to bracket this study of lithographic caricatures to show the context within which marriage was portrayed. Several new visual themes appeared suddenly in nineteenth-century France, seemingly without precedent, directly criticizing the abuses of marriage. In multitudinous examples, the practice of marrying for dowries was condemned both in images and in prose. The reformers Doin and Charton remarked "This oriental trafficking of our sisters and our daughters is the ruin of all tender and virtuous

56   Charles Philipon, "Love by Inclination," *Compensations*, 1, 1828. Lithograph. Lith. Wattier & Ducarme, Dist. Ostervald l'aîné & Hautecoeur-Martinet. Bibliothèque nationale de France, Paris. ("Amours d'inclination")

57   Charles Philipon, "Love by Calculation," *Compensations*, 1 *bis*, 1828. Lith. Wattier & Ducarme, Dist. Ostervald l'aîné & Hautecoeur-Martinet. Lithograph. Bibliothèque nationale de France, Paris. ("Amours de convenance")

illusions, of all sentiments born of simple morality and generous confidence in human values. A woman seems to have no value other than that of her beauty and her fortune."[54] One of the prints in Philipon's *Parisian Classified Ads* (Figure 55) illustrates this criticism, cynically listing the relative financial attractions of a young orphan and a middle-aged widow as though they were property for sale.

Another new subject of social criticism often treated by Grandville and Philipon was the "marriage of reason," or "marriage of convenience," invariably represented as between an unattractive old man and a pretty young woman, and inevitably shown in pendant with the "marriage for love" in which

59 *(facing page bottom)*   Grandville, "A Marriage according to Nature," *Les Métamorphoses du jour*, 62, 1828–29. Handcolored lithograph. Lith. Langlumé, Dist. Bulla. Bibliothèque nationale de France, Paris. ("Un Mariage suivant la nature")

58 (*above*) Grandville, "A Marriage according to the Law," *Les Métamorphoses du jour*, 61, 1828–29. Handcolored lithograph. Lith. Langlumé, Dist. Bulla. Bibliothèque nationale de France, Paris. ("Un Mariage suivant les lois")

60   "The Husband Highly Delighted with His Supposed Fruits," 1790.
Etching. Dist. Robt. Sayer. British Museum, London

two young and attractive lovers are happily united (Figures 56–59). These pendants present the image of arranged marriage from the viewpoint of young men:
Philipon was twenty-two when he drew these, Grandville was twenty-six. Both
dwell on the negative aspects of such "rational" marriages. For Philipon, the
husband is old and unattractive, an inappropriate match for the pretty young
girl who recoils from his touch. Grandville goes further by showing the results
of such a marriage, with the old husband lurking behind a tree, spying on the
young couple whose adulterous union may be "according to nature," but is
certainly not sanctioned by the law. A visual alternative is now being offered
to the loveless arranged marriage, namely the idealized "marriage of inclination," as the love match was then called. Such caricatures attacking arranged
marriages disappeared in the course of the nineteenth century, as the practices
they depicted waned.

Even seemingly traditional imagery was not current in all places at all times.
A theme commonplace in eighteenth-century England was that of illegitimate
birth as a peril of adultery. A typical example is "The Husband Highly
Delighted with His Supposed Fruits" (Figure 60), an anonymous etching of
1790, with the antlered deer head on the wall representing the traditional
symbol of the cuckold. Images like these would have been unthinkable in pre-

Coucou!......ah le voilà!!!

61 (*above*) "Cuckoo! There it is!!!! / Cuckold! There he is!," 1815–30. Lithograph. Bibliothèque nationale de France, Paris. ("Coucou! . . . ah le voilà!!!")

62 Charles Philipon, "Excellent Friend!!," *Amourettes*, 4, 1827. Lithograph. Lith. Ducarme, Dist. Ostervald l'aîné & Hautecoeur-Martinet. Bibliothèque nationale de France, Paris. ("Excellent ami!!")

63 Jean-Michel Moreau le jeune, gr. Jean-Charles
Bacquoy, "It's a son, Monsieur," 1776. Etching with
engraving from *Seconde Suite d'estampes pour
servir à l'histoire des modes et du costume en
France, dans le dix-huitième siècle. Année 1776*
(Paris: Prault, 1777). Bibliothèque nationale de
France, Paris. ("C'est un fils, Monsieur.")

64 Grandville, "Hurry, hurry, nurse! Good Lord,
how he looks just like Monsieur!," *Les Métamorphoses du jour*, 11, 1828–29. Handcolored lithograph. Lith. Langlumé, Dist. Bulla. Bibliothèque
nationale de France, Paris. ("Arrivez, arrivez nour-
rice! – Dieux comme y r'semble a Mosieu!")

Revolutionary French art, where the only children present in light-hearted
Rococo fantasies were little love cupids. Considering that there was a thriving
international print trade between England and France, one might have expected
to find similar images on both sides of the Channel, but the theme was never
taken up in France until after the generational warfare that had been brewing
through the Revolutionary period had erupted in cultural warfare as well.[55] The
Civil Code's abolition of primogeniture intensified the problem, which now
became "visible." Suddenly children, the inevitable – but heretofore invisible –
consequence of love made their appearance in these prints of husbands, wives,
and lovers. The pornographic French lithograph "Cuckoo! . . . There it is!!!! /
Cuckold! There he is!" (Figure 61) presents a graphic illustration of this situation, while Philipon's "Excellent Friend!!" (Figure 62) offers a sanitized
version of the same theme.

The arrival in visual consciousness of the child as the fruit of illicit love can be seen by comparing two prints on the subject of the birth of a son. Moreau le jeune's famous etching "It's a son, Monsieur" (Figure 63) shows the eighteenth-century socially condoned response to the event: great joy. Grandville's lithograph (Figure 64) dates from several decades later, when the joy is replaced by the fear and threat of adulterine children. Under the new laws of the Civil Code, all offspring born to a wife were legally the children of her husband and inherited equally. So when the nurse in this caricature says to the proud papa stag who is holding a young bird, "Good Lord, how he looks just like Monsieur!," an entire audience is brought into complicity with the joke. The viewer can see what the father cannot, namely that the son looks nothing at all like his putative father. A cuckoo has been in the nest, and a cuckold is now the father.

Statistically this may not have occurred very often. Even a single occurrence of a dreaded event, however, can provoke a widespread underlying anxiety out of all proportion to the statistical probability of its reoccurrence. Within a few decades the very possibility of fathering an adulterine child had come to assume a major importance in the psychic life of both old husbands and young lovers, as fear, as threat, and as desire. The result was the creation of a new major theme in visual production.

The full extent of this, however, can be comprehended only by considering both the traditional and the innovative themes as part of the same visual nexus. As should be clear from even this brief overview of marital imagery prevalent from the mid-eighteenth century to the mid-nineteenth, the husband, wife, and lover theme must be seen as part of the entire spectrum of images focusing on contemporary marriage customs.

Images bear a complicated relationship to social reality, for they construct it from factors such as tradition and imagination, technology, audience, markets, and lived experience. To understand the variety of possible relationships, one might draw a parallel to dream imagery, which can reflect lived experience as it is perceived by the dreamer, but can just as easily construct a nightmare of fears and anxieties, the incarnation of the dreamer's worst-case scenario. Dreams can also be wish-fulfillment, expressing hopes and desires. Visual imagery functions across this spectrum, which is why interpretation always must be dependent on an assessment of its role and function within the culture. I suspect that these lithographic images of young men stealing old men's wives partake a little of all these basic types, lived experience, desires, threats, and fears, and that, as a result, these images gained currency in a culture where they were supercharged with meaning.

4

For Money or For Love:
Theatrical Alternatives

Provided one did not trifle about God, or about priests, or about the king, or about men in high places, or about artists patronized by the court, or about the establishment in general, provided one spoke well neither of Béranger, nor of the opposition newspapers, nor of Voltaire, nor of Rousseau, nor of anyone who indulged in a bit of plain speaking; provided, especially, one never talked politics, one might discuss any subject freely.

Stendhal, The Red and the Black[1]

We no longer witness the triumph of virtue anywhere but at the boulevard theaters.

George Sand, preface to Indiana[2]

THE SAME CONCERNS THAT EMERGED in other cultural forms also made their appearance on the stage. The issue of marriage, whether arranged or chosen, whether for money or for love, was debated on the boards night after night. The titles of plays staged in Paris during the 1820s are revelatory: *The Marriageable Young Lady, Inheritance and Marriage, The Marriage of Reason, The Marriage for Money, The Marriage for Love, The Results of a Marriage of Reason.*[3] Love was hardly a new subject in the theater, which in France had traditionally enjoyed the patronage of an aristocratic class that proclaimed the importance of love, although not necessarily in combination with marriage. In French theater from Molière to Marivaux, when young love triumphed it tended to be between individuals of the same class, made all the more piquant by the disguises and subterfuges that hid the lovers' true identities. During the Enlightenment, however, philosophers attempted to harness the didactic power of the theater to their belief in the artificiality of social rank. First Marivaux in his *False Confessions* (1737), then Voltaire in his *Nanine, or Prejudice Overcome* (1749), and Diderot in *The Father of the Family* (1758) went so far as to propose that love could overcome even the dreaded *mésalliance*, as marriage with a social inferior was termed.[4] The idealistic combination of love, marriage,

facing page Louis Boilly, "The Effect of Melodrama," 1830 (detail of Figure 71).

and a mixture of social classes was a proposition utterly different from previous theatrical dénouements, however, and such idealistic notions did not long survive the Revolution. In the post-Revolutionary world of the Restoration, theatrical love would have a much harder time vanquishing prejudice. The bourgeoisie now made up the principal audience for theatrical productions, and they had little interest in idealist fantasies of marriage with the lower classes. A proper and prosperous marriage became the preferred subject of bourgeois theater.

Theatrical conventions from the time of Molière had pitted young lovers against a father or guardian who vainly attempts to substitute a reasonable but loveless match for their mutual affection. During the Restoration, this plot was transposed into the young lovers' conflict with the father/guardian who wisely and successfully protects their honor and happiness by ending their ill-considered attachment, thus warding off an inappropriate marriage. The pertinence of this newly revised trope was demonstrated by the hundreds of plays devoted to myriad variations on this theme.

In the nineteenth century, theater came in many modes: vaudeville, comedy, drama, melodrama, and tragedy, along with infinite combinations and permutations of these. Theater had been strictly controlled in France since the seventeenth century, with the Académie royale de musique given, from its founding in 1671, a monopoly on opera. The Théâtre-Français, founded in 1680 (now the Comédie-Française) was given the monopoly on tragedy. Fairground entertainment of pantomimes and street shows sufficed for the lower classes until the late eighteenth century, when independent theaters began to be licensed, but with strict controls on what kinds of plays each theater was permitted, how many actors could be included, and whether they could speak or sing.[5] The monopolies enjoyed by the government-sponsored theaters were ended after the 1789 Revolution and, as a result, the number and variety of productions burgeoned. Tragedy remained the most prestigious of the genres, but it was the least popular, playing only at the government-subsidized Théâtre-Français. Other theaters needed audience support in order to survive, and so served more popular fare. The *comédie de moeurs*, the heir to the late eighteenth-century *drame bourgeois* praised by Diderot and Voltaire, dealt with issues of contemporary life, but the favorite theatrical entertainment of the bourgeoisie was vaudeville. With its combination of music and topical plots, the equivalent of the modern musical comedy, it triumphed everywhere. Melodrama, with its extremes of emotion, was the polar opposite of the cerebral tragedies at the Théâtre-Français; it attracted the lower classes and more than a few of the social élite as well. Grand opera, during this period, was focused more on historical tragedy than on domestic drama, and, except for the bowdlerized librettos of Beaumarchais's *Marriage of Figaro* (1786) and *Barber of Seville* (1816) bore little relation to the genre subjects discussed here.[6]

Major theaters had two thousand or more places to fill at each performance.[7]

As the public wanted new plays each week, theaters sold season subscriptions to guarantee themselves a steady audience. Subscribers knew in advance what to expect as each theater specialized in a particular genre, one playing melodrama, another vaudeville. While it would be an exaggeration to say that all social classes went to the theater, nonetheless, during most of the nineteenth century it constituted the principal form of public entertainment and enjoyed broad support from a wide spectrum of social classes. The cheapest seats cost less than a franc while luxurious private loges were subscribed for the entire season (Figure 65).

During the Restoration, theater was the only authorized site of public meetings other than religious services, but unlike churches, theaters represented a kind of liberated space, offering a public forum and an audience that might be receptive to unorthodox ideas. As a result, government censors were as active in policing theater as they were in overseeing the press. To no avail, it would

65   Charles Philipon, "High Society in the Loges," *Compensations*, 20 *bis*, 1828. Lithograph. Lith. Wattier & Ducarme, Dist. Ostervald l'aîné & Hautecoeur-Martinet. Biliothèque nationale de France, Paris. ("Beau Monde des loges")

66   Charles Philipon, "The Rabble in Paradise," *Compensations*, 20, 1828. Lithograph. Lith. Wattier & Ducarme, Dist. Ostervald l'aîné & Hautecoeur-Martinet. Bibliothèque nationale de France, Paris. ("Canaille du paradis")

seem, for, despite their efforts, theaters were the scene of many public distur-
bances and scandals that often originated in the boisterous and rowdy "paradise" (Figure 66), the popular inexpensive section, ironically so-called because
it was close to the ceiling and, therefore, closer to God. As a result of the
omnipresent censorship, the plays of this period cannot be discussed without
determining what was permissible.

Censorship existed in France from the Middle Ages but had been abolished
by the National Assembly in 1791.[8] Bonaparte, as Premier Consul, re-
established it in April 1800, and, as Emperor, decreed on June 8, 1806 that
"No play can be performed without authorization by the Minister of Police."[9]
The following year, convinced that the little theaters of Paris bred unrest and
immorality, he suppressed them, leaving only eight authorized theaters.[10] These
little theaters reopened during the Restoration, with a resultant increase in the
number of productions. Like all theaters, however, they were under the surveillance of the Office of Censorship, which continued to function, virtually
unchanged, until the twentieth century.[11]

During the Restoration, plays had to be approved by the Office of Censorship before they went into rehearsal. Once the plays had opened, government
spies attended every performance to verify that censored lines did not find their
way back into the script.[12] Even *Hamlet* was censored when it played in Paris.
The procedure was that fifteen days before the opening of a play, the director
of the theater had to deposit the manuscript at the Office of Censorship, which
would then either accept it as written, demand corrections, or reject it outright.
The most common verdict was acceptance with corrections, which then had to
be made within two days. Fewer than two dozen plays were actually banned
during the Restoration as most playwrights either self-censored in advance,
steering clear of potentially dangerous topics, or hastily agreed to whatever
changes were demanded of them so that their plays could open. Enforcement
was not uniform throughout the period, however. There were periods of relative laxness, and other periods of draconian severity, usually provoked by some
political crisis such as the assassination of the duc de Berry in 1820.

During the Restoration the censors were aristocratic and ultra-royalist, more
vigilant in censoring political or religious ideas than in censoring morality.
Provided that plays contained no mixing of classes, no immorality or suicides,
censors could even be lenient.[13] In the early years of the Restoration they were
concerned mostly with politics, in the 1820s with religion, while towards 1830
they fretted over Romanticism.[14] As Stendhal noted, censored subjects included
any mention of royalty, revolution, ideas of liberty and independence, controversial names such as Voltaire or Napoléon, or certain official positions such
as minister, prefect, or senator.[15] The list was interminable because audiences
could, and did, turn virtually any character or event into a plebiscite by hissing,
booing, cheering, or applauding during the performance, thus effectively defeat-
ing censorship and "rewriting" the play to its own purposes. Sheryl Kroen has

written extensively of how performances of Molière's *Tartuffe* were demanded and applauded all over France during these years as a vehicle for criticizing the role of the Church in government affairs; censored lines were shouted out by audience members, and, when the play was banned, the audience even conducted noisy readings in the parterre while the actors on stage attempted to perform the officially sanctioned production.[16]

Because theater was considered a didactic force, on-stage transgressions were discouraged, or at least had to be punished by the end of the play. The theater historian E. J. H. Greene has pointed out that the *commedia dell'arte* plots on which French comedies were based always featured cuckolded husbands; the strictures of censorship in France, however, resulted in their transformation into the ubiquitous "guardians" who, in plays from Molière well into the nineteenth century, vainly attempt to separate their young wards from their lovers.[17] Among the hundreds of plays during the Restoration that took marriage as a theme, there was never any open treatment of adultery until after the "Three Glorious Days" of 1830 had ushered in the July Monarchy and a more liberal Office of Censorship.[18] The word "adultery" could not even be uttered on stage.[19] No *mésalliances* were permitted on stage unless they were cast in the disapproving light that demonstrated their inevitable unfortunate consequences. Each class had to be encouraged to marry within itself. It is miraculous that in these circumstances any plays could be written at all, and yet writers proved resourceful in avoiding censorship either by elliptically referring to taboo subjects, by tacking unrealistic endings onto realistic plays, by distancing the action through situating it in another period or country, or by ingenious recourse to a whole host of other evasions. Censorship was a cat-and-mouse game where sometimes the playwright won, sometimes the censors, and, as Sheryl Kroen has shown, audiences retained the power to transform the theatrical experience so that, even in winning, the censors sometimes lost.

Because of the problems of censorship, any discussion of plays is fraught with difficulty. The scripts of popular plays were published, and since censorship of texts was more lenient than censorship of theatrical performances, these texts often restored lines or scenes that had fallen before the censor's scissors. As a result, one cannot assume that the published text corresponds to the theatrical promptbook. The most accurate information on what audiences actually saw or heard is provided by theatrical reviews that often narrate the plot of the play under discussion. And yet, as Sheryl Kroen has shown, the public often knew the uncut text and interpolated it into the production, either actually, as in *Tartuffe* where they shouted out the lines, or mentally, as in many other plays whose texts circulated at the same time as their productions.

Only with this caveat in mind, can I discuss the theatrical ambience of the Restoration and that which preceded it, first looking briefly at the work of Pierre-Augustin Caron de Beaumarchais (1732–99), the major playwright of the earlier period.[20] His plays are well known for their stinging social and political criticism, but it has been noted less often that his plots revolve around the marriage question. His first success was *The Barber of Seville* (1775), a traditional play of courtship and intrigue where the old Dr. Bartolo wants to marry his young ward Rosine; she, however, is loved by Count Almaviva who eventually wins her hand. E. J. H. Greene neatly summarized this familiar plot: "The spontaneous loves of the Young, traversed by the Old, are aided and abetted by the Servants."[21] Playwrights of the Restoration reversed this time-honored script to show age triumphing over youth, and the bourgeoisie over the aristocracy. Beaumarchais's *Barber of Seville* was followed by *The Marriage of Figaro* (1784), the theatrical *cause célèbre* of its age, still censored well into the

67 Emile Bayard, gr. Adrien Nargeot, "*The Guilty Mother*. The Countess: 'Accept the loathing that I feel as atonement for my fault.' Act IV, scene xiii," 1876. Handcolored etching. Bibliothèque nationale de France, Paris. ("*La Mère coupable*. La Comtesse: 'Accepte l'horreur que j'éprouve en expiation de ma faute!' Acte IV, sc. xiii")

LA MÈRE COUPABLE.

LA COMTESSE.

Accepte l'horreur que j'éprouve,
en expiation de ma faute!

Acte IV, sc. XIII.

Imp. Salmon, Paris

following century. This play picks up the story of Count Almaviva several years later, by which time he is a philanderer, neglecting his wife and determined to seduce the Countess's maid Suzanne before she can marry his valet Figaro. Beaumarchais mercilessly and wittily lambasted the aristocracy as stupid, lazy, and debauched. The servant Figaro wins every interchange with his master, thus reversing the "normal" relations between masters and servants, and in the process foiling, for once, the Count's adulterous escapades. As was to be expected, the play was condemned by the censors, but, in the pre-Revolutionary period, the aristocracy formed the principal audience for theater and often sponsored their own private theatrical productions outside the reach of royal censors. Fashionable society found Beaumarchais's satire and sparkling wit vastly amusing, and *The Marriage of Figaro* found a ready audience there, among its very targets. As the play's celebrity grew, the pressure to perform it publicly increased, until finally, in 1784, the weakened King Louis XVI agreed to a softened, censored, but still powerful public production that proved to be an enduring favorite. The third play of the trilogy, *The Guilty Mother* (1792), is the one of principal concern here as it focuses directly on the double standard of adultery and familial conduct. Although Beaumarchais regarded it as his masterpiece, it has been the least popular of the trilogy and was not made into an opera until 1965, when Darius Milhaud's setting received its première.[22] The plot develops along parallel lines: Countess Almaviva is revealed to have borne an adulterine child, and so is condemned by the Count (Figure 67) and resigned to entering a convent. Then the Count is revealed to have done the same thing. In its frank treatment of marital infidelity, its powerful argument against the double standard of conduct for husbands and wives, and its condemnation of moral hypocrisy, the play is typical of the idealism of the Enlightenment and Revolutionary periods.

Playwrights of the Restoration, however, had to contend with very different conditions. After the Revolution, neither of the propertied classes, the aristocracy and the bourgeoisie, was willing to risk the ingenuous attitude towards social criticism that had been widespread in the waning years of the Old Regime, nor would an insecure restored monarchy allow it. The aristocratic class no longer played the leading role in cultural, particularly theatrical, patronage, and its successor, the bourgeoisie, was not adventurous in supporting radical forms of cultural production. As a result, with the omnipresent censorship, playwrights of the Restoration were obliged to speak in innuendo, allusively, elliptically. Until Victor Hugo's *Hernani*, the play that closed the period, the stage lacked a *cause célèbre* of the magnitude of Beaumarchais's trilogy. This does not mean that the Parisian stage was dark; far from it. There were in fact more productions and larger audiences than ever before.

I now look at the work of three celebrated playwrights of the period, each of whom examined the institution of marriage and its discontents, and then conclude this chapter with a brief examination of Hugo's *Hernani*. Casimir Delavigne (1793–1843), often characterized as *juste-milieu*, expressed sympathy for both arranged marriages and for the marriage of love. As befitted his *juste-milieu* status, he wrote his plays in the alexandrine verse of high classical tragedy. The result was that he was praised across the political spectrum and became the most successful and respected playwright of the period. Eugène Scribe (1791–1861), in contrast, celebrated only the "marriage of reason" so dear to the bourgeoisie and, in play after play, he demonstrated the dire consequences of allowing young people to choose their own mates. Lionized by the bourgeoisie, though scorned by intellectuals, his plays were so successful that there were often several running concurrently at Paris theaters. At the other extreme was Victor Ducange (1783–1833), an acclaimed author of melodramas, who took a critical view of arranged marriages; he appealed to liberals and to women, but, probably because of that, he never reaped the honors accrued to these other more acceptable playwrights. Each of these men worked in a different theatrical genre: Ducange wrote melodramas, Scribe wrote vaudevilles, and Delavigne wrote comedies, a designation that did not imply that the plays were humorous, merely that they ended happily rather than tragically.

Delavigne, "The Molière of Our Time"

As Delavigne enjoyed the greatest respect and celebrity during the period, I begin with an examination of his work.[23] His first success was in poetry; his odes to antiquity on patriotic subjects, *The Messinian Women*, brought him renown in 1818. He then turned to the theater: *The Sicilian Vespers*, applauding the revolt of Palermo against the Dukes of Anjou, opened at the Odéon in 1819; Alexandre Dumas recalled that people waited in line for three hours to see it.[24] This success was followed by *The Pariah* of 1821, an attack on religious intolerance. From the beginning, Delavigne was adopted as a hero by Bonapartists and liberals in order to oppose Hugo and Lamartine who, at the time, were royalists.

It was his *School for Old Men*, however, that became the major theatrical sensation of the Restoration, long before Victor Hugo's *Hernani*.[25] First performed on December 6, 1823 at the Théâtre-Français, the national theater, it featured the two major stars of the period, Talma and Mademoiselle Mars, who appeared together for the first time (Figure 68). It was Talma's first role outside tragedy. "*The School for Old Men* was an immense success," wrote Alexandre Dumas in his memoirs, while Alphonse de Lamartine published a long letter in alexandrine verse praising the work.[26] Comtesse Dash (1804–72) wrote in her memoirs, "this comedy, *The School for Old Men*, had all Paris running to see it."[27] The play immediately established Delavigne as a major force in French theater.

The plot recounts the story of Danville, an elderly widower from Le Havre, a retired armaments manufacturer who has recently married Hortense, a young woman of twenty, younger even than his son. Hortense has convinced Danville to move to Paris, but, because his business concerns would detain him for two months in Le Havre, she has gone on ahead. When Danville arrives, he learns that Hortense has not only spent an extraordinary amount of money, but also that she has rented an apartment for them in the townhouse of the young duc d'Elmar. The duke, as Danville's old friend Bonnard tells him, is a dangerous man much feared by husbands, "Very gallant, a good dancer, and an excellent swordsman."[28] The duke seduces wives right under the noses of their husbands, whose complicity he buys with appointments to high government posts. The most dramatic moment in the play arrives when the duke sneaks into the Danville apartment late one night in an attempt to seduce Hortense. Danville returns, unexpectedly and just in time. He sends Hortense away and challenges the duke to a duel:

> So, monsieur, you think that you can safely attack
> The tranquillity and the happiness of a household
> By disguising your vile intentions as a bit of fun!
> You thought you were being amusing
> But you have become a criminal.
> The death of an honorable man is an eternal reproach.[29]

68 Charles Aubray, *"The School for Old Men* by Casimir Delavigne. Talma in the role of Danville, Mlle Mars in the role of Hortense (Act 5)," 1823. Lithograph. Lith. Villain. Bibliothèque nationale de France, Paris. (*"L'Ecole des vieillards* par M. Casimir Delavigne. Talma, rôle d'Anville, Mlle Mars, rôle .d'Hortense [acte 5]")

Danville is disarmed but not injured and, in the dénouement, he acknowledges the problems of such May–December marriages. Then, *deus ex machina*, he discovers a letter proving that his young wife had actually rejected the duke's advances because she really does love her old husband. And *mirabile dictu*, she even wants to leave Paris and move back to the provinces, because, as she says, "In this fascinating world, snares have too many charms."[30] The play ends with Danville describing how happy they will be in the provinces and, echoing Voltaire's *Candide*, prophesying that "all will be for the best."[31] The very last lines, however, go to Danville's elderly friend Bonnard, who has decided not to marry a young woman:

> To marry so late in life a young and pretty woman,
> That might succeed, but it usually doesn't.
> You're happy of course,
> But you have found one in a thousand.[32]

And on this ambiguous note the play ends.

Delavigne's *School for Old Men* was clearly modeled on Molière's *School for Husbands* (1661), where the guardian who wants to marry his young ward succeeds in winning her love through his understanding and indulgence, while his brother, a jealous and overly protective guardian, loses his ward to a young

lover. Molière, however, took care to present the situation as predating marriage, while Delavigne alludes to the possibility of adultery.

The play spawned several parodies, and within a few weeks Paris audiences
had witnessed *The School for Dunces*, *The School for Cripples*, and *Cadet
Buteux at The School for Old Men*, each of which satirized the many incon-
sistencies and unrealistic aspects of Delavigne's plot.[33] None of them was anywhere nearly as successful as *The School for Old Men*. Delavigne's script was pur-
chased almost immediately for the immense sum of 14,000 francs and, even
before its publication, three thousand copies were sold by advance subscription;
another two thousand were sold on the first day of publication.[34] A second edition
was printed and also sold out, nearly four thousand additional copies in two days.[35]
Le Journal des débats commented "it is found in the hands of every theater-lover,
of every critic, of all his competitors, and of all the envious."[36] Within a few weeks
the play had opened in Marseilles, in Tours, in Abbeville, and in Dijon.[37] It was
no longer just a Parisian success, it had become a national success, with Delavigne
being hailed everywhere as "the poet of our epoch, the Molière of our times."[38]
The satirical "Cadet Buteux after the performance of *The School for Old Men*"
(Figure 69) had the irreverent young man tipping his hat to Molière's bust in the
foyer of the Théâtre-Français. Delavigne was even compared with Corneille.[39] His
play enjoyed what was at the time an extended run: forty-eight Parisian performances in 1824 alone. Even *Hernani* had only thirty-nine in 1830, the year of
its début.[40] In the year following the triumph of his play, Delavigne, at thirty-
two years old, was deemed immortal and was elected to the Académie française. In
the face of this unexpected success, the critic of *Le Journal des débats* wondered,
"If the play, as everyone claims, has no

69   A. D. [Achille Devéria?], "Cadet Buteux after the performance of *The School for Old Men*. 'Before the portrait of this great man whom I admire, / I take off my hat when I pass in the foyer; / I think I see him smiling . . . / Perhaps with joy at having found an heir!'," 1824. Lithograph. Lith. A. Cornillon, Dist. Duvernois. Bibliothèque nationale de France, Paris. ("Cadet Buteux après la représentation de l'*Ecole des vieillards*. 'Devant l'portrait de c'grand homme qu'on admire, / Je me découvre en passant dans l'foyer; / Il m'a semblé que je l'voyais sourire . . . / C'est p'tetr' de joie d'avoir un héri-tier!'")

CADET BUTEUX *après la représentation de l'Ecole des Vieillards.*

Devant l'portrait de c'grand homme qu'on admire,
Je me découvre en passant dans l'foyer;
Il m'a semblé que je l'voyais sourire....
C'est p'tetr' de joi d'avoir un héritier!

Lith de A. Cornillon.   Chez Duvernois, libraire, cour des Fontaines.

merit other than its style, is this merit, no matter how great in the eyes of the true connoisseur, sufficient to explain the popularity of *The School for Old Men?*"[41] Obviously he thought not.

The School for Old Men has been seen as affirming bourgeois values, but so did scores of other plays.[42] That alone would not have ensured its overwhelming success. I propose instead that its success was due to its ability to entertain several contradictory readings at the same time, to allow each segment of its audience, in effect, to construct a different play from what it had seen and heard. Liberals applauded its frank acknowledgment of the problems of the "marriage of convenience" in which a dowryless young woman marries a wealthy, older man. Charles-Guillaume Etienne, the drama critic for the liberal and anti-clerical *Le Constitutionnel*, claimed in an article appearing in *Le Mercure du dix-neuvième siècle* that "the author's intention was to depict the dangers of inappropriate marriages; his sixty-year-old dotard was wrong to marry a woman of only twenty."[43] Criticizing arranged marriages such as this was standard liberal practice. *Le Journal de Paris* opened its review by citing a verse from, it claimed, the Opéra-Comique: "Young wives and old husbands / *always* make bad marriages."[44] In the play, the duke himself defends the liberal position, arguing that spouses should be the same age:

> Even in his tolerance, an old man is severe.
> His advice is good, of course, but . . . stern.
> One is less tolerant of tastes one no longer shares.
> At the same age, young people understand and forgive each other.
> In an equal exchange one gives as well as receives.[45]

On the other hand, Balzac's famous quip that during the Restoration there were only two ages, youth and senility, was confirmed by the pleasure expressed by the legitimist press that, in this play, age, if not exactly senility, had triumphed over youth.[46] The legitimist journal *Le Drapeau blanc* announced that it had decided to praise the playwright, even though he was called "our Delavigne" by the opposition. The reason for this uncharacteristic abandonment of political battlelines was, as the journal explained, that Delavigne had taken the stock situation of an old man tormented by his love for a young girl, material for farce in the tradition of Molière, who always identified the old man as an object of ridicule. Delavigne, however, had reinterpreted it: "He knew enough to disdain the easy solution of ambiguity and to give the finest role to the voice of the highest morality."[47] There was the small matter of the lowest morality in the play being represented by an aristocrat; the fact did not go completely unnoticed. The critic for the legitimist *Journal des débats* wrote:

> I've heard Monsieur Delavigne blamed for having given an illustrious title in our social order to a blameworthy individual. I share this opinion, not that a young duke would be incapable, like any other young man, of letting himself be carried away by a guilty passion, but the title is not at all neces-

sary to the author's plot. At the moment when our society, shaken by such long and terrible convulsions, is attempting, and has already begun, to restructure itself on the basis of our new institutions, the political hierarchy that has been established needs to be treated with respect. It cannot be too carefully shielded from attacks that are always dangerous for newborn institutions. [...] Now nothing demands that the nephew of a minister, that a powerful protector, be a duke. I think that it would have been better not to so identify the seducer. But a very important consideration mitigates the offense with which Monsieur Delavigne has been charged: his duke is guilty, but he is not at all vilified.[48]

The duke is actually presented quite sympathetically, as a warm and generous fellow so apologetic at having disarmed Danville in their duel that Danville's servant praises him as an honorable man. Nonetheless, even a liberal like Etienne wondered about the duke's character: "It is indeed quite odd that the author of *The School for Old Men* was permitted to make a duke the seducer."[49] Since the censorship report has not survived, it is impossible to know precisely why Delavigne was allowed to do this, other than that the play opened at a lenient moment, but it might also have been because he so carefully balanced praise and blame. Danville, for example, has a long soliloquy expressing scorn for aristocrats and their pretentious way of life:

> I lose my appetite when in my dining-room,
> I must contend with all the bother of aristocratic manners;
> My tongue hesitates to break the silence
> When it becomes necessary to say "Your Excellency" instead of "You."[50]

This attitude would usually identify a play with the political opposition and might well bring down the full force of censorship. But Danville's conclusion is that "My household suits me." He explains:[51]

> Nothing is better, I will admit, than a fine name well carried;
> I respect the nobility at its proper value.
> To receive in one's home a marquis, a duke, or a duchess,
> That is fine, if one is a duke – but I am not.[52]

In other words, Danville is quite happy to maintain the status quo, with each class remaining in its own stratum. One segment of the audience could appreciate his sentiments, while another could appreciate his conclusions – and perhaps that is why the censors spared his play.

The critical response to this play differed from that which customarily greeted ideologically engaged works of art, which usually took clear positions that critics could applaud or contest. Scribe's play *The Marriage of Reason* (1826), for example, treated the same theme as did Delavigne, namely that of an arranged marriage, a mismatch between a young woman and an older man, but Scribe clearly supported such marriages, giving all the best lines and best roles to its proponents.[53] Delavigne's *School for Old Men*, on the other hand, even-handedly divided praise and blame so that no one would be offended, apparently not even the censors. *La Pandore* suggested that the play's success was due precisely to this skillful imbrication of contradictory ideologies:

> Those who criticize most vehemently what a few days before they praised just as fervently have said that the author of *The School for Old Men* knows how to show the dangers of such inappropriate marriages without vilifying the play's protagonist, or making him ridiculous. At the same time he knows how to provoke our moral indignation against men who amuse themselves by destroying the harmony of households. The most severe critics are saying, and I agree with them, that this double lesson is an original conception, a daring project carried out with a superior talent.[54]

For this "daring project," Delavigne was richly rewarded during his lifetime. *The School for Old Men* was the biggest theatrical success since Beaumarchais's *Marriage of Figaro*; it remained the most popular comedy throughout the Restoration, and contemporary journals even ranked Delavigne ahead of Victor Hugo.[55] Delavigne has since been largely forgotten, but in any study of the vast unknown arena of nineteenth-century popular culture, he should surely be singled out as an important innovator who, standing at the threshold of modern republics with their many and varied constituencies, understood that he could create an immense audience on a national scale by appealing simultaneously to mutually opposed factions across the political and cultural spectrum.

Scribe, "The Respectable Bourgeois"

Eugène Scribe, on the other hand, focused his plays exclusively on the bourgeoisie, espousing their values and depicting their world. As a result, he was widely identified with this class and, although universally acknowledged as a major force in theater during these decades, his success, even in his own day, never transcended the borders of class and style. On the contrary, partisans of Romanticism such as Alexandre Dumas and Théophile Gautier (1811–72) loathed him. Gautier wrote that Scribe's plays were especially pleasing, not to sophisticated audiences, but to "the respectable bourgeois, more-or-less family man who, with no interest in art, in style, or in poetics, wants to spend a relaxing evening at the theater after his day's work is done."[56]

During the fifteen years of the Restoration, Scribe wrote 148 vaudevilles, many with collaborators, and most for the Théâtre du Gymnase, sometimes called the Théâtre de Madame because it was patronized by the duchesse de Berry. It was the favorite theater of the wealthy bourgeoisie of Paris. In addition, beginning in the 1820s he produced dozens of librettos for opera.[57] Perhaps this is why, despite the scorn of the Romantics, he was elected to the

70   Octave Tassaert, "*The Marriage of Reason* (Gymnase dramatique, Act II, Last Scene, By Scribe and Varner)," *Album théâtrale*, 1, 1827. Lithograph. Lith. Ducarme, Dist. Ostervald l'aîné. Bibliothèque nationale de France, Paris. ("*Le Mariage de raison* [Gymnase dramatique, Acte II, Scène dernière, par Scribe et Varner]")

Académie française in 1834. His plays were in such demand that the Paris stage was never without at least one current production, and he became the first French playwright to earn a living solely through writing plays. His *comédies-vaudevilles* broke with tradition by treating contemporary subjects with highly developed plots but with songs adapted from familiar tunes. This was the opposite of the *opéra-comique*, in which originality was limited to the music with plots of secondary importance.

In Scribe's plays romance was always subjugated to reason, sentiment and passion to the cold light of rationality. In these beliefs he espoused the world-view of the bourgeoisie. As the arrangement of advantageous marriages for their children was the principal preoccupation of bourgeois families, it was Scribe's favored subject as well. His first play to deal directly with the marriage question was *The Marriage of Reason*, a vaudeville (comedy with song) that opened at the Gymnase on October 10, 1826 (Figure 70).[58] It was his major success during these years, reprinted four times in its first year and provoking parodies and rejoinders. Originally written by Antoine-François Varner

(1790–1854), the play was rewritten by Scribe and bears both their names as co-authors, standard practice in a period when plays were often written in collaboration to meet the exigencies of production.

The Marriage of Reason tells the story of pretty, charming Suzette, an impoverished young orphan and a paragon of virtue, who was taken into the household of the General de Brémont as chambermaid, and then, after the death of Madame de Brémont, raised as a sister to Brémont's son Edouard. Suzette and Edouard, both eighteen, are now in love, but the General, who was made a count by Napoléon and thus is one of the "new aristocrats" characteristic of the period, regards the match as a *mésalliance*, a humiliating degradation of his new status. This unacceptable mixture of social classes was dreaded by propertied families, and was considered a disaster many shades worse than the simple *mariage mal-assorti* of two spouses of the same class but inappropriately matched in age or in temperament. General de Brémont had planned an advantageous marriage between Edouard and Mademoiselle de Luceval, a woman of their own class. To remove the impediment to his plans, he forces Suzette to marry his retainer Bertrand, a man twice her age, a retired soldier with a wooden leg, the symbolism of which, in those pre-Freudian days, seems to have escaped author, audience, and critics alike.

Scribe's play functioned as a vehicle for a whole range of arguments in support of arranged marriages. Unlike Delavigne's *School for Old Men*, Scribe provided no counter-weight of arguments extolling the contrary position, the *mariage d'inclination*, or marriage for love. As a result, the play constitutes a brutal defense of the principles of the propertied classes – which is probably why it was such a success among both the bourgeoisie and the aristocracy. The *frisson* of the play comes from the fact that Suzette's beauty and virtue have caused Edouard and all his friends to be smitten with her. It would seem natural, then, for her to ascend the social ladder through an advantageous marriage. She is a social hybrid, however, raised in the aristocracy but lacking family or dowry, and so she is instead forced to marry the older Bertrand who, although honest and brave, is uneducated and from the peasant class. His cousins the Pinchons provide comic relief.

General de Brémont bolsters his anti-romantic position by recounting the story of his own *mésalliance*. When he was eighteen, he fell in love with a woman from the working classes. His father refused to allow them to marry, and so, influenced by Goethe's *Werther* (1774), they attempted suicide together. They survived, however, and his father eventually relented. They were soon married, but, he tells Edouard: "One year later we were filing for separation and I was the unhappiest of men. There you are, my boy, that is how most marriages of inclination begin and end."[59] Fortunately for Brémont, his inappropriate wife died shortly thereafter, leaving him free to contract a marriage of reason. "I married your mother," he tells Edouard, "whom I esteemed, whom I respected, but whom I did not love."[60]

Love came later, you know; not the love that sweeps you away with sensuality or imagination, but true love that was strengthened by time, by our
mutual happiness, by all the virtues that I discovered in her. This constant
happiness, this inner harmony of our family, you have witnessed it. Let this
memory guide you. Think of your mother and make your choice.[61]

Brémont's defense of reason over passion is repeated throughout the play.
He warns Edouard: "when this first ardor has faded, when your love for her
has waned, there will be nothing left for you other than an awareness of
your mistake and your regrets."[62] To Suzette he says bluntly, "Such a union is
impossible," going on to paint a grim picture of the social consequences:

There are proprieties that must be respected, and society avenges itself on
those who dare to defy them. If my son were to marry his mother's chambermaid, in the world where he would want to introduce you, public opinion
would reject you. He would realize this himself, he would be humiliated
because of you, and soon he would no longer love you, for unfortunately
self-esteem is the primary motive of love. Then, disdained by society,
abandoned by your husband, you would have only me, my daughter, and
I am very old and would not be able to console you for very long.[63]

Scribe is at pains to show that the benefits of the marriage of reason are
universal, not limited merely to the upper classes. He has Bertrand's peasant
cousin, Madame Pinchon, espouse the same sentiments as the General and offer
Suzette the same advice:

But mark my words, lovers last only for the moment. Now husbands, they
last for ever. So for this you've got to choose someone good and solid, because
once you've chosen, you can never change your mind. And that's what I did.
[. . .] And in your home, in your daily life, when you realize how happy he
makes you, you will be like me. This love that you don't yet feel, it will come,
little by little, little by little.[64]

Despite the steady barrage of arguments such as these, the young lovers remain
unconvinced, and so General de Brémont forces Suzette to sign the marriage
contract with Bertrand while imprisoning Edouard to prevent him from
dissuading her. When Edouard finally meets with Suzette, too late, he pleads
with her in the sentiments of Romanticism:

No one has ever loved you as I do. And what are these obligations that have
been imposed on you against your will, despite your feelings? Are they any
more sacred than the promises you made to me? Yes, Suzette, it is I who have
received your vows, it is I who am your lover, your spouse. Come, let us flee
together. If you love me, follow me.[65]

The unhappy Suzette is saved from temptation only by the unexpected arrival
of Bertrand. This is how adultery makes its appearance in plays of the Restora-

tion, invariably prevented "just in the nick of time" by an unlikely set of coin-
cidences that audiences and critics could simply disregard as the censor's figleaf.

By the end of the play, the party of reason has been proven correct: Edouard
is exposed as a frivolous young man who has already courted several young
women before Suzette – including even Madame Pinchon! Scribe, like Delavigne, has identified the ideals of romantic love with the seductive lies of an
irresponsible young man, an aristocrat whose whims would destroy the true
happiness of families. In contrast to Edouard, Bertrand is revealed as a solid
and worthy husband, so devoted to Suzette that he had made her his heir long
before their marriage, a financial gesture of true affection not lost on bourgeois
audiences. Both Delavigne and Scribe identify marital happiness – and the
censors would concur – as proceeding from marriage within one's own class.
Unlike Delavigne, however, Scribe focuses on differences in class and not in age
as the potential disrupter of ideal marriage. While Delavigne's subject is the
mariage mal-assorti, Scribe's is the more serious transgression of a *mésalliance*.
The Marriage of Reason resolves that problem with the marriage of Suzette
and Bertrand, and so all ends well in this rationally arranged universe with the
entire cast – except for Edouard – singing together as the curtain falls: "Ah,
what happiness there is in marriage!"[66]

The critical response to this play focused exclusively on the arranged
marriage between Suzette and Bertrand and, as might be expected, the play as
a whole was judged by whether the critic agreed with Scribe's views on marriage. Several critics, instead of analyzing the play or the production, presented
lengthy exegeses of their own views on the marriage question, and used Scribe's
play as a vehicle to discuss current social practice. The anonymous critic for
La Pandore, after recounting the plot, concluded: "This is what is called 'the
marriage of reason,' although it should instead be called 'the marriage of
absurdity.' After all, why punish this unfortunate girl against whom one cannot
reproach even one of the faults of flighty young women?"[67] The anonymous
critic for *Le Globe*, the Saint-Simonian journal, referred to "the marriages of
reason, so called, no doubt, because they are usually the most *unreasonable* of
all."[68] Of the character of the General de Brémont, *Le Globe* stated:

> This character is realistic: don't we see certain gentlemen, raised up by
> an imperial decree, sons, brothers and husbands of dressmakers, who fear
> nothing so much as a marriage beneath their new rank? Aside from that
> they're extremely liberal – when they are not directly involved. I know a great
> partisan of equality who was made a baron in 1813. For sons-in-law, he
> wants only counts or marquises, old or new, it doesn't matter to him. He
> feels that if you don't have any titles, then you should buy them. And this
> baron is perfectly right, since the reason titles are sold is so that they will be
> bought.[69]

Le Figaro, at that time a liberal journal, published a diatribe in guise of a review,
noting the private carriages lined up in front of the theater: "Everywhere you

hear titles announced: *Count! Marquise! Baron!*" The review concluded, "This play is not a fantasy: the original of these attitudes can be found in the faubourg St-Germain."[70] Scribe's play, in fact, so realistically depicted these attitudes that it was cited even in court proceedings. Two months after *The Marriage of Reason* opened, the *Gazette des tribunaux* reported on a love match that had turned sour and, like that of the General de Brémont, had ended up in court with a plea for a legal separation. The *Gazette* editorialized:

> Who, by now, hasn't seen *The Marriage of Reason* more than once? Monsieur Scribe, in the opinion of excellent judges, has risen to the rank of moralist through this witty vaudeville, and he has served society well by teaching our youth how they ought to undertake this most pleasant of contracts. *The School for Husbands* and *The School for Old Men* have found their pendant: *The Marriage of Reason* is truly *The School for Youth*. And so fathers are bringing their sons to see it, and every mother takes her daughters because it is the gentlest and most effective sermon, even though they risk interrupting the spectacle (as we have seen) with fits of hysteria and fainting. We have even heard that many husbands are taking their wives to see it, in order to show them that they are the most fortunate of women, and that a marriage of inclination would have been catastrophic for them.
>
> In any case, few days pass without the law courts giving striking confirmation of the charming moral lesson of the Théâtre du Gymnase.[71]

A complicated set of issues governed the reception of the play, making it palatable to all the propertied classes however much they might disagree on other issues. The General is an aristocrat, a count, but of such recent vintage that the Old Regime aristocracy would feel contemptuous of his lineage; meanwhile his bourgeois background was contradicted by his current aristocratic status. In his own way he is as much of a hybrid as Suzette, existing between two classes. Through the persona of the General de Brémont, Scribe's play could thus emphasize and applaud the values that the two classes shared, and attract a large and enthusiastic following from both quarters. The General is clearly the hero of the play, a wise patriarch like Danville in *The School for Old Men*. The young men of both plays, Edouard de Brémont in *The Marriage of Reason*, the duc d'Elmar in *The School for Old Men,* are irresponsible, fickle, and callow. These are not just men's plays, they are old men's plays, where women play passive roles at best. The hysteria and fainting that the *Gazette des tribunaux* reported among daughters taken to see *The Marriage of Reason* indicates that such marriages of reason did not appeal equally to all members of the family. Such intense reactions could have been provoked only by an acute identification with Suzette's plight.

One thing all the critics could agree upon was that, whether they approved or not, Scribe had accurately described a common social practice among the propertied classes, and one that had not found its way previously onto the stage. "He is one of the greatest *cynics* in the world," wrote the critic for *Le Mercure du dix-neuvième siècle,* "he is a man who believes neither in puppy love, nor in mysterious attractions, nor in irresistible passions."[72] He imagines a young working-class woman reproaching Scribe:

> Before you, in the theater, love always triumphed over the prejudices of fortune or of birth. There, the equality that the world has destroyed was re-established; and if, in society, uncles and fathers opposed our desires, at least in the theater and in the novel we enjoyed a safe haven. There, no more tyrannical prejudices. There, dressmakers, when they were pretty, could marry dukes and peers, for neither titles nor distinctions have any place in philosophy. [. . .] You have changed everything. Now it is fathers and uncles who triumph in the theater. No more irresistible love, no more victories over prejudice. One should marry within one's own class.[73]

This young woman's memory was selective, since, while novels routinely indulged in fantasies of dressmakers marrying aristocrats, theater transgressed such class boundaries only during the Enlightenment. The critic's conclusion, however, was accurate: "Monsieur Scribe describes the world as it is. When men practice equality, he'll put it on stage."[74] Scribe's play he called "today's society presented with incisive accuracy in the finest depiction of manners we have ever seen."[75]

Ironically, the most glowing appreciation of the play came from the anonymous government censor whose report began by praising the relationship of Bertrand and Suzette:

> The play is performed with so much art that we share the strong friendship that she feels for him. We remain convinced that it is personal qualities and the observation of social conventions that bring happiness to marriage, and not the fleeting and shameful passions of a heedless and immoderate love. The second part of the lesson is no less valuable. It comes from Monsieur de Brémont who conveys to Suzette all the dangers of an inappropriate alliance, warning her that fortune and education cannot eradicate differences in rank. [. . .] In short, the play is charming for the public and irreproachable for the Office of Censorship.[76]

Le Journal des débats pronounced the play a total success:

> *The Marriage of Reason* was announced a month ago, and the Gymnase had high hopes for it. Favorable advance publicity about this new work had attracted a considerable crowd to the theater, and the public has not been disappointed. The play's success is complete, and it will be durable because it is legitimate. [. . .] It has been a long time since we've seen a play welcomed with such heartfelt pleasure by the patrons of the Gymnase.[77]

The Marriage of Reason remained popular for years, reprinted several times well into the 1860s; its conservative sentiments about marriage did not soon go out of date. The party of Romanticism was slowly gaining ground during these years, however, and while the marriages Scribe described remained customary for the propertied classes, the practice continued to be attacked relentlessly by Romantics and liberals alike.

Although applauded in some quarters for his realistic portrayal of the marriage of reason, Scribe was nonetheless criticized for his unrealistic appraisal of the chances of happiness in such marriages. His opponents, as shown in chapter 3, were most conspicuous in the realm of the visual arts, producing quantities of lithographic caricatures on the subject of the marriage of reason versus the marriage for love. Even in the theater, however, he did not go unchallenged. When, two years after *The Marriage of Reason*, Scribe wrote *Malvina, or A Marriage for Love*, a play that once again demonstrated that only unhappiness could result from allowing a woman to choose her husband, the playwriting team of Dartois, Léon Brunswick, and Lhérie produced, in response, *The Results of a Marriage of Reason.*[78]

Their play revisits Bertrand and Suzette three years after their arranged marriage, and begins with the General priding himself on having successfully arranged two marriages of reason, one for Suzette and the other for his son Edouard. It soon becomes clear, however, that both young people are miserably unhappy. Suzette, raised in an upper-class household, has nothing in common with either Bertrand or with his rural cousins the Pinchons. Edouard's society wife, the former Mademoiselle de Luceval, thoroughly detests him because she also was forced into this marriage by her parents; in retaliation she has taken a lover. In the published version of the play, Edouard has entrapped them *in flagrante delicto* and killed her lover, an act that would be a crime during the Old Regime, but had become legal under the new Penal Code (article 324). Censors would not allow these events, even off stage, and so, as played, it is the discovery of his wife's infidelity that causes Edouard, at the beginning of the play, to seek his father's advice.[79] Despite the general's aristocratic title, his advice is typical of bourgeois families, that Edouard should avoid scandal by maintaining the appearance of a happy marriage.

Disregarding this advice, Edouard, who has always truly loved Suzette, arranges to meet her again, but, through a series of contretemps, Bertrand bursts in upon their meeting, once again arriving just in time. Assuming, incorrectly, that Edouard has already seduced Suzette, Bertrand challenges him to a duel. Suzette throws herself at Bertrand's feet, begging him to think of their children, but he rushes off, pistol in hand. The play ends as shots are heard and Bertrand, the sole survivor, returns, falling to his knees in front of the General. He has murdered his benefactor's son. General de Brémont, because of his insistence on the marriage of reason, has been the cause of deaths and ruined lives – including his own. The curtain falls.

The play's "message" was trumpeted by the political opposition. The Saint-Simonian journal *Le Globe* applauded the play with these words: "Do you still doubt that marriages for love are the only truly reasonable ones? Here then is the proof."[80]

Ducange and the "Mode of Excess"

Although Victor Ducange's *Thirty Years, or The Life of a Gambler* was only tangentially about marriage, it also showed, strongly and graphically, the negative consequences of the marriage of reason.[81] Ducange, the oldest of the playwrights considered here, was considered the heir of Guilbert de Pixérécourt (1773–1844), the father of French melodrama, a new theatrical form that had arisen during the Revolutionary period (Figure 71). It was a "mode of excess," as Peter Brooks termed it, a theater "of dramatic conflict and clash, of grandiose struggle represented in hyperbolic gestures."[82] In short, it was a genre befitting its times. Pitting personifications of Good against Evil, earlier melodramatic plots tended to espouse a patriarchal conception of the family by reasserting the authority of the father. Ducange's liberal politics, however, led him to revise these traditional plots to propose instead a family structured on love and equality instead of on rights and authority.[83] In many ways his vision of the family was more typical of Revolutionary idealism than of Restoration conservatism. The "fathers and uncles" who had regained their absolute power in Scribe's plays were transformed in those of Ducange into deeply caring human beings. Marriage should be freely entered into, he proposed over and over again in his plays: husbands should not abuse their legal authority; love and mutual

71   Louis Boilly, "The Effect of Melodrama," 1830. Lithograph. Lith. Villain. Bibliothèque nationale de France, Paris. ("L'Effet du mélodrame")

L'EFFET DU MÉLODRAME.

respect, not a master–slave relationship, should govern family relations. That his plays achieved a popular success equal to Scribe's, although not with the same constituency, is testimony to the increasing fragmentation of audience during the period, with each ideological faction applauding its own theaters, heroes, plots, and plays.

Thirty Years, or The Life of a Gambler was one of Ducange's major successes, frequently revived during the rest of the century. Written in collaboration with Jacques-Félix Beudin and Prosper-Parfait Goubaux (1795–1859), it was first presented on June 19, 1827 at the Théâtre de la Porte-Saint-Martin, a theater specializing in melodrama, and it starred two well-known actors of the period, Frédérick Lemaître and Marie Dorval. While the typical audience for Scribe was described as the bourgeois businessman and family patriarch, Ducange's melodrama, four hours long, was said to appeal mainly to women, who were said to comprise 90 per cent of its audience.[84] The press reported that handkerchiefs and smelling-salts were everywhere, as women wept and fainted throughout each performance.[85] As *La Pandore* pointed out: "Everything that defines the art of melodrama, violent contrasts, hideous vice, loathsome crime, is included in this work. There is filial ingratitude, corruption, rape, theft, forgery, murder and arson."[86] This was, apparently, a winning combination: "The crowd of ticket-sellers is considerable, the size of the audience is immense, the composure of the gate-men is shattered, the sword of the policeman is drawn, his horse is wild. The gates give way, the women scream, the men swear. They push and shove but the queue does not move. The spectacle at the entrance is frightening, but the one inside is appalling."[87]

The play's three acts portray three days in the life of Georges de Germany, a gambler whose vice leads him to destroy everything and everyone around him. The three days are situated fifteen years apart, in 1790, 1805, and 1820. On the first "day," Georges, twenty-five years old, is about to enter into an arranged marriage with Amélie, a rich orphan of sixteen who was raised in the same household. Like Suzette, she is lovely, loyal, and kind, "an angel" as the critics described her. Unlike Suzette, however, she is rich. For Georges her principal attraction is her dowry, which will provide the money that he needs to cover his gambling debts. In true melodramatic style, Amélie's uncle Dermont, who has discovered Georges's vice and is trying to stop the marriage, arrives moments too late, finding the couple united forever in unholy wedlock. Scoundrel that he is, Georges immediately exercises his legal rights over Amélie by telling her: "You no longer have any master here other than me."[88] Such words referred directly to Civil Code article 213: "The wife must obey her husband."[89] When expressed in this way by the despicable Georges, however, the playwright's condemnation of women's inferior legal position becomes manifest. A husband's rights over his wife's property are even further implicitly criticized when Georges flies into a rage against Amélie's uncle Dermont, who wants to have the marriage annulled:

Break up my marriage! You would have already paid with your life . . . if this Amélie, whose spouse and master I now am, were not your blood relation. So – you have come here to denounce me? And by what right do you think you can pass judgment on my conduct, manage my affairs, curb my desires? I am now free, I have wealth. The law has given it to me. I am here in my own household, and remember that I have the right to eject anyone who insults me.[90]

The act ends with Georges's father cursing him with his dying breath: "The fate of a gambler is written on the gates of hell. Ungrateful son! Murdering, parricidal son! You will be a corrupt husband and an unnatural father! Your life will end in misery, blood and remorse!"[91] And as the curtain falls, he drops dead.

As the play progresses, the curse of Georges's father quickly becomes reality. Georges spends all his own inheritance as well as Amélie's dowry on his gambling debts. When, on the second "day," fifteen years later, Amélie says "We have spent fifteen years without even one day of peace, much less of happiness," Ducange is again making a searing indictment of the system of arranged marriages.[92] In the intervening period, Georges has become as brutal as he is corrupt, even striking Amélie. While "moderate correction" is within his rights as husband, it is here represented as an unquestionably vile and cowardly act.[93] Georges's friend Warner, having led him into corruption and vice, attempts to seduce Amélie by sending Georges away and hiding in her bedroom. On discovering him, Amélie, horrified, seizes his sword to kill herself but, upon grasping it, she faints. Georges returns, finds the sword, and shouting "treacherous, adulterous spouse!" he rushes out to seek vengeance – as did both Edouard and Bertrand in *The Results of a Marriage of Reason*.[94] In *Thirty Years*, however, the evil Warner tells George that Amélie's supposed seducer was none other than Rodolphe, her devoted and chaste admirer, who has just arrived to warn Georges that the police are pursuing him for forging banknotes. In a frenzy, Georges kills Rodolphe and drags Amélie away just as the police burst in and the second-act curtain falls. This entire episode can be seen as a tragic commentary on the provision of the Civil Code permitting a husband to kill his wife and her lover caught *in flagrante delicto* (article 324). The circumstances here are presented in such a way that the avenging husband's "crime of honor" is exposed as simply murder.

On the third "day," in 1820, the couple is living in Bavaria, reduced to destitution. Georges is disliked and feared by the local villagers who suspect him, correctly, of preying upon travelers in the mountains. The couple's son Albert, left behind with Amélie's uncle Dermont when they fled, is now twenty-one. The heir to his uncle's fortune, he is searching for his lost family, which now includes a sister under ten. When Albert arrives, Georges does not even recognize his own son but, thinking him a wealthy traveler, plots with Warner to kill him for his money. As originally written, soldiers arrive, a moment too late.

Albert is dead and Amélie is in despair. Georges drags Warner into the house that they have set on fire to conceal Albert's murder, shouting "Now you will never leave me! I swear to you by hell itself!"[95]

Needless to say, the censors found much to dislike in this play. The production was delayed while, in two successive reports, they worked out a compromise.[96] Their criticism touched on all the obvious points: Georges's mistreatment of his virtuous wife, Georges's father's paternal malediction and death on stage, Georges's murder of Rodolphe, also on stage, the filicide of Georges's own son Albert and, most objectionable of all, the final suicide/murder of Georges and Warner. The censors' reports note that melodramas were usually permitted more violence than other productions – that was, no doubt, their principal attraction. In this case, the censors concluded that, since the play presented a strong moral message against gambling, it was, on the whole, "more salutary than harmful."[97] They proposed, however, that Georges should rush into the burning building to save his son and drag him out, leaving it undetermined whether he was alive or dead. According to the critics' reviews, that is how it was staged, although in the published text, Albert survives the assault.[98] The final murder/suicide was more problematic, as suicide, never acceptable in Catholicism, was banned on stage. The censors concluded that the building should be struck by lightning, not intentionally set on fire: "In this ending, the conflation of suicide and divine vengeance can be tolerated on condition that the staging of the scene does not make it too clear." The desired result would be that "the spectator, as well as the reader, should be struck by his horrible death, without knowing precisely how it came about."[99] Despite this concession, the reviews described the play, as staged, ending with the soldiers rushing into the burning building, seizing and arresting Georges and Warner, and taking them away.[100] A less melodramatic ending, perhaps, but one that did not prevent the women in the audience from screaming and fainting as the final scene unfolded in all its horror, leaving Amélie and her daughter Georgette alone, bereft, destitute, and homeless in a foreign land. So extreme were the audience reactions that the critic for the *Journal des débats* reported rumors that even the fainting had been staged to increase the melodramatic effect.[101]

In comparing this play with those of Delavigne and Scribe, one notes that the friction between classes is softened. While the particle in Georges's name signals his aristocratic origins, Uncle Dermont is identified only as a rich merchant and Amélie as a rich orphan. No characters in the play are titled and, unlike Delavigne and Scribe, Ducange included no discussion of class differences or *mésalliances*. Although class does represent a subtext, in true melodramatic tradition Ducange's play presents the conflict as simply between virtue and vice.

While the degeneration of Georges through the evils of gambling is the central thread of Ducange's *Thirty Years*, a powerful subtheme is the mistreatment of women. Everything that Georges did to Amélie was completely legal and within his rights as her husband – to the extent that, aside from noting their disapproval, the censors did not require any changes in their relationship. And yet, because Georges is presented as weak, corrupt, and dishonest, the play implicitly condemns his behavior towards Amélie.

Republished thirteen times by 1866, the play seems to have had an enduring appeal to women. Perhaps, ultimately, only a melodrama could adequately criticize the marriage of reason. And perhaps all the tears and fainting by the women in the audience was, in fact, an implicit acknowledgment of their own vulnerability in the face of their epoch's unjust laws and customs.

Hugo and "The Extremes of Aberration"

Victor Hugo's *Hernani* was premièred on February 25, 1830.[102] It is universally acknowledged as the theatrical landmark that concluded the period and eclipsed the theater of the preceding decades. It would cast a long shadow over the rest of the century. The play has been valued for its challenge to the conventions of French theater, to the purity of the alexandrine verse form, to the unities of time, place, and action, and to the prohibition on mixing comedy and tragedy as well as on showing violence on stage, but, as Marie Le Hir has shown, these conventions had already been challenged by melodrama, and particularly by Ducange.[103] Hugo (1802–85), however, brought these innovations directly into the Théâtre-Français, the most respected theater in France, and into the genre of the five-act tragedy in alexandrine verse, the highest form of theater. In its own sphere, this event was very like the Revolutionary assault on the Bastille. What has received relatively little attention, however, is Hugo's treatment of the marriage question, for, whatever else the play may be, it is essentially the story of an arranged marriage and a doomed love. It is appropriate, then, to conclude this discussion of theater during the Restoration with a brief glance at the play that was, for contemporaries as well as for posterity, the landmark theatrical event of the period.

In *Hernani*, Doña Sol de Silva, a beautiful young woman of eighteen, is betrothed to her aged uncle Ruy Gomez de Silva, the Duke of Pastrana, a man over sixty. She loves Hernani, however, who is her own age but is an impoverished bandit, or so she believes. He is actually Jean d'Aragon, a grandee of Spain in disguise. The plot is tortuously complicated, with Hernani leading an uprising against the king, Don Carlos, who at the end of the play becomes the Holy Roman Emperor Charles V and forgives him. While proscribed, however, Hernani hid in the castle of the duke who, in return for his hospitality, extorted from him an oath that his life would henceforth belong to the duke. Hernani and Doña Sol eventually marry with the new emperor's blessings, but then the duke demands Hernani's life, and so, on their wedding night the two young lovers take poison and die. The duke stabs himself in despair as the curtain falls, leaving the stage littered with bodies. Although overshadowed by the melodramatic action (I have omitted numerous incidents of duels, hiding in armoires, disguises, kidnappings, and so on) the major elements of the *comédie de moeurs*, the play of manners and morals, are present. There is the tension between the loveless marriage of reason arranged between a young woman and a much older man, and the idealized marrage of inclination of two young people who love each other. In this way, *Hernani*, despite its ambitions to classical tragedy, is just as much a hybrid theatrical form as the work of Delavigne.

Because Hernani leads a revolt against the king, and because the play opened only five months before the very real revolt that toppled the Restoration regime, *Hernani* has often been read as a commentary on politics, but Hugo's play can also be seen as a further development of the *comédie de moeurs*. Molière had provided the model for the comedy of two young people whose mutual love is endangered by an inappropriate arranged marriage, but in Molière's plays, set in the bourgeoisie but produced for an aristocratic audience, love always triumphed in the end, albeit in someone else's social class. Shakespeare's *Romeo and Juliet* (which played in Paris in June 1827), did offer a "doomed love" scenario similar in spirit to *Hernani*, but Hugo's plot is actually closer to the standard trope used by Molière, Delavigne, and Scribe than to that of Shakespeare. These French playwrights all portray young people who love each other despite the interference of their elders, and all feature, as *Romeo and Juliet* does not, an arranged marriage between the young woman and a man two or three times her age. Hugo provides a dénouement even more tragic and less innocent than Shakespeare's, however, and completely different from the happy endings of Molière, Delavigne, and Scribe. No longer, as in Molière, does young love triumph in the end, nor, as in Scribe, does a marriage of reason resolve the threat of a *mésalliance*; nor even, as in Shakespeare, do the two young lovers kill themselves as the tragic result of a misunderstanding. In *Hernani*, Hugo mounts a brutal frontal attack on the older, propertied generation, in the person of the duke, for being directly responsible for the death of the young lovers. Although their deaths are more precisely suicides, Hugo clearly presents them as murder, the result of Don Ruy Gomez's evil tricks (Figure 72).

Hugo "distanced" his plot in a way that Scribe never did, by locating it in sixteenth-century Spain instead of in contemporary Paris, a historicization that placed it in the tradition of classical tragedy. In addition to the Romantic predilection for historicized periods and locations, and the high classical theater's insistence on the avoidance of contemporary settings, there was the additional factor that censors were always more lenient towards plays depicting an earlier period.[104] Despite this, the censors were extremely negative towards *Hernani*, calling it "a web of excesses, to which the author has tried in vain to give a character of grandeur, but that is not only vulgar but often crude."[105] They allowed it to be produced anyway, feeling that "it is good that

72   Achille Devéria, "*Hernani* (Last Scene)," 1830. Lithograph from *La Silhouette*, 1/11 (1830). Lith. V. Ratier. Bibliothèque nationale de France, Paris. ("*Hernani* [scène dernière]")

the public should see the extremes of aberration to which the human mind can reach when all principles and decency are abandoned."[106]

Their hopes that the play, with all its extravagances, would shame the young Romantics proved incorrect, and the play's opening night made theatrical history. Under cover of its chronological and geographical distancing, *Hernani* accurately conveyed the resentment and hostility of the young Romantic generation towards the gerontocracy that ruled the Restoration. Hugo, just as much as the other playwrights discussed here, rewrote the classic scripts of love and marriage to demonstrate new values and attitudes. He was the only one of these playwrights who was actually part of that "French Generation of 1820," for in 1820 he was eighteen, while Delavigne was already twenty-seven, Scribe was twenty-nine, and Ducange thirty-seven. For Hugo's generational cohort, it was not grounds for rejoicing that fathers and uncles had regained the authority they had enjoyed under the Old Regime. For them, the classic plot pitting the old man against the young lovers could not be so easily resolved with the victory of the old man. Even Balzac, who panned *Hernani* in two review articles, finding the plot unrealistic to an extreme, nonetheless dwelt approvingly and at length on Hugo's portrayal of Don Ruy Gomez as what Balzac called "a stupid old man."[107]

   In the earlier plays discussed here, respect for old age was constantly reiterated. But, in contrast to the admiration accorded to Danville in *The School for Old Men*, to Brémont in *The Marriage of Reason*, to both the elder Germany and to Dermont in *Thirty Years*, Don Ruy Gomez in *Hernani* is repeatedly called a "foolish old man," even by his intended bride Doña Sol.[108] Here is Hernani's description of him:

> Oh, the foolish old man,
> With head drooped down to finish out his days!
> Wanting a wife, he takes a girl; himself
> Most like a frozen specter. Does he not see,
> The fool, that while with one hand he
> Marries you, the other mates with Death!
> Yet without a shudder he comes between our hearts!
> Seek out the gravedigger, old man, and give
> Your measure.[109]

In contrast to the euphoric gerontocracy characteristic of the Restoration period, a sentiment that Scribe exploited to the full, Hugo throughout his play heaped abuse on old men and their love for young women. Hugo has Don Ruy Gomez repeat the platitudes in the conduct manuals and advice books discussed in chapter 2, praising the marriage of reason over the marriage of mutual attraction:

> Oh! this love of mine
> Is not a plaything made of glass, which gleams
> And trembles: Oh no! it is a love severe and sure,
> Solid, profound, paternal – strong as
> The oak that forms my ducal chair![110]

By giving the metaphor only a slight twist, Hugo has the old man in effect calling his love wooden and autocratic. This was quite different from the speech of General de Brémont, or even of the simple Madame Pinchon who advised choosing a "good and solid" spouse.[111] Hugo addresses the same marriage issues as do the other playwrights, but, by ridiculing the representative of the old values, he set out a manifesto for youth and passion against age, "reason," and worldly position. A telling example comes in Act III, aptly entitled "The Old Man," where he presents an ironic revision of a parallel scene in Delavigne's *School for Old Men*. In both scenes, old men who love young women speak of their dilemma, and they both ask pardon for an old man's love of youth. Danville, in *The School for Old Men*, says that he realizes:

> That the heart of an old man, deprived of ecstasies,
> Succumbs to all the raptures of a heedless love.

When one loves apprehensively, one loves excessively.
When young we knew that we were attractive, we were sure of success;
But old, but love-struck in the autumn of life,
Possessing a treasure that is envied by all
We become miserly, we try to hide it away.[112]

Don Ruy Gomez says almost the same thing:

> Listen, one cannot be
> The master of himself, so much in love
> As I am now with you. And I am old
> And jealous, and I am cross – and why? Because
> I'm old. Because the beauty, grace or youth
> Of others frightens, threatens me. Because
> While jealous of others, of myself
> I am ashamed.[113]

But while Danville's love is paternalistic, tender, and in the end triumphant, Don Ruy Gomez, by jealously demanding the death of his rival Hernani, becomes in effect the murderer of both young lovers. Because he forces Hernani to take his own life to satisfy a wrongful oath that was extorted from him, Don Ruy Gomez becomes responsible even for the suicide of Doña Sol, who cannot live without Hernani, and refuses to live as the wife of his murderer. Could Hugo have more powerfully demonstrated that Don Ruy Gomez's love for Doña Sol is evil and perverse? And, although *Hernani* is at the other end of the literary spectrum from the vicomte de S***'s *Conjugalism, or The Art of Marrying Well*, their warnings were identical, that the inevitable tragic result of forced marriages will be suicide.[114]

In ways large and small, the plays of Delavigne, Scribe, and Ducange all treat the theme of class conflict, the *mésalliance*. Vice is represented by the aristocracy, virtue by the bourgeoisie, and never the twain should marry. In the comedies of Delavigne and Scribe, the villains are aristocrats who threaten the family happiness of the lower orders. Ducange's *Thirty Years* differs only in that it can be read as a cautionary tale of what would have happened had the villains prevailed. Here, the wicked Georges de Germany was not foiled by the virtuous bourgeois, Uncle Dermont, but succeeded in winning Amélie and ruining her life. This success, followed by the inevitable downward spiral of misery, tragedy, and death, was the same fate that would have befallen Hortense or Suzette had the duc d'Elmar or Edouard de Brémont carried out their schemes of seduction. The message throughout is the same: one should marry within one's own class.

Hugo differs from these playwrights in that he came from an aristocratic family, albeit a recently ennobled one. His father, like the General de Brémont, was a Napoleonic general who received his title in compensation for military service.[115] During most of the 1820s Hugo remained a royalist, finally

announcing himself as a liberal only three days before the première of
Hernani.[116] In *Hernani*, set completely among the aristocracy, he ignores the
plot possibilities of the *mésalliance* theme, so important to bourgeois audiences,
and refers to it only elliptically, through the traditional Old Regime plot device
where Doña Sol is temporarily under the illusion that she loves a commoner,
Hernani in disguise.

Intertwined with the plots of *mésalliances*, real or imaginary, in the plays
discussed in this chapter, and complicating them still further, is the theme of
generational conflict. These plays all challenge the trend, begun in the late eighteenth century, towards the empowerment of youth over age.[117] In the work of
Delavigne, Scribe, and Ducange, wisdom is represented by father figures, while
young men signify immorality, even wickedness. The old men, Danville, General
de Brémont, Bertrand, Uncle Dermont, all are presented with sympathy and
admiration. The young men, the charming duc d'Elmar, the dashing but irresponsible Edouard de Brémont, the evil Georges de Germany, all illustrate
varying degrees of criminality. These plays, and hundreds like them, reversed
and "corrected" the Old Regime theme of the old man duped by a pair of young
lovers. In the work of the Restoration playwrights, either the young lovers are
trumped by the old man (as in the comedies of Delavigne or Scribe), or, if the
young couple is united, disaster inevitably follows (as in the melodramas of
Ducange). If there were, as Balzac said, only two ages during the Restoration,
youth and senility, then it is obvious that youth was not the audience for these
plays.

In its own way, *Hernani* also demonstrates the triumph of age over youth,
but Hugo, unlike Delavigne and Scribe, does not applaud this victory. He presents it as tragedy, and perhaps that was another reason why *Hernani* became
the battle standard for Hugo's generation. For Hugo, the major conflict of his
period was generational, youth versus age. In comparing *Hernani* with contemporaneous works, it is clear that the issues involved were more than simply
literary. And so, only months before the July Revolution of 1830 ended the
Restoration regime, the battle between the generations, smoldering for decades,
erupted on stage in *Hernani* – with the marriage question as the catalyst.

5

Happily Ever After . . . Or Not:
Novels and Their Readers

The novels [. . .] were invariably about love affairs, lovers, mistresses, harassed ladies swooning in remote pavilions. Couriers were killed at every relay, horses ridden to death on every page; there were gloomy forests, broken hearts, vows, sobs, tears and kisses, skiffs in the moonlight, nightingales in thickets; the noblemen were all brave as lions, gentle as lambs, incredibly virtuous, always beautifully dressed, and wept copiously on every occasion.

Gustave Flaubert, *Madame Bovary*[1]

The most dangerous enemy of a young woman's happiness, and, by extension, of a husband's repose, is imagination.

Horace Raisson, *Conjugal Code*[2]

BY THE LATE 1820s, the marital literature discussed in chapter 2 was being replaced in popularity by the novel. Despite its position in the modern literary canon, however, the novel was not then considered a major artistic genre. Both drama and poetry were accorded a higher status because they were thought to be more universal than the novel, which focused "merely" on the inner lives of specific individuals.[3] Individuality itself was a new and not entirely welcome concept in the nineteenth century; traditionalists rejected it as equivalent to egotism and emblematic of modernity.[4]

"For the educated classes, the novel remained clandestine reading," wrote Marc Angenot in his study of nineteenth-century French popular literature.[5] Deemed light, even frivolous, entertainment, novels were judged fit only for women either as authors or as audience.[6] *The Princess of Clèves* (1678) by Marie-Madeleine Pioche de la Vergne, comtesse de La Fayette (1634–1692), usually cited as the first French novel, had immediately established this identification, and by the early nineteenth century women authors not only produced half the novels written in the period, but were also its most renowned authors.[7] The writings of Caroline-Stéphanie-Félicité Du Crest, comtesse de Genlis (1746–1830), Adélaïde de Souza (1761–1836), Germaine de Staël-Holstein

73 Louis-Léopold Boilly, "Reading the Novel," 1828. Lithograph. Lith. Delpech. Bibliothèque nationale de France, ("La Lecture du roman")

74 Louis-Léopold Boilly, "Newspapers," 1826. Lithograph. Lith. Delpech. Bibliothèque nationale de France, Paris. ("Les Journaux")

(1766–1817), and Sophie Ristaud Cottin (1770–1807) filled the *cabinets de lecture*, the public reading-rooms that predated public libraries in France.[8] The widespread assumption that only women read novels caused men to be embarrassed to have it known that they either read or wrote them. Men were assumed to occupy themselves with more serious reading, as can be seen in Boilly's pendants "Reading the Novel," and "Newspapers" (Figures 73 and 74), where the male audience for the novel comprises a young boy and a fop, while their more respectable elders occupy themselves with newspapers. Until the early decades of the nineteenth century, when Sir Walter Scott's historical novels brought new respectability to the medium and made him the most popular novelist of the period, men who wrote novels took care to let it be known that their more serious endeavors lay elsewhere.[9] Nonetheless, novels enjoyed great popularity, their numbers increasing year by year to the point where, by the early nineteenth century, they comprised 80–100 per cent of the books in the *cabinets de lecture*.[10]

Since no one could ignore the vast number of popular novels with their huge audiences, "serious" authors attempted to distinguish their own production from this pulp fiction.[11] Stendhal divided novels into two classes: those written for provincial chambermaids, filled with extravagant fantasies and flawless heroes (very like those Flaubert described in the epigraph to this chapter); and those written for sophisticated Parisian salons, accurately depicting contemporary life.[12] Needless to say, Stendhal considered his novel *The Red and the Black* (1830) to be among the latter, claiming that "The author in no way treats Julien like the hero of a *chambermaid's* novel. He exposes all his faults, all his base impulses."[13] Nor was he the only author making wry references to the servant class as the audience for novels. In Balzac's "At the Sign of the Cat and Racket" (1829), for example, the young Augustine Guillaume, strictly brought up by her parents, secretly reads romances left behind by the family cook.[14] Augustine's cook's novels, *Hippolyte, Count of Douglas* and *The Count of Comminges*, were actual novels of the seventeenth and eighteenth centuries, typical of the genre that focused on the romantic exploits of dashing young aristocrats.[15] Despite the predilection of Balzac's fictional cook, however, literary historians have pointed out that, in reality, servants could rarely afford to buy books, or even to pay the modest lender's fees of the *cabinets de lecture*; at best they might listen to the after-dinner readings common in the bourgeois and petit-bourgeois households as depicted by Boilly (Figure 73). The real audience for romantic novels consisted of women of the petite bourgeoisie and bourgeoisie, in both the provinces and in Paris.[16] Whether their cooks read them or not, Madame Bovary, the convent-educated daughter of a prosperous provincial farmer, and Augustine Guillaume, the daughter of a well-to-do Parisian draper, certainly did.

The success of the chambermaid's novel tainted all the others and challenged Charles Nodier's dictum that "The novel is the expression of the customs, characters, and events of a century."[17] This conviction pervaded the critical writing of the Restoration, with the attendant idea that good novels had a special mission to be a more faithful reflection of society than did other literary genres.[18] Nodier (1780–1844) went so far as to call the novelist "a social historian."[19] In her study *The Idea of the Novel in France: The Critical Reaction 1815–1848*, Margaret Iknayan wrote: "The idea that the modern novel completes and complements history, since it depicts the private life of the people while history occupies itself with the public life, had become a truism, and good novels were often said to be "truer than history."[20] To this end, reviews of novels focused on whether they presented an accurate portrayal of society, the same criterion, as described in chapter 4, that was used to evaluate bourgeois theater. Authors emphasized the realism of their works, as in Stendhal's famous description of a novel as "a mirror moving along the road."[21]

During the decades from the late eighteenth century to the early nineteenth, there was a shift in the focus of French novels. The literary historians J. S.

Wood and Priscilla Clark have both noted that the protagonists of earlier novels were aristocrats, with bourgeois characters limited to minor roles.[22] In the post-Revolutionary period, however, French novels began to focus on bourgeois rather than aristocratic lives, and on the reality of marriage rather than the sentimentality of courtship. Since the bourgeoisie had two contradictory aspirations for marriage, seeing it as both an institution for organizing the distribution of wealth and as the source of individual happiness and fulfillment, the tension between these aspirations became the subject of the novel in France. And as the new literary criteria that gave novels respectability emphasized their accurate portrayal of society, the "chambermaid's" narrative – where *mésalliances* always worked out at the end, with the young lovers succeeding in overcoming all obstacles – was soon replaced by more realistic plots that harshly criticized the tyrannical social conventions that in the contemporary world actually kept lovers apart.[23] This parallels the working-class woman's observation, cited in the previous chapter, that in Scribe's plays the fantasies of love were discarded in favor of a grim reality.[24]

During these years, the social activity of reading aloud in groups (Figure 73) gradually declined in favor of reading as a solitary pursuit of pleasure (Figure 75).[25] It is testimony to this new experience of reading as a private affair, as opposed to the social experience of theater-going, that such opposite dénouements to the standard Molière plot would be operative in the two media. In the bourgeois theater, the marriage of reason triumphed and even brought happiness to its participants, while novels favored either the sentimental "love conquers all" plot (the chambermaid's novel), or its realist counterpart in which love is destroyed by rigid social conventions (the literary novel). In either type of novel, the ascendancy of individual happiness over social conventions is assumed. It is only the compatibility of the two concerns that is at issue.

Social conventions demanded that marriages should be arranged by the parents of individuals of the same social class. The result was often the mismatch, the *mariage mal-assorti* of incompatible spouses. This situation, as noted in previous chapters, provoked apprehension over the possibility of adultery, exacerbated by the new inheritance laws.[26] Novels articulated these fears and anxieties. As the literary historian Tony Tanner, in his study *Adultery in the Novel*, has pointed out, while eighteenth-century novels abounded in seduction, fornication, and rape, in the nineteenth-century novel adultery became the main theme.[27] In France, arranged marriages remained the norm well into the nineteenth century, while the courtly love tradition continued to assume that romantic love would follow, not precede, marriage – but rarely with one's lawful spouse.[28] As a result, from Stendhal's *The Red and the Black* (1830), through Balzac's *The Woman of Thirty* (1832), George Sand's *Indiana* (1832), Flaubert's *Madame Bovary* (1857) – the list could go on indefinitely – the French novel took adultery as its theme. In England, where stricter moral codes discouraged such themes, and where different social patterns gave young people more freedom to choose a spouse, the novel of adultery was less com-

75 Octave Tassaert,
"The Novel," 1829.
Lithograph.
Lith. Lemercier, Dist.
Ostervald l'aîné.
Bibliothèque nationale
de France, Paris.
("Le Roman")

mon. There the standard novelistic plot focused on pre-marital courtship, with the plot ending at the altar – where the French novel usually began.[29]

Although it has been convincingly argued that the libertine text of the eighteenth century was aristocratic while the nineteenth-century novel of female adultery was bourgeois, this reading overlooks the complicated post-Revolutionary morality whereby the aristocracy attempted to demonstrate its right to rule by virtue of its reformed morality.[30] A striking literary example of this is the character of the Marquise de Carvajal, who serves as mentor to Indiana in George Sand's novel. Sand (1804–76) described Madame de Carvajal as someone who has successfully made the transition from Old Regime morality to that of the Restoration, when all the propertied classes adopted stricter moral codes, at least in public.

> The Restoration had given a virtuous impulse to minds of that stamp; and as *conduct* was demanded at court, the marquise detested nothing so much as the scandal that ruins and destroys. Under Madame du Barry she would have been less rigid in her principles; under the dauphine she became one of the *high-necked*.[31]

Cuckoldry has often been a common literary theme, but the fact that adulterous wives in nineteenth-century novels were all punished for their transgressions either with death or with life-threatening illness, either for themselves or for their children, shows that there had developed a new social attitude towards this offense.[32] One may recall the horrible agonizing suicide suffered by Flaubert's Madame Bovary, whose husband dies of grief in her wake, leaving the sins of the mother to be visited upon their innocent daughter, who ends up poor and orphaned, sent to work as child labor in a factory. Or Madame de Rênal in Stendhal's *The Red and the Black* who, having given her solemn promise not to die by her own hand, nonetheless expires of grief while embracing her legitimate children; these children have been represented as so sickly that, deprived of her constant solicitude, they too will certainly die. Or what may be the most shocking literary retribution of all: in Balzac's *The Woman of Thirty*, the young Charles, the adulterine son of Madame d'Aiglemont, described as the most adorable little boy imaginable, with blond hair, a fair complexion, graceful bearing, and a sweet disposition, is, before the horrified eyes of his mother and her lover, pushed by his legitimate sister down a rocky slope, and, screaming, bloody, and torn, falls into the muddy waters of a rapidly flowing river, his pitiful cries abruptly terminated by a loud sucking sound as he is swallowed up in the mud and disappears for ever. Now *that* is retribution.

And yet, despite the inevitable "moral" conclusions that terminated adulterous affairs with punishment only for the wives, novels were considered dangerous reading for an impressionable female audience (Figures 76 and 77). Families could shelter daughters from dangerous social experience, but novels subverted that by giving them imaginative entry into situations they could not yet negotiate in reality. On these grounds, Claire-Elisabeth-Jeanne Rémusat in her influential *Essay on the Education of Women* (1824) counseled against allowing young women to read novels. "Licentious novels overheat their imagination, agitate their mind, undermine their affection," she wrote.[33] For her and her contemporaries, however, "licentious novels" did not mean only pornography, although that certainly existed in quantity. The term was widely used to describe novels that presented any illicit love, or even an unfulfilled temptation. There is a long tradition in French philosophy of suspicion of the imagination, particularly women's imagination. Etienne Bonnot de Condillac (1715–1780) in his influential "Essay on the Origin of Human Knowledge" (1755) included a chapter "On the Vices and the Advantages of Imagination" in which he wrote:

> This explanation will reveal how dangerous the reading of novels is for young females whose brain is yet unformed. Their intelligence, which their education usually neglects, seizes hungrily on fiction that flatters the natural passions of their age. They find there material for the most beautiful castles in the air, and they put them into effect with the greatest of pleasure, encouraged by the desire to please and the gallantries that surround them. Then all

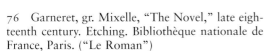

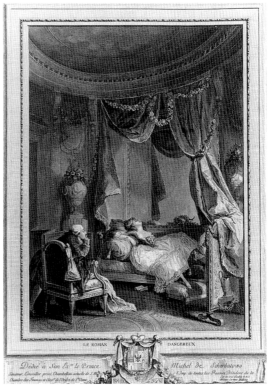

76   Garneret, gr. Mixelle, "The Novel," late eighteenth century. Etching. Bibliothèque nationale de
France, Paris. ("Le Roman")

77   Lavreince [Niklas Lafrensen], gr. Antoine-Jean
Duclos and Isidore-Stanislas Helman, "The Dangerous Novel," 1781. Etching. Bibliothèque nationale
de France, Paris. ("Le Roman dangereux")

that is necessary is perhaps a slight misfortune to turn a young girl's head,
to persuade her that she is Angélique or some such heroine whom she fancies,
and to cause her to mistake for Médor every man whom she meets.[34]

The notorious prude La Rochefoucauld-Doudeauville (1785–1864), in his
later but equally influential *Family Guide*, had a mother advise her daughter:
"You should not read novels. They encourage you to believe in a kind of happiness that doesn't exist, and, by weakening your moral fiber, they detach your
mind and heart from reality."[35]
As both Condillac and La Rochefoucauld-Doudeauville predicted, Augustine
Guillaume in Balzac's "At the Sign of the Cat and Racket" was, in fact, influenced by the cook's novels to make the romantic decision to marry someone
outside her social class, a decision that brought her unhappiness and led to her
premature death. Yet how could she not fall in love with the aristocratic

Théodore de Sommervieux, of whom her cousin declared: "His behavior to Augustine is seen only in novels."[36]

The ultimate case study of the tragic results of novel-reading was given not by the authors of moralizing conduct manuals, but by Gustave Flaubert (1821–80). Madame Bovary's persistent attempt to live her life as a romantic novel leads her only to disaster; at every turn of plot, and especially in the harrowing suicide scene, lived experience is starkly contrasted with the romantic fantasies of the chambermaid's novel. When Madame Bovary has taken poison, for example, her first thought is "I'll fall asleep, and everything will be over!"[37] Her idyllic conception of suicide, as described in so many romantic novels and plays, is followed by an ultra-realistic description of her agonized suffering and death: "Soon she was vomiting blood. Her lips pressed together more tightly. Her limbs were contorted, her body was covered with brown blotches, her pulse quivered under the doctor's fingers like a taut thread, like a harp string about to snap. Then she began to scream, horribly."[38] Just as the power of this passage comes from its contrast to Madame Bovary's earlier contemplation of the peaceful suicide of the chambermaid's novel, so too do the adulterous affairs in these nineteenth-century novels depend for their effect on their audience's familiarity with both the chambermaid's novel's romantic liaisons, and the courtly love tradition. The nineteenth-century reality was quite different.

The existence of romantic love within marriage was itself controversial and by no means considered necessary. La Rochefoucauld-Doudeauville might as well have warned that novels detached a woman's heart and mind, not from *reality* but from *duty*, which for him was the only reality and the only virtue incontrovertibly demanded of wives. Traditionalists assumed that romantic love was shallow and fleeting and neither could nor should have any role in marriage. Novels, despite their transgressive aura, reinforced this same idea through consistent portrayal of the grim consequences of passionate love. But whereas traditionalists preached self-abnegation for women, thus covering with a veil of silence the female sexual transgressions that they feared would follow loveless marriages, novels went so far as to depict the guilty deed, or at least its attractions. Regardless of the outcome of these illicit liaisons, invariably presented as disastrous during this period (at least partly because of censorship), novels, at the very least, articulated the possibility of a course of action other than "duty." They raised the specter that women, regardless of their marital status, wanted – and deserved – a degree of personal happiness beyond the mere fulfillment of duty. That was their offense.

Because of the perceived link between novels and female behavior, most of the advice manuals discussed the problem of women's reading. Balzac, for example, devoted the "Eleventh Meditation" in his *Physiology of Marriage* to "Education in Married Life," and took such an extreme position against women's literacy that it demands to be read as satire. He advises husbands: "'Away with civilization! Away with thought!' ... that should be your cry. You should look with horror upon the idea of educating women, for the reason, so fully realized by the Spaniards, that it is easier to govern a nation of idiots than a nation of wise men."[39] He suggests "various ways of consuming your wife's time so as to leave her no time for reading."[40] "To leave a woman free to read such books as the bent of her mind would lead her to choose . . . is to drop a spark in a gunroom. Nay, it is worse than that, it is to teach your wife how to do without you, to live in an imaginary world, a paradise. For what do women read? Works relating to the passions, Jean-Jacques' *Confessions*, novels, and all things that are likely powerfully to agitate their feelings."[41] Balzac went on to summarize the arguments against women's reading of novels in terms similar to those of Condillac, La Rochefoucauld-Doudeauville, and a whole host of predecessors and followers:

> In reading plays and novels, the woman, being a creature far more suscep-tible to loftier feelings than we are, must experience the most intoxicating ecstasies. She creates around her an ideal existence that makes everything else look pale; it is not long before she tries to realize this voluptuous life, and convey its magic into her actual life. Almost involuntarily she passes from the spirit to the letter, and from the letter to the senses.[42]

Ever the cynic, Balzac concludes by noting: "Many husbands find it difficult to keep their wives from reading, and there are even some who contend that reading has this advantage, that at least they know what their wives are doing when they are thus engaged."[43]

The authors of conduct manuals discussed in chapter 2 often compiled inventories of acceptable and non-acceptable novels. Their lists of unacceptable novels usually included Voltaire's *Candide* (1759), Rousseau's *Julie, or The New Héloïse* (1761), Laclos's *Dangerous Liaisons* (1782), Chateaubriand's *René* (1802), and that masterpiece of pornography, *Julie, or I Saved My Rose* (1807). These same novels were usually included on official lists of books for-bidden to the *cabinets de lectures*.[44] Charles Chabot, in his *Conjugal Grammar*, identified as the only acceptable reading the works of vicomte Louis de Bonald (1754–1840), a notorious legitimist who wanted to return to the Old Regime in every way except its licentiousness, and "the good books of Madame de Genlis" where morality always triumphed in the end. Balzac's list was even more extreme, listing fairy tales and works on mathematics, botany, and geog-raphy as among the only safe readings for women.[45] To be sure, these gestures were at least partly satirical; nonetheless, the result was to fix in the public mind the clear division of women's reading matter into the didactic on the one hand, and the objectionable on the other. Prints accentuated this by empha-sizing the corrupting influence of literacy, novels being the main target (Figures 76 and 77). When uncensored, these images showed women reading and mas-turbating at the same time, as though these two activities were indubitably intertwined, but even sanitized images served to underscore the popular asso-ciation between women, novels, and the dangers of the imagination.

Early nineteenth-century *romans de moeurs*, the novels of manners and morals, are revelatory. Those set in the Restoration, even if written subsequently, can flesh out the cold statutes of the Civil Code as well as the icy justice dispensed in its adultery trials. Tony Tanner, the first scholar to make an extensive study of the phenomenon of adultery in the novel, was so focused on the texts alone that he even denied that adultery was prosecuted in the nineteenth century.[46] He credited a formal literary device as the motive behind novelists' neglect of divorce as a possible solution to marital problems – during a century when divorce was outlawed in France! Subsequent literary scholars such as Judith Armstrong, Bill Overton, Naomi Segal, and Nicholas White have continued to explore the adultery theme in novels of the period.[47] My methodology is more that of the cultural than the literary historian in that I am concerned with how the situations presented in the novels interface with the situations presented in the law courts.

As already noted, contemporary theatrical productions presented schematic renderings of the conflicts that arose when the desires of individuals clashed with the proprieties of wealth and position. In novels, the reader is taken into the intimate thoughts of the parties involved. The French literary tradition, insofar as it was based on courtly love, presented adultery (or at least its temptations) as the normal result of arranged marriages in which the desires of the individual were subservient to the necessities of families.[48] In these literary narratives, women become symbolic of individuality, in all its contradictory meanings in French social thought. Individuality in general had been seen as a negative concept, synonymous with selfishness, egocentricity, and private pleasures, and contrasted with the positive virtues of universality and the public good.[49] During the early nineteenth century, the concept of individualism became identified with Romanticism, but it was also coded as female, while universality was identified as male.[50] An important subtext of many novels thus became the clash between the nascent value of individualism (represented by the female protagonist) and the traditional value of universality (represented by her husband). George Sand, in her preface to the 1832 edition of *Indiana*, explained: "Indiana, if you insist upon an explanation of everything in the book, is a type; she is woman, the feeble being whose mission it is to represent *passions* repressed, or, if you prefer, suppressed by *the law*; she is desire at odds with necessity; she is love dashing her head blindly against all the obstacles of civilization."[51]

In the propertied classes, marriages were arranged for the benefit of families, not of individuals. Because property, wealth, and titles followed the chain of alliances and descent, the marriage contract was in essence a corporate contract uniting the futures of two families.[52] In contemporary lived experience, a woman's desire usually bowed before the necessity of this orderly transfer of property, which demanded female monogamy to ensure the legitimacy of the line of inheritance. These desires, however, no matter how much repressed or suppressed by her marriage vows, were fully explored in novels.

Novelists of the period, like the law itself, focused on the sexual transgressions and inevitable punishment of married women and not of their husbands. As the husband's infidelity went unpunished except in certain extreme situations, his experience of adultery could not provide the vehicle for exploring the opposition between the desires of the individual and the exigencies of society. A novel presenting a wife's adultery without punishment would have provoked a scandal, however, and certainly would have been subject to censorship. Even with the wife duly punished, as in Flaubert's *Madame Bovary*, there was scandal at the mere portrayal of such behavior, and in novels such as Balzac's *Lily of the Valley* (1836), where no adultery actually occurred, the wife is punished for merely considering it.[53] Only in *Indiana* is there a happy ending, but that is because it was written by George Sand, whose avowed aim was to demonstrate the social evils attendant upon arranged marriages. "I had not to write a treatise on jurisprudence but to fight against public opinion; for it is that which postpones or advances social reforms," Sand wrote of *Indiana*.[54] She understood the complicated relationship between literature and society, claiming that she wrote this novel from "a deep and genuine feeling that the laws that still govern woman's existence in wedlock, in the family and in society are unjust and barbarous."[55] While women's experience of love and desire could become the carrier of a larger social issue, namely the friction between the needs of the individual and of society, George Sand noted in a letter to Alexandre Dumas (5 July 1866) that novels rarely portrayed a wife's negative feelings of anger, betrayal, or abandonment in the face of her husband's adultery.[56] Sand (1805–1876) and Genlis both alluded to this problem in their novels, as did such successors as Marie de Flavigny, comtesse d'Agoult (1805–1876, writing as Daniel Stern) and Flora Tristan (1803–1844), but it was not an issue that had any social resonance in the overwhelmingly male world of letters, and so was largely ignored.[57]

As noted above in the context of the theater, critics were quick to point out where fictional events struck a responsive chord, or where they were ill-conceived to the point of absurdity. In novels, the schematic presentation of moral values offered in the conduct manuals had to be transmuted by the medium's necessity of presenting more nuanced characters. Abstractions had to become personified, and the three characters of this study's title, the husband, the wife, and the lover, had to take on flesh-and-blood characteristics. That these novels usually ended badly for the protagonists, particularly the women, is understandable if one accepts the novelists' claim both to mirror society and to tell the stories of individuals. As George Sand pointed out, the novelist's insoluble problem was "reconciling the welfare and the dignity of individuals oppressed by that same society without modifying society itself."[58]

In the rest of this chapter I discuss two types of novel, those that were highly esteemed during their own period (despite their neglect by subsequent generations) and those that have become part of the literary canon. Most of the novels written during the nineteenth century have simply vanished, leaving little trace. Genlis, for example, who was the governess of the children of the duc d'Orléans, Philippe Egalité, was the most popular French novelist of her period, outranking even Sir Walter Scott in the number of her books in the *cabinets de lecture*.[59] Although her works have not survived with anywhere near the acclaim with which they were initially greeted, they are worth reading, for they often provide the missing female point of view on the marriage question. Her novel *The Parvenus, or The Adventures of Julien Delmours, Written by Himself* (1819) is a good example of a novel once esteemed, now forgotten.[60] Sand has fared better with the modern reader, at least partly because her scandalous private life has struck a responsive chord in our own transgressive age. *Indiana*, set in the Restoration, is an indispensable work for any study of marriage and its discontents during this period. Of the novels forming the canon of earlier nineteenth-century French literature, Balzac's *Scenes of Private Life* (1830), his first collection of novellas, has much to say of contemporary mores, while Stendhal's *The Red and the Black* (1830) is surely the major canonical work of the period. A brief analysis of each of these works will enable the reader to compare the strategies of fictional characters with those of the theater and the law courts.

Genlis and "The Sacred Principles of Morality"

Genlis's *The Parvenus, or The Adventures of Julien Delmours* developed out of the earlier French picaresque tradition where there are many adventures but little character development or introspection. Genlis, however, clearly wanted to participate in the new trend towards realism, and so, in her preface, she rejected the obvious comparison of *The Parvenus* with Alain-René Lesage's *Gil Blas* (1715–35), the classic eighteenth-century picaresque novel.[61] The public, she wrote, would find in her work, unlike in earlier novels, "reality, truth of observation and the portrayal of manners and mores."[62] To validate this claim, she added to *The Parvenus* numerous footnotes linking its events and opinions to the historical record. Set in the aristocracy, as were most novels of the earlier period, it recounts the "eye-witness" experiences of its fictional protagonist, Julien Delmours. Born a commoner, the son of a confectioner, he was taken into the family of the marquis d'Inglar at the age of seven, becoming what Priscilla Clark has termed "a pseudo-aristocrat" who shared the values, if not the titles and wealth, of this class.[63] *The Parvenus* is a long novel, two volumes, covering a broad historical spectrum from the protagonist's birth in 1767 to the time of the book's publication in 1819 during the Restoration. With an immense cast of characters drawn from all social classes, the novel provides a kaleidoscopic view of society from the Old Regime through the Revolution, the Reign of Terror, the Directory, the Empire, and into the Restoration. It takes the reader into exile with the émigrés, weaves back and forth through the experiences of different social classes during those troubled years, and ends happily with the return of the exiles to France. Julien recounts his life from the vantage point of the later decades, viewing historical events in hindsight. In the course of the novel, he reveals as much about Restoration values as about Old Regime society and Revolutionary events. There are, for example, several delectable licentious interludes in the style of eighteenth-century novels, but, after recounting them in all their titillating detail, Julien invariably condemns them with the puritanical (and, one might add, hypocritical) rectitude of the Restoration. The result is a clear revision of an earlier literary trope, similar to Flaubert's strategy in *Madame Bovary* of revising the romantic suicide scene for a later realist audience.

The Parvenus was an immediate success; it sold 1900 copies in four days and quickly went into a second edition and an English translation.[64] Genlis's audience was largely female, and perhaps that is the reason why, although the historical backdrop to *The Parvenus* provides a rich and colorful setting, the real focus of the novel is on the romantic histories of the principal characters. Without exception, they are unhappily married. His father died when Julien was eight, and, in order to maintain an income, his mother married Simon Landry, the principal assistant in their confectionery shop; after their marriage Simon became a brutal, drunken philanderer who tormented his wife by employing his mistress in their shop. Julien's patroness, the marquise d'Inglar is unfaithful to her bumbling but good-natured husband, the marquis. This couple arranges "marriages of reason" for both their children, although each loves someone else. Edélie, their daughter, loves Julien despite their class differences; nonetheless, she is married off to the worthless comte Joseph de Velmas. Eusèbe, their son, loves the married duchesse de Palmis, who was also sacrificed in an arranged marriage, to a man three times her age. Her sister-in-law, the marquise de Palmis, has a similar loveless arranged marriage, as do a broad assortment of other characters from various classes. The characters in this novel would certainly not join the chorus of Scribe's *Marriage of Reason*, singing "Ah, what happiness there is in marriage!"[65]

Genlis was approved by the authors of advice manuals because, although her characters' marriages might be unhappy, she always counseled fortitude and always condemned and punished adultery.[66] Nonetheless, in *The Parvenus*, the institution of marriage is under constant criticism by (unlike Scribe's plays) the novel's most sympathetic characters. Edélie, after a year of marriage to the philandering Joseph, announces "There is nothing good in matrimony but the fortnight that precedes and the two months that follow it."[67] After six weeks of marriage, she had discovered that her husband was: "careless, frivolous, extravagant, and incapable of participating in a sincere attachment."[68] Her conclusion was: "I know my duty and will not depart from it, but I shall not be at a loss what steps to take, much less be so foolish as to fret about the offenses of a husband who has not even the delicacy of concealing them."[69] Arranged marriages are criticized even by the male protagonists, although only insofar as they lead to unfortunate consequences for themselves. Eusèbe, for example, tells Julien: "We can only deplore the caprice of destiny, and the tyranny of social contracts! Had it not been for the unnatural cruelty of these, I should have been permitted to name a brother-in-law, for the happiness of a beloved sister as well as my own."[70] Here Lynn Hunt's theory of the "Family Romance of the French Revolution" is played out: the sons and brothers want to replace the father's patriarchal authority, but without sharing that authority with women.[71] In reflecting on the aristocratic imperative of marrying daughters to wealthy husbands, Eusèbe tells Julien:

> For instance, if a banker, whose father was a *porter*, marries his daughter to a lord, or a female of high birth weds a rich plebeian, the world approves of such alliances; but should anyone at court become acquainted with a man, who happens to have no fortune, though he be young, amiable, well-bred, educated, witty, sensible and virtuous, should he venture to give him his daughter, after having put both their inclinations to the test, he would be universally accused of having committed an act of the greatest degradation. So people do not lower themselves by giving up a child for the sake of money, or sacrificing her to ambition, but they are guilty of a crime if they marry her to someone whose manners, principles, mind and character they most esteem![72]

Unlike George Sand, Genlis took great care to prevent her novels from being read as feminist manifestos, and yet passages like this do represent criticism of the institution of marriage. Her criticism is mitigated by her coupling Eusèbe's conclusion, "Would it be possible to cite a more odious prejudice!" with his resignation, "But my dear Julien, continued he, let us be resigned to evils that are without any remedy!"[73] This "resigned" conclusion, while contradicting the previous criticism, can be seen as identical with the strategy used by Delavigne to make palatable Danville's criticism of the aristocracy in *The School for Old Men.* There, Danville ends his attack on the pretensions of the aristocracy by announcing that he is, nonetheless, content with his own lower station in life; here Eusèbe ends his criticism of marriages of convenience by accepting the injustices as "without any remedy." Neither Danville nor Eusèbe, in other words, intends to upset the status quo. It might be recalled that Natalie Zemon Davis has identified this strategy as standard in repressive societies for keeping resistance alive; at the same time as acceptance of contemporary social injustice is recommended, criticism of it is reiterated and reinforced.[74] In the nineteenth century this strategy was often effective in disarming censorship as well.

The Parvenus depicts a moral universe very different from that reported in the *Gazette des tribunaux.* In Genlis's novel, married male characters who commit adultery are presented negatively and, one way or another, are punished with death; in real life they rarely faced even opprobrium, much less prosecution. While Genlis also punishes married women who stray, they are dealt with much less severely than their husbands, and perhaps this is an indication of her latent feminism. In *The Parvenus*, only the baronne de Blimont is punished with death. An impoverished widow who has become a society courtesan, she entertains a succession of married lovers who support her financially. By the end of the novel, she has lost both her beauty and her lovers, and poisons herself, dying in a shockingly realistic scene that Flaubert may well have known and remembered when writing *Madame Bovary*. Julien's early patroness, the unfaithful marquise d'Inglar, ends up deaf, senile, and embittered. The marquise de Palmis, a more sympathetic figure who sincerely regrets her past sins of adultery, is treated more kindly. She is allowed to retire from society altogether and move to the country, where she will spend the rest of her life doing good works to expiate her past. Genlis does not, however, allow her to marry Julien despite her sincere love for him. Nor is the angelic Edélie, who has remained pure and chaste despite her illicit love for Julien, permitted to marry him either. Guilt-ridden after the death of her odious and unfaithful husband during the Revolution, Edélie makes a trip to the Holy Land where she has a transformative religious experience. She realizes that, although her conduct was blameless, in her heart she has sinned: "God, who sees into all hearts, has he not perceived in mine an adulterous passion, nay, and the most violent that ever existed? I nourished this criminal flame in secret. [. . .] I have cherished it, while it has occupied my heart and imagination."[75] As a result of this, Edélie decides to enter a convent to spend the rest of her life atoning for her sins of imagination.

Among the working-class characters, Simon Landry's mistress Lise, who had four adulterine children by him while he was still married to Julien's mother, retires to the country alone with her children after Simon is executed during the Reign of Terror of 1794. In a moral sense, Simon has merited his fate because of his treatment of Julien's mother, as has Joseph because of his behavior towards Edélie. Another character, Mathilde, enters the novel when, at seventeen, she seduces and marries Julien's aging uncle, a rich jeweler, only for his money. She then cuckolds him with a variety of consorts, marrying, after his death, a prince (before the Revolution), and Julien's cousin, the butcher Le Dru (during the Revolution), cuckolding each in turn. At the end of the novel, she is penniless and abandoned. It is truly remarkable the variety of ways Genlis finds to punish the wicked so that they do not "live happily ever after."

Two of her unhappily married characters do manage to find happiness, however, but only because they have remained chaste. Eusèbe was as filled with adulterous longing for the duchesse de Palmis as his sister Edélie was for Julien, but he is excused because, although married, he never acted on his desires; imaginative adultery for men is, apparently, excusable. Eusèbe's love, the duchesse de Palmis, remains, against all probability, completely unaware of his love for her until after both her husband and Eusèbe's wife have conveniently died. Because she, unlike Edélie, does not commit "imaginative adultery," she and Eusèbe are allowed to happily marry in the end.

Throughout the novel, Julien has his own sexual adventures, but apparently they are excusable because neither he nor his partners were married. After he loses Edélie to the convent, he is allowed to find happiness with the widowed comtesse de Valmis who loves him in return, but since her desire, like that of the duchesse de Palmis, was not awakened until after she was widowed, she has remained pure and is therefore entitled to happiness. Her stepson, Tiburce, a Cherubino-like character, was at one time the lover of his aunt, the marquise de Palmis (she who is punished for this transgression with exile in the country and a lifetime of good works). Tiburce, however, was single at the time, and during the Old Regime, bachelors escaped punishment provided that their adulterous liaisons were with women of their own or a lower social class. And so, despite the adultery and the incest, Tiburce is permitted a happy marriage to Julien's sister Casilda, who, needless to say, is pure as the driven snow. With an almost mathematical sense of precision, each character in the novel gets exactly what he or she deserves, and worthy members of the lower classes, such as Julien and Casilda, are even rewarded with wealth and titles, thus becoming the *parvenus* of the novel's title.

Like Sand, Genlis frankly avowed the didactic intention of her writing. In the preface to *The Parvenus*, she announced that her work "offers to young readers of all classes some history, some striking images, and some stories whose principal aim is to convey to them the importance of virtue and the love of work."[76] The last sentence of the novel extends the hope that "the friends of truth" might find in it "the courage to defend and maintain without fear or equivocation the sacred principles of morality."[77] No wonder she was the only novelist considered virtuous enough for female readers!

Balzac's "Lessons on the Dangers of Marriage"

Balzac (1799–1850) shared with Genlis plots that tended towards melodrama, plots that were, as Peter Brooks has described, full of violent and dramatic contrasts, with characters that represented Manichaean abstractions of good and evil.[78] Although Genlis related her plots and characters to the historical events of the epoch, Balzac, being more "modern" found them in individual sensibility and psychology. The theme of marriage and its discontents fascinated Balzac throughout his career, beginning as early as his *Physiology of Marriage* in the 1820s. During the time that he was completing this witty and sardonic analysis of marriage, he was also composing the collection of stories known as *Scenes of Private Life*. Published in 1830, they deal concretely with many of the situations first sketched out in the *Physiology of Marriage*.[79] Balzac esteemed these stories so greatly that he later placed them at the very beginning of the section "Studies of Manners" that opens his life's work, *The Human Comedy*, a novelistic attempt to portray the totality of his own epoch. He saw his work as a realist corrective to contemporary literature, and claimed to present in these stories "a true picture of the manners and morals that families of our times cloak in secrecy, and that the observer can discern only with great effort."[80] And yet, as noted above, Genlis did much the same thing with her portraits of marital unhappiness throughout all levels of society.

It is typical of Balzac that in the six tales of *Scenes of Private Life* he would attempt to summarize all the various possibilities of the marriage theme in a single work, claiming "to depict faithfully the events preceding and following marriage."[81] His preface states that he intended them especially for the education of women: "This work has thus been written out of hatred for the stupid books that mediocre minds have given women up to now."[82] The noted Balzac scholar Bernard Guyon called them "six lessons on the dangers of marriage."[83]

During his lifetime, Balzac constantly retitled his works, rewrote them, and changed the order of their appearance in *The Human Comedy*. As already noted, although he wrote *Physiology of Marriage* in the 1820s, he eventually placed it at the end of *The Human Comedy* as the summation of his life's work. *Scenes of Private Life* underwent more drastic metamorphoses. It originally included six novellas, each demonstrating the problems of marriage in a different way. Between his publication of this collection in 1830 and its incorporation into *The Human Comedy* in 1842, Balzac not only changed the titles of the stories, but also replaced some and added others. The original collection included "The Vendetta," "Gobseck" (earlier titled "The Dangers of Misconduct"), "The Sceaux Ball, or The Peer of France," "At the Sign of the Cat and Racket" (earlier "Glory and Misfortune"), "A Double Family" (earlier "The Virtuous Wife"), and "Domestic Peace."[84] Taken together they constitute an indictment of contemporary marriage in all its pitfalls and inequities. While the plots of these works, especially "At the Sign of the Cat and Racket" and "The Sceaux Ball," echo those of chambermaids' novels, Balzac substitutes the icy water of a grim, virtually melodramatic, reality for the warm glow of happily-ever-after.[85] Arranged marriages are the cause of much of the unhappiness in these stories, but love matches fare no better; both cause not just personal unhappiness, but often tragedy. All Balzac's protagonists suffer, whether they marry for love or for money, whether their marriages were arranged or freely chosen. This can be demonstrated by a brief survey of the varieties of unhappiness Balzac saw as afflicting marriage in his time.

"At the Sign of the Cat and Racket," written in 1829, has often been called Balzac's first realist novel, and, by extension, the first in French literature. While not the earliest of the tales, it was always Balzac's favorite, by all accounts based on the tragic early death of his beloved sister Laurence.[86] It was fourth in the original 1830 edition, but Balzac then rearranged the order, placing it first, as the opening work of *The Human Comedy*. It recounts the life of Augustine Guillaume who, at the beginning, is eighteen years old and leading a sheltered life within her family of well-to-do Parisian drapers. She is courted and falls in love with Théodore de Sommervieux, an artist of noble family, over-comes her family's opposition, and marries him despite their class differences. Her marital bliss is shattered, however, when Théodore, after their first love has faded, becomes embarrassed by her ignorance and lack of social graces, and begins to treat her with contempt. This was the fate that Scribe had the General de Brémont warn Suzette against in his *Marriage of Reason*, as seen in the previous chapter, and Balzac's Théodore de Sommervieux thoroughly justifies Brémont's dire predictions. Reverting to his aristocratic way of life, Théodore neglects his wife and instead frequents the salon of the older, more sophisticated, duchesse de Carigliano. Augustine dies of unhappiness at twenty-seven, still feeling that the eighteen months of happiness she enjoyed was worth her subsequent misery.

Into these bare bones of a plot, Balzac poured his attitudes towards the various types of marriage. Augustine's sister Virginie is set up in an arranged marriage with Joseph Lebas, the chief apprentice in their shop, whom Augustine has rejected for Théodore. When Augustine visits them, she was "touched to the heart [. . .] by the equable happiness, devoid to be sure, of all emotion, but equally free from storms, enjoyed by this well-matched couple."[87] Their union illustrates the widespread preference, which Balzac shared, for a marriage of friendship over a marriage of passion: "Having by degrees learned to esteem and care for his wife, the time that his happiness had taken to germinate was to Joseph Lebas a guarantee of its durability."[88] A contrast to their marriage is presented in the attitude of the duchesse de Carigliano, whom Augustine visits in a vain attempt to reclaim her husband's affection. " 'My dear child,' the great lady went on in a serious tone, 'Conjugal happiness has in all times been a speculation, a business demanding particular attention. If you persist in talking passion while I am talking marriage, we shall soon cease to understand each other.' "[89] Augustine then visits her parents, but she is repelled by the vacuity of their lives. These are the possibilities: a solidly based marriage of friendship between spouses of the same class, or the business arrangements characteristic of both the upper classes (with sexual freedom for the spouses) and the artisanal classes (with mutual fidelity but little else). Augustine dies searching, unsuccessfully, for something new, for a marriage based on love, passion, and companionship.

In "The Vendetta," Ginevra Piombo, like Augustine, insists on marrying for love, with the same tragic results. Balzac underscored this by originally writing it in four distinct scenes like a play: "The Studio," where Ginevra is a happy and talented young art student; "The Disobedience," when she defies her father's will by choosing her own husband; "The Marriage," which details her initial happiness; and "The Punishment," which chronicles her slide into poverty and, eventually, death.[90]

Ginevra was born into a Corsican family that owed its wealth to its support of Bonaparte; she falls in love with Luigi Porta, the son of a sworn enemy of her family, and she defies her father's will by insisting on marrying him. Ostra-cized by her family, the young couple struggles for several years to survive, but eventually both Ginevra and her infant die of cold, poverty, and starvation. Like Augustine, Ginevra feels that her brief happiness was worth the price: "Happiness so great as mine had to be paid for," she says with her dying breath.[91] The introduction to the first compilation of the "Studies of Manners" (1835) underscores the stern moral message of this tale: "The daughter is guilty of disobedience even although she has the law on her side."[92] Balzac's position on paternal authority was so conservative that in "The Vendetta" he even con-demned the reform in the Civil Code that allowed marriage without parental consent for men over twenty-five and women over twenty-one. The same intro-duction explains: "Here the author has shown that a child is wrong to marry by making the respectful notifications stipulated by the Code. He agrees with our customs and is opposed to an article of law so rarely applied."[93] The law was not that obscure, however, since Ginevra knew enough to avail herself of it in order to marry Luigi. It required merely that an adult over the age of majority who wanted to marry without parental approval should first solicit parental counsel "by a respectful and formal notification."[94] In Balzac's moral economy, however, it is not Ginevra's personal happiness that sentences her to death, but her flouting of paternal authority by availing herself of this provi-sion of the Civil Code.

In "The Sceaux Ball," the plot of "At the Sign of the Cat and Racket" is reversed in gender; here an aristocratic woman falls in love with an untitled husband.[95] Emilie de Fontaine, from a brilliant and wealthy family, is deter-mined to marry only a peer of France; as a result, she refuses to follow her heart and marry the man she really loves, Maximilien de Longueville, because she has seen him working in a draper's shop. After rejecting all the suitors her father proposes to her, she marries instead her aged uncle, only because he is noble and wealthy. By an unexpected series of events, however, Maximilien, who had sacrificed his share of the family fortune in order to enable his elder brother to enter the diplomatic corps, eventually becomes a peer of France. In the end Emilie is forced to recognize that she has ruined her life by denying her true love only because of her social prejudices. This is the "realist" version of the time-honored literary trope in which one of the young lovers pretends to be poor to test the sincerity of the other. In Molière's *Tartuffe*, for example, the avaricious hypocrite Tartuffe immediately loses interest in marrying Mariane when he is told (falsely) that her family has lost all its wealth, while in Victor Hugo's *Hernani*, Doña Sol truly loves Hernani, who is a grandee of Spain, despite his disguise as an impoverished outlaw. The twist in "The Sceaux Ball" is that what appears to be Balzac's approval of a *mésalliance*, a marriage across class lines, proves to be no such thing. Had Maximilien, for example, really been a member of the commercial classes and not an aristocrat idealistically sacrificing himself for his brother, it is unlikely that Balzac would have approved their liaison – or punished Emilie for refusing to follow her heart.

For the purposes of this book, "A Double Family" is the most revelatory of the *Scenes of Private Life*. This tale reveals the evils that attend loveless arranged marriages. Caroline Crochard, an impoverished young seamstress, agrees to become the mistress of the unhappily married comte de Granville; he had entered into a marriage of reason with a rich provincial heiress from the bourgeoisie who has since become fanatically religious. Granville sets up a second household with Caroline, and they live together happily for several years, eventually having two children. One day, however, the comtesse, who has become suspicious, follows Granville, discovers this second family, and confronts him in a melodramatic scene. Although close to death, she has enough remaining energy to enter into a long and erudite debate with her husband on the nature of love and marriage. They each propose a different definition of marriage. She holds to the traditional definition of duty and faithfulness, long the only virtues required of a wife; he, however, is searching for the new ideal of romantic love. An excerpt from their discussion will demonstrate aptly the changing definitions of marriage. The comtesse begins by asking:

> "What have you to reproach me with? Have I deceived you? Have I not been a discreet and virtuous wife? My heart has preserved only your image, my ears have heard only your voice. In what duty have I failed? What have I refused you?" "Happiness!" replied the count in a firm voice. [. . .] "Have I not then loved you?" she asked. "No, madame." "What then is love?" asked the countess involuntarily. "Love, my dear," replied Granville with a sort of ironical surprise, "you are not in a condition to comprehend it. [. . .] To yield to our caprices, to divine them in advance, to find pleasures in misfortune, to sacrifice the opinion of the world, self-love, even religion, and to regard these offerings only as grains of incense burned in honor of the idol, that is love . . ." "The love of opera dancers," said the countess in horror. "Such fires as those should be but little durable, and leave you very soon with only cinders or coal, regrets or despair. A wife, monsieur, should offer you, it seems to me, a true friendship, a lasting warmth."[96]

They are speaking at cross-purposes. Like Augustine and the duchess in "At the Sign of the Cat and Racket," they will never understand each other.

Despite being founded on love, Granville's second family fares no better than his first. After six years together, their peaceful domestic life is shattered when Caroline falls passionately in love with Solvet, a complete scoundrel described as a gambler "endowed with all the vices possible."[97] "A Double Family" might almost appear to illustrate Etienne de Senancour's warning in his enduringly popular *On Love*. There, as noted in chapter 2, he counseled the marriage of reason and pointed out this very problem with love matches: "For this union to be bitterly troubled, all that is necessary is for one of the spouses to be seized by a new and uncontrollable passion."[98] Balzac's melodramatic streak can be seen in his depiction of Solvet as a complete villain who not only destroys Caroline's and Granville's happiness together, but also reduces Caroline and her children by Granville to poverty, hunger, illness, and eventually, death.

By the end of the story, Caroline is dying in misery while Granville, now alone and in despair, has aged horribly. Their son Charles has been arrested as a thief, and is brought before Granville's legitimate son Eugène, who has become, fittingly, the King's Prosecutor (*procureur du roi*). The contrast could not be stronger between these two offspring: Eugène, the product of a loveless but legitimate marriage, has become honest and respectable; Charles, the off-spring of a passionate but illicit union, has become criminal. The story ends with Granville leaving France for exile in Italy, telling Eugène that "A want of union between two married people, by whatever cause it may be produced, brings about frightful evils."[99]

"Gobseck" has a similar plot.[100] It follows the downfall of the comtesse Anastasie de Restaud, the daughter of a rich bourgeois who marries into the aristocracy. Instead of accepting her fate and resigning herself to a loveless mar-riage, however, she, like the comte de Granville, seeks personal happiness. She gives in to passion and becomes involved with Maxime de Trailles, a fashion-able dandy and scoundrel. His financial demands drive her to the usurer Gobseck, and set in motion the events that eventually destroy her marriage and family fortune. The tale is usually cited for its unforgettable portrait of Gobseck, but it also offers the familiar cautionary tale of the disasters that befall women who marry above their class and, in consequence, cannot balance the demands of husbands and lovers. In contrast to Anastasie de Restaud, the duchesse de Carigliano, in "At the Sign of the Cat and Racket," was born into the aristocracy and so has no problems managing her "business arrangement" marriage and a succession of lovers as well.

The last of the tales, "Domestic Peace," has always been considered the weakest. Written first, it is the only one that does not end tragically.[101] It recounts a wry tale of infidelity, in which Madame de Soulanges, a virtuous and faithful wife, retrieves a valuable ring that her husband has stolen from her in order to present it to his society mistress, Madame de Vaudremont, who, in turn, has made a gift of it to her current favorite, Martial. Madame de Soulanges, usually a shy and retiring woman, learns all this and arranges to attend a glittery society ball given by Madame de Vaudremont, where both her husband and Martial are in attendance, and where Martial is flaunting the ring without realizing that it is hers. Madame de Soulanges, although virtuous throughout, pretends to be receptive to Martial's advances in order to obtain her ring, after which she returns home and, without comment, wears it so that her husband realizes that she knows all. Balzac's friend Davin (with assistance from Balzac himself) wrote: " 'Domestic Peace' is a fine sketch, a portrait of the Empire period, a warning to wives to be indulgent towards their husband's errors."[102]

In all of these novellas Balzac insisted that a woman should marry a spouse chosen by her father from her own class. The duchesse de Carigliano, despite her cynicism, seems to have a satisfactory marriage, as do Ginevra Piombo's parents and Augustine's sister Virginie. They represent different social strata, but all have successfully married within their own class. Balzac made quite clear his conviction that, if the marriage is not a success, the unhappy spouses should resign themselves or tragedy will certainly follow. Although he acknowledged "At this strange period commerce and finance were more than ever possessed by the crazy mania for seeking alliance with rank," there is no doubt that, in Balzac's opinion, marriages that transgress class boundaries or defy parental authority will never succeed.[103] Balzac gave his own point of view to Monsieur Guillaume in "At the Sign of the Cat and Racket": "His favorite saying was that, to secure happiness, a woman must marry a man of her own class."[104] Granville in "A Double Family" also speaks for Balzac when he concludes sadly: "We are, sooner or later, punished for not having obeyed the social laws."[105] Balzac is often quoted as having announced in "At the Sign of the Cat and Racket" that "there are *mésalliances* of the spirit as well as of rank and habits," but, in fact, these *mésalliances* all have at their root the issue of class.[106]

Stendhal, "A Mirror Moving Along the Road"

In Stendhal's *The Red and the Black*, melodramatic turns of plot are still present, as they were in the contemporaneous works of Genlis and Balzac, but here they are subordinated to the development of richly nuanced characters. Like Genlis and Balzac, Stendhal (pseudonym of Henri Beyle, 1783–1842) emphasized the historicity of his novel, calling it "a mirror moving along a road," and subtitling it *A Chronicle of the Nineteenth Century*.[107] *The Red and the Black* has, however, established its place in the canon of nineteenth-century literature more through the brilliant exposition of its protagonists' most intimate emotions and reflections than through its historicity.

Although the prefatory editor's note (which Stendhal himself wrote) states "We have reason to believe that the following pages were written in 1827," the novel was published in November 1830 and was most probably written in 1829–30.[108] The date 1827 no doubt referred to his inspiration for the plot. On December 28–31, 1827 the *Gazette des tribunaux* carried the story of Antoine Berthet of Brangues (Isère), a twenty-five-year-old tried for the attempted murder of Madame Michoud, a married woman thirteen years his senior.[109] Berthet, a poor boy adopted by the local curé, had abandoned his seminary studies because of illness, and had become tutor to the children of the Michoud family. What transpired between Berthet and Madame Michoud was never fully explained, but he was asked to leave the family. He returned for a while to the seminary and then became tutor for a Monsieur Cordon.

When he was dismissed from that job because of a letter written to Cordon by Madame Michoud, the young man bought two pistols, waited in the church near the pew where she worshiped, and fired two shots at her. Although she survived, Berthet was executed, probably as much for his violation of class barriers as for his crime.

In Stendhal's transformation of these events, Julien Sorel, the son of a peasant, educated by the local curé, becomes tutor to the children of the aristocratic Rênal family. The novel begins when Madame de Rênal is thirty and Julien eighteen; her husband, however, is "forty-eight or fifty," which means that when she married him at sixteen, her husband was more than twice her age.[110] When the novel begins fourteen years later, Madame de Rênal's continued ignorance of love is attributed not only to her unfortunate marriage but, Stendhal's wry joke, also to the paucity of novels she had been able to read meanwhile.[111]

In literary terms, Stendhal's novel is more modern than Genlis's, dispensing with the rambling plot of loosely connected adventures characteristic of the previous century; nonetheless, their attitude towards sexual transgression is similar. Shortly after Madame de Rênal begins her affair with Julien, her son falls ill; she becomes convinced that this is divine retribution for her sins, although the male protagonists, her husband and lover, dismiss this possibility. Julien tries to dissuade her from confessing to her husband by providing a "realist" counterpoint, assuring her that "nothing you can say will cure our little Stanislas's fever."[112] Nonetheless, she throws herself at her husband's feet, crying "Heaven is punishing me; in God's eyes I am guilty of murder." Uncomprehending, he replies: "Romantic notions, all that! Julien, have the doctor sent for at daybreak."[113] The irony of this realist response to the standard romantic plot is that, despite this disclaimer, Stendhal did in fact implement the same harsh moral code as Genlis. If anything, he is even more harsh since both his protagonists, Madame de Rênal and Julien Sorel, die in the end.

In its portrayal of the inner thoughts of his male characters, *The Red and the Black* gives a valuable portrait of Stendhal's age. Julien, a bachelor, has much less at stake in their affair than does Madame de Rênal, and he plans his seduction with the coldness of a military campaign, describing it in terms of combat, enemies, advantages, and victory.[114] The language, in fact, is similar to that of Balzac, whose *Physiology of Marriage* describes as generational warfare the young men's campaigns to seduce older men's wives. Julien seeks revenge on Rênal through the conquest of his wife. He plans his strategy: "Wouldn't it be a good way to get even with this creature, on whom fortune has heaped every advantage, by taking hold of his wife's hand right under his nose? Yes, I'll do it – I, the man for whom he has shown such contempt."[115] Eve Kosofsky Sedgwick has aptly characterized this rivalry "between men" as the primary emotional bond in the triangle of husband, wife, and lover.[116] For Julien, Madame de Rênal is merely a pawn in his rivalry with her husband.

Julien's affair with Madame de Rênal is revealed by an anonymous letter mailed to her husband. Anonymous letters played an important role both in fiction and in court cases. In a case in Rouen, reported in the *Gazette des tribunaux* in January 1827 without names, the husband claimed that he learned of his wife's adultery through anonymous placards tacked to his door.[117] Monsieur de Rênal had a similar experience: "That same night, M. de Rênal received from town, along with his newspaper, a long anonymous letter, which informed him in the greatest detail of what was going on in his house."[118] In the following chapter, Julien and Madame de Rênal create a second accusatory letter that she will show to her husband in order to demonstrate her innocence. The letter, no doubt generic of its kind, was made up of words cut out of a book and pasted on a sheet of paper. It began: "Madame: All your sly carryings-on have been found out; but the persons whose concern it is to put an end to them have been warned."[119] The next chapter is devoted to Rênal's reaction on receiving the letter. As he contemplates the possibilities open to him, he reviews the entire spectrum available to a betrayed husband of the period. Legalized murder is, of course, his first thought. He ponders his decision:

> 'I have no daughter, and the way I mean to punish the mother will not hurt my boys' chances for making good matches; I can catch that little peasant with my wife and kill them both; in that case the tragic aspect of the affair may cancel out its ridiculous side.' This idea appealed to him; he explored it in detail. 'The Penal Code is on my side, but whatever happens, our congregation and my friends on the jury will save me.'[120]

While Rênal is attracted to the romantic idea of murder as vengeance, the pedestrian reality is that the thought of bloodshed frightens him. In his attitude towards Julien, "that little peasant," he is representative of the class attitudes of Old Regime adultery law. In the pre-Revolutionary period, the major determinant of a man's punishment for an adulterous union was his social class *vis-à-vis* that of his accomplice: a man of a lower social class could be severely punished, even with death, but if his lover were either his social equal or his inferior, he (although not she) would escape punishment altogether.[121] While in theory the Civil Code had suppressed all such class distinctions, making all equal before the law, they were clearly still operative, as the case of Stendhal's prototype Berthet had demonstrated.

Despite the Penal Code's dispensation for a husband who murders his wife caught *in flagrante delicto* with her lover, Rênal broods incessantly about the scandal that would result. Thinking no doubt of the *Gazette des tribunaux*, and possibly even of the recent Cairon affair, he reflects:

> 'A man of good family like me, whose name means something to him, is bound to be hated by plebeians. I can see myself in those awful Paris newspapers; oh, my God! what humiliation! to see the ancient name of Rênal

dragged through the mud of ridicule . . . If ever I traveled, I would have to change my name; what! give up the name that has been my glory and my strength. That would be the height of misery!"[122]

While Rênal was wallowing in humiliation over this affair, at least partly because Julien came from the peasantry, Julien, on the other hand, felt himself elevated by being chosen by a woman of a higher class: "His mistress's rank seemed to raise him above himself."[123] He wonders: "But how could I have inspired such a love – I, so poor, so badly brought up, so ignorant, sometimes so boorish in my ways?"[124] He comforts himself with the assurance that "It means nothing to her that she is noble and I a working man's son; she loves me . . . For her, I am not a valet who has been assigned the duty of lover."[125]

Rênal meanwhile is mentally cataloguing all his possible courses of action. Unlike the schematic rendering of emotion in *The Parvenus*, here mental anguish is given full expression, another innovation of the modern novel. Rênal reflects that even unceremoniously evicting Julien from their household, with or without giving him a thrashing, would cause a scandal. He obsesses: "If I do not kill my wife, and I drive her away in disgrace, she has her aunt in Besançon, who will hand over her entire fortune to her without a will. My wife will go and live in Paris with Julien; it will get back to Verrières, and I will still be taken for a dupe."[126] He broods: "What, they will say, he didn't even know how to get revenge against his wife!"[127]

In the end, however, his desire for his wife's inheritance prevents him from confronting either of them. Madame de Rênal, however, is unaware of her husband's cowardice. She imagines his revenge in a lurid image from a thirteenth-century romance that, in legend, took place in the village of Vergy; appropriately enough, Stendhal has the Rênal family taking up residence there.[128] "Over and over she pictured her husband killing Julien in the hunt, as though by accident, and then at night making her eat his heart."[129]

Reality proves a good deal less dramatic, however, and Rênal's revenge takes the form merely of ransacking his wife's bedroom and destroying her cherished possessions. When she discovers the damage, she reflects, still in the grip of Romantic fantasies, "He would have shown me no mercy!"[130] Stendhal's project, however, was, like Flaubert's after him, to contrast the melodramatic romance with the banal reality of adultery. While Rênal is consumed with suspicion of his wife, Stendhal breaks into the story to editorialize, using an orientalist image typical of Romanticism to contrast the two distinct modes of revenge:

> In spite of everything, an odalisk in a harem may love the sultan; he is omnipotent; she can have no hope of escaping his authority by a series of little ruses. The master's vengeance is terrible, bloody, yet military, generous. A blow of the dagger ends all. In the nineteenth century, a husband kills his wife with blows of public scorn, by closing every salon door to her.[131]

Ultimately, Rênal proves incapable of acting at all and thus the tragedy unfolds: Julien leaves their household, and Madame de Rênal's confessor forces her to write the defamatory letter that ruins Julien's chances of making a brilliant marriage to the wealthy and aristocratic Matilde de La Mole. Like the real-life Berthet, Julien attempts to kill his former protectress, and, like him, he is executed, not so much for the attempted murder as for his violation of class proprieties. Although the identification of *The Red and the Black* as a "novel of adultery" has been challenged, it is Julien's affair with Madame de Rênal that lies at the heart of the work.[132] In terms of nineteenth-century morality, this is the event that drives the plot; this is the transgression that must be avenged.

George Sand and the "Craving for Happiness"

Although completed in the early years of the July Monarchy, George Sand's first novel, *Indiana* (1832), is included here because it is set in the Restoration and provides an excellent portrayal of its manners, as well as an explicitly feminist point of view on the marriage question. Throughout her career, Sand criticized the institution of marriage and challenged the novelistic tradition of divine retribution for female sexual transgressions, even imaginary ones.[133] While male novelists such as Balzac, Stendhal, and Flaubert resolved their novels of female adultery with disaster and death for the adulteress, and Genlis punished hers with isolation and social exile at the very least, Sand's Indiana and her lover live happily ever after, albeit in a distant land. In this way she managed to portray, simultaneously, contemporaneous French social mores and her own utopian ideals.

As the novel opens in 1828, Indiana, at nineteen, has been unhappily married to Colonel Delmare for three years. He is sixty, a former officer in the Napoleonic armies, uneducated, crude, and violent. Indiana describes her marriage as "the chain that has crushed my life and withered my youth."[134] Sand comments, "He had taken a wife as he would have taken a housekeeper."[135] Slowly dying from lovelessness, she falls passionately in love with Raymon de Ramière, an unscrupulous and opportunist legitimist, who, Sand frankly acknowledges, stands for "the false morality by which society is governed."[136] Indiana irreparably dishonors herself by running away to be with him, but, despite this sacrifice, Ramière rejects her in order to make a lucrative but loveless marriage of reason with the wealthy aristocrat Laure de Nangy. Just when all seems lost, however, and Indiana lies dying, alone and miserable in a Paris boarding-house, her husband dies suddenly and unexpectedly, and her cousin Sir Ralph, the baronet Rodolphe Brown, finds her, rescues her, and takes her back to Ile Bourbon (now Réunion) where they had grown up together. Once there she realizes that she has always loved him, her childhood companion, mentor, and friend. Ralph, in turn, has always loved Indiana, but he too had been forced into an arranged marriage, although his wife had conveniently died. In the end they go to a wild and uninhabited area of Ile Bourbon, where they will spend the rest of their lives, isolated from society but happy in each other's company. This tacked-on *deus ex machina* ending follows the "realist" conclusion of the novel, a suicide attempt by Ralph and Indiana when they realize that, because they have broken society's laws and flouted public opinion, there is no place where they can live together in peace.

Despite this contrived ending, Sand emphasized its realism. Like Genlis, Balzac, and Stendhal, she claimed verisimilitude for her work. In the preface to the 1832 edition, she wrote of herself (in the masculine as befit her pseudonym):

> The author has invented almost nothing. If, in the course of his task, he has happened to set forth the lamentations extorted from his characters by the social malady with which they were assailed; if he has not shrunk from recording their aspirations towards a happier existence, let the blame be laid upon society for its inequalities, upon destiny for its caprices! The author is merely a mirror that reflects them, a machine that traces their outlines, and he has no reason for self-reproach if the impression is exact, if the reflection is true.[137]

Like Stendhal's "mirror moving along the road," Sand's "mirror that reflects" puts forth the claim of realism to protect the author from charges of social criticism or immorality. Sand described herself as "an historian who forces his way brutally through the midst of facts, elbowing right and left, with no more regard for one camp than for the other."[138] In the first edition of *Indiana*, she wrote: "You see that I am telling you an extremely realistic story, one that experience confirms on a daily basis."[139] She called herself "an historian of the heart," and claimed to show "needs, desires and human passions at odds with the exigencies of a law-abiding life."[140] To the charge that *Indiana* presented "a deliberate argument against marriage," Sand defended herself by later claiming "I was not so ambitious."[141]

This is not quite true, however, for her characters and her anonymous narrator often articulate her criticisms of marriage. Of Raymon, whose legitimist politics are intended to signal his unworthy character, Sand wrote: "These positive reflections made plain to him the utter coldness of heart that characterizes marriages of reason, so called, and the hope of having some day a companion worthy of his love entered only incidentally into his prospects of happiness."[142] Indiana says to the Colonel: "I know that I am the slave and you the master. The laws of this country make you my master. You can bind my body, tie my hands, govern my acts. You have the right of the stronger, and society confirms you in it."[143] To Raymon she says, speaking of all men: "You deem yourselves the masters of the world; I deem you only its tyrants. You think that God protects you and authorizes you to possess the empire of the earth; I think that He permits that for a little time, and that the day will come when His breath will scatter you like grains of sand."[144] She tells him, "all your morality, all your principles, are simply the interests of your social order that you have raised to the dignity of laws and that you claim to trace back to God himself."[145] Throughout the novel, her sympathetic characters argue for equality of women's rights, and her scoundrels make every effort to deny them.

In her 1832 preface to *Indiana*, Sand defended herself against charges of immorality: "You will think that I have done wrong in not casting into misery and destitution the character who has transgressed the laws of mankind through two volumes. In this regard, the author will reply that before being moral he chose to be true."[146] Sand later reversed herself, claiming that there had been no adultery while Indiana's husband remained alive.[147] That readers then – and now – assume otherwise probably speaks to Sand's ability to hint at a situation that, if articulated, would have prevented her happy ending, either through censorship or through scandal. Indiana and Ralph must go off to a distant island to find happiness because, realistically, there was no way that the novelist could have had them remain together and participate in respectable society in France. The limits of fiction as opposed to lived experience can be seen, however, in reflecting that the real-life marquise de Cairon and her lover François Soubiranne, discussed in chapter 1, did manage to do just that, although they had to wait until her husband had died and the harsh Restoration regime had been replaced by the more lenient July Monarchy before they could return to France. Their tale, however, insofar as it is atypical of the usual fate of adulterous couples, would be unsatisfactory as a vehicle for all the polemics that George Sand poured into her text.

Sand's Indiana and Ralph are cousins; this intimate and egalitarian relationship was the subject of many warnings in advice books, and was often depicted satirically in the cartoons of the period (Figures 9 and 10). Sand clearly agreed with Balzac that passion is to be mistrusted for, throughout the novel, Indiana's feelings of trustful affection for Ralph are contrasted with her passionate and ill-fated love for Raymon. Indiana's half-sister Noun serves as a dreadful example of the tragic results of unbridled passion, in that she commits suicide when, madly in love with Raymon and pregnant by him, she is abandoned by him for Indiana. For Sand and for contemporaneous novelists and playwrights, it seems, the only two emotional possibilities for heterosexual relationships are dangerous sexual passion or paternal/fraternal affection.

"I love my cousin like a brother," says Indiana of Ralph.[148] Together they read Bernardin de Saint-Pierre's novel *Paul and Virginia* (1787), about the tragic love of two young people raised as siblings.[149] One might contrast Indiana's feelings for Ralph to those of Madame de Rênal, who asks Julien: "Shall I love you like a brother? Is it in my power to love you like a brother?"[150] The fact that the answer is a resounding "no!" prefigures the tragedy that then unfolds inexorably. Ralph, on the other hand, describes himself as Indiana's father and guardian, the very model for the bourgeois marriage relationship at the time.[151] The kaleidoscope of possible male/female relationships swings from parent to child to sibling to lover, everything, in fact, except spouse, for that relationship had not yet been defined as one of equality and affection. In commenting on this, George Sand in her 1842 preface to *Indiana* stated that she had written "a series of novels, almost all of which were based on the same idea: the ill-defined relations between the sexes, attributable to the constitution of our society."[152]

What set *Indiana* apart from contemporaneous novels was Sand's positive attitude towards human happiness. Although she shared with her contemporaries a suspicion of passion, she believed that the pursuit of happiness was always justified. In the last pages of *Indiana* the word "happiness" (*bonheur*) is repeated like a mantra: "You are young," Ralph tells the narrator, "because your conscience is ingenuous and pure and unsoiled by the world, in your eyes our happiness is the proof of our virtue; in the eyes of the world it is our crime."[153] This contrast between a "soiled" worldliness, namely civilization, and an "ingenuous and pure" human nature is underscored throughout the novel. It takes the reader from sophisticated but unhappy France to the simple happiness of a wild and unspoiled island in the Indian Ocean. Sand wrote in the conclusion: "Thus all Indiana's reflections, all her acts, all her sorrows were a part of this great and terrible struggle between nature and civilization."[154] The issue had again become that of individualism, that embattled quality so trumpeted by the modernists, so decried by traditionalists. Sand left no doubt about where she stood in the matter: "But it may be that this craving for happiness that consumes us, this hatred of injustice, this thirst for liberty that ends only with life, are the constituent elements of *egotism*, a term by which the English designate love of self, considered as one of the rights of mankind and not as a vice."[155]

The French novel of the nineteenth century, in the end, took as its subject this "egotism," this "craving for happiness," as the individual attempted to make her or his way in the modern world. On the one hand, there was the search for companionate marriage, on the other, the search for love and passion. Novelists such as Genlis and Balzac, Stendhal and Sand, explored their contemporary world, observing for their audiences, and for us today, all the various ways men and women could bring each other joy . . . or grief.

6

Many Ways to Ride a Horse:
Mazeppa

Mazeppa, tied naked to a horse, became a symbol and an
interpretation of the sufferings of the artist – of the man of genius who
endures so much for the sake of his art.
                    Jürgen N. Schultze, *Art of Nineteenth-Century Europe*[1]

[. . .] this theme which, for the romantics, symbolized the transports of
the poet carried away by inspiration. The hellish course results in
freedom and leads the hero to the realms of genius.
                    Paris: Grand Palais, *French Painting 1774–1830:*
                    The Age of Revolution[2]

THERE IS A KIND OF fugal counterpoint running through cultural production, with the same themes often articulated in both popular and high art.
In caricature, the themes considered in this book are presented in an explicit
and straightforward manner. Painting, however, is more attenuated in its relation to social history. In the high art of the early nineteenth century, the same
themes appeared, but mediated, sometimes even obfuscated, by classical or literary references. Artists of the Academy tended to choose moral themes redo-
lent of the *exemplum virtutis*, the "example of virtue," typical of neoclassical
painting. In *Phaedra and Hippolytus* (Figure 78) by Pierre-Narcisse Guérin
(1774–1833), for example, Hippolytus "just says no" to the advances his stepmother makes to him, while in *Antiochus and Stratonice* (Figure 79) by
J.-A.-D. Ingres (1780–1867) Antiochus is so honorable that he is dying of
unspoken love for his equally virtuous stepmother. *Paolo and Francesca* (Figure
80) shows Ingres preaching more visibly against adultery: the two young lovers
are surprised by Francesca's ugly and deformed old husband, who kills them
both – just in time, it would seem. Their murder prevents, in Ingres's version,
the adultery that in its source, Dante's *Divine Comedy*, had already taken place.
Ingres did fifteen versions of *Paolo and Francesca* and nine of *Antiochus and
Stratonice*.[3] In works such as these, the audience receives a double message: on
the one hand, the inevitability and attractiveness of adulterous young love; on
the other, its illicitness. Balzac's *Physiology of Marriage* could state it no clearer.

facing page   Théodore Géricault, *Mazeppa*, 1823 (detail of Figure 88).

78　Pierre-Narcisse Guérin, *Phaedra and Hippolytus*, 1802. Oil on canvas, 257 × 335 cm. Musée du Louvre, Paris.

It is fascinating to note how often the married woman's adultery in its various guises is the theme of Western art – Tintoretto (1518–94), for example, was among the artists to paint *Joseph and Potiphar's Wife*, in which the virtuous Joseph, like Hippolytus, refuses the advances of a bad wife.[4] In the Renaissance, *Lucretia* represented the ideal wife because, in preference to being slandered as an adulteress, she submitted to rape – and then cleared her honor by committing suicide.[5] Such themes, besides offering a didactic lesson on moral behavior, show the constant anxiety of husbands who wanted to be reassured that adultery could not happen. Surely, the art seems to proclaim, either the wife or her putative lover would be, certainly should be, too virtuous to behave like that. The court cases of nineteenth-century France, however, show the reality to be otherwise, and, indeed, the young men who were most likely to become involved with a married woman were often, like Antiochus or Paolo, Joseph or Hippolytus, relatives or members of her household. To underscore the ideological and didactic function of these images, one might note that there are relatively fewer images in Western art, and virtually none in nineteenth-century French art, of the familiar Bible story of Christ forgiving the woman taken in adultery.[6] Forgiveness, it would seem, was not part of the agenda.

79 J.-A.-D. Ingres, *Antiochus and Stratonice*, 1840. Oil on canvas, 57 × 98 cm. Musée Condé, Chantilly.

Whatever their stylistic differences, artists of the two major movements of early nineteenth-century France, Classicism and Romanticism, chose structurally similar themes of the old husband, his young wife, and her putative, potential, or actual lover. Despite the similarity of the cast of characters, however, paintings by Classicists such as Ingres chose themes where no adultery actually took place: Phaedra, Stratonice, Francesca were all innocent, in deed if not in intention. The Romantics, on the other hand, openly acknowledged this taboo subject and even dwelt on its unpleasant consequences. Although revisionism has made it fashionable to elide the differences between these two styles, such differences are apparent in their choice of thematic protagonist. Not only did no Romantic artist treat *Antiochus and Stratonice*, but no Classicist portrayed *Medea* (Figure 81), as did Eugène Delacroix (1798–1863) in two major paintings and numerous drawings, showing her about to kill her children in revenge for her husband Jason's infidelity. This subject would, no doubt, be just as repugnant to husbands as that of Christ forgiving the woman taken in adultery. It is worth noting that Ingres, born in 1780, was part of the older generation and was married for more than fifty years, while Delacroix, born in 1798, was part of the French generation of 1820 and remained a lifelong bachelor.

    In chapter 3, I traced marriage and its discontents from the carefree lovers of Old Regime France, through the happy mothers and devoted fathers of the Enlightenment, to the angry husbands, bad mothers, and invisible fathers of early nineteenth-century art. During the years of the Restoration, however, when the new bourgeois morality and laws on inheritance and divorce resulted in unprecedented prosecutions of adultery, there was an important, though heretofore unidentified theme that spoke to the issue of marriage and its discontents. This theme, a *cri de coeur* from the young Romantic generation, protested the plight of the unjustly punished lover in the persona of Mazeppa. While this theme does not, at first, seem related to marriage and adultery, it is nonetheless a prime example of how social concerns can be transmuted into high art. It is therefore a fitting subject for this penultimate chapter.

80 *(facing page)*
J.-A.-D. Ingres, *Paolo and Francesca*, 1819.
Oil on canvas, 48 × 39 cm. Musée d'Angers, Angers.

81   Eugène Delacroix, *Medea*, 1838. Oil on canvas, 260 × 165 cm. Musée des beaux-arts, Lille.

The History

Traditional explanations of the Mazeppa theme, for example the two epigraphs to this chapter, derive from Victor Hugo's poem "Mazeppa," published in his collection *Les Orientales* (1829).[7] This was ten years after Byron's narrative poem "Mazeppa" had already inspired a generation of Romantic artists including Théodore Géricault, Eugène Delacroix, Horace Vernet, and Louis Boulanger.[8] Art historians have tended to privilege literary readings over social and political ones, however, and so a retrospective view of history has tended to see the earlier paintings in terms of the later poem. The theme also had an enormous popular appeal, as evidenced by the Cirque olympique production of *Mazeppa, or The Tartar Horse* (1825) and numerous lithographic print edi-

82 Anon., *Ivan Stepanovych Mazeppa*, 1703. Oil on canvas. Special Collections, New York Public Library.

tions by various artists.[9] While members of Hugo's cenacle saw Mazeppa as symbolic of the suffering artist, it is unlikely that the audience at the Cirque olympique was particularly interested in the sufferings of the man of genius who endured so much for the sake of his art. The theme had to have conveyed other meanings. In this chapter I explore the multivalence of the Mazeppa theme in France in the decade before Hugo flattened its semiology into the "artist-genius," and investigate how the theme was communicated to a wide variety of audiences.[10] The theme is particularly appropriate for a study of the ways in which art mediates social experience, for it demonstrates how an historical social issue can become a cultural theme.

Ivan Stepanovych Mazeppa (Figure 82), the inspiration for so much literature and art, really existed.[11] He was born into the Ukrainian gentry some time between 1632 and 1644 in that part of the Ukraine ruled by Poland. His family was so favored by the Polish king Jan Kazimierz that the young Mazeppa spent some years in his court, leaving there in 1665. Eventually he was elected Hetman, leader of the Ukraine. The Ukraine (literally "borderland") was traditionally divided between Poland and Russia, with Turkey and its Tartars also seeking control. The Ukrainian Cossacks had been organized to provide self-defense from the constant warfare, taxes, and levies, and they freely changed allegiances according to circumstances. As allies of Peter the Great of Russia, Mazeppa and his Cossack army had fought Charles XII of Sweden; then, fearing that Peter intended to dissolve the Hetmanate and disband its forces, they changed sides, joined Charles against Peter and were defeated at Poltava in 1709. Mazeppa died a few months later in Moldavia, then Turkish territory but now Romania. After his defeat and death, the Ukraine was partitioned and the Hetmanate ceased to be a strong political force as the Ukraine was not reunified until 1919 and did not regain its political autonomy until 1991. These are the undisputed facts of Mazeppa's life. The disputed facts concern two events: one is his departure from the Polish court, and the other is his change of allegiance from Russia to Sweden. The first event provided the material for Western European interpretations of Mazeppa, the latter for those of Eastern Europe.

According to the memoirs of a Polish gentleman named Jan Chryzostom Pasek (?1636–1701), whom Mazeppa had denounced for having conspired against the Polish king, Mazeppa was caught in an affair with the wife of a high official named Falbowski.[12] Falbowski had Mazeppa stripped naked and tied backwards to his horse, which was then whipped into a frenzy and turned loose to race home through wild and rough undergrowth. When recovered from his injuries, Mazeppa left Poland in shame and humiliation and returned to the Ukraine where he began his military career. This story of near-death and regeneration, although historically dubious, captured the imagination of the Romantic generation in Western Europe to the exclusion of any other aspect of Mazeppa's career. In Central Europe, however, Mazeppa has always been regarded primarily as a political figure, either a hero of Ukrainian nationalism ("an ardent patriot and the great Hetman of Ukraine"[13]) or a traitor to Peter the Great ("a man almost born to be a traitor, a moral monster who had long ago set out on the path of perfidy"[14]). Thus the word *Mazepyntsi* in Eastern Europe, literally "follower of Mazeppa," has always meant either "freedom fighter" or "traitor" depending on who is saying it. The question of patriot or traitor, however, is of less concern here than the fact that Eastern Europe concentrated on his politics and Western Europe on his passions.

Before Byron's poem, the major Western source of knowledge about Mazeppa was Voltaire's *History of Charles XII*, first published in 1731; in a volume of several hundred pages including an extensive discussion of Mazeppa's military and political career, Voltaire added a short paragraph relating the legend of Mazeppa's wild ride.[15] It was this paragraph that Byron used as an epigraph to his poem "Mazeppa," the last of his *Oriental Tales*. Written in Venice in 1818, it was immediately published in France, both in English and in French translation. By the Salon of 1827–8, when Vernet and Boulanger showed their *Mazeppa* paintings, French readers had their choice of six French or eight English editions of Byron's poem.[16]

George Gordon, Lord Byron (1788–1824), was the ideal Romantic hero, a man whose life and art were inseparable. He held a seat in the House of Lords and scandalized polite society with his drinking, temper tantrums, drugs, suspected insanity, and his sexual adventures, which included homosexuality, incest with his sister, and highly public adultery with numerous partners. When his wife of one year left him in 1816, it caused such overwhelming gossip and animosity that he was forced to leave England to continue his wild life abroad. He traveled with Percy and Mary Shelley and her stepsister Jane Clairmont; his liaison with Clairmont, by whom he had a child, led to rumors in England that Byron and Shelley "had formed a League of Incest."[17]

While Byron was in Venice, he had the last great love affair of his life, with the contessa Teresa Guiccioli whose name, anglicized, he gave to Mazeppa's great love.[18] Both Theresas were unhappily married to men much older than themselves; the real Teresa, contessa Guiccioli, was eighteen and her husband fifty-seven when they married. Conte Guiccioli's violent and vengeful nature terrified Byron, who, no doubt, feared meeting a fate similar to Mazeppa's.[19]

Byron's fate was different, however; he went to Greece in 1823 to take part in the struggle for Greek independence, and died at Missolonghi the following year.

Byron's life and writing appealed to the younger French generation that came of age during the repressive Restoration, "the French Generation of 1820."[20] For this generation of young French Romantics, Byron was an individual in revolt against society, and *Byronisme* in France has been defined as just that.[21] Unlike the heroes of the neoclassical age, Byron appealed to a generation that had seen idealism turn sour and had replaced self-sacrifice for the good of society with self-gratification as the prime reality. Byron had political appeal as well: like Napoléon, whom he admired greatly and to whom he dedicated several poems, he was an exile from his native land.[22] Numerous French critics mentioned this aspect of Byron's career, for "exiled by England" carried an attractive cachet in France.[23] Although the Romantic fad for all things English was general in France throughout the early nineteenth century, although Shakespeare and Sir Walter Scott were admired, it was Byron who was adored.

"Mazeppa" was more esteemed and more influential in France than in England where the poem was roundly condemned as immoral. While "Mazeppa" may be symbolic of the man of genius who suffers for his art, it clearly did not escape Byron's contemporaries that it was also quite literally the story of a man sent into exile as punishment for adultery, and that it was, at least in part, an apologia for Byron's own life. As one English critic wrote: "When we sympathize with suffering virtue, we are excited to follow a noble example, and when we are unintentionally made to sympathize with an offender, by a poet of so high an order as Lord Byron, there's a hazard that our sense of his offence may be proportionally diminished."[24] The first French translator of Byron, Amédée Pichot, in his "Essay on the Genius and the Character of Lord Byron" counterattacked: "Some of these men who look for shameful motives everywhere, and they are numerous in today's England, have cried out that Lord Byron wants to sanctify adultery and incest."[25] Pichot defended the poet: "Lord Byron has so identified himself with his writing, much of which is like a mirror reflecting all his moods, that the critic really ought to make sure he is being objective before making judgments that condemn the man at the same time as the poet."[26]

While his contemporaries read Byron's poem as a thinly disguised apologia for his own adulterous liaisons, a modernist bias in twentieth-century cultural studies has completely suppressed this aspect of the poem. As a result, the literary historian Hubert F. Babinski, who wrote the only full-length study of the Mazeppa theme, could state, "there is no explicit reason, according to the evidence, why Byron should write about Mazeppa at all, especially as he was in the middle of his 'Italian Period.'"[27]

French Romantics, on the other hand, admired both the man and his poetry. Alfred de Vigny, in the first French review of the poem, praised it, stating that "*Mazeppa* is an extraordinary effort of an extremely rich imagination. Who else besides Lord Byron would dare to compose a poem based on the simple tale of a man carried away by a wild horse? Who else could succeed?"[28] Not only did Byron's poem begin with a passage from the great French philosopher Voltaire, but its first stanza alluded sympathetically to the French defeat in Russia, linking Mazeppa and France in humiliating defeat.[29] In Byron's poem, Mazeppa, now over seventy, recounts his life to Charles XII as they pause for rest after the débâcle at Poltava. Mazeppa tells how in his youth as a page to John Casimir (the anglicized Jan Kazimierz), he fell in love with Theresa, the young wife of the aging Count Palatine. When their affair was discovered, in punishment he was tied naked backwards to a wild horse and sent off into the wilderness to die. The body of the poem describes the wild ride. Mazeppa was carried through forests and streams and over mountains, menaced by wolves and ravens, and subjected to "Cold, hunger, sorrow, shame, distress" (531), until his horse dropped dead from exhaustion under him. Found by a Cossack maiden, he awakened to become ruler of the Ukraine. Mazeppa concludes his tale with the moral message: "What mortal his own doom may guess? / Let none despond, let none despair!" (853–54).

The last lines of the poem are: "And if ye marvel Charles forgot / To thank his tale, *he* wonder'd not, – / The king had been an hour asleep" (867–69). The implication is clear: Mazeppa's tale of regeneration, of hope, of assurance that virtue (as it were) will triumph, has proved a deadly bore. It is the rambling of an old man and Charles, the political ruler, has simply fallen asleep. So "Mazeppa" exists on two levels: Byron has given his readers a rousing tale of suffering rewarded, but at the same time he has put it in a cynical framework, as though no one could possibly believe in such an outcome. Since the poem ends with the defeat at Poltava, the implication is that Mazeppa's triumph was of no lasting value anyway. Byron is having it both ways, which constitutes in part the appeal of the poem. Translated into French as a novel, the narrative is even further strengthened by the loss of formal poetic devices such as meter and rhyme.

Byron's "Mazeppa" could be – and was – read across a broad interpretative spectrum ranging from individual experience to national allegory. The *littérateur* Edgar Quinet (1803–75) even compared the French nation to Mazeppa:

> In their bitter imagination, I have often heard them say that France, tied to its Revolution, resembles *Mazeppa* carried far away from all the beaten paths by a horse that cannot be controlled. [. . .] That is perhaps true; only it must be added that at the moment when all seems lost, it is then that he rises up to the sound of the cheers of those who made him king.[30]

In the years after Waterloo, this symbolic message proved more popular in defeated France than in victorious England.

"Mazeppa" had an immediate appeal to French artists. The painters who worked with this theme in the 1820s, including Géricault, Delacroix, Vernet, and Boulanger, also produced related lithographs. Of all the possible scenes in Byron's long poem, they each chose the same one, Mazeppa's "wild ride." This chapter will investigate each of these images in turn, but it is important to look first at the general cultural background that informed all the manifestations of the theme.

The Horse . . .

I start with the classical significance of horses and riders, for Western culture was suffused with the classical tradition. Plato's image in *Phaedrus* underlies the Western equestrian tradition in myth and literature:

83   Jacques-Louis David, *Count Stanislas Kostka Potocki*, 1781. Oil on canvas, 304 × 218 cm. Muzeum narodowe, Warsaw.

84   Lust. Capital figure from St-Pierre-de-Montmartre, Paris, *c.* 1147. Lithograph by Louis Courtin from *Eglise Montmartre: Détails*, 1841. Bibliothèque nationale de France, Paris.

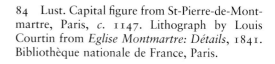

Of the nature of the soul [. . .] let me speak briefly and in a figure. And let the figure be composite – a pair of winged horses and a charioteer. [. . .] the human charioteer drives his in a pair; and one of them is noble and of noble breed, and the other is ignoble and of ignoble breed; and the driving of them of necessity gives a great deal of trouble to him. [. . .] The right-hand horse is upright and cleanly made; he has a lofty neck and an aquiline nose; his colour is white and his eyes dark; he is a lover of honour and modesty and temperance, and the follower of true glory; he needs no touch of the whip, but is guided by word and admonition only. The other is a crooked lumbering animal, put together anyhow: he has a short thick neck; he is flat-faced and of a dark colour, with gray eyes and a blood-red complexion; the mate of insolence and pride, shag-eared and deaf, hardly yielding to whip and spur. Now when the charioteer beholds the vision of love, and has his whole soul warmed through sense, and is full of the prickings and tickings of desire, the obedient steed, then as always under the government of shame, refrains from leaping on the beloved; but the other, heedless of the pricks and of the blows of the whip, plunges and runs away, giving all manner of trouble to his companion and the charioteer.[31]

The classical and neoclassical horse is the "lover of honour and modesty and temperance." The horsemen on the Parthenon frieze and in *Count Stanislas Kostka Potocki* (Figure 83) by Jacques-Louis David (1748–1825) represent such composite images of rational behavior, with the "lower" bodily instincts of the horse held in check by the "higher" intellect and rationality of the rider. The Romantic horse, however, "plunges and runs away," overcome by passions, uncontrolled by the rider-intellect. The colors white and black encode these classical attitudes, towards race to be sure, but also towards mind and body, intellect and emotion, the former being as desirable in the classical world as the latter was suspect, the one leading to the rationality of the clear light of day, the other to the mysteriousness of night. These attitudes became so embedded in Western culture that over the centuries the white horse became the very symbol of probity, while the black horse came to embody eroticism and transgression.[32]

. . . and the Rider

A function of this encoding of horse and rider as metaphor for body and mind is the parallel image of the backward rider, a version of "world upside-down" imagery encountered in chapter 3.[33] Ruth Mellinkoff has traced the backwards rider motif from antiquity, pointing out that the backwards ride was often punishment for crimes of a sexual nature, adultery in particular.[34] In popular culture throughout the Indo-European region, the *chevauchée sur l'âne*, the naked rider mounted backwards on an ass, was the standard punishment for such crimes,

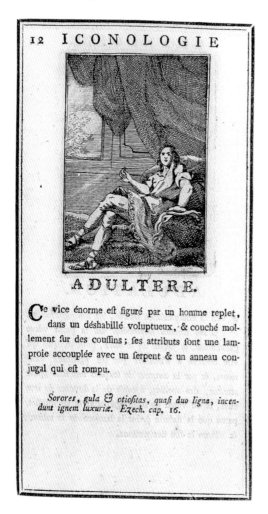

85 "Adultery." Engraving from Jean-Baptiste Boudard, *Iconologie tirée de divers auteurs, ouvrage utile aux gens de lettres, aux poëtes, aux artistes, et généralement à tous les amateurs des beaux-arts* (Parma and Paris: Tilliard, 1759). Bibliothèque nationale de France, Paris.

the ass being seen as a degraded horse, an "inversion" of the noble mount of the warrior-citizen.[35] Lust (Figure 84) was often portrayed as a backwards rider on a goat, an even more degraded version of the horse. Religious preachers, meanwhile, often described the adulterer as a horseman galloping straight to hell in pursuit of pleasure.[36] As in France punishment was reserved for married females and their bachelor accomplices, ritually turned into females for the occasion, Mazeppa's soft, almost effeminate body riding backwards can be read as the allegorical type of the adulterous young lover.[37] In Cesare Ripa's *Iconologia*, a compilation of allegorical representations for artists first published in the sixteenth century and translated into all European languages, "Adulterium" is represented as a plump young man, with the legend:

> He is young, for youth is the age most interested in matters sexual, and so most tempted to commit adultery. He is richly dressed, for such pleasures are reserved for those who can afford a great deal of leisure. He is plump because of his sins of sloth (indicated by his being seated), which generates libidinous thoughts, and greed for food, which also leads to lewd thinking.[38]

The illustration here (Figure 85) is drawn from the French edition by Jean-Baptiste Boudard (1710–68), which shows an almost identical image with a slightly condensed legend: "This heinous vice is represented by a plump man in voluptuous dishevelment, lying languidly on cushions. His attributes are a lamprey mating with a serpent and a broken wedding ring."[39]

And so Mazeppa's wild ride, bizarre though it may seem to modern eyes, is a pastiche of iconographic traditions deeply embedded in the European culture of earlier centuries. With this in mind, one can better understand the images of Mazeppa created by the major French Romantic artists, Géricault, Delacroix, Vernet, and Boulanger.

Théodore Géricault (1791–1824), the first French artist to use themes from Byron, had much in common with the poet, not least of which was, according to French reviewers, a passion for horses.[40] Both men had gone into exile in Italy in 1816, Byron because of his dissolute life in England, Géricault to escape his liaison with his young aunt. In 1819–20 Géricault did lithographs based on Byron's "Lara Wounded" and "The Giaour" and repeated them in 1823 in a series to which he added prints illustrating Byron's "The Bride of Abydos" and "Mazeppa," the latter based on his own painting of the same title.[41] Besides *Mazeppa*, Géricault painted two other Byronic subjects, *The Bride of Abydos* and *Gulnare Visiting Conrad in Prison (The Corsair)*. All of Géricault's Byronic works are based on themes of exile and tragic love, themes that had specific meanings in the lives of both men.

Géricault's life is similar to Byron's in that it also offers evidence of a deeper motivation for his interest in the Mazeppa theme. In 1815 Géricault had begun his affair with the young wife of his maternal uncle, Jean-Baptiste Caruel.[42] Caruel had, at fifty, married Alexandrine-Modest de Saint-Martin, an orphan of twenty-two. She was only six years older than Géricault. "This liaison had a fatal influence on Géricault's entire life, and explains his moody, restless, tormented existence, full of anguish and sorrow," Henri Houssaye later wrote.[43] The following year both Byron and Géricault were fleeing their unhappy love affairs for the more sympathetic atmosphere of Italy, a site that, as Robert Viscusi has pointed out, represented a double destination in the nineteenth century, the locus both of antiquity (Rome) and of relaxed sexual mores (Italy).[44] In this sense, Géricault's destination was both Rome and Italy, for during the years 1816–17 he became preoccupied with the antique subject of a centaur abducting a nymph.[45] Centaurs, violent sexual creatures in Greek mythology, were slaves to their lower appetites, and so were graphically represented with their lower-half animal and upper-half human. Lorenz Eitner has identified Géricault's motif in Figure 86 as inspired by the frieze of the Apollo Temple at Bassae Phigalia that the artist knew through engravings.[46] His sixteen tracings of these engravings bear obvious witness to their source, but also suggest a far deeper motivation, particularly as Géricault had left for Italy repenting the "terrible situation into which I have recklessly thrown myself."[47] Géricault was evidently not interested in the theme of Chiron, the only well-behaved centaur, but he often drew the centaur Nessus who, ordered by Hercules to carry his wife Deianira across the river, instead attempted to abduct her. Hercules killed Nessus with a poisoned arrow but the dying centaur gave Deianira a poisoned cloak that, he said, would restore her husband's fidelity should he stray. Hercules strayed, Deianira gave him the cloak, and Hercules died in agony.[48] Like the legend of Mazeppa, this is a story of adultery punished and avenged, and its appeal to Géricault at this time is revelatory.

Some time during these years Géricault painted *The Death of Hippolytus* (Figure 87). According to Euripides, Hippolytus was torn apart by horses after

87 (*below*)   Théodore Géricault, *The Death of Hippolytus*, c. 1816–17. Oil on canvas, 260 × 380 cm. Musée Fabre, Montpellier.

86 *(facing page top)*
Théodore Géricault,
*Centaur Abducting a
Woman*, 1816–17.
Pen, wash, and gouache,
175 × 274 cm. Musée du
Louvre, Paris.

88 Théodore Géricault,
Mazeppa, 1823. Oil/paper
applied to canvas,
285 × 215 cm. Private
collection, Paris.

being falsely accused of an adulterous love for his stepmother. An earlier moment in this narrative was treated by Guérin (Figure 78), but Géricault shifted the focus of Guérin's painting from Phaedra to Hippolytus, specifically the latter's gruesome death in the wake of Phaedra's accusation.[49] Géricault himself was not falsely accused, however, for within a year of his return to Paris in 1817, his aunt bore him a son whom he named Georges-Hippolyte (his own father's name was Georges). As already noted, under Penal Code article 337 both Géricault and Madame Caruel could have been sent to prison for up to two years, but their families, like most of the bourgeoisie, preferred to hush up the scandal and deal with it privately. Madame Caruel's newborn son was taken away from her and registered as "of unknown parents," in violation of Civil Code article 312, which stated that any child born into a marriage was legally the husband's. Despite this, the child was raised anonymously, supported by Géricault's father.[50] He did not regain the Géricault name until 1840. Madame Caruel was sent away to a country estate, where she lived out her life in isolation and disgrace, dying in 1875 at age ninety.

This solution to the problem of adultery might be contrasted with that of the marquis de Cairon, discussed in chapter 1. During the years 1816–19, the marquis had his wife imprisoned for the same offense, and he also had her newborn son taken away from her and registered as "of unknown parentage." Cairon went even further, however, arranging the winter voyage that resulted in the infant's death, and eventually filing criminal adultery charges against his wife and her lover. The Caruel solution was a less scandalous and, no doubt, more customary way of dealing with this problem among the propertied classes.

Géricault went unpunished but, after the scandal was suppressed, he barricaded himself in his studio to paint *The Raft of the Medusa*, exhibited at the Salon of 1819 as *A Shipwreck*. Seen in this context, his choice of this subject assumes a wider resonance, particularly as he had left for Italy just after the Medusa tragedy had become known.[51] And, although the legendary Mazeppa survived to become king, Géricault himself became so depressed in the months following his personal "shipwreck" that he left France for England, where he was rumored to have repeatedly attempted suicide; he remained there, with brief visits to the continent, until the end of 1821.[52]

Some time between 1819 and 1823 (he died in January 1824), Géricault painted his *Mazeppa* (Figure 88), which he then repeated in the 1823 lithograph.[53] It is a private image of a defeated Mazeppa who, in a moment of stillness, seems almost crucified. It is an interior image, lacking setting and supporting characters. It does not so much narrate the story as communicate the mood. Géricault's *Mazeppa* is bound to the dark horse of untamed passion; he does not hold the reins but is carried along helplessly by his horse, very like the centaur ruled by his "lower" instincts. It is a small, intimate painting, not intended for the public, and it was never exhibited. A comparison of this image to his centaur drawing of several years earlier (Figure 86) shows the changed relationship between the man and his "animal instincts." Earlier he was actively, successfully pursuing them. Now they have defeated him.

This implicit connection between Mazeppa, centaurs, and debauchery was later made explicit by Alfred de Musset (1810–57) in his autobiographical *Confession of a Child of the Century* (1836). Speaking of the libertine atmosphere that surrounded his generation, he wrote:

> They are bound to debauchery like Mazeppa to his wild beast. They are pinioned there, turned into centaurs, and they see neither the bloody trail that their shredded flesh is leaving on the trees, nor the eyes of the wolves that gleam crimson in pursuit, neither the desert, nor the vultures.[54]

For Musset, debauchery had reached a point where the rational charioteer no longer existed; existence was one long wild ride with Mazeppa as its emblem.

Géricault's passion for horses is well known, and so strongly did he identify with them that his biography has even been traced through such images, from the passionate spirited horses of his youth to the broken down, dying, and dead workhorses of his last years.[55] The passive backwards ride of Géricault's *Mazeppa* should assume a major position in this equine autobiography, as it

89   Eugène Delacroix, *Mazeppa*, 1824. Watercolor, 22.5 × 31 cm. Ateneum, National Gallery of Finland, Helsinki.

combines in a single emblematic image, both his autobiographical concerns and the dilemma of his generation.

Delacroix's version of *Mazeppa* is similar to Géricault's in that it is also a small private image, unexhibited during his lifetime, and focuses on the isolation of the sufferer in a timeless setting. The earliest catalogue raisonné of his work listed nine Mazeppa studies dated around 1824, but most have since disappeared.[56] There remain, however, a watercolor in the Finnish National Gallery in Helsinki (Figure 89), an oil painting after Géricault's version in the Mahmoud Khalil Museum in Cairo, and two drawings.[57]

Delacroix read Byron in English even before the first French translations appeared, and he painted Byronic themes throughout his life.[58] He had a number of English friends, including the artists Richard Parkes Bonington and the four Fielding brothers, and in 1825 he visited England. So one could interpret his paintings of *Mazeppa* as manifestations of the general fad for all things English during the period, or, as several scholars have done, as formal exercises, presenting, according to Alfred Robaut "a fine pretext for a superb linear development, for bold rhythms, for a rare display of energy, and, at the same time, for valuable dramatic contrasts."[59] I argue, however, that Delacroix's interest in the theme had a more personal genesis.

Like Géricault, Delacroix did small, intimate versions of Mazeppa set in unspecified landscapes, icons rather than narratives. And like Géricault, Delacroix placed Mazeppa on the dark horse of unbridled passion, in pictures that, as Lee Johnson has pointed out, were obviously not intended to reach a wide audience as they were unsigned, unexhibited, and disposed of privately.[60] Although Johnson refers to the Cairo picture as "essentially a personal exercise," an examination of Delacroix's biography suggests some more telling reasons for his interest in this theme in 1824.

Edouard Soulier, whom Delacroix had known since 1816, was one of his closest friends.[61] Raised in England, he taught Delacroix both English and the watercolor technique that he had learned from Copley Fielding (1787–1855). In 1820 Soulier went to Florence and remained there until 1822. During that time Delacroix took up with Soulier's lover, who has since been identified as Madame de Coetlosquet.[62] On his return there ensued a long and tormented period during which Delacroix was alternately filled with guilt, shame, and desire.[63] He wrote in his journal: "My first reaction was delight in seeing him again. Then I felt a terrible pang. [. . .] I hope that my wrong to him will not affect his relationship with . . . I hope to God that he never finds out! And why do I, at this very moment, feel something like satisfied vanity? Oh! If he were to hear of it he would be devastated."[64] During this period Delacroix painted *Louis d'Orléans Showing His Mistress* (Fondación Colección Thyssen-Bornemisza, Madrid), an image that combines the theme of adultery with the "satisfied vanity" he felt towards Soulier: in the painting, Louis d'Orléans displays his naked mistress, Mariette d'Englien, to her own husband.[65] A year later, as the situation worsened, Delacroix wrote of Madame de Coetlosquet: "Say that your heart is big enough for two friends, that neither of us is your lover. Then I will not be jealous, then I will not consider myself guilty for possessing you."[66] Madame de Coetlosquet who, in addition to her two lovers also had a husband, toyed with both Soulier and Delacroix until December 1823, when Delacroix broke off the affair – and abruptly began working on the Mazeppa theme.

Delacroix's *Mazeppa* was among his earliest Byronic subjects; he had painted *The Castaways* in 1821 but most of his other paintings on Byronic themes were done in 1827 or later. The confluence of Byron and Mazeppa, the English influence of his friend Soulier, and his anguished affair with Soulier's lover, all serve to reinforce a reading of Delacroix's *Mazeppa* as being more about sexuality and guilt than about the artist's genius. Interestingly enough, the Cairo

Mazeppa was long dated, incorrectly, to 1828; on biographical evidence alone that date should have been reconsidered.[67] Only in 1824 was Delacroix intrigued by this theme so closely related to his private life, and so ambivalent about producing a large public version of it. His other Byronic themes presented no such problems.

To comprehend Géricault's and Delacroix's identification with Mazeppa adequately, one must remember the perilous situation in which the new penal code placed bachelor lovers of married women. Under the Old Regime, punishment for adultery was prescribed only for married women; married men could behave as they pleased, and a bachelor was punished only if his social class fell below that of his married lover, as was the case of Mazeppa. The new Civil Code, however, ruled that the bachelor accomplice of the married woman should receive a punishment equal to hers, namely imprisonment of three months to two years; in addition, he would be fined.[68] Although the proofs needed to convict a married woman's bachelor lover were much more stringent than those needed to convict the woman herself, the fact remained that there were now two classes of philandering men: the married ones, who would go free, and the unmarried ones, who could be severely punished. Géricault and Delacroix both fell into the latter category, and so, added to whatever personal anguish their unhappy love affairs brought them, there was this new and additional worry.

Despite the new regulations of the Penal Code, the courts continued, as discussed in chapter 1, to punish adulterous wives more severely than their lovers. Nonetheless, there is a sense in which Mazeppa can be seen as being unjustly punished in comparison with what would have happened to the Count Palatine in similar circumstances. "Theresa's doom I never knew," Byron wrote in "Mazeppa" (340), and she is of no further interest in this unfolding allegory of male victimization and regeneration. Before the entire symbolic superstructure of the Mazeppa legend can be made socially legible, however, it must be understood that, although Mazeppa was punished for adultery (which he did in fact commit), from the point of view of young men, it was unjust that they should be punished when married men who committed the same offense would go free. In their own view, they were the real victims of injustice.

While Géricault and Delacroix both invested *Mazeppa* with biographical meaning and never exhibited their small and moving testimonials to personal experience, Horace Vernet and Louis Boulanger exhibited large-scale public paintings of Mazeppa at the Salon of 1827–28. At this point the Mazeppa legend began to move away from personal biography to become invested with universal significance, in the process becoming metaphor in a public sphere. It is as full-fledged "mythologies" in the Roland Barthes sense that these later paintings must be examined.

When Vernet and Boulanger showed their *Mazeppa* paintings at the Salon, they became rallying points for the liberal opposition. This particular exhibition is well known for its juxtaposition of Delacroix's *Death of Sardanapalus* and Ingres's *Apotheosis of Homer*, and yet it also represented the apotheosis of Mazeppa, both because of the paintings exhibited and because they, in turn, inspired Victor Hugo to write his poem "Mazeppa."

Horace Vernet (1789–1863) was the third of the Vernet family to make his mark as a painter.[69] The son of Carle Vernet and grandson of Joseph Vernet, he carried on the family tradition, and was honored and successful from his Salon début in 1812. In contrast to Géricault and Delacroix, Vernet held strong political opinions; throughout the Restoration he was a dedicated Bonapartist whose studio became a meeting-place for the political opposition. In 1822 a scandal occurred when seven paintings that he had sent to the Salon were refused on the basis of their inflammatory anti-royalist themes. To show his opposition to both the Academy and the regime, Vernet held an open studio exhibition of these and other paintings, an event that further identified him as an opponent of the repressive Restoration government.[70]

Vernet painted at least four versions of *Mazeppa*. The first of these, *Mazeppa and the Horses* (Figure 90), was completed in 1825 and was exhibited the following year at the *Exhibition of Paintings for the Benefit of the Greeks* held at the Galerie Lebrun in Paris.[71] The government had cancelled the previous Salon, and in protest the artists had organized this exhibition. Writing in *Le Globe*, Louis Vitet explained the event:

> As soon as they had conceived of the project, they determined to hold an open exhibition. They had already begun securing the loans when they heard the anguished cries of the unfortunate Greeks. To consecrate an enterprise organized for the benefit of art to the relief of misfortune, to convert an act of independence into a work of charity, such was the spontaneous desire of all the artists, and the exhibition was designated for the benefit of the Greeks.[72]

Vitet left no doubt that the unhappy artists identified with the unhappy Greeks and that their act of protest in holding their own exhibition was also an act of political protest – as witness the many Bonapartist subjects shown. In this context the exhibition of over two hundred paintings took on added political significance, particularly as so many of them came from collections of prominent members of the liberal opposition. Included, for example, were David's *Death of Socrates* and Gérard's *Portrait of General Foy*, Gros's sketch for *The Pesthouse at Jaffa* and Delacroix's *Marino Faliero*. Of Delacroix's work the catalogue explained: "The Doge of Venice Marino Faliero, having, at the age of more than eighty, conspired against the Republic, was condemned to death by the Senate."[73] Vernet sent his *Apotheosis of Bonaparte* and *Mazeppa and the Horses*, the latter described in the catalogue as a "subject drawn from a novella by Lord Byron."[74]

The scene depicted by Vernet is the incident in Byron's poem when Mazeppa, tied to his horse, is surrounded by a herd of wild horses; his own horse drops

90   Horace Vernet, *Mazeppa and the Horses*, 1825. Oil on canvas, 195 × 279 cm. Destroyed.

dead of exhaustion and all the others flee. Byron's description echoes the Platonic concept of the unruly passionate dark horse:

> The steeds rush on in plunging pride;
> But where are they the reins to guide?
> A thousand horse and none to ride!
> With flowing tail, and flying mane,
> Wide nostrils never stretch'd by pain
> Mouths bloodless to the bit or rein,
> And feet that iron never shod,
> And flanks unscarr'd by spur or rod,
> Like waves that follow o'er the sea.
>   Came thickly thundering on. (676–86)

While Byron does not have Mazeppa riding the black horse of passion, the troop of wild horses is led by such a horse:

> Then plunging back with sudden bound,
> Headed by one black mighty steed,
> Who seem'd the patriarch of his breed,
>   Without a single speck or hair
> Of white upon his shaggy hide. (701–05)

In Vernet's painting the two horses face each other, the black horse of passion wild and free, the white horse of rationality defeated and dead. When the painting was exhibited in the Salon of 1827–28, this confrontation seems to have been on the minds of many of the critics.[75] Auguste Jal began by noting the painting's instant acclaim: "This work was a success even before it was finished, for Monsieur Horace is no less fortunate than the poet of whom it was said 'His verses are recited even while he is still writing them.' "[76] He noted that some critics had found the horses "too polished and polite," referring no doubt to Antoine-Nicolas Béraud, who had written that the depiction of the horses contradicted their "wild nature."[77] Jal preferred the figure of Mazeppa in Vernet's second version, *Mazeppa and the Wolves* (Figure 91), exhibited in the same Salon, because it was "less of an *académie*," meaning less like the Greek-sculpture-inspired nudes that staffed classical history painting.[78]

These two criticisms taken together imply that the conflict between Classicism and Romanticism was inscribed onto *Mazeppa and the Horses*: the academic figure and his white classical horse have fallen exhausted before the unfettered, wild, and free forces of Romanticism, represented by the black horse. The iconography of the painting is an example of how Romantic artists used the classical tradition for their own ends. Had they not done so, images such as this would lose much of their resonance. The meanings of this painting are not wholly articulate but float around the concept of bound versus free; symbolically that could stand for Classicism versus Romanticism, or for the helpless Greeks versus the savage Turks. This latter reading would be underscored by the purpose of the exhibition in which the painting first appeared. To the younger Romantic generation, the motif presented in this painting could also stand for the bondage of social conventions versus the freedom of natural desires.

Vernet's second version of this theme, *Mazeppa and the Wolves* (Figure 91), became the best-known Mazeppa image throughout Europe and America, copied, used in posters, clocks, cameos, vases.[79] He considered it "one of his better productions," sending it to the Universal Exposition of 1855 as well as to the Salon of 1827–28.[80] It is undoubtedly the one that Alfred de Musset had in mind when writing his *Confession of a Child of the Century*. Vernet painted it in 1826 as a gift for the Musée Calvet in Avignon because the museum had named a gallery in honor of his grandfather, Joseph Vernet. The museum curator had suggested other subjects, but Vernet decided to repeat the Mazeppa theme and to choose a different moment in Byron's tale.[81] When the painting

91   Horace Vernet, *Mazeppa and the Wolves*, 1826. Oil on canvas, 100 × 138 cm. Musée Calvet, Avignon.

was exhibited in the Salon of 1827–28, Jal described it thus: "All the dangers besetting Mazeppa's route, the raging river, the fallen trees, the dense forest and the night that, leaving his steed without direction, might perhaps deliver him to the wolves, all these dangers are excellent inventions."[82]

In the eyes of all the critics, this second version was much better than the first, for, as Jal noted, it is thrillingly imagined as a moment of sublime terror.[83] Vernet treated his theme almost emblematically, compressing the various trials of Mazeppa – the wolves, the night, the forest, the torrential river – into a single image. In this way it takes on a "voyage through life" quality that would have been impossible had Vernet limited himself to a single moment in the narrative as he had done in *Mazeppa and the Horses*. The body of Mazeppa is no longer the carefully articulated *académie* to which Jal objected in the first version: it is now soft and limp, lacking bone and muscle – and for those reasons all the more vulnerable to the dangers of his journey. The painting evokes sensations of helplessness, vulnerability, and peril, and so it is no surprise that a lithograph of it was published after the July Revolution of 1830 carrying the caption: "The proceeds from the sale of this lithograph are designated for the relief of families of victims of the momentous events of July 1830."[84] The families of the victims of the Revolution were in the same symbolic situation as Mazeppa, helpless and exposed to grave dangers over which they had no control. When the painting was exhibited at the Musée Calvet in Avignon in 1826 in the newly dedicated Galerie Vernet, it was "for the benefit of the poor" who, metaphorically, are always in the same vulnerable situation as Mazeppa.[85] And so within four years, Vernet's image of Mazeppa, the young page caught in adultery with his lord's wife, had become publicly identified with the cause of the Greeks, the poor, and the victims of the July Revolution of 1830.

Mazeppa and the Wolves could function politically and "mythologically," however, only if Mazeppa were seen as the victim, unjustly punished and thus sharing the fate of these other victims. "Theresa's doom I never knew," wrote Byron, but it can be assumed that she, like Géricault's Madame Caruel, did not have a future as glorious as Mazeppa. It was not her fate that would be universalized to symbolize injustice towards an entire generation. And yet, for many of his contemporaries, Vernet had created an image with universal resonance. It wasn't even necessary to know Byron's poem in order to respond to this image, as there are times when everyone has the feeling of being naked and defenseless against hungry wolves. That, no doubt, accounts for the enormous popularity that Vernet's *Mazeppa and the Wolves* enjoyed in the nineteenth century, for this *Mazeppa* eclipsed all the rest.

Louis Boulanger (1806–67) was the last major painter to treat the Mazeppa theme during this period. It was his painting *The Punishment of Mazeppa* (Figure 92), shown in his Salon début in 1827, that inspired Victor Hugo's "Mazeppa" and was thus responsible for the shift in interpretation that followed.[86] The painting was enthusiastically received and earned him a second-class medal, a major achievement for a twenty-one-year-old neophyte. Even more impressive, Hugo's "Mazeppa," written shortly after the Salon closed in 1828, was dedicated, not to Byron, but "to M. Louis Boulanger."[87] The identification of Boulanger and Hugo with Mazeppa and Romanticism was so strong that Baudelaire in his "Salon of 1845" got them all with one shot. He wrote of Boulanger:

> Here we have the last ruins of the old Romanticism. This is what it means to come at a time when received wisdom holds that inspiration suffices and replaces everything else; this is the abyss to which the unbridled course of Mazeppa has led. It is Monsieur Victor Hugo who has ruined Monsieur Boulanger, after having ruined so many others. It is the poet who has tumbled the painter into the ditch.[88]

To understand what attracted Hugo and his cenacle to Boulanger's painting, the writings of Petrus Borel are illuminating. In his article "Intellectual Artists

92 Louis Boulanger, *The Punishment of Mazeppa*, 1827. Oil on canvas, 525 × 392 cm. Musée des beaux-arts, Rouen.

and Shallow Artists," Borel discussed Boulanger at greater length than David, Ingres, Géricault, or Delacroix:

> Louis Boulanger is not only a man of thought and a painter of conviction, but he also possesses a quality that is worth everything else, a prodigious imagination. [. . .] What erudition, what energy, what life, what excitement, what terror, what dread! [. . .] his compositions are always marked by gravity, by sadness, by reverie, they charm us, they seduce us. They are always expressive and boldly poetic. [. . .] From his first appearance with his paintings of *Mazeppa*, Boulanger revealed all these remarkable qualities.[89]

Although posterity has not shared this high esteem, in a narrative sense Boulanger's *Mazeppa* is the most complete of all the versions. Its composition, seemingly crowded and fragmented, is the only one that represents the dialectic of the event. There is the struggle between youth and age, the dynamic and energetic lower group juxtaposed with the stilted and static upper group. There is the class division, where the lower figures represent servants, executioners, soldiers, and Mazeppa the criminal, all in various degrees of undress, while the upper figures, fittingly enough, represent the upper classes, clad in robes of state. This dialectic is underscored by the legend included in the Salon catalogue: "Mazeppa is tied to a wild horse, by order of the Count Palatin whom he outraged. (Lord Byron, Mazeppa, stanza 10)."[90] Boulanger has even included a female figure with child at the upper right, a reminder of the *raison d'être* of adultery laws. Although the kind of prodigious imagination necessary to compose such a picture is clearly now out of favor, it should be recognized that this painting is the most complete in terms of an external narrative, just as the Géricault, pared down of all extraneous elements, is the most complete in terms of an internal reality.

The striking homoerotic content of all these Mazeppa images can be seen as a function of the appropriation of the female role as victim, the effeminization of Mazeppa signifying his surrogate female status in the eyes of husbands and the law. As specified in the traditional iconography of *Adultery*, his body, soft like a woman's, is made for love. There was, in fact, a long tradition in European common law of symbolically transforming the bachelor adulterer into a female by shaving his body and dressing him in female clothing as prelude to his backwards ride.[91] In the painting, Mazeppa's effeminization occludes the female role in the drama and focuses attention on even this crime of adultery as a drama "between men."[92]

The Romantic artist's self-identification as victim, replacing and excluding the female, can be seen in a comparison of Boulanger's *Mazeppa* with Nicolas Poussin's *Christ and the Adulterous Woman* (Figure 93). Poussin's painting, like that of Boulanger, assumed an importance in this period that it is no longer accorded. E.-J. Delécluze, for example, the doyen of French critics, wrote at length in 1819 of the genius of Poussin (1594–1665) in counterposing the good

93   Nicolas Poussin, *Christ and the Adulterous Woman*, 1653. Oil on canvas, 122 × 125 cm. Musée du Louvre, Paris.

and the bad woman, noting that the juxtaposition of the good mother with her child makes the nature and consequences of the adulterous woman's crime all the more obvious.[93] As discussed in chapter 3, the visual trope contrasting the good with the bad mother invaded lithographic imagery during these years. Boulanger borrowed that device of the good mother with her child, but he here juxtaposed her with Mazeppa, who now replaces the bad mother, the adulterous woman, as both sinner and victim. And Theresa's fate remains unknown.

It is easy to see how Victor Hugo (1802–85) extrapolated from this painting his image of the artist suffering in the face of a hostile audience. In the Géricault and Delacroix paintings there was no audience, there was just suffering; in the Vernet paintings it was nature, i.e. life, that caused Mazeppa's suffering. Boulanger, however, specifically portrays the enemy: old entrenched authority. Boulanger's painting aptly illustrates Balzac's often-quoted quip that during this period there were "only two ages, youth and senility."[94]

Hugo's poem is based at least as much on Byron as on Boulanger, for the painter showed only the prelude to Mazeppa's ride, while Hugo described it at length, following Byron's poem in all its details, and even including Byron's line "Away! – Away!" as an epigraph.[95] The title of Hugo's collection of poems, *Les Orientales*, is an obvious reference to Byron's collection of *Oriental Tales* that had proved so popular in France. What Hugo took from Boulanger is the dialectic of the situation, recasting it as that of genius and his audience. Hugo has the troop of wild horses follow Mazeppa, as do the ravens, eagle, osprey, and owl. Mazeppa suffers, but he leads the way. The others are deaf or hostile, but they follow. In Part II of the poem, Hugo leaves Byron's narrative to weave his own symbolic interpretation:

> Thus when a mortal whom God protects,
> Is bound alive to your fateful back,
>   Genius, ardent steed,
> In vain he struggles, alas! You leap, you carry him off
> Away from the real world, whose barriers you smash
>   With your hooves of steel![96]

After another description of Mazeppa's sufferings, parallel with the earlier narrative, but this time in symbolic rather than literal terms, the poem ends:

> He cries out, terrified. You pursue, implacably.
> Pale, exhausted, gasping, on your flight that overwhelms him,
>   He twists with fear.
> Each step you take seems to dig his grave.
> Finally, the end comes . . . He runs, he flies, he falls,
>   And he rises up king![97]

This interpretation of Mazeppa as triumphant suffering genius was given wide currency in the Saint-Simonian periodical *Le Globe*. Saint-Simonians believed in the artist's role as prophet, and their leader, Pierre Leroux, wrote of this poem:

> Thus is accomplished the fusion of a moral idea with a corporeal image. The assimilation is perfect. The genius, his interior torments, the hatred that first pursues him, the adoration that then follows that hatred, all these pure conceptions of intelligence have been made visible. We have a symbol and not a comparison.[98]

Hugo succeeded in doing what no other poet or painter had done: he completely articulated the meaning he found in the theme into a clear, simple message. This distillation of experience is one of many things art can do, but art can also present a multi-faceted image, allusive, elusive, and polyreferential in nature, as the various earlier manifestations of Mazeppa had done. There are many ways to ride a horse, but, in a kind of Gresham's law of critical inquiry, simpler explanations tend to drive out more complex ones. As a result, Hugo's "Mazeppa" has retroactively obscured all the rest.

These manifestations of the Mazeppa theme occurred within the hallowed precincts of high art, and yet popular audiences also had their readings of the theme, primarily expressed through theatrical productions. The earliest was

LE MONDE DRAMATIQUE.

Cirque Olympique de Franconi.

94   "Franconi's Cirque olympique," *Le Monde dramatique*, 1815–30.
Lithograph. Lith. Caboche. Bibliothèque nationale de France, Paris.
("Cirque olympique de Franconi")

Mazeppa, or The Tartar Horse, an equestrian *mimodrame*, premièred at the
Cirque olympique on January 11, 1825.[99] These *mimodrames*, half play, half
equestrian acrobatic feats, were the featured entertainment at the Cirque
olympique (Figure 94), and starred Adolphe Franconi who, in this production,
played Mazeppa. It was a form of popular entertainment that Géricault and
Delacroix often attended; Géricault even rode at the Cirque olympique.[100] The
play (without the acrobatic feats) proved to have international appeal, and was
subsequently plagiarized by the American actor John Howard Payne in an
English translation entitled *Mazeppa, or The Wild Horse of Tartary*; H. M.
Milner did the same thing in England.[101] In all three versions, Mazeppa is identified with the wild horse, both in the title of the play and in numerous explicit
comparisons made by various characters. By casting the Cossack Mazeppa as
a Tartar, these plays hopelessly muddled Central European history, for the two
groups not only represented different ethnic groups, Ukrainians and Turks, but
they were sworn enemies as well. Historical accuracy, however, was not the
point of these productions.

In all three of these popular versions of the Mazeppa legend, Olinska (Byron's
Theresa) is affianced to Count Prémislas but not yet married to him. As a result,

the driving motivation of the "high art" plot, Mazeppa's and Theresa's adultery, is elided. Mazeppa is now an orphan, discovered after a battle with the Tartars and raised in Poland where, under the name Casimir, he becomes a page in the court of the Castellan de Laurinski. He falls in love with the Castellan's daughter, Olinska, and forces his rival Prémislas into a duel in an attempt to kill him. He fails to do so and is captured – but not *in flagrante delicto* as Byron would have it. The Castellan orders Mazeppa to be tied to a wild horse and driven out into the wilderness to die – but here he is punished for ambition, not for adultery. After many equestrian torments, all ably performed by Frasconi, Mazeppa collapses, only to awaken to cries of "Long live Mazeppa!"[102] He finds himself in Tartary, miraculously recognized as the long-lost grandson of Abder Kan who, coincidentally, was just about to name his successor. Now recognized and reinstated to his high social class, Mazeppa returns to Poland with his Tartar army to wreak vengeance and to claim Olinska as his bride. He attacks just as her wedding to Prémislas begins, and he proclaims: "I am no longer that obscure Casimir, unworthy of your love. I am Mazeppa, Prince of Tartary! Come, follow me to my camp, there to be proclaimed my wife and my queen."[103] Olinska refuses because he is the enemy of Poland, the despoiler of her country. A pitched battle ensues in which Mazeppa kills Prémislas and is about to kill the Castellan when Olinska begs: "Mazeppa, spare my father and take Olinska as the pledge of peace."[104] The play ends with Mazeppa receiving both Olinska's hand in marriage and the blessing of her father.

Mazeppa here is Everyman – in his dreams. Mazeppa the weak and obscure has become Mazeppa the omnipotent. He avenges his humiliations, he seizes what he wants. The production was a major success with *la foule*, the unsophisticated public who, according to contemptuous critics, queued up to get into the theater, applauded from beginning to end, and didn't care at all about the implausibility of the plot.[105] The ease with which common-law marriages were entered into and dissolved, as well as the absence of any appreciable property to complicate inheritance, made the issue of adultery inappropriate as a symbolic vehicle for audiences of the lower classes. The motivational forces in the drama have been transformed into upward social mobility and revenge, sentiments more charged with meaning in the popular classes than was adultery. Even here, however, the structure of the narrative is based on the assumption that Mazeppa should be able to appropriate whatever and whomever he wants for his own use. Even here the fate of Olinska/Theresa remains irrelevant.

All of this took place in France, and it is surprising how little artistic influence Byron's poem had in England. Richard Westall (1765–1836) and George Cruikshank (1792–1878) both did illustrations for Byron's *Mazeppa*, Westall in 1819 and Cruikshank in 1825 (Figure 95).[106] Although Byron never specified exactly how Mazeppa was tied to the horse, both artists made Mazeppa appear ridiculous by showing him securely trussed, implying that it took a lot

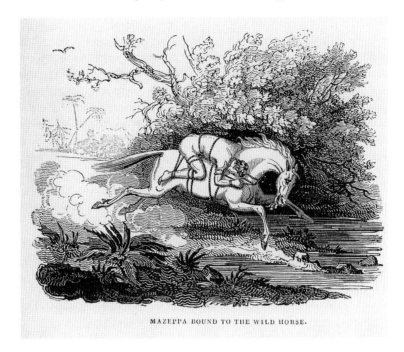

MAZEPPA BOUND TO THE WILD HORSE.

95   George Cruikshank, "Mazeppa Bound to the Wild Horse." Etching
from *Forty Illustrations of Lord Byron* (London: J. Robins & Co., 1825).
Print Collection, Miriam and Ira D. Wallach Division of Art, Prints, and
Photographs; New York Public Library, Astor, Lenox, and Tilden Foundations.

more rope to tie an English Mazeppa to the wild horse of passion. Both artists
avoided the explicit eroticism of the back-to-back spread-eagled pose used by
all the French artists, a pose that symbolically transforms the horse's tail into
a phallic symbol and thus intensifies the eroticism of the image. Several minor
painters did Mazeppa images, now lost, and Milner's play was not staged until
1831.[107]

The evident lack of English enthusiasm for Mazeppa could have a social
explanation. In 1820, one year after the publication of Byron's poem, George
IV of England had his wife Queen Caroline tried for adultery before the House
of Lords.[108] In one of the stranger quirks of history, Byron, who as Lord Gordon
was a hereditary peer, was summoned back to England to sit in judgment on
the Queen.[109] Although he resolutely refused to go, he followed the trial from
Italy, and his correspondence from Venice kept up a lively commentary on the
court proceedings, for he had known both Caroline and her consort Bartolomo
Bergami during their residence in Italy.[110] George IV was a notorious rake, and,
although Caroline was hardly the chaste and devoted wife, the king's efforts to

condemn her did not meet with popular support. "It was a business with which I should have been sorry to have had anything to do," wrote Byron, "they who voted her guilty cut but a dirty figure and those who call her innocent a not very clean one."[111] The trial went on for months and kept all of England transfixed as a succession of witnesses (some of them reportedly paid by George's agents) recounted every lurid detail of the queen's liaison. Byron remarked slyly that it was even more scandalous than his *Don Juan*.[112] French observers were just as fascinated by this unfolding drama, and at least nine French lithographs were produced during the trial depicting George, Caroline, and Bergami, sometimes all three as a wry "royal family" portrait, sometimes only Bergami as a rakish British Mazeppa (Figure 96).[113]

The final parliamentary vote was so close (109 to 99) that the bill was withdrawn, even though it had carried, because the peers had demonstrated an obvious lack of support for George. The public had shown even less support for the king's scheme, for during the entire proceedings there had been a steady stream of pamphlets and demonstrations in Caroline's defense. When she died suddenly a few months later, the affair was considered closed, but the scars remained.[114]

The Mazeppa in the case, Bartolomo Bergami, was described in the "Bill of Pains and Penalties" presented to the peers as "a foreigner of low station."[115] He was, in fact, Caroline's chamberlain, a member of her entourage while she was living in Italy. In a letter of 1817 Byron commented that the queen's relationship with Bergami was scandalizing polite society in Italy primarily because Bergami was lowborn.[116] Byron has Mazeppa, in the poem, make a similar comment on the Count Palatine:

> 'Sdeath! with a *page* – perchance a king
> Had reconciled him to the thing;
> But with a stripling of a page –
> I felt, but cannot paint his rage. (354–57)

The correlation is indeed very close, although literary critics have not noted the relationship between the Queen Caroline scandal and Byron's poem. Needless to say, unlike Mazeppa, Bergami went unpunished, although Caroline, like Theresa, paid dearly for her transgression. It is possible that this rude intrusion of life into art made the theme unattractive both politically and psychologically to British artists and the British public, or perhaps artists simply could not compete with the scores of caricatures that flooded England commenting upon this event. As noted earlier, "Theresa's doom I never knew," wrote Byron, and that freed him to focus on the fate of Mazeppa. But everyone in England knew what had happened to Caroline. Had there been an equivalent to the Queen Caroline affair in France in the 1820s, it is unlikely that the theme could have become as popular as it did. Being flawed in its internal structure, in direct contradiction to an obtrusive social reality, the Mazeppa theme could assume

Lith. de G. Engelmann.

De Bergami.

96 "Bergami," 1820. Lithograph. Lith. Engelmann. Bibliothèque nationale de France, Paris. ("De Bergami")

widespread cultural validity only through the repression and denial of that consciousness. This proved impossible in England.

The multivalence of the Mazeppa theme in the decade following Byron's poem demonstrates how cultural themes can become invested with social meanings that shift according to audience and circumstance. So who was Mazeppa? To the Ukrainians he was a patriot, to the Russians a traitor, to Delacroix he was himself suffering and to Géricault himself defeated. To Vernet he was the poor, the Greeks, the victims of Revolution, to Boulanger and Hugo, the artist-genius – and to the British, an adulterer and a fool.

7

The Marriage of Contradiction: Some Conclusions

If you persist in talking passion while I am talking marriage, we shall soon cease to understand each other.

Comtesse de Carigliano in Balzac,
"At the Sign of the Cat and Racket"[1]

THE SENTIMENTS EXPRESSED BY Balzac's duchesse de Carigliano succinctly express the traditional view of marriage encountered throughout this study. The courtly definition of marriage as a business arrangement between families or between individuals, with love as something that happened, if at all, outside its parameters, was challenged during the nineteenth century by the modern ideal of the companionate marriage, freely chosen and based on equality and sentiment. Most historians date the beginnings of this redefinition of marriage in France to the late eighteenth century; the onset of the idea of what was then called the "marriage of inclination" was encouraged by both the new Enlightenment emphasis on individual happiness and the concomitant weakening of familial, especially paternal, authority. Throughout the turbulent period of Revolution and its aftermath, laws on marriage, family, inheritance, and divorce were made, revised, and unmade, while debate on these issues increased. These debates provided the background and often the inspiration for the works of art and literature discussed in this book, and these works should be seen as the continuation of the debates into the media of cultural production.

The prints, plays, novels, and tracts I have discussed argue the superiority of either the marriage of reason or its opposite, the marriage of inclination. Only happiness was predicted for the preferred form, only disaster for its converse. The marriage of reason was based on a more solid foundation simply because it was not passionate, argued its proponents, who believed that passionate attachments were inherently unstable because they cooled as readily as they ignited. Marriages of reason, they felt, were based on mutual respect and would eventually develop into deep and permanent attachments. By this logic, marriage was much too important an affair to be left to callow youth, who, carried away by momentary infatuation, might even make a *mésalliance*, a marriage with a member of an inferior social class. Only parents could safely choose a child's spouse.

The opposite camp felt that marriages of reason were inherently doomed simply because the spouses lacked the mutual attraction necessary for a successful long-term union. In this view, marriages of reason were merely mercenary alliances of family fortunes. Although families might be spared the *mésalliance* of an inappropriate class relationship, spouses would be chosen for the wrong reasons, usually financial, and would undoubtedly be *mal-assorti*, mismatched in age or in temperament. Such a marriage of reason could never be happy and would inevitably lead to adultery, for who would, or should, feel loyalty to a spouse whom one had not chosen?

I have termed this situation "the marriage of contradiction," in that each camp produced excellent reasons why marriages failed, and yet each was unwilling to compromise its polarized position. The bourgeoisie was determined to have it both ways, to have parents arrange materially advantageous marriages that would, at the same time, function as a site of emotional support and refuge for the spouses, a "haven in a heartless world," to use Christopher Lasch's phrase.[2] What they wanted was, in essence, a marriage of contradiction. These ideological positions, staked out most clearly in the pendant caricatures in chapter 3, illustrate the extreme polarities of the marriage of reason contrasted to the marriage for love. They appear again in the "pendant" plays, *The Marriage of Reason* and *The Results of the Marriage of Reason*, discussed in chapter 4. The novels of Sand and Genlis, discussed in chapter 5, show us the unhappiness of wives caught in arranged marriages with husbands they had not chosen and do not love, while in Balzac's *Scenes from Private Life* love matches can just as easily end in unhappiness.

These opinions had a generational basis. As pointed out several times in the course of this book, the younger generation, which Alan Spitzer has called "the French generation of 1820," was in the forefront of the attack on the old system of arranged marriages.[3] Young men born around the turn of the century were the most vocal in claiming their rights and attacking what they perceived as the injustices of the current regime. Their voices are heard in the codes and physiologies by Raisson and Balzac, the poetry and plays of Hugo, caricatures by Grandville and Philipon, paintings by Delacroix – to name but a few representatives of this generation. In all media, they depicted handsome young bachelors, very like themselves, represented as adulterous lovers successfully seducing attractive young wives, whose husbands were inevitably represented as old and ugly. Fictional young men such as Stendhal's Julien Sorel in *The Red and the Black* or Byron's quasi-historical Mazeppa, or even "real-life" figures such as François Soubiranne, the young lover of the marquise de Cairon encountered in chapter 1, chose to challenge older men's prerogatives towards "their" women. For these young bachelors, stealing the wives of married men was a symbolic as well as a real act, for this threat could conceal many other kinds of competition, such as Julien Sorel's use of women for class warfare and social advancement. This hostility of bachelors to husbands, pervasive throughout the culture of the period, should be seen as a subset of their antagonism to fathers. Carol Duncan has traced this latter phenomenon in the visual arts in her article "Fallen Fathers: Images of Authority in Pre-Revolutionary French Art," and Lynn Hunt has termed it *The Family Romance of the French Revolution*.[4] Needless to say, in reality not all husbands were old, although, since men of the middle and upper classes tended to marry late, they would indeed be older than the artists and writers described here. It is more likely that the trope of always presenting husbands as old was less sociological reportage than a symbolic aspect of the generational warfare already under way. Once more, it is relevant to cite Balzac's quip that there were only two ages in contemporary France, youth and senility, an opinion shared by the younger generation of men across the spectrum of cultural production.[5] And yet, to repeat again, this younger generation of men denounced laws and customs less to assert the rights of women than to appropriate to themselves the authority of the old men whom they criticized so harshly. Genlis was well aware of this. In her novel *The Parvenus*, the young Eusèbe criticizes the marriage arranged by his parents for his sister Edélie, by saying that brothers, namely himself, could do a better job of this and should do it instead; he does not suggest that Edélie should be allowed to choose her own mate.[6]

The voices of men, young and old, are heard throughout the art and literature of the period, but where are the female voices? They are found in both likely and unlikely places, sometimes directly, sometimes only in reflection, like the shadows in Plato's cave. They are often heard in court, attempting to survive poverty and abandonment, like Madame Guichard, who, charged by the judge trying her for adultery, "You had an illicit relationship with Tendre," responds simply: "He saved me from destitution and we lived together."[7] They are seen attempting to find more satisfactory emotional relationships, as did the marquise de Cairon whose long-term relationship with the young medical student François de Soubiranne brought her, despite her aristocratic title, into the same criminal court as the street-vendor Madame Guichard. The *Gazette des tribunaux* tells of an incident in which anonymous women in the judiciary waiting-room rose up *en masse* and attacked a husband who has sent his wife to jail for adultery.[8] Their voices are heard especially in the many novels written by women, a practice that, as Joan DeJean has pointed out, began with the very earliest novels.[9] George Sand, slightly younger than the generation of men discussed here, was even more insistent than they in her criticism of contemporary marriage, but, unlike her male colleagues, she championed women's rights and, in her novels, had her female characters point out all the injustices of current laws and customs. Genlis was older and more conservative, but all her characters, male and female, suffer from arranged marriages and search for love.

While debates over the "marriage question" entered into a wide spectrum of cultural production, it should also be noted that each medium had its own characteristics, its own advantages, its own limitations; individual concerns were expressed according to audience and constituency. In the visual arts, lithographic caricature was dominated by young men like Grandville and Philipon, who used their art to espouse the concerns of their generation and mercilessly ridicule their elders. The codes and physiologies written by a host of young men, Balzac and Raisson chief among them, did the same thing. The younger generation of Romantic artists, Géricault, Delacroix, Vernet, and Boulanger, took up Byron's theme of Mazeppa, a young man punished for an adulterous liaison with his master's wife, and they universalized its symbolism to stand for all the injustices of their epoch. In contrast, older artists of the period such as Guérin and Ingres adopted narratives that denied the very existence of adultery.

Like the audience for visual arts, that for theater was polarized. But whether discussing the vaudeville of Scribe, the comedy of Delavigne, the melodrama of Ducange, or even the tragedy of Hugo, it is striking to note how many plots revolve around the marriage question, contrasting the results of marriages arranged or freely chosen, between spouses of the same or widely disparate ages. Regardless of differences in plot, playwrights did not seem capable of constructing happy endings that were believable; the plays therefore either end tragically, as do *Hernani* and *Three Days in the Life of a Gambler*, or they have happy endings that critics might have accepted, but did not believe, as in *The Marriage of Reason* and *The School for Old Men*.

As theater after the Revolution was firmly in the grip of the bourgeoisie, it is not surprising that successful productions and preferred plots upheld the values of this class. On stage, old men now had to be treated with respect and dignity, and it was no longer acceptable to mock them, as comedies had done in the past. Now they were shown as wise patriarchs, and it is the young men who are derided, presented as irresponsible, even immoral or criminal. This was the gerontocracy of the Restoration that the generation of 1820 so detested, a loathing that erupted on stage in 1830 in Hugo's *Hernani*. Throughout the spectrum of theatrical production, however, from vaudeville to tragedy, woman's role was passive, "between men" who disputed her possession.[10]

As befitted an audience of women readers, the novel was the medium that explored most fully the ramifications of the marriage of reason and the marriage for love. As already noted, the issue of personal happiness was central to novels of the period, appropriate to a medium that was increasingly being experienced through solitary silent reading, not in the social groups in which reading aloud had formerly taken place, or in which theater was experienced. While much attention has been given to the novel of adultery in nineteenth-century France, its true subject is this quest for personal happiness, with marriage, as it was then defined, invariably blocking the path. For young wives in these novels, especially those written by women authors, adultery was an attempt to bypass this obstacle despite the strictures of the new Civil Code, to take an active role in shaping one's own life. For Balzac as novelist, however, in a departure from his younger libertine persona as physiologist, those who break society's rules must be punished, women with death, men with unhappiness. While demonstrating that marriages for love always end badly, Balzac was equally harsh in his judgment of marriages of reason – unless they were between members of the same economic and social class. Stendhal explored a different aspect of liaisons, the coldly calculated desire for social advancement that sometimes determined a young man's affair with an older married woman. This was a subject ignored by the caricaturists, who single-mindedly focused their attack on older men, but it certainly constituted an aspect of the Mazeppa theme. Women novelists even explored the ramifications of a husband's adultery, a subject that playwrights avoided and that few authors of conduct manuals even broached.

The literary works progressed from the schematic to the individualistic, from the types of the codes and physiologies, through their theatrical versions, to the individual characters of the novels, which presented the broadest possible arena for exploring all the thoughts, feelings, and motivations of husband, wife, and lover.

George Sand claimed that relations between the sexes were ill-defined, and she attributed this to the constitution of contemporary society.[11] In one way or another, all the artists and writers of the period agreed, although they were not all equally critical of this situation. The art and literature of the time bear out her observation, for the proposed model for male/female relationships oscillated from parent to child to sibling to cousin. There was a certain logic to the depiction of the paternal husband, lauded in the plays of Delavigne and Scribe, lampooned in the lithographic caricatures, because a wife was usually younger than her husband and always his legal inferior. She was, in fact, more like a daughter than a wife. It is striking, however, that younger artists and writers should be so inarticulate in expressing their concept of the ideal marital relationship. While the new drive towards literary realism was responsible for much of the contemporaneous literature, especially its harsh depictions of the reality of loveless marriages, there was also an almost romantic attitude towards the marriage of inclination, as is clear in the "happily ever after" mode of the pendants discussed in chapter 3, in the ubiquitous "chambermaid's novel," and in the conclusion of *Indiana*. The closest model for this new relationship, proposed by friend and foe alike, was that of a cousin with whom one could be both intimate and equal. Perhaps this is the reason why cousins were the subject of such dire warnings in codes, physiologies, and caricatures. George Sand even has Indiana turn away from her passionate relationship with the unworthy Raymon de Ramière to find happiness with her cousin Ralph. This is as far as artists and writers of the period could go in articulating a strong emotional relationship that would be spared the shoals of momentary infatuation, yet be passionate and companionate at the same time. Fictional characters, both male and female, expressed their yearning for this kind of relationship, even when, as in Balzac's novels, it brings them personal disaster.

In this study I have proposed to refute the assumption that the theme of adultery is timeless and eternal, or is simply a literary trope with no historical significance. It is important to remember, first of all, that when adultery was discussed in the pre-modern period, only the wife's adultery was at issue, for that of the husband was traditionally tolerated as "normal." No doubt the wife's adultery was a long-term concern, continuing for centuries, but this was because arranged marriages were a long-term tradition, and because women displayed a long-term resistance to them – a resistance that threatened the stability of both property relations and the hierarchical social structure. As I have shown in the visual arts, the particular trope of old husband, young wife, and her young lover was by no means timeless and eternal, but arose in the eighteenth century concurrent with ideas of companionate marriage and economic modernity. In its previous incarnations (most famously in the comedies of Molière), the love triangle was situated chronologically *previous* to marriage, as the old tutor or guardian vied with the young lover for his ward's hand. During the period of the Restoration, however, a particular combination of historical circumstances led to the apogee of this relatively new trope of husband, wife, and lover. These circumstances included not only the growing emphasis on individual rights and happiness, but the restoration of many of the Old Regime's harsh punishments for female adultery in the new Civil Code, which also instituted severe penalties for bachelor lovers regardless of class, abolished primogeniture, and established equal inheritance for all children born in a marriage. The repeal of divorce and the installation of the stern religious morality of "Throne and Altar" at the advent of the Restoration served only to create a situation where the older ecology of the marital relationship no longer prevailed. In many ways the values of this period had much in common with the melodramas that were then so popular. Its religious and moral fundamentalism led to Manichaean alternatives, with women's behavior perceived as good or evil, with no nuances or latitude. The new print pendants of the Good and Bad Mother amply demonstrate this.

While this study has focused on the issue of adultery during the Restoration, it should be evident by now that the issue had symbolic as well as social consequences. It became the nexus of concerns about marriage because it stood at the crossroads between the old values and the new. The lack of individual marital choice was by no means new, and yet it was, no doubt, felt more keenly in this post-Revolutionary period when reaction followed hard upon liberalization, and when fissures had developed in paternal authority. The new model of companionate marriage had already begun to replace the older model of corporate marriage, but during these decades the two shared an uneasy coexistence in the hybrid ideal of the marriage of contradiction. Without the escape clause of divorce, but with new laws not only stipulating that a wife's child will be her husband's heir, but also severely punishing female adultery, there was less leeway for individual solutions to the problem of unsuccessful marriages. This is not to say that adultery was less common in the nineteenth century than in the Old Regime, but it is to acknowledge that, in the later period, attitudes and laws had changed. One of the major changes in the laws was the criminalization of young men; the popularity of the Mazeppa theme was one cultural response by the younger generation to its new, legally precarious, status.

In addition to the very real issue of immediate personal happiness, the symbolism of adultery differed for each group. For bachelors, an adulterous relationship with the young wife of an older man could exemplify generational warfare; its prohibition could typify the many ways in which the gerontocracy of the Restoration limited their lives, choices, and careers. For old husbands, the adultery of a wife could epitomize property theft, an attack against their own authority, and indeed against the entire established social order, as seen most vehemently in the memoir of the marquis de Cairon discussed in chapter 1. For wives, their own adulterous liaison, in addition to whatever personal happiness it brought them, could represent individual freedom and self-determination, since a woman could choose a lover but not a husband.

Battle lines and issues were drawn more clearly during this period than at any other time during the post-Revolutionary years. A telling example of this is the Cairon affair that, during the Restoration, was resolved by the flight into exile in 1826 of the marquise de Cairon and her lover François Soubiranne, in order to avoid two-year prison sentences for adultery. Although the marquis died the same year, the proscribed couple could not return to France until 1831, after the July Revolution of 1830 had toppled the repressive Restoration regime and ushered in a more liberal constitutional monarchy. Under this subsequent regime, the couple not only returned, but even managed to marry, although the law prohibiting marriages between convicted adulterers was not repealed until the twentieth century.[12] Clearly the atmosphere had changed and, if the laws were not yet liberalized, their enforcement was.

The Enlightenment concern for the rights of individuals, even female individuals, included personal happiness, but these concerns, at least as far as women were concerned, often conflicted with the provisions of the Civil Code that enforced a morality that many did not feel or accept. The interlude of legal divorce in France, from 1792 to 1816, provided an experience of another social order, however, and, no matter how much divorce was criticized, its temporary existence cast a long shadow across the rest of the nineteenth century.

Between 1830 and 1834 five motions to reintroduce divorce were voted by the Chamber of Deputies, all rejected by the Chamber of Peers.[13] Bills proposing the legalization of divorce were regularly proposed, debated, and rejected in subsequent decades, until the Naquet Law of 1884 resumed the process, begun during the Revolutionary period, of redefining marriage as a civil con-tract between equals.[14] This process was not completed until 1975, when divorce by mutual consent was re-established in France for the first time since 1792, and all references to adultery were removed from the legal code.[15] As late as 1899 approximately one-third of those prosecuted for adultery spent time in jail, with the others being fined, and it was not until 1904 that adul-terous couples were legally entitled to marry.[16] The French equivalent of the "great leap forward" in the social legislation of the Revolutionary period was indeed partly undone during the Restoration, to the great unhappiness of many individuals, but in the long term it proved impossible to return fully to the past.

The cultural milieu of the Restoration offered a clear choice between opposed ideologies of marriage, the old and the new. Works of art and literature were more nakedly ideological than during periods when distinctions and positions are blurred by laxity either in articulation or in execution, or when unchal-lenged assumptions about the "normal" and the "natural" blind one to the ideological foundations of all art and social institutions. The Restoration was incontrovertibly a period of reaction, and yet, as Emmanuel de Waresquiel, Benoît Yvert, Marie-Claude Chaudonneret, and Sheryl Kroen have shown, it was also a period when many of the forward-looking reforms and innovations of the Revolutionary period, though contested, were assimilated into French culture and society and took root there.[17] The "marriage of inclination," for example, though still controversial, emerged from the period firmly established as an ideal, if not yet a reality.

In my exploration of the ways in which cultural tropes change, I have com-pared examples from different periods, most notably in chapter 2 on conduct manuals and in chapter 3 on graphic imagery. What is retained across time is always of equal importance with what is eliminated; transformations are as important as innovations. In the modern period, and especially in the study of the visual arts, audiences are more attuned to innovation than to revision, and yet, in the study of cultural history the two should have equal importance. During the Restoration, the maintenance of the focus on female adultery shows that the issue continued to be of concern, as were the perceived dangers of women's imaginative excursions through reading and the risks of her having friends of either sex; warnings on these perils were repeated from one century to the next. What was new in post-Revolutionary France were warnings about adulterine children, images of angry, stalking, murderous husbands, and the pendants comparing arranged and chosen marriages. What was revised were the standard escapist literary plots of young love conquering all: during the Restoration, it was old men who triumphed over young lovers, either happily, as in the plays of Scribe and Delavigne, or tragically, as in Hugo's *Hernani*. And what disappeared were the light-hearted references to cuckoldry. As Dumas said, it was no longer something to laugh about.

There are also shifts in tropes according to media. While the sly etchings and engravings of the Old Regime were often based on paintings, by the nineteenth century the two media of painting and prints were clearly distinct. Lithographs continued the Rococo tradition, witty and cynical, but paintings no longer depicted such risqué subject matter. High art, exhibited in the official government Salon, was now obliged to present a moral, public façade, while the "low" art of caricature never appeared in such hallowed precincts and so could be as vulgar and ribald as its creators and its audiences desired.

Perhaps the clearest commentary on the continuation of tropes across the centuries was evidenced by these prints, in which the images plainly continue old concerns, while also inflecting them, abandoning them, inventing new ones. In chapter 3, I traced marriage and its discontents across a century of such images, from the light-hearted lovers of the Old Regime through the happy mothers and fathers who replaced them, to the angry, vengeful husbands and bad adulterous wives of the nineteenth century. Paintings of the early nineteenth century, however, comment on sexual mores only by cloaking them with the veil of literature, myth, or history; this is how the Mazeppa theme assumed such significance in the period. The relation of high art themes to similar concerns in the more popular lithographic caricatures would go unnoticed without a comparison of the two media.

The purpose of this study has not been to claim that any of these tropes disappeared at the end of the Restoration. Far from it. In most cases they continued throughout the nineteenth century, as Zola insisted when he wrote, as late as 1881: "Adultery is the plague of the bourgeoisie just as prostitution is the plague of the lower classes."[18] The problem continued to "plague" the bourgeoisie, and would do so for some time to come – at least until divorce provided a solution to marital woes. When the Manichaean harshness of the Restoration period ended in 1830, the subject gradually lost the multivalent symbolism that had overlaid it and had brought it to the fore in the *mentalité* of this earlier period. Daumier's lithograph "The Adultery Complaint" (Figure 97) displays an almost benign good humor replacing the edgy hostility that had characterized earlier works on similar themes. The husband's lawyer addresses the judges, stating: "Magistrates, my client is certain of the facts. But this personal conviction was not enough for him, he felt it necessary to share it with your tribunal, with the large audience that is here present . . . with all of France. This is the task that I have undertaken out of solicitude for my client, and I believe that I have succeeded in rendering his situation clear to everyone. Now the only thing missing is for my client to see his . . . social situation confirmed by a legal judgment, and you are too equitable, Magistrates, to refuse him this ultimate satisfaction." By 1846, Gavarni, and probably most viewers, regarded the subject as a bore, as can be seen in "At the Théâtre-Français: The Hundred-and-First Performance of 'The Husband, the Wife, and the Lover'" (Figure 98). In the following year, Balzac's *Splendors and Miseries of Courtesans* was completed and published in its entirety. For the rest of the century, prostitution

Chez Bauger Rue au Croissant 16.   Chez Aubert gal. Vero-Dodat.   1840-3854.   Imp. d'Aubert & C.ie

LA PLAINTE EN ADULTÈRE.

"Magistrats, mon client est sur de son fait. Mais cette conviction personnelle ne lui suffisait pas ;
il fallait encore qu'il la fit partager à votre tribunal, au nombreux auditoire qui nous entoure . . . . . .
à la France entière. Telle est la tache que je me suis chargé d'accomplir dans l'intérêt même de mon
client, et je crois avoir réussi à rendre la chose claire à tous les yeux. Maintenant il ne manque plus à
mon client que de voir sa . . . . position sociale constatée par un jugement authentique, et vous êtes trop
justes, Magistrats, pour lui refuser cette dernière satisfaction."

97   Honoré Daumier, "The Adultery Complaint. Magistrates, my client is certain
of the facts. But this personal conviction wasn't enough for him, he felt it
necessary to share it with your tribunal, with the large audience that is here present . . . with all of France. This is the task that I have undertaken out of solicitude
for my client, and I believe that I have succeeded in rendering his situation clear
to everyone. Now the only thing missing is for my client to see his . . . social
situation confirmed by a legal judgment, and you are too equitable, Magistrates,
to refuse him this ultimate satisfaction." *Moeurs conjugales*, 30, in *Le Charivari*,
29 Nov. 1840. Lithograph. Lith. Aubert, Dist. Bauger & Aubert. Bibliothèque
nationale de France, Paris. ("La Plainte en adultère. Magistrats, mon client est sûr
de son fait. Mais cette conviction personnelle ne lui suffisait pas, il fallait encore
qu'il la fit partager à votre tribunal, au nombreux auditoire qui nous entoure . . .
à la France entière. Telle est la tache que je me suis chargé d'accomplir dans
l'intérêt même de mon client, et je crois avoir réussi à rendre la chose claire à tous
les yeux. Maintenant il ne manque plus à mon client que de voir sa . . . position
sociale constatée par un jugement authentique et vous êtes trop justes, Magistrats,
pour lui refuser cette dernière satisfaction.")

ŒUVRES NOUVELLES DE GAVARNI

Chez Aubert Pl. de la Bourse. 29

AU THEATRE FRANÇAIS,

La Cent-et-unième Représentation de.

LE MARI, LA FEMME ET L'AMANT.

98   Gavarni, "At the Théâtre-Francais: The Hundred-and-First Performance of 'The Husband, the Wife, and the Lover.'" *Affiches Illustrées: Annonces, réclames, enseignes*, in *Le Charivari*, 28 May 1846. Lithograph. Lith. & Dist. Aubert. Bibliothèque nationale de France, Paris. ("Au Théâtre-Français: Le Cent-et-unième Représentation de *Le Mari, la femme et l'amant*")

would occupy the role that adultery had earlier played as the sexual transgression that symbolized society's ills.

This study has explored the many ways in which art and history can interact and intersect, from the most literal to the most abstract. Works of art and literature permit an imaginative acting out of social scenarios through articulation, recognition, allusion, or even negation, and provide a model of experience in uncertain times. If mothers brought their daughters to Scribe's *Marriage of Reason* as a warning against ill-considered passionate attachments, how many other young women, despite the warnings of their parents and their conduct manuals, were learning of the existence of love, both licit and illicit, through reading novels? Experience is often evaluated through the prism of art. It helps us to think about our lives. It speaks to us on many levels, as distinctly different as reading a newspaper, visiting an art exhibition, attending a play with family or friends, or reading a novel alone.

And yet works of art look different when seen, or heard, or read against the fabric of lived experience, woven into its quotidian concerns. This is how contemporaries experience works of art, and what I have tried, in this study, to convey. Over time, however, these threads of lived experience fade, and subsequent generations experience the same works differently. This does not imply that, stripped of their contemporaneity, they somehow become better or purer. Far from it, they merely assume the contemporaneity of another period, with different patterns emerging from their warp and weft.

Notes

Preface

1 Stendhal, *De l'amour* [1822], ed. Henri Martineau (Paris: Garnier frères, 1959), 218. [Il est absurde de dire à une jeune fille: vous serez fidèle à l'époux de votre choix et ensuite de la marier par force à un vieillard ennuyeux.]

2 See, for a discussion of this project, Pierre Bourdieu, *The Field of Cultural Production: Essays on Art and Literature* (New York: Columbia University Press, 1993), 29–73, 254–66.

3 Alexandre Dumas, "Le Cocuage, l'adultère et le code civil," *Mes Mémoires* [1852–55], ed. Pierre Josserand, 5 vols. (Paris: Gallimard, 1954–68), 4, CC, 304–05.

4 Patricia Mainardi, "Why is Caricature Funny?," *Persistence of Vision*, 14 (1997), 8–24.

5 Patricia Mainardi, "Impertinent Questions," *French Historical Studies*, 19/12 (Fall 1995), 399–414.

6 Patricia Mainardi, "Husbands, Wives and Lovers: *Mazeppa*, or Marriage and Its Discontents in Nineteenth-Century France," in Régis Michel, ed., *Géricault*, 2 vols. (Paris: La Documentation française, 1996), 1, 273–92, 312–17.

7 Patricia Mainardi, "Mazeppa," *Word & Image*, 16/4 (Oct.–Dec. 2000), 335–51.

Introduction

1 It should be noted that "cuckoldry" (extra-marital cheating) was the vernacular term, while "adultery" was the legal offense. Alexandre Dumas, "Le Cocuage, l'adultère et le code civil," *Mes Mémoires*, [1852–55], ed. Pierre Josserand, 5 vols. (Paris: Gallimard, 1954–68), 4, CC, 304–05. [Il est vrai que, du temps de Molière, cela s'appelait le cocuage, et qu'on en riait; que, de nos jours, cela s'appelle l'adultère, et qu'on en pleure. / Pourquoi donc ce qui s'appelait cocuage, au XVIIe siècle, s'appelle-t-il adultère au XIXe? / Je vais vous le dire. / C'est qu'au XVIIe siècle, le code civil n'était point inventé. / Le code civil? Bon! que vient faire ici le code civil? / Ce qu'il vient y faire, vous allez le voir. / Au XVIIe siècle, on avait le droit d'aînesse, les majorats, les fidéicommis, les substitutions; au XVIIe siècle, l'aîné des fils héritant du nom, du titre et de la fortune, les autres fils étaient M. le chevalier, M. le mousquetaire, M. l'abbé. / On attachait au premier une croix de Malte à la boutonnière, on affublait le second de la casaque de buffle, on dotait le troisième d'un petit collet. / Quant aux filles, on ne s'en occupait même pas; elles épousaient qui elles voulaient lorsqu'elles étaient jolies, qui elles pouvaient lorsqu'elles étaient laides. Pour celles qui n'épousaient ni qui elles voulaient ni qui elles pouvaient, restait le couvent, ce grand cimetière des cœurs. / Or, quoique les trois quarts des mariages fussent des mariages de convenance, et se contractassent entre gens qui se connaissaient à peine, le mari était presque toujours sûr que son premier enfant mâle était de lui. / Ce premier enfant mâle, c'est-à-dire ce fils héritier de son nom, de son titre et de sa fortune, une fois fait par lui, que lui importait qui faisait M. le chevalier, M. le mousquetaire ou M. l'abbé? La chose, par ma foi! lui était bien égale; souvent même il ne s'en enquérait pas. [. . .] / De nos jours, c'est bien différent, peste! / La loi a aboli le droit d'aînesse; le code proscrit les majorats, les substitutions, les fidéicommis. / Le partage de la fortune est égal entre les enfants; il n'y a même plus d'exception pour les filles: les filles, comme les garçons, ont droit à l'héritage paternel. / Or, du moment où le *quem nuptiae demonstrant* sait que les enfants nés pendant le mariage partageront sa fortune en portions égales, il tient à ce que ces enfants soient de lui; car l'enfant qui, n'étant point de lui, partage comme ceux qui sont de lui, est tout simple-

ment un voleur. / Voilà pourquoi l'adultère est un crime au XIXe siècle, et pourquoi le cocuage était une plaisanterie au XVIIe.]

2   While the Civil Code legislated equal inheritance among all children born in a marriage, previous customary and written law usually provided that all children had to inherit some of the family assets, though not necessarily an equal share. There had been prosecutions for adultery in the seventeenth century, but Dumas was referring to the frequent and severe prosecutions of the wife's lover that were occurring more often in the nineteenth century. Prosecution of a philandering husband was rare at any time. On Old Regime inheritance, see Ralph E. Giesey, "Rules of Inheritance and Strategies of Mobility in Prerevolutionary France," *American Historical Review*, 82/2 (April 1977), 271–89; Paul Ourliac and J. de Malafosse, *Histoire du droit privé*, 3 vols. (Paris: PUF, 1968), 3: *Le Droit familial*; André Burguière, "La Famille et l'état: Débats et attentes de la société française à la veille de la Révolution," in Irène Théry and Christian Biet, eds., *La Famille, la loi, l'état: De la Révolution au Code civil* (Paris: Imprimerie nationale, 1989), 147–56; Margaret Darrow, *Revolution in the House: Family, Class and Inheritance in Southern France, 1775–1825* (Princeton: Princeton University Press, 1989). For later nineteenth-century commentary on adultery as a social phenomenon, see, for example, Hippolyte Lucas, "La Femme adultère," in *Les Français peints par eux-mêmes*, 8 vols. (Paris: L. Curmer, 1840–42), 3, 265–72; Emile Zola, "L'Adultère dans la bourgeoisie," *Le Figaro*, 28 Feb. 1881; Félix Fénéon, "L'Adultère dans le roman contemporain" [1887], in his *Oeuvres plus que complètes*, ed. Joan U. Halperin, 2 vols. (Geneva: Librairie Droz, 1970), 2, 692–95. Literary scholars have long been interested in this subject; see, for example, Tony Tanner, *Adultery in the Novel: Contract and Transgression* (Baltimore: Johns Hopkins University Press, 1979); Naomi Segal, *The Adulteress's Child: Authorship and Desire in the Nineteenth-Century Novel* (Cambridge: Polity Press, 1992); Bill Overton, *The Novel of Female Adultery: Love and Gender in Continental European Fiction, 1830–1900* (New York: St. Martin's Press, 1996); Nicholas White and Naomi Segal, *Scarlet Letters: Fictions of Adultery from Antiquity to the 1990s* (London: Macmillan, 1997); Nicholas White, *The Family in Crisis in Late Nineteenth-Century French Fiction* (Cambridge: Cambridge University Press, 1999).

3   The literature on family history in the late eighteenth century and the early nineteenth is vast. For histories of pre-Revolutionary family law, see Ourliac and Malafosse, *Histoire du droit privé*, 3: *Le Droit familial*; Jean-Louis Halpérin, *Histoire du droit privé français depuis 1804* (Paris: PUF, 1996). For analysis of specific issues, see James F. Traer, *Marriage and the Family in Eighteenth-Century France* (Ithaca, N.Y.: Cornell University Press, 1980), and several articles by Sarah Hanley: "Engendering the State: Family Formation and State Building in Early Modern France," *French Historical Studies*, 16/1 (Spring 1989), 4–27; "The Monarchic State in Early Modern France: Marital Regime, Government and Male Right," in Adrianna E. Bakos, ed., *Politics, Ideology, and the Law* (Rochester, N.Y.: University of Rochester Press, 1994), 107–26; "Social Sites of Political Practice in France: Lawsuits, Civil Rights, and the Separation of Powers in Domestic and State Government, 1500–1800," *American Historical Review*, 102/1 (Feb. 1997), 27–52; "'The Jurisprudence of the Arrêts': Marital Union, Civil Society and State Formation in France, 1550–1650," forthcoming in *Law History Review*, 21/1 (2003). For the Revolutionary period, see Marcel Garaud and Romuald Szramkiewicz, *La Révolution française et la famille* (Paris: PUF, 1978) and Théry and Biet, eds., *La Famille, la loi, l'état*. For the later nineteenth century, see Rachel G. Fuchs, "Seduction, Paternity and the Law in Fin-de-Siècle France," *The Journal of Modern History*, 72/4 (Dec. 2000), 944–89.

4   See Hanley, "Monarchic State" and "Social Sites," Lynn Hunt, *The Family Romance of the French Revolution* (Berkeley and Los Angeles: University of California Press, 1992), 1–16; Sarah Maza, *Private Lives and Public Affairs: The Causes Célèbres of Prerevolutionary France* (Berkeley and Los Angeles: University of California Press, 1993), 262–311.

5   Natalie Zemon Davis, "Women on Top," in her *Society and Culture in Early Modern France* (Stanford, Calif.: Stanford University Press, 1975), 124–51.

6   Official concern about prostitution was not culturally reinforced until after Alexandre-J.-B. Parent-Duchâtelet's proto-sociological study, *Prostitution in the City of Paris*, was published in 1836. Balzac read Parent-Duchâtelet's book and wrote *Splendeurs et misères des courtisanes* (1838–47). From then on, prostitution constituted not only a political issue, but provided a seemingly inexhaustible subject for art and literature as well. See

Parent-Duchâtelet, *De la prostitution dans la ville de Paris* (1836), annotated and edited by Alain Corbin as *La Prostitution à Paris au XIXe siècle* (Paris: Seuil, 1981). See also Corbin, *Les Filles de noces: Misère sexuelle et prostitution (19e et 20e siècles)* (Paris: Aubier Montaigne, 1978); Jill Harsin, *Policing Prostitution in Nineteenth-Century Paris* (Princeton: Princeton University Press, 1985); Charles Bernheimer, *Figures of Ill Repute: Representing Prostitution in Nineteenth-Century France* (Cambridge, Mass., Harvard University Press, 1989); Hollis Clayson, *Painted Love: Prostitution in French Art of the Impressionist Era* (New Haven: Yale University Press, 1991). On Balzac's *Splendors and Miseries of Courtesans*, see Bernheimer, *Figures of Ill Repute*, 35. Hugo's play *Marion de Lorme* (1829) tells the tragic tale of a former prostitute's attempts to become respectable, but government censors refused to allow its production; according to Keith Wren, this was more because of its references to politics than because of its treatment of prostitution; see his *Hugo: Hernani and Ruy Blas* (London: Grant & Cutler, 1982), 17–18.

7   *Le Palais-Royal, ou les filles en bonne fortune* (Paris: Bocquet, 1815) lists seven levels of prostitute: kept women and mistresses of financiers and men of rank; dancers, actresses, singers, and so on, who are half mercenary and half in love with their protectors; bourgeois wives with lovers; servants who sleep with their employers; working women, usually in the needle trades, who are part-time prostitutes; street-walkers; and, finally, the most degraded urban whores; see 64–67.

8   See Maza, *Private Lives*, 283. On bourgeois marriage, see also Adeline Daumard, *La Bourgeoisie parisienne de 1815 à 1848* (Paris: SEVPEN, 1963), 329.

9   For a discussion of changing expectations from marriage, see Roderick Phillips, *Putting Asunder: A History of Divorce in Western Society* (Cambridge: Cambridge University Press, 1988), 354–60. Jean-Louis Flandrin has noted that the expression "amour conjugal" rarely appeared in France before 1770; see his *Familles: Parenté, maison, sexualité dans l'ancienne société* (Paris: Seuil, rev. 1984), 165. Other scholars who have stressed the late eighteenth-century origins of romantic marital love include Edward Shorter, *The Making of the Modern Family* (New York: Basic Books, 1975), 56–65, and Lawrence Stone, *The Family, Sex and Marriage in England, 1500–1800* (New York: Harper & Row, 1977), 325–404. For a literary study, see Denis de Rougemont, *Amour et l'Occident*

[1939], trans. Montgomery Belgion as *Love in the Western World* (New York: Harcourt Brace, 1940).

10   Condorcet [Antoine Caritat, marquis de Condorcet], *Oeuvres de Condorcet*, ed. A. Condorcet O'Connor and F. Arago, 12 vols. (Paris: Firmin-Didot frères, 1847–49), 6: *Esquisse d'un tableau historique des progrès de l'esprit humain*, "Fragment de l'histoire de la xe époque," 523.

11   The standard histories of the Restoration are Guillaume de Bertier de Sauvigny, *La Restauration* [1955], trans. Lynn M. Case as *The Bourbon Restoration* (Philadelphia: University of Pennsylvania Press, 1967), and André Jardin and André-Jean Tudesq, *La France des notables*, 2 vols. [1973], trans. Elborg Forster as *Restoration & Reaction 1815–1848* (Cambridge: Cambridge University Press, 1983). For a revisionist approach, see Emmanuel de Waresquiel and Benoît Yvert, *Histoire de la Restauration, 1814–1830: Naissance de la France moderne* (Paris: Librairie académique Perrin, [1996]).

12   Although the ideological ferment of the early 1800s has generated relatively little interest from cultural historians, two welcome additions to the meager historiography of cultural history, focusing on different issues, are Sheryl Kroen, *Politics and Theater: The Crisis of Legitimacy in Restoration France, 1815–1830* (Berkeley and Los Angeles: University of California Press, 2000), and Marie-Claude Chaudonneret, *L'Etat et les artistes: De la Restauration à la monarchie de Juillet, 1855–1833* (Paris: Flammarion, 1999).

13   Quoted in Antoine Le Roux de Lincy, *Le Livre des proverbes français, précédé de recherches historiques sur les proverbes français et leur emploi dans la littérature du moyen âge et de la renaissance*, 2 vols. (Paris: Adolphe Delahays, rev. 2/1859), 2, 267. [Chacun est roy en sa maison.]

14   André Burguière has divided pre-Revolutionary French family law into three broad types: in the north and west there were more egalitarian nuclear families (*modèle nucléaire*); in the south, patriarchal, inegalitarian families (*modèle de la famille-souche*); and in the center, communal families that pooled resources and maintained a horizontal indivisible front (*modèle communautaire*); see Burguière, "La Famille et l'état." For thorough analyses of pre-Revolutionary family law, see Ourliac and Malafosse, *Histoire du droit privé*, 3; Traer, *Marriage and the Family*. For the process whereby jurisdiction over French marriage law was transferred gradually from the

Church to the State, see Hanley, "The Jurisprudence of the Arrêts."

15   Maza, *Private Lives*, 286. Phillips, *Putting Asunder*, 351, points out that European élites in general were permissive about extramarital sexuality; see also Gérard Duplessis-Le Guélinel, *Les Mariages en France*, Cahiers de la Fondation nationale des sciences politiques, 53 (Paris: Armand Colin, 1954), 37.

16   Duplessis-Le Guélinel, ibid., 21–24; Daumard also makes this point in *La Bourgeoisie parisienne*, 329.

17   See Arlette Farge and Michel Foucault, eds., *Le Désordre des familles: Lettres de cachet des archives de la Bastille* (Paris: Gallimard, 1982); Traer, *Marriage and the Family*, 139–42; Hunt, *Family Romance*, 19–20.

18   Hanley, "Social Sites," 31.

19   On chivalry and marriage, see Rougemont, *Love in the Western World*, trans. Belgion, 32–35.

20   For a discussion of these new ideas, see Hunt, *Family Romance*, esp. chaps. 2, "The Rise and Fall of the Good Father," and 6, "Rehabilitating the Family." The new "family values" are also discussed extensively by Traer, *Marriage and the Family*, and in Part 3 of Jean Delumeau and Daniel Roche, eds., *Histoire des pères et de la paternité* (Paris: Larousse-HER, rev. 2000).

21   See Duplessis-Le Guélinel, *Mariages en France*, 21–28.

22   Traer, *Marriage and the Family*, 39–40; Ourliac and Malafosse, *Histoire du droit privé*, 3, 188. Hanley, in "The Jurisprudence of the Arrêts" and "Social Sites," makes the point that there was no royal law *per se*, but through case law and precedent the State gradually succeeded in gaining jurisdiction over marriage.

23   On Pothier's importance, see Ourliac and Malafosse, *Histoire du droit privé*, 3, 16–17.

24   Robert-Joseph Pothier, "Traité de la puissance du mari sur la personne et les biens de la femme" [1768], in *Oeuvres complètes de Pothier*, ed. Saint-Albin Berville, 26 vols. (Paris: Thomine & Fortic, 1821–24), 10, 653. For examples of how it worked in practice, see Hanley, "Social Sites." [Le mariage, en formant une société entre le mari et la femme, dont le mari est le chef, donne au mari, en la qualité qu'il a de chef de cette société un droit de puissance sur la personne de la femme, qui s'étend aussi sur ses biens.]

25   Ibid., 10, 654. [La puissance du mari sur la personne de la femme consiste, par le droit naturel, dans le droit qu'a le mari d'exiger d'elle tous les devoirs de soumission qui sont dus à un supérieur.]

26   On Roman family law, see Beryl Rawson, "The Roman Family," in Beryl Rawson, ed., *The Family in Ancient Rome: New Perspectives* (Ithaca, N.Y.: Cornell University Press, 1986); see also Traer, *Marriage and the Family*, 24–26.

27   Pothier, "Traité du contrat de mariage," in *Oeuvres complètes*, 10, Part 6, chap. 3, art. 1, no. 516. For examples of how this worked in practice, see Hanley, "Social Sites." [L'adultère que commet la femme est infiniment plus contraire au bon ordre de la société civile, puisqu'il tend à dépouiller des familles, et à en faire passer les biens à des enfants adultérins, qui y sont étrangers; au lieu que l'adultère commis par le mari, quoique très-criminel en soi, est à cet égard sans conséquence. Ajoutez qu'il n'appartient pas à la femme, qui est une inférieure, d'avoir inspection sur la conduite de son mari, qui est son supérieur. Elle doit présumer qu'il lui est fidèle, et la jalousie ne doit pas le porter à faire des recherches de sa conduite.]

28   Jean-François Fournel, *Traité de l'adultère considéré dans l'ordre judiciaire* (Paris: Jean-François Bastien, 1778); Pothier, "Traité du contrat de mariage," in *Oeuvres complètes*, 10, Part 6, chap. 3, art. 2, no. 527. On the relation to Justinian's Novelle 134, see Ourliac and Malafosse, *Histoire du droit privé*, 3, 149.

29   Fournel, *Traité de l'adultére*, 3.

30   On Old Regime law, see Ourliac and Malafosse, *Histoire du droit privé*, 3; Michèle Bordeaux, "Le Maître et l'infidèle: Des Relations personnelles entre mari et femme de l'ancien droit au Code civil," in Théry and Biet, eds., *La Famille, la loi, l'état*, 432–46, and Fournel, *Traité de l'adultére*, 354–59. Several histories were written around the time that the Naquet Law (1884) re-established divorce; see Henri Coulon, *Le Divorce et l'adultère: De l'abrogation des lois pénales en matière d'adultère* (Paris: Marchal & Billard, 1892), 8–10, and his *Le Divorce et la séparation de corps*, 3 vols. (Paris: Marchal & Billard, 1890), 1, 166–68.

31   Voltaire, "Adultère," *Questions sur l'Encyclopédie, par des amateurs*, 6 vols. (1775), 1, 60–71.

32   Bordeaux, "Le Maître et l'infidèle," 437; Hanley, "Engendering the State," 18–19;

Florence Laroche-Gisserot, "Pratiques de la dot en France au xixe siècle," *Annales ESC* (Nov.–Dec. 1988), 6, 1433–52.

33 Pothier, "Traité du contrat de mariage," in *Oeuvres complètes*, 10: see the sections "Des effets de la séparation d'habitation," 500–501, and "De la séparation d'habitation qui intervient sur la demande du mari," 502–04.

34 See Hanley, "Social Sites," for examples of such suits in the Old Regime. The practice seems to have continued unabated into the nineteenth century.

35 Voltaire, "Adultère," 60–71; see also Hanley, "Social Sites," 44–46.

36 Maza, *Private Lives*, 15.

37 See Duplessis-Le Guélinal, *Mariages en France*, 29.

38 See J. Mulliez, "La Volonté d'un homme," in Delumeau and Roche, eds., *Histoire des pères*, 289–90.

39 This is the main thesis of Hunt, *Family Romance*. For the art-historical ramifications, see Carol Duncan, "Fallen Fathers: Images of Authority in Pre-Revolutionary French Art," in her *The Aesthetics of Power: Essays in Critical Art History* (Cambridge: Cambridge University Press, 1993), 27–56.

40 For an analysis of the complicated inheritance laws of the pre-Revolutionary period and the results of the changes wrought by the Civil Code, see Suzanne Desan, "War between Brothers and Sisters: Inheritance Law and Gender Politics in Revolutionary France," *French Historical Studies*, 20/4 (Fall 1997), 597–634, and her "Reconstituting the Social after the Terror: Family, Property and the Law in Popular Politics," *Past and Present*, 164 (Aug. 1999), 81–121. For an overview of the nineteenth-century practice of dowry, see Laroche-Gisserot, "Pratiques de la dot."

41 "15 mars 1790: Décret relatif aux droits féodaux," in J.-B. Duvergier, *Collection complète des lois, décrets, ordonnances, règlements et avis du Conseil d'état*, 91 vols. (Paris: Guyot & Scribe, 1824–91), 1 *(1788–1790)*, 114–21.

42 "8 avril 1791: Décret relatif au partage des successions *ab intestat*," in ibid., 2: *(1790–1791)*, 348–49.

43 "7 mars 1793: Décret qui abolit la faculté de tester en ligne direct," in ibid., 5: *(1792–1793)*, 185.

44 "12 brumaire an 2 (2 novembre 1793): Décret relatif aux droits des enfants nés hors du mariage," in ibid., 6: *(1793–1794)*, 269–71.

45 On Old Regime customs, see Ourliac

and Malafosse, *Histoire du droit privé*, 3, 290. For changes during the Revolutionary period, see Desan, "War between Brothers and Sisters," and "Reconstituting the Social." See also "5 brumaire an 2 (26 octobre 1793): Décret contenant plusieurs dispositions relatives aux actes et contrats civils," in Duvergier, *Collection complète des lois*, 6: *(1793–1794)*, 256–57; and "17 nivôse an 2 (6 janvier 1794): Décret relatif aux donations et successions," in ibid., 373–84, art. 13.

46 "16–26 mars 1790: Décret concernant les personnes détenues en vertu d'ordres particuliers," in ibid., 1: *(1788–1790)*, 121–23. See also Burguière, "La Famille et l'état," 153; Farge and Foucault, eds., *Le Désordre des familles*, 359–63.

47 See James F. Traer, "The French Family Court," *History*, 59 (June 1974), 211–28; also his *Marriage and the Family*, 139–42.

48 Traer, *Marriage and the Family*, 164.

49 See Titre II, article 7 of "Constitution Française: 3 septembre 1791," in Duvergier, *Collection complète des lois*, 3: *(1791)*, 242. [La loi ne considère le mariage que comme contrat civil.]

50 On article 13, "Projet de loi sur la police municipale," see Pierre Lascoumes, Pierrette Poncela, and Pierre Lenoël, *Au Nom de l'ordre: Une Histoire politique du code pénal* (Paris: Hachette, 1989), 144–45; see also the text and discussion in Darlene Gay Levy, Harriet Branson Applewhite, and Mary Durham Johnson, *Women in Revolutionary Paris* (Urbana: University of Illinois Press, 1979); Etta Palm d'Aelders, "Adresse des citoyennes françoises à l'Assemblée nationale" (1791), in *Recueil sur les femmes* [n.d.], Bibliothèque historique de la ville de Paris, 1/15, 37–40, trans. in Levy, Applewhite, and Johnson, 75–77.

51 Palm d'Aelders, "Adresse des citoyennes françoises," 38; see also Hanley, "Social Sites," 27–28. [surpasse tout ce qui a été fait de plus injuste dans les siècles barbares.]

52 *Archives parlementaires de 1787 à 1860: Recueil complet des débats législatifs et politiques des chambres françaises*, ed. Jérôme Mavidal and Emile Laurent, 1st ser.: *(1789–1799)*, 96 vols. (Paris: Paul Dupont, 1879–87), 28: *(6 juillet au 28 juillet 1791)*, 7 July 1791, 29. [Les peines proposées par le comité sont sans contredit beaucoup plus douces que les peines prononcées par les anciennes lois, mais je les trouve encore injustes, ces peines; parce que très certainement, par la con-

naissance que nous avons de la société, il est très vrai de dire que souvent les hommes sont beaucoup plus coupables que les femmes.]

53   Ibid., 29. [il y aurait même de l'injustice après avoir bien établi les droits des hommes dans ce contrat réciproque, d'avoir oublié ou négligé quels pourraient être les droits des femmes.]

54   Louis-Antoine-Léon de Saint-Just, "Esprit de la Révolution et de la Constitution de France" [1791], in his *Théorie politique*, ed. Alain Liénard (Paris: Seuil, 1976), 77–78. [je veux une bonne fois qu'on m'explique pourquoi le mari qui met des enfants adultérins dans la maison d'un autre, ou de plusieurs autres, est moins criminel que la femme qui n'en peut mettre qu'un dans la sienne.]

55   "20 septembre 1792: Décret qui détermine les causes, le mode et les effets du divorce," in Duvergier, *Collection complète des lois*, 4: *(1791–1792)*, 476–82. Divorce was first discussed in the National Constituent Assembly on April 8, 1790; for summaries, see Phillips, *Putting Asunder*, 175–90, 256–76; Francis Ronsin, *Le Contrat sentimental: Débats sur le mariage, l'amour, le divorce, de l'Ancien Régime à la Restauration* ([Paris]: Aubier, 1990), 39–51; Traer, *Marriage and the Family*, 105–36; Hanley, "Social Sites," 49–50; Theresa McBride, "Public Authority and Private Lives: Divorce after the French Revolution," *French Historical Studies*, 17/3 (Spring 1992), 747–68.

56   Hanley, "Social Sites," 49.

57   Statistics from Gérard Thibault-Laurent, *La Première Introduction du divorce en France sous la Révolution et l'Empire (1792–1816)* (thèse pour le doctorat, Clermont-Ferrand: Moderne, 1938), 189–90. Phillips, *Putting Asunder*, 256–78, estimates that there were almost 20,000 divorces granted in France in the nine largest cities alone from 1792 to 1803; see also Traer, *Marriage and the Family*, 188, n. 55.

58   Jean-Etienne-Marie Portalis, "Exposé des motifs du projet de loi sur le mariage, formant le titre v du Code civil, présenté le 16 ventôse an XI" [March 7, 1803], in *Discours, rapports et travaux inédits sur le Code civil*, ed. Frédéric Portalis (Paris: Joubert, Librairie de la cour de cassation, 1844), 184. [Les pères et les aïeuls sont toujours magistrats dans leurs familles.]

59   On the circumstances leading up to the formulation of the Civil Code, see Jean-Louis Halpérin, *L'Impossible Code civil* (Paris: PUF, 1992).

60   See Traer, *Marriage and the Family*, 166–91.

61   See Bordeaux, "Le Maître et l'infidèle," and P.-Antoine Fenet, *Pothier analysé dans ses rapports avec le Code civil, et mis en ordre, sous chacun des articles de ce code* (Paris: L'Auteur, Dépôt, rue Saint-André des arts, 1826). 75 per cent of the Civil Code was taken directly from Pothier; see Hanley, "Social Sites," 50, n. 84.

62   Ibid., 49.

63   Hunt, *Family Romance*, 193–204.

64   Traer, *Marriage and the Family*, 92–97.

65   "20–25 septembre 1792: Décret qui détermine le mode de constater l'état civil des citoyens," in Duvergier, *Collection complète des lois*, 4: *(1791–1792)*, 482–88.

66   See Traer, *Marriage and the Family*, 105–36, and McBride, "Public Authority."

67   Previously, adultery had been prosecuted through case-law precedents, but there was no law *per se*. See "30 ventôse–11 germinal an XI (21–31 mars 1803): Loi sur le divorce," in Duvergier, *Collection complète des lois*, 14: *(1803–1804)*, 40; Phillips, *Putting Asunder*, 185.

68   Traer, *Marriage and the Family*, 188, n. 55; Thibault-Laurent, *La Première Introduction du divorce*, 189–91.

69   "Procès-verbaux du Conseil d'état: Séance du 15 novembre 1808," in Jean-Guillaume Locré, *La Législation civile, commerciale et criminelle de la France, ou Commentaire et complément des codes français*, 31 vols. (Paris: Treuffel & Würtz, 1827–31), 30, 397–98. [En effet, dans le projet, on rentre dans le système de l'ancien droit. Autrefois le divorce n'était point admis. En conséquence, la loi permettait au mari de poursuivre la punition de la femme adultère, sans que le lien qui les unissait fût rompu. Il pouvait même la reprendre, et faire ainsi cesser la peine. / Le Code Napoléon, au contraire, suppose que la peine de l'adultère ne sera prononcée contre la femme qu'après que le mari aura obtenu le divorce, et que la preuve du crime aura été acquise par la procédure sur laquelle le jugement de divorce est rendu. / C'est dans cette doctrine qu'il convient de se renfermer: l'action en adultère ne doit être admise que comme moyen de parvenir au divorce. Il serait scandaleux qu'un mari fît condamner sa femme comme infidèle, et que néanmoins il ne voulût pas rompre avec elle.]

70   Ibid., 30, 398. [Il faut laisser libre le mari que veut la faire châtier, sans divorcer ni se séparer.]

71 Ibid., 30, 399. Eugène de Beauharnais was the stepson of Napoléon, Josephine's son by her first husband, Alexandre de Beauharnais. [S.A.S. Le Prince Archichancelier de l'Empire [. . .] Il semble aussi à S.A.S. qu'un crime qui a des suites aussi désastreuses que l'adultère, doit être puni d'une peine plus sévère qu'un emprisonnement de trois mois à deux ans.]

72 Ibid., 30, 399–400. [Ce renvoi serait encore plus inconvenant, si la personne accusée comme complice de l'adultère tenait un rang distingué dans l'Etat.]

73 Ibid., 30, 397. [Il serait très fâcheux qu'un sénateur, qu'un conseiller d'état, qu'un juge, pût être traduit devant les tribunaux sur un simple soupçon de connivence.]

74 "Exposé de motifs du Chapitre Ier du Titre II, Livre III, du Code Pénal, fait par M. le chevalier Faure, Conseiller d'état et orateur du gouvernement, dans la séance du Corps législatif du 7 février 1810," in ibid., 30, 480. Article 298 of the Civil Code specified that a spouse divorced for adultery could never marry the accomplice. [Parmi les attentats aux moeurs est compris la violation de la foi conjugale, soit que ce délit ait été commis par la femme, soit qu'il l'ait été par le mari. L'adultère de la femme est un délit plus grand, parce qu'il entraîne des conséquences plus graves, et qu'il peut faire entrer dans la famille légitime un enfant qui n'appartient point à celui que la loi regarde comme le père. Le Code Pénal, en énonçant la peine qui doit être prononcée contre la femme, n'a fait que se conformer á l'art. 298 du Code Napoléon, de ce Code où l'on remarque partout le respect le plus religieux pour les moeurs: il porte un emprisonnement, par voie de police correctionnelle, de trois mois au moins et de deux ans au plus. / On a rappelé dans le projet l'art. 309 de ce même Code, qui laisse le mari maître d'arrêter l'effet de cette condamnation, en consentant à reprendre sa femme. En effet, la femme n'est coupable qu'envers son mari; il doit donc avoir le droit de lui pardonner. / Si la femme n'est coupable qu'envers le mari, lui seul est en droit de se plaindre; l'action doit être interdite à tout autre, parce que tout autre est sans qualité et sans intérêt. / Bien plus, le mari serait privé de cette action s'il avait été condamné lui-même pour cause d'adultère. Alors la justice le repousserait, comme indigne de sa confiance; et n'ayant pu, comme on va le voir, être convaincu d'adultère que sur la plainte de sa femme, il serait trop à craindre qu'il n'agît par récrimination. / La complice de la femme sera condamné

à la même peine, et, de plus, à l'amende. / A l'égard de la poursuite contre le mari pour cause d'adultère, elle ne peut avoir lieu que sur la plainte de la femme, parce qu'elle seule est intéressée à réclamer contre l'infidélité de son époux, et la femme ne peut intenter cette plainte que lorsqu'il a entretenu sa concubine dans la maison conjugale. Dans tout autre cas, les recherches dégénéreraient souvent en inquisition: mais dans celui prévu par la loi, le délit est notoire; c'est d'après le même esprit que le Code Napoléon n'admet la femme à demander le divorce pour cause d'adultère de son mari, qu'en rapportant la même preuve à l'égard de la concubine. Quant au délit, il sera puni d'une amende. / La loi de 1791 avait gardé le silence sur la violation de la foi conjugale de la part de l'époux ou de l'épouse. Les dispositions du nouveau Code rempliront cette lacune.]

75 On adultery, see Penal Code articles 336–39; on recidivism, see Penal Code article 56.

76 Penal Code article 324. Fournel, *Traité de l'adultère*, 264–65, pointed out that the husband does not have the right to kill his wife even if caught *in flagrante delicto*. [le meurtre commis par l'époux sur son épouse, ainsi que sur le complice, à l'instant où il les surprend en flagrant délit dans la maison conjugale, est excusable.]

77 See A. Bedel, *Nouveau Traité de l'adultère et des enfans adultérins, selon les lois civiles et pénales* (Paris: Warée fils aîné, F. Bernard, 1826), 110–11. Bedel announced his intention of updating Fournel's Old Regime tract. He identified many of the loopholes and anomalies in the Civil and Penal Codes.

78 On young men and older women, see Gabrielle Haubre, "L'Entrée dans le monde: Le Jeune Homme et les femmes (première moitié du XIXe siècle)," in Alain Corbin, Jacqueline Lalouette, and Michèle Riot-Sarcey, eds., *Femmes dans la cité 1815–1871* (Grâne, France: Créaphis [1997]), 261–77.

79 Civil Code article 298: "Dans le cas de divorce admis en justice pour cause d'adultère, l'époux coupable ne pourra jamais se marier avec son complice."

80 See Bedel, *Nouveau Traité*, 64, n. 1, and Pothier, "Traité du contrat de mariage," in *Oeuvres complètes*, 10, Part 6, chap. 3, art. 2, no. 527.

81 On dowry practice, see Laroche-Gisserot, "Pratiques de la dot."

82 See J. Mulliez, "La Volonté d'un homme," 310.

83 Bonald was quoting from his own

book, *Du Divorce considéré au dix-neuvième siècle* (1801); see Chambre des députés no. 115. *Proposition faite à la chambre des députés, par M. de Bonald, Député du département de l'Aveyron: Séance du 26 décembre 1815* (Paris: Hacquert, n.d) [tolérer le divorce, c'est légaliser l'adultère, c'est conspirer avec les passions de l'homme contre sa raison et avec l'homme lui-même contre la société.]

84   "8 mai 1816: Loi sur l'abolition du divorce," in Duvergier, *Collection complète des lois*, 20: *(1815–1816)*, 379; Ronsin, *Le Contrat sentimental*, 235–55. [dans l'intérêt de la religion, des moeurs, de la monarchie et des familles.]

85   "27–29 juillet 1884: Loi qui rétablit le divorce," in ibid., 84: *(1884)*, 231–38. See Phillips, *Putting Asunder*, 422–28; McBride, "Public Authority"; Francis Ronsin, *Les Divorciaires: Affrontements politiques et conceptions du mariage dans la France du XIXe siècle* (Paris: Aubier, 1992), 181–284.

86   "Procès-verbaux du Conseil d'état: Séance du 15 novembre 1808," in Locré, *La Législation civile* 30, 398–99. [Jamais en France la plainte en adultère n'a été admise si le mari ne concluait en même temps à la séparation.]

87   Ibid., 30, 398. [Il serait scandaleux qu'un mari fît condamner sa femme comme infidèle, et que néanmoins il ne voulût pas rompre avec elle.]

1   Unhappy Families

1   Horace Raisson, *Code conjugal, contenant les lois, règles, applications et exemples de l'art de se bien marier et d'être heureux en ménage* (Paris: J.-P. Roret, 1829), 146. [Il faut qu'un mari soit bien sot pour craindre sa femme; mais une femme est cent mille fois plus sotte encore de ne pas craindre son mari.]

2   The opening line of Tolstoy's *Anna Karenina* is "Happy families are all alike; every unhappy family is unhappy in its own way"; see Leo Tolstoy, *Anna Karenina* [1873–76], trans. Constance Garnett [1901] (New York: Modern Library, 1965), 3.

3   Court records for the period of the Restoration (1815–30) were destroyed during the 1871 Commune.

4   Accounts of this trial, that of Antoine Berthet, were published as "Justice criminelle: Cour d'assises de l'Isère (Grenoble)," *Gazette*

des tribunaux (hereafter *GT*), 28, 29, 30, 31 Dec. 1827. The articles are reprinted in Stendhal, *Le Rouge et le noir: Chronique du XIXe siècle* [1830], ed. Béatrice Didier (Paris: Gallimard, 1972), 623–46. For a complete account, see René Fonvieille, *Le Véritable Julien Sorel* (Paris: Arthaud, 1971).

5   "Cour de cassation (section civile) Pourvoi de M. le marquis de Cairon contre l'arrêt de la Cour royale de Rouen, qui a prononcé la séparation de corps," *GT*, 16 Nov. 1825, 1. [un journal qui est dans toutes les mains, que tout le monde lit.]

6   See, for example, AN F7 3868/9/70/71: Police générale. Rapports de la Préfecture de police (1825–27), and AN F7 3877/8/9/80/81: Police générale. Bulletins de Paris (1823–27).

7   See, for example, *Compte général de l'administration de la justice criminelle en France, pendant l'année 1825: Présenté au roi, par le garde des sceaux, ministre secrétaire d'état au département de la justice* (Paris: Imprimerie royale, 1827), 60. The 1825 report was the first compiled, with subsequent reports published annually. See also P. Fayet, *Observations sur la statistique intellectuelle et morale de la France pendant la période de vingt ans (1828–47)* (Paris: Bureau du correspondant, 1851).

8   For example, Madame Costerousse was arrested on January 10, 1826 and sentenced to four months in prison on February 11; see AN F7 3868: Préfecture de police, Rapport général à son excellence le ministre de l'intérieur, 10 janvier 1826, and "Paris, 11 février," *GT*, 12 Feb. 1826, 4. Madame Chatard was arrested for adultery on April 7, 1826, and sentenced to a year in prison on May 31; see "Interrogatoire des individus," AN F7 3869: Préfecture de police, Rapport général, 7 avril 1826, and "Paris, le 31 mai," *GT*, 1 June 1826, 3.

9   "Police correctionnelle de Paris," *GT*, 7 May 1827, 787. [cet affront que les maris trompés se décident si rarement à déférer aux tribunaux.]

10   "Paris, le 31 mai," *GT*, 1 June 1826, 3. [ou les dames de Paris deviennent plus infidèles que jamais, ou les maris parisiens deviennent plus ennemis de l'adultère et plus amis du scandale. Ce qu'il y a de certain, c'est que, depuis quelques temps, nous voyons juger une foule d'infractions au pacte conjugal.]

11   "Police correctionnelle de Paris," *GT*, 15 Sept. 1826, 3. [Ses favoris noirs tombent sous le rasoir; d'énormes moustaches les remplacent, de larges lunettes couvrent ses yeux,

une polonaise verte est substituée au froc habituel et pour achever le déguisement, sa manche entr'ouverte lui donne l'air d'un militaire récemment blessé; son bras est soutenu par une cravate noire en écharpe.]

12   "Police correctionnelle de Paris," *GT*, 29 Oct. 1826, 4. [Le mari restera le maître d'arrêter l'effet de cette condamnation en consentant à reprendre sa femme.]

13   See, for example, "Justice criminelle: Cour royale de Caen," *GT*, 27 Sept. 1826, 1–2; "Justice criminelle: Cour de cassation," *GT*, 18 Aug. 1827, 1217; "Chronique judiciaire," *GT*, 29 June 1827, 1016; "Justice criminelle," *GT*, 5 July 1827, 1041–42. The most common (although not unanimous) decision was that if the husband forgave his wife before judgment was handed down, her accomplice was also forgiven, but after judgment he would have to serve his sentence.

14   Penal Code, Section III, art. 324. [Le meurtre commis par l'époux sur son épouse, ainsi que sur le complice, à l'instant où il les surprend en flagrant délit dans la maison conjugale, est excusable.]

15   "Paris, le 31 mai," *GT*, 1 June 1826, 3–4. For their arrest record, see AN F7 3869: Interrogatoire des individus, Préfecture de police. Rapport général, 7 avril 1826, where his name is given as Peschet. [eussent atteint le dernier degré de criminalité en pareille matière.]

16   "Cour d'assises de l'Hérault (Montpellier)," *GT*, 24 Dec. 1826, 218. [blessures graves]

17   "Cour royale de Rouen," *GT*, 27 Oct. 1827, 1501–02. The plaintiff was identified only as "P." [Il n'en est pas besoin pour la femme coupable; il en est autrement pour le complice; mais pour la femme, le délit d'adultère se prouve par tous les moyens possibles; il suffit que les magistrats aient l'intime conviction de la culpabilité. [. . .] Il doit nécessairement en être ainsi; car on sent la difficulté énorme qu'on éprouverait en semblable occurrence, s'il fallait toujours obtenir des preuves du flagrant délit: souvent la chose serait impossible; le libertinage en serait la conséquence, et l'impunité d'une vie scandaleuse le résultat.]

18   "Chronique judiciaire," *GT*, 24 Oct. 1827, 1492. Madame Lemaire met the same fate in 1826; see "Paris, 2 août," *GT*, 3 Aug. 1826, 4. [ce procès offre cette circonstance remarquable, bien que fréquente, que le sieur Lejeune, son complice, n'était pas poursuivi avec elle, la chambre de conseil n'ayant pas

trouvé dans les faits de l'accusé les preuves indispensables à l'égard de l'homme prévenu d'adultère, c'est-à-dire, le flagrant délit ou une correspondance.]

19   "Cour royale (Ire chambre)," *GT*, 19 March 1826, 2–3. [absous en sa qualité de mari [. . .] injure grave.]

20   "Cour royale de Rouen," *GT*, 23 Oct. 1827, 1486–87; "Justice criminelle: Cour royale de Rouen," *GT*, 25 Oct. 1827, 1494; "Cour royale de Rouen," *GT*, 27 Oct. 1827, 1501–02.

21   "Cour royal de Nîmes," *GT*, 2 Aug. 1827, 1156–57; "Justice civile: Cour royale de Nîmes," *GT*, 17 Sept. 1827, 1340–41.

22   "Chronique judiciaire: Départemens," *GT*, 22 Sept. 1826, 4.

23   "Police correctionnelle de Paris," *GT*, 29 Oct. 1826, 23. For their arrest record, see AN F7 3870: Préfecture de police, Rapport général, Interrogatoires des individus, 12 octobre 1826. Madame Amelle was sentenced to four months, but Theuriet was condemned to a year's imprisonment because he was convicted of theft as well.

24   "Police correctionnelle de Paris," *GT*, 22 Nov. 1826, 82–83.

25   The verse is here quoted by the lawyer for Madame Faure in the adultery prosecution her husband brought against her and Monsieur Empéraire in Valence, reported in "Départemens," *GT*, 28 Jan. 1826, 4. The verse was also cited by the vicomte de S*** [J. P. R. Cuisin], in *Le Conjugalisme, ou L'Art de se bien marier* (Paris: Mansut, 1823), 272, where it was attributed to Jean-Baptiste-Louis Gresset (1709–77), a poet, *littérateur*, and Academician, whose most famous work was the poem "Vert-Vert." [Le bruit est pour le fat, le craint est pour le sot; / L'honnête homme trompé, s'éloigne et ne dit mot.]

26   See Katherine A. Lynch, *Family, Class, and Ideology in Early Industrial France: Social Policy and the Working-Class Family, 1825–1848* (Madison: University of Wisconsin Press, 1988), chap. 3; Jean-Louis Halpérin, *Histoire du droit privé français depuis 1804* (Paris: PUF, 1996), 86.

27   See Adeline Daumard, ed., *Les Fortunes françaises au XIXe siècle* (Paris: Mouton, 1973), 175–95; for the statistic, 195.

28   "Départemens," *GT*, 10 June 1826, 4; 27 June 1826, 3.

29   "Police correctionnelle de Paris (6e chambre)," *GT*, 7 May 1827, 787. [les poursuites intentées á raison de ces délits, devant les

tribunaux correctionels, sont très rares dans la classe ouvrière.]

30 Ibid., 787. [Deux pauvres ouvriers comparaissaient aujourd'hui sous la prévention de ce délit. L'extérieur des deux prévenus, assis tristement l'un à côté de l'autre, avant les débats, ne pouvait à l'avance faire présumer qu'il dût s'agir pour eux d'une semblable accusation. Monsieur Tendre (c'est le coupable) est âgé de 41 ans. Il n'a de joli et de séduisant que son nom. Mme Guichard, sa complice, a depuis 20 ans au moins passé l'âge des illusions. Sa figure rouge et bourgeonnée, sa pétulance quand on l'interroge, forment un contraste frappant avec l'extrême pâleur et l'impassibilité de son complice.]

31 Ibid., 787. [Ecoutons Jean-Denis Guichard exposer sa plainte interrompue à chaque mot par les brisques réparties de la prévenue.]

32 Ibid., 787. [*Guichard*: Je suis marié avec Madame depuis dix ans . . . *La femme vivement*: Oui, et pour mon malheur. *M. le président*: N'interrompez pas. Plaignant, êtes vous marié légitimement? *Guichard*: Oui, M. le président, au civil et à la sainte église catholique. *La femme*: Oui, c'est vrai, et je le répète, malheureusement pour moi.]

33 Ibid., 787. [Qu'avez-vous à répondre? [. . .] Ce que j'ai à répondre, parbleu, c'est qu'il me battait plus souvent qu'à mon tour. Il me laissait sans existence, moi et trois pauvres petits enfants. Quand je lui demandais de l'argent, il me donnait des coups et il me disait: *Va ce soir en gagner*.]

34 Ibid., 787. [*M. le président*: Vous avez fui le domicile conjugal en emportant le mobilier. *La femme*: Beau mobilier! Je demande la huitaine pour faire venir des témoins. Il avait tout vendu, article par article. Je suis sortie en plein jour avec un enfant sur mes bras et dix sous dans ma poche. *M. le président*: Vous aviez une coupable liaison avec Tendre. *La femme*: Je ne le connaissais pas avant de quitter ce g . . . -là [gredin?]. En vendant dans les rues, j'ai fait sa connaissance. Il m'a retirée de la misère et nous avons vécu ensemble.]

35 Ibid., 787. While Tendre's fine is within the limits allowable (100 to 2000 francs), it is so high that this may be a misprint for 100 francs. [Bien obligée! Et ce monsieur, qui m'a tant battue, il n'y a donc rien pour lui?]

36 "Police correctionnelle de Paris," *GT*, 19 Sept. 1827, 1351.

37 See William R. Reddy, "Marriage, Honor, and the Public Sphere in Post-

Revolutionary France: *Séparations de corps, 1815–1848*," *Journal of Modern History*, 65/3 (Sept. 1993), 437–72; see also his *The Invisible Code: Honor and Sentiment in Postrevolutionary France, 1814–1848* (Berkeley and Los Angeles: University of California Press, 1997).

38 "Cour royale," *GT*, 9 Aug. 1826, 1; for the decision on the appeal, see "Justice Civile: Cour royale de Paris," *GT*, 18 Nov. 1826, 65.

39 "Cour de cassation," *GT*, 14 Aug. 1826, 1; "Justice civile: Cour de cassation," *GT*, 31 Aug. 1826, 1. [Une femme à qui un arrêt enjoint de réintégrer la domicile conjugal peut-elle y être contrainte par l'emploi de la force publique? [. . .] Faudrait-il des gendarmes pour réintégrer la femme dans le domicile et dans le lit conjugal?]

40 See "Tribunal de Ire instance," *GT*, 13 Aug. 1827, 1195. For an analysis of French family law, see Paul Ourliac and J. de Malafosse, *Histoire du droit privé*, 3 vols. (Paris: PUF, 1968), 3: *Le Droit familial*.

41 "Tribunal de Lyon," *GT*, 18 Aug. 1827, 1217. [excès et les mauvais traitmens]

42 "Cour royale d'Aix," *GT*, 25 April 1827, 736. [Plusieurs arrêts ont jugé que la séparation de corps n'empêchait pas que la femme ne pût être poursuivie comme coupable d'adultère.]

43 See Penal Code articles 57–58 on probation and recidivism.

44 Natalie Zemon Davis notes this as a wife's standard complaint in her *Fiction in the Archives: Pardon Tales and Their Tellers in Sixteenth-Century France* (Stanford, Calif.: Stanford University Press, 1987), 77–110; since moderate wife-beating was legal, the wives' complaints were probably founded. [excès, sévices et injures graves]

45 "Paris, 2 août 1826," *GT*, 3 Aug. 1826, 4. [L'un des témoins de l'enquête a déposé, entre autres faites, qu'ayant voulu s'interposer entre les deux époux dans un de leur combats, le sieur Perrier lui saisit la main avec violence: Vous me cassez la main! s'écria le témoin. – *Ah! pardon, dit Perrier, je croyais que c'était celle de ma femme.*]

46 "Justice criminelle: Police correctionnelle de Paris," *GT*, 14 June 1827, 953–54.

47 Ibid. [Le mari, en sortant de la salle, se plaignait de l'indulgence du Tribunal. Quelques-uns de ses voisins lui ayant conseillé d'aller rechercher sa femme, il a répondu *qu'il payerait plutôt pour la laisser en prison*. Ce propos a failli lui causer une mauvaise affaire dans la salle des pas-perdus, où un grand nom-

bre de femmes se sont élancées sur lui. Il se serait avec peine échappé de leurs mains sans la protection de son avocat.]

48 *GT*, 1 Nov. 1825, 4. [On sait que M. le marquis de Cairon a déposé au parquet de M. le procureur du Roi une plainte en adultère contre son épouse.]

49 In addition to the *Gazette des tribunaux*, other newspapers that published articles on the Cairon affair included *Le Moniteur universel*, *Le Constitutionnel*, *Le Drapeau blanc*, *Le Journal des débats*, *La Quotidienne*, and *Le Journal de Paris*. The most extensive coverage was provided, appropriately enough, by the *Gazette des tribunaux*, although the official government newspaper, *Le Moniteur universel*, also published the court record.

50 Sarah Maza, *Private Lives and Public Affairs: The Causes Célèbres of Prerevolutionary France* (Berkeley and Los Angeles: University of California Press, 1993), 14. Sarah Hanley has argued that the practice had been going on since at least the 1660s; see her "Social Sites of Political Practice in France: Lawsuits, Civil Rights, and the Separation of Powers in Domestic and State Government, 1500–1800," *American Historical Review*, 102/1 (Feb. 1997), 27–52.

51 Maza, *Private Lives*, 103, 141, 166.

52 Ibid., 264, 311.

53 According to Maza, this custom began in the eighteenth century; ibid., 124.

54 "Police correctionnelle (6e Chambre)," *GT*, 21 Jan. 1826, 1. [La ville de Rouen, les campagnes, Paris en sont inondés. Les voitures publiques, les cafés, les cabinets littéraires regorgent de ces écrits signés Augustin de Cairon.]

55 [Factum: Adélaïde Hays-Delamotte de Cairon], *Aux magistrats composant la Cour royale de Rouen; Madame de Cairon contre Monsieur de Cairon son mari, signé Barthe et Billecocq* (Paris: A. Vovée, 1823), 1–2. This memoir was re-used in 1825 for the later proceedings; the marquis cites it several times in his own 1825 memoir. The marquise also published an additional memoir, which seems to be either identical or a slightly rewritten version of that of 1823; see [Factum: Adélaïde Hays-Delamotte de Cairon], *Observations pour Madame de Cairon sur le dernier mémoire de M. de Cairon* (Paris: Plassan [1825]); excerpts from the 1825 memoir were published as "Observations de Madame de Cairon sur le dernier mémoire de M. de Cairon," *GT*, 15 Nov. 1825, 3–4. There is also *Arrêt rendu par*

la Cour royale de Rouen le 28 avril 1824, au profit de la dame Hays-Delamotte, épouse du sieur Augustin de Cairon et attaqué en cassation par ce dernier (Paris: Le Normant Fils [1825]), which, while not technically a factum as it was published after the decision, gives all the facts of the case. [Si quelqu'un osait écrire en s'adressant à des magistrats chargés d'offrir à tous une protection égale: "Magistrats, une femme issue d'une famille respectable, propriétaire d'une grande fortune, mère de cinq enfans, a été tout à coup, sans jugement, sans accusation, sans mandat légal, et seulement sur les ordres de son mari, jetée dans une prison consacrée à recevoir des criminels; après huit jours d'une détention dont chaque circonstance était un nouveau crime, elle a été enlevée au milieu de la nuit, conduite avec violence dans une autre prison à quarante lieues de son domicile, et là confondue avec des filles publiques déjà flétries par des condamnations, privée de son nom, de ses vêtemens, couverte de bure, assujettie aux travaux les plus rudes, nourrie dans les premiers temps d'un pain noir tel qu'on en donne aux animaux domestiques; elle a été retenue pendant trois années entières, jusqu'au moment où une protection tardive lui fut accordée par l'autorité supérieure. D'autres attentats plus odieux encore ont été commis. Des cinq enfans qu'elle avait mis au jour, deux disparurent, en même temps que leur mère: au moment où elle fut enlevée, elle était enceinte: ce dernier enfant n'a pas péri, il est vrai, dans son sein, par les horribles traitemens dont celle qui le portait a été l'objet; mais à peine venu au monde, il a été arraché aux soins maternels, et jeté, comme né de parens inconnus, dans un hospice d'Enfans trouvés." / Après avoir entendu un tel récit, ne serait-on pas disposé à reconnaître le produit d'une imagination égarée, qui transporte dans notre siècle, sous un gouvernement protecteur, des faits qui ont pu déshonorer des temps de désordre et de barbarie. Toutefois, ce récit ne contient que vérité; ces violences, ces manoeuvres criminelles existaient il y a quelques années, elles se continuent encore: cette femme si cruellement traitée, plongée pendant plus de trois ans dans les prisons, sans jugement, sans accusation, cette mère à qui malgré ses larmes, on a arraché son enfant, c'est moi, l'épouse de M. de Cairon, qui jouit encore de ma fortune.]

56 Although the newspaper accounts give various ages (probably because of the shift from the Revolutionary calendar), their marriage records show that he was born in

Panneville on July 14, 1775, and she in Rouen on October 18, 1787; they were married in Panneville on 14 brumaire an XIII (November 5, 1804). See Rouen, Archives départementales de la Seine-Maritime, 5 MI 1998: 1804, no. 4: Mariage de Augustin de Cairon et de Adelaïde Haïs Delamotte.

57 "Cairon, (De)," in E. de Magny, ed., *Nobiliaire de Normandie*, 2 vols. (Paris: Librairie héraldique d'Auguste Aubry, n.d.), 2, 42–43. The seat of the family was the chateau de Quévreville, near Rouen.

58 [Factum: Adélaïde Hays-Delamotte de Cairon], *Aux magistrats composant la Cour royale de Rouen*, 3. [Mes parens voulurent cette union, et j'y donnais mon consentement.]

59 [Factum: Adélaïde Hays-Delamotte de Cairon], *Observations pour Madame de Cairon*, 2. [il n'avait vu en moi qu'une riche héritier; il m'épousa par calcul; son âme n'avait aucune affection à me donner.]

60 See "8 mai 1816: Loi sur l'abolition du divorce," in J.-B. Duvergier, *Collection complète des lois, décrets, ordonnances, règlements et avis du Conseil d'état*, 91 vols. (Paris: Guyot & Scribe, 1824–91), 20: *(1815–1816)*, 379. The police commissioner's name is spelled Rolet in some documents. [dans l'intérêt de la religion, des moeurs, de la monarchie et des familles.]

61 [Factum: Adélaïde Hays-Delamotte de Cairon], *Aux magistrats composant la Cour royale de Rouen*, 5–6. [débauche, et défaut de papiers]

62 Civil Code articles 299–300 (abrogated in 1816) specified that the spouse against whom the divorce was obtained would lose all benefits given by the marriage contract.

63 The Refuge Saint-Michel was the convent of the Visitation Sainte-Marie; see "Jacques (rue Saint-) No. 193," in Félix Lazare and Louis Lazare, *Dictionnaire administratif et historique des rues et monuments de Paris* [1855], 2 vols. (Paris: reprint, Maisonneuve & Larose, 1994). For the convent's pre-Revolutionary history, see "Postes (rue des) No. 52." [maison de correction pour les jeunes filles repenties, et pour celles qui sont détenues par mesure de police ou par inconduite, à la demande de leurs parents.]

64 See [Factum: Adélaïde Hays-Delamotte de Cairon], *Aux magistrats composant la Cour royale de Rouen*, 25.

65 Although Madame de Cairon's memoir referred to twenty-two months in the class of penitents, the Rouen court decision gives the dates as June 25, 1816 to the end of February 1818, totaling slightly over twenty months.

66 See *Arrêt rendu par la Cour royale de Rouen*.

67 Madame Cairon was speaking figuratively about the *lettre de cachet* that the marquis had obtained against her. In fact, he had simply conspired with the Rouen police commissioner Rollet to have her arrested without any legal proceedings, a process she compared with the hated Old Regime practice. [Factum: Adélaïde Hays-Delamotte de Cairon], *Aux magistrats composant la Cour royale de Rouen*, 7–8. For a similar version of this passage, see "Observations de Madame de Cairon sur le dernier mémoire de M. de Cairon," *GT*, 15 Nov. 1825, 3–4; for the Rouen decision and a summary of the case, see *Arrêt rendu par la cour royale de Rouen*. [On me dépouilla de mes vêtemens, on me donna une robe de bure noire, on mit sur ma tête un bonnet rond destiné aux femmes condamnées. On me conduisit ainsi vêtue dans la classe des pénitentes. Dans la maison de Refuge Saint-Michel, la classe des pénitentes est destinée aux femmes condamnées, à des filles publiques, reprises de justice, et qui n'ont pas les moyens de se racheter des travaux que l'Etat leur impose; comme on leur fait acheter péniblement le pain noir dont on les nourrit! . . . En quelques mots voici leur existence. / En hiver, elles sont levées à six heures du matin, et dans des exercices religieux elles attendent le jour. Quand le jour est venu, les pénitentes descendent à leur classe transies de froid, et elles doivent travailler dans le plus profond silence, à de grosses chemises de soldat, ou à d'autres travaux de ce genre. A neuf heures du matin, on leur donne du pain bis quelquefois si dur, que des animaux le rejetteraient. Le besoin le plus pressant peut seul déterminer à le manger. A onze heures, elles ont la permission de parler en travaillant, mais on ne doit montrer aucune préférence, et il faut s'adresser indistinctement à chacune d'elles, quelque soit le motif de leur condamnation. Le réfectoire où l'on descend pour dîner, ne reçoit point de feu, il est humide et très froid, et le repas qu'on y fait se compose de légumes cuits à l'eau ou de harengs salés. / Telle est la vie à laquelle M. le marquis de Cairon, de sa seule autorité, en abusant de l'influence que son nom et ma fortune peuvent lui donner a condamné sa malheureuse épouse. Oui, sur trois ans et un mois que j'ai passés dans cette prison, j'ai vécu vingt-deux mois du régime des pénitents, avec des femmes, avec des filles publiques condamnées, et que

l'Etat nourrissait à ses frais. J'ai porté leurs vêtemens, j'ai vécu de pain bis dont on les nourrit, j'ai travaillé avec elles malgré ma foiblesse et mon état de souffrance, et quelquefois j'en ai vu qui, au milieu de leurs travaux, malgré leur dépravation, jetaient sur moi un regard de pitié, et auraient voulu m'apporter quelque consolation. [. . .] M. le marquis de Cairon seul a été inexorable, il a réalisé un exemple de barbarie inconnu de nos jours. Après avoir obtenu contre son épouse une lettre de cachet, comment l'a-t-il exécutée? Pendant qu'il jouissait de toute sa fortune, qu'il la privait de ses enfans, il donnait de l'argent non pour la dispenser d'un séjour malsain, des travaux, des alimens les plus grossiers, mais pour qu'on l'y condamnât chaque jour avec violence.]

68 "Observations de Madame de Cairon sur le dernier mémoire de M. de Cairon," *GT*, 15 Nov. 1825, 4. This was also noted by the lawyer Barthe in his summation: see "Police correctionnelle," *GT*, 21 Jan. 1826, 3.

69 [Factum: Adélaïde Hays-Delamotte de Cairon], *Aux magistrats composant la Cour royale de Rouen*, 24–26, 48.

70 All parties agreed on that date; see ibid., 26. The marquis claimed that she emerged from the Refuge Saint-Michel on August 29, 1819, but the *Gazette des tribunaux* contradicted this and gave the July date; [Factum: Augustin de Cairon], *Mémoire et consultation pour M. Augustin de Cairon, signé Charles Ledru, Berryer fils, Garnier, Bourguinon, Dupin* (Paris: J. Tastu, 1825), 15, and "Plainte en adultère," *GT*, 3 Nov. 1825, 2.

71 "Départemens," *GT*, 16 Feb. 1826, 4.

72 [Factum: Adélaïde Hays-Delamotte de Cairon], *Aux magistrats composant la Cour royale de Rouen*, 26. [Le premier usage que je fis de cette liberté si longtemps attendue, fut de présenter requête pour former contre mon époux, une demande en séparation de corps. Qui ne comprend que la vie commune était désormais impossible entre cet homme et moi?]

73 The marquis wrote that Madame de Cairon's separation suit began on September 27, 1819; see [Factum: Augustin de Cairon], *Mémoire et consultation*, 15, and "Cour de cassation (section civile), *GT*, 16 Nov. 1825, 1–2. The *Arrêt rendu par le cour royale de Rouen* stated that the hearing took place on October 9, 1819, but the decision was not announced until June 15, 1821.

74 *Arrêt rendu par la Cour royale de Rouen*, 4–6; "Police correctionnelle (6e chambre)," *GT*, 21 Jan. 1826, 1–2.

75 *Arrêt rendu par la cour royale de*

Rouen; see also "Police correctionnelle," *GT*, 21 Jan. 1826, 3.

76 [Factum: Adélaïde Hays-Delamotte de Cairon], "Consultation," *Aux magistrats composant la Cour royale de Rouen*, 39–40.

77 For the appeal of the Rouen separation agreement, see "Cour de cassation (Section des requêtes)," *Le Moniteur universel*, 13 Feb. 1825, 188. For the announcement of the adultery suit, see *GT*, 1 Nov. 1825, 4.

78 The marquis's memoir lists their addresses as 40, rue de Bussi [Buci]; 17, rue Monsieur-le-Prince; 10, rue Saint-André-des-arts; and at Antony, a suburb of Paris; [Factum: Augustin de Cairon], *Mémoire et consultation*, 17.

79 "Police correctionnelle, 20 janvier," *GT*, 21 Jan. 1826, 1–3.

80 See [Factum: Augustin de Cairon], *Mémoire et consultation*, 1–2.

81 See "Cour de cassation (section civile)," *GT*, 16 Nov. 1825, 1–2; 17 Nov. 1825, 1; *Le Moniteur universel*, 17 Nov. 1825, 1540. [excès et sévices graves [. . .] l'indemnité, l'amende et les dépens]

82 "Police correctionnelle (sixième chambre)," *GT*, 12 Nov. 1825, 1–4. See also *Journal des débats*, 12 Nov. 1825, 4. [Depuis longtemps les amateurs de scandale attendaient impatiemment l'ouverture de ces débats. Le rang du plaignant, la déplorable célébrité qu'avaient acquise de précédens débats devant une Cour de province et qu'on espérait entendre renouveler aujourd'hui, avaient attiré dans l'auditoire une affluence considérable de curieux.]

83 "Police correctionnelle (sixième chambre)," *GT*, 12 Nov. 1825, 1–4.

84 "Police correctionnelle (6e chambre)," *GT*, 21 Jan. 1826, 1. For the appeal, see also "Police correctionnelle (6e chambre)," *GT*, 14 Jan. 1826, 2–4; 21 Jan. 1826, 1–3; 22 Jan. 1826, 2–3, 28 Jan. 1826, 2–4; 29 Jan. 1826, 4. [parmi lesquels on remarquait plusieurs dames d'une mise élégante. Tous les bancs étaient occupés par des avocats en robe.]

85 "Police correctionnelle," *GT*, 14 Jan. 1826, 3. [Un public nombreux remplissait la salle lorsque les prévenus sont entrés; on leur a, par l'offre de deux chaises, épargné le désagrément de s'asseoir sur le banc où figurent d'habitude les voleurs et les escrocs. La mise de madame de Cairon est fort élégante; cette dame porte une robe de velours violet, que couvre à demi un cachemire blanc; son chapeau de velours noir est orné de marabouts blancs, et un grand voile noir descend, suivant l'usage,

jusque sur ses genoux. [. . .] un jeune homme d'un physique très-agréable [. . .] c'est un homme déjà âgé, qui a les cheveux gris, le visage rouge et des lunettes vertes.]

86   "Cour de cassation (section civile)," *GT*, 17 Nov. 1825, 1. [le sieur de Cairon s'est rendu coupable envers sa femme d'excès et sévices graves, et que dans cette appréciation de faits, abandonnée à sa conscience, elle n'a pu violer aucune loi.]

87   "Police correctionnelle (6e Chambre)," *GT*, 28 Jan. 1826, 3. Sarah Hanley has traced this concept of "civil society" back to the seventeenth century; see her discussion of Claude Le Prestre's *Questions notables* (1645), in " 'The Jurisprudence of the Arrêts': Marital Union, Civil Society and State Formation in France, 1550–1650," forthcoming in *Law History Review*, 21/1 (2003). [C'est en effet, Messieurs, de la famille que la vie se répand dans la société: c'est par le respect qui est dû aux liens qui la protègent, que se maintient cette grande chaîne qui attache l'homme à tous ses devoirs. Ce premier anneau rompu, on ne trouve plus que la licence; l'état est ébranlé du coup qui dissout les devoirs de la famille, et dans cette cause où la liberté a été souvent nommée, il nous sera permis de finir en rappelant que la vraie liberté ne peut reposer que sur les bonnes mœurs.]

88   "Police correctionnelle," *GT*, 29 Jan. 1826, 4. [Que les excès, sévices et injures graves, alors même qu'ils ont été admis comme cause de séparation de corps sur la demande de la femme, ne rentrent pas dans la cause déterminée par l'art. 339 et ne privent point le mari du droit de rendre plainte en adultère.]

89   "Cour royale (Appels de police correctionnelle)," *GT*, 14 March 1826, 3. [Attendu que la peine prononcée par les premiers juges n'est pas proportionnée à la gravité du délit.]

90   "Paris, le 25 avril," *GT*, 27 April 1826, 4.

91   "D'hier, 14 mars," *Journal de Rouen et du département de la Seine-Inférieure*, 15 March 1826, 1. The article was identified as reprinted from the Paris journal *L'Etoile*, but never appeared there; the false attribution was possibly a way to deflect questions of how the local newspaper learned of the marquise's flight. In any case, *L'Etoile* was much too serious a journal, reporting only national and international news, to have reported on the marquise's flight to Belgium. [On assure que Mme de Cairon s'est réfugié en Belgique.]

92   [Factum: Augustin de Cairon], *Mémoire et consultation*, 1. Cairon quoted the

verse from Proverbs in Latin, which undescored the "Throne and Altar" relationship. [Talis est via mulieris adulterae, quae comedit et tergens os suum, dicit: Non sum operata malum. Lib. Prov. 30, 20.]

93   [Factum: Augustin de Cairon], *Mémoire et consultation*, 1–2; sections of his memoir were published in "Plainte en adultère," *GT*, 3 Nov. 1825, 2; 5 Nov. 1825, 1–3. [Tout à coup, des faits nouveaux se dévoilent à mes yeux. Je croyais que la haine de mon épouse s'était épuisée entièrement sur moi, et j'apprends qu'elle va s'exercer encore contre mes enfans; j'apprends que ce n'est pas assez pour madame de Cairon d'avoir flétri leur nom, mais qu'elle se flatte de se venger un jour sur eux des larmes qu'ils mêlent aux larmes de leur père; j'apprends qu'elle veut les dépouiller quand je ne serai plus, au profit de bâtards adultérins dont elle environne l'existence d'un affreux mystère, de peur qu'il ne me reste encore assez de force pour réclamer au nom des saintes lois de la nature contre l'attentat qu'elle a médité.]

94   [Factum: Augustin de Cairon], *Mémoire et consultation*, 18.

95   "Observations de Madame de Cairon," *GT*, 15 Nov. 1825, 4.

96   On the history of *recherche en paternité* and *recherche en maternité*, see Rachel G. Fuchs, "Seduction, Paternity and the Law in Fin-de-Siècle France," *The Journal of Modern History*, 72/4 (Dec. 2000), 944–89.

97   [Factum: Augustin de Cairon], *Mémoire et consultation*, 21 [dépouiller cinq enfans légitimes en faveur de ses deux bâtards adultérins.]

98   Ibid., 21. [nos débats devaient se renouveler devant le tribunal imposant de l'opinion publique. [. . .] Madame de Cairon ne réussira plus à soulever contre moi une opinion puissante qu'elle avait trompée, comme elle trompa la justice jusque dans son temple.]

99   Ibid., 3. [Elle s'offre aux yeux de toute la France, comme une infortunée qui a brisé ses fers et qui demande justice contre ses oppresseurs: parce qu'elle a foulé aux pieds tout ce qu'il y a de plus sacré, elle croit qu'il lui appartient d'invoquer la liberté; séduit à ce mot, le talent lui-même vient lui prêter secours, et à l'aide de ce levier tout puissant, elle réussit à soulever en sa faveur l'esprit de parti qui me réclame pour victime.]

100   See "Cour de cassation (Section des requêtes)," *Le Moniteur universel*, 13 Feb. 1825, 188.

101   [Factum: Adélaïde Hays-Delamotte de Cairon], *Aux magistrats composant la Cour*

royale de Rouen, 21–22. Madame de Cairon wanted to underscore her husband's use of the "royal we." [M. le marquis de Cairon a feint d'ignorer ce que tout le monde sait aujourd'hui: à ses yeux, *les lettres de cachet* sont encore existantes. Il a pu me faire détenir trois années entières sans aucune espèce de formalité, et il avait le droit de me dire que ma *détention serait éternelle*. Tel est le sens de ces paroles, *le ministre ET NOUS, avons eu toute espèce de droit.* Que M. le marquis de Cairon ait été de bonne foi en prononçant ces paroles, que confondant les temps dans son esprit, il ait pu penser qu'un mari pouvait de nos jours, faire enlever son épouse dont il prétendait avoir à se plaindre, et la plonger *à jamais* dans une prison, pendant qu'il jouissait paisiblement de sa fortune; une pareille erreur, si elle était possible, ne servirait pas certainement d'excuse aux mauvais traitemens dont j'ai été l'objet. Le régime de la classe des pénitentes que m'a fait imposer M. le marquis de Cairon eût été toujours un acte de barbarie, dans le temps même où les lettres de cachet étaient en vigueur. Mais, ajoutait-il, *ses droits avaient été reconnus par moi*; quelle odieuse défaite!]

102 *Arrêt rendu par la Cour royale de Rouen*, 2. [La liberté individuelle des français est garantie, personne ne pouvant être poursuivi ni arrêté que dans le cas prévus par la loi et dans les formes qu'elle prescrit.]

103 "Observations de Madame de Cairon," *GT*, 15 Nov. 1825, 3. [O vous, s'écrie-t-elle, vous qui m'offriez il y a à peine quelques jours, de me recevoir dans votre domicile, où je trouverais amour et bonheur, et qui aujourd'hui, jetant le masque de l'hypocrisie, m'accuse avec le plus révoltant cynisme, parce que j'ai refusé de laisser dans vos mains ma fortune, devenue nécessaire au désordre de vos affaires, qui pourrait ne pas avoir lu dans votre âme? Cessez de parler de morale et de religion. La cupidité vous dictait de fausses promesses, si cruellement démenties par vos faits; la cupidité dicte aujourd'hui vos accusations!]

104 *Arrêt rendu par la Cour royale de Rouen*, 19. [C'est aux applaudissemens de toute la France que la Cour de Rouen a écarté certains actes *ténébreux* de police que le sieur de Cairon invoquait, et déclaré *que de pareils actes ne poudroient soutenir les regards des magistrats qui ne connaissent que la loi et les formes protectrices qu'elle consacre, formes rappelées et sanctionnées par l'art. 4 de la Charte qui garantit à tous les Français que le régime des lettres de cachet est proscrit sans retour.*]

105 Ibid., 19. [Serait-il vrai que ce monument élevé par la Cour de Rouen aux principes, à la justice, serait frappé de censure et renversé par la Cour suprême? Nous ne pouvons le craindre.]

106 [Factum: Joseph-François Soubiranne], *Observations pour François Soubiranne, présentées par lui à l'audience du Tribunal correctionnel, 6e chambre, pour servir de réponse à un mémoire signé Augustin de Cairon* (Paris: A. Boucher, 1825), 12. [Ce nom, quoique inconnu, suffira à leur honneur, et ne vous y trompez pas, s'il existe en France des familles titrées, il en est de plébéiennes qui ne donneraient pas leurs vertus et la considération dont elles jouissent, en échange d'*une noblesse* assez souvent méritée, mais qui n'est aussi quelquefois qu'*héréditaire*.]

107 Ibid., 15. [livré tout entier aux devoirs de sa profession, passait tous les jours des heures entières dans le premier hôpital de Paris auprès de ces lits de douleur occupés par l'infortune [. . .] tandis que vous étiez riche et oisif.]

108 Ibid, 9. [offrir de l'argent et sa protection, pour obtenir des renseignemens qu'ils ont l'impudeur de dicter d'avance.]

109 [Factum: Joseph-François Soubiranne], *Du Dernier Procès de l' "Indis-cret": Explication* (Paris: A. Belin [1836]).

110 [Factum: Joseph-François Soubiranne], *A MM. le président, juges, et substitut de procureur impérial composant la sixième chambre* (Paris: E. Brière [1856]).

111 Ibid., 42–44. [des dettes contractées dans les mauvais jours de ma vie, soit à France, soit à l'étranger.]

112 "D'hier, 14 mars," *Journal de Rouen et du département de la Seine-Inférieure*, 15 March 1826, 1.

113 Although Soubiranne stated in the 1856 factum that they married at Pont de l'Arche on January 3, 1831, there is no such record at the mairie. They probably married in one of the rural communes in the canton of Pont de l'Arche in order to avoid publicity; see [Factum: Joseph-François Soubiranne], *A MM. le président, juges, et substitut de procureur impérial*, 46–47.

114 See Joseph-François Soubiranne, *Le Chaos: Réponse au plus grand des Hugolins* (Paris: Tous les libraires, 1853).

115 P. Soubiranne de La Motte, *A propos de la crise financière: La Banque de l'avenir. Délégations commerciales* (Marseilles: Blanc & Bernard, 1882).

2 The Art of Keeping
Wives Faithful

1 Horace Raisson, *Code galant, ou Art de conter fleurette* (Paris: Charpentier, 1829), 159. [Les hommes qui ont perdu leur femme sont tristes, les veuves au contraire gaies et heureuses. Il y a même un proverbe parmi les femmes sur la félicité du veuvage. Il n'y a donc pas égalité dans le contrat d'union.]

2 Honoré de Balzac, *Physiologie du mariage, ou Méditations de philosophie éclectique, sur le bonheur et le malheur conjugal. Publiées par un jeune célibataire* [1829], in *La Comédie humaine,* ed. Pierre-Georges Castex, 12 vols. (Paris: Gallimard, 1976–81), 11, 903–1205; trans. as *The Physiology of Marriage* [1904], ed. Sharon Marcus (Baltimore: Johns Hopkins University Press, 1997). All translations are taken from this English edition, sometimes with minor revisions.

3 Vicomte de S*** [J.-P.-R. Cuisin], *Le Conjugalisme, ou L'Art de se bien marier: Conseils aux jeunes gens d'épouser une femme jeune, belle et riche; aux demoiselles de s'unir à un joli homme, bien fait et fortuné: Code des leçons matrimoniales, appuyées de préceptes moraux, d'anecdotes très curieuses touchant le lien si important du mariage* (Paris: Mansut, 1823).

4 Ibid., 1. Sophie Arnould was renowned as a singer of Rameau and Gluck and for her beauty and wit. [comparait le mariage à un sac rempli de serpens dangereux, entre lesquels se trouvaient à peine une ou deux bonnes anguilles: 'On met, ajoute-t-elle, la main dans ce sac, les yeux bandés, et il faut être née sous une étoile bien heureuse, pour éviter d'en tirer quelque serpent cruel, en ne tombant uniquement que sur la *bonne anguille*.]

5 Ibid., vii–viii. [Plus de divorce pour séparer deux êtres, dont *jusqu'à l'haleine* [. . .] semble à l'un et à l'autre une odeur insupportable.]

6 Ibid., vii. [les haines, les dégoûts, les infidélités, les querelles, les récriminations tardives, les reproches sanglans]

7 Ibid., viii. [Il faut enfin que ces deux époux portent le joug indéfini d'une chaîne jumelle, rivée par les lois.]

8 Ibid., chap. vi. [Des mariages d'inclination, d'amour, d'intérêt, de convenances, des unions forcées par les parens. – Conduite à tenir dans toutes ces hypothèses.]

9 Ibid., 153. [Il est vraiment fatal, pour la cause du sentiment, pour le crédit de l'amour, que les *mariages d'inclination* soient presque

tous malheureux. Ces grandes passions gigantesques, qui prétendent se suffire du charme des pures extases platoniques, subsister de soupirs, de métaphysique, de tournoiement d'yeux, de spasmes et de verres d'eau sucrée, ne peuvent presque jamais passer sans un trépas subit, au creuset de l'hymen.]

10 Ibid., 164. See also Horace Raisson, *Code conjugal, contenant les lois, règles, applications et exemples de l'art de se bien marier et d'être heureux en ménage* (Paris: J.-P. Roret, 1829), 15, 78. [il fuit de sa maison à l'aspect du froid calcul, de l'égoïsme, du sordide intérêt, de l'avarice, qui, des balances à la main, se sont installés d'avance dans l'alcôve, pour en chasser à jamais les ris, les jeux et les amours.]

11 Ibid., 167–69.

12 Ibid., 169. [c'est qu'en contraignant une jeune femme à des noeuds qu'elle abhorre, vous affranchissez pour toujours sa conscience, qui, à l'autel, ne prête plus qu'un serment forcé de fidélité et de vertu. Je vois déjà, à peine après un mois de mariage, des *rameux de cerf* ombrager le frontispice de l'alcôve conjugale.]

13 Stendhal, *De l'amour* [1822], ed. Henri Martineau (Paris: Garnier frères, 1959), chap. lvi-*bis*: "Du mariage," 219. [Il n'y a qu'un moyen d'obtenir plus de fidélité des femmes dans le mariage, c'est de donner la liberté aux jeunes filles et le divorce aux gens mariés.]

14 Balzac, "First Meditation: The Subject," *Physiology of Marriage,* 20–21 [Méditation 1: Le Sujet, 919: N'est-ce pas une entreprise neuve et à laquelle tout philosophe a renoncé que de montrer comment on peut empêcher une femme de tromper son mari?]

15 Etienne de Senancour, *De l'amour, selon les lois primordiales et selon les convenances des sociétés modernes* [1806], 2 vols. (Paris: Vieilh de Boisjoslin, rev. 3/1829), 2, 213–14. This book remained popular into the twentieth century; by 1925 it had been republished five times. [Pour que cette union soit troublée amèrement, il suffira que l'un des deux époux se voie saisi d'une passion nouvelle qu'il croira indomptable [. . .] Les probabilités d'un heureux mariage sont beaucoup plus fortes en faveur de ceux qui n'admettent qu'un attachement conciliable avec la prudence. Une affection justifiée en grande partie par les qualités morales, une affection douce, mais non exempte de retenue, pourra se prolonger jusque vers le temps où on ne désirera pas même de la remplacer. Dans la première jeunesse on a ordinairement et trop d'espoir, et trop d'impétuosité pour juger de toutes les convenances du mariage.]

16   See, for example, Stendhal, *De l'amour*, chap. LVI-*bis*, and the vicomtesse de G***, *L'Art de se faire aimer de son mari: Recueil de préceptes à l'usage des femmes qui ont serré le lien conjugal, et très utiles aux demoiselles qui désirent s'engager sous les lois de l'hymen* (Paris: Librairie française et étrangère, 1823), 4.

17   Ibid., 4. [à l'époque où nous vivons, le mariage, cette institution si noble, qu'elle paraît émanée de la divinité, n'étant plus qu'un acte purement commercial, où les traitans calculent froidement, le barème à la main, une union mercantile et intéressée, les mauvais ménages ont dû être la suite de la ridicule manie de s'épouser sans se connaître, et de subordonner la fidélité conjugale aux sacs d'écus que la future apporte en mariage. Il est donc nécessaire de chercher à diminuer les inconvéniens de ces unions mal assorties, si l'on ne peut parvenir à les détruire entièrement, et c'est le but que je me propose dans cet ouvrage.]

18   During the Old Regime, women could bring paternity suits to gain child-rearing expenses (except in cases of adultery or incest); this right was not regained until 1912. See Rachel G. Fuchs, "Seduction, Paternity and the Law in Fin-de-Siècle France," *The Journal of Modern History*, 72/4 (Dec. 2000), 944–89.

19   Maurice Bardèche, *Honoré de Balzac: Physiologie du mariage pré-originale (1826)* (thèse complémentaire pour le doctorat ès lettres, Paris: G. Droz, 1940), 12–13.

20   Madame Pariset, *Manuel de la maîtresse de maison, ou Lettres sur l'économie domestique* (Paris: Audot, 1821). This manual was reprinted in 1822, 1825, 1852, and 1913.

21   Ibid., 14–16. [Croyez en mon expérience: il n'y a point de sentiment qui mette à l'abri de l'incommodité d'un trop grand rapprochement dans certains détails de la vie journalière.]

22   The vicomte de S*** agreed with her; see his *Le Conjugalisme*, chap. X, "De l'art nécessaire d'une certaine coquetterie dans une femme, afin de conserver longtemps l'amour et le coeur de son époux," 227–71. Balzac disagreed; see *Physiology of Marriage*, "Twenty-Seventh Meditation: Final Symptoms," 322 [Méditation XXVII: Des Derniers Symptômes, 1176].

23   Madame la comtesse de G*** [Caroline-Stéphanie-Félicité Ducrest, comtesse de Genlis], *Manuel de la jeune femme: Guide complet de la maîtresse de maison* (Paris: Charles-Béchet, 1829), 343. [Devinez les désirs de votre famille, et satisfaites-les.]

24   Claire-Elisabeth-Jeanne Rémusat, *Essai sur l'éducation des femmes* (Paris: Ladvocat, 1824); Caroline-Stéphanie-Félicité Du Crest, comtesse de Genlis, *Adèle et Théodore, ou Lettres sur l'éducation* [1782], 4 vols. (Paris: Lecointe & Durey, 1827), 3, 323; Pauline Guizot, *Education domestique, ou Lettres de famille sur l'éducation,* 2 vols. (Paris: Bechet aîné, 1826), 2, 27.

25   See Voltaire, "L'Education des filles" [1761], in *Oeuvres complètes de Voltaire,* 52 vols. (Paris: Garnier frères, 1877–85), 24: *Mélanges III*, 284–87; Condorcet [Antoine Caritat, marquis de Condorcet], *Oeuvres de Condorcet*, ed. A. Condorcet O'Connor and F. Arago, 12 vols. (Paris: Firmin Didot frères, 1847–49), 7: *Sur l'instruction publique,* 215–28; see also Jacques-Henri-Bernardin de Saint-Pierre, "Discours sur cette question: Comment l'éducation des femmes pourrait contribuer à rendre les hommes meilleurs" [1777], in *Oeuvres posthumes de Jacques-Henri Bernardin de Saint-Pierre*, ed. L. Aimé-Martin [Louis-Aimé Martin] (Paris: Lefèvre, 1833), 447–62.

26   Rémusat, *Essai sur l'éducation des femmes*, 118, 24. [les trois états de fille, épouse et mère, qui composent l'existence des femmes. [. . .] L'homme doit être formé pour les institutions de son pays; la femme pour l'homme.]

27   Virginia Woolf, *A Room of One's Own* [1929] (New York: Harcourt Brace Jovanovich, 1981).

28   Vicomtesse de G***, *L'Art de se faire aimer de son mari*, 16–18. [un homme en place [. . .] égayer les soucis qui lui causent les affaires. [. . .] une compagne douce, vertueuse qui, par ses soins affectueux, son attachement, lui fait oublier ses fatigues et surtout le console de l'injustice de la fortune.]

29   Ibid. [Il arrive, sa femme court au devant de lui, portant dans ses bras le fruit de leurs amours, essuie la sueur qui coule de son front, l'embrasse, et toutes ses peines sont oubliées.]

30   See the many examples included in P. Cuisin, *Le Nouveau Secrétaire universel, ou Le Code épistolaire, présentant des modèles de lettres d'amour, de mariage, de commerce, d'affaires; placets au roi, aux princes, etc.; un exposé des encres sympathiques de la sténographie, et généralement tout ce qui rentre dans les attributions du cérémonial et du style épistolaires* (Paris: Corbet aîné, 1824). See also Roger Chartier, Alain Boureau, and Cécile Dauphin, *Correspondence: Models of Letter-Writing from the Middle Ages to the Nineteenth*

Century, trans. Christopher Woodall (Cambridge: Polity Press, 1997), esp. Cécile Dauphin, "Letter-Writing Manuals in the Nineteenth Century," 112–57.

31 Stendhal, *Le Rouge et le noir* [1830], ed. Béatrice Didier (Paris: Gallimard, 1972); trans. Lloyd C. Parks as *The Red and the Black* (New York: Signet, New American Library, 1970), chap. XXIV onwards.

32 Vicomtesse de G***, *L'Art de se faire aimer de son mari*, 111–12. For a similar model, see comte de P., *L'Art de se faire aimer de sa femme* (Paris: Delaunay, 1823), 44–48. [Mon cher Adolphe, / Trois jours seulement se sont écoulés depuis ton départ, et chaque jour me semble une année; tous les objets qui m'entourent ont perdu leur charme; ceux-là seuls qui me rappellent ta présence ont le don de me distraire; rien ne peut faire diversion au chagrin cruel que me cause notre séparation, et si elle devait durer longtemps encore, je ne sais ce que je deviendrai: jamais je n'ai senti aussi vivement combien je t'aime, que depuis l'instant où je suis privé de ta présence; hâte le plus que tu le pourras les maudites affaires qui te retiennent loin de ton Eléonore, et une fois terminées part au plus vite.]

33 See [Factum: Adélaïde Hays-Delamotte de Cairon], *Aux magistrats composant la Cour royale de Rouen: Madame de Cairon contre Monsieur de Cairon son mari, signé Barthe et Billecocq* (Paris: A. Vovée, 1823), 13–15; [Factum: Cairon], *Arrêt rendu par la Cour royale de Rouen le 28 avril 1824, au profit de la dame Hays-Delamotte, épouse du sieur Augustin de Cairon et attaqué en cassation par ce dernier* (Paris: Le Normant fils [1825]), 15.

34 [Factum: Cairon], *Arrêt rendu par la cour royale de Rouen*, 7.

35 In addition to the vicomtesse de G***, *L'Art de se faire aimer de son mari*, see Eugène de Pradel, *L'Art de se faire aimer de son mari, à l'usage des demoiselles à marier* (Paris: Bailleul aîné, 1823); L'Ami [J. M. Mossé], *L'Art de se faire aimer des femmes et de se conduire dans le monde, ou Conseils aux hommes* (Paris: rue des filles Saint-Thomas, no. 5 [1822]).

36 [E.-Charles Chabot, *Grammaire conjugale, ou Principes généraux à l'aide desquels on peut dresser la femme, la faire marcher au doigt et à l'oeil, et la rendre aussi douce qu'un mouton. Par un petit-cousin des Lovelaces* (Paris: J. Bréauté, 1827).

37 Ibid., 30: "Des défauts de la femme" [l'amour de la liberté].

38 Horace Raisson, *Code conjugal*; [Horace-Napoléon Raisson], *Code des boudoirs, ou Moyens adroits de faire des conquêtes, de devenir bientôt heureux en amour, et d'acquérir un certain aplomb auprès des femmes, par un jurisconsulte de Cythère* (Paris: Bréaute, 1829); Raisson, *Code de la cravate: Traité complet des formes, de la mise, des couleurs de la cravate; Ouvrage indispensable à tout homme de bon ton* (Paris: Audin, 1828).

39 On Horace-Napoléon Raisson, see Bardèche, *Honoré de Balzac*, 12–14, and Albert-Pierre Prioult, *Balzac avant la "Comédie humaine" (1818–1829): Contribution à l'étude de la genèse de son oeuvre* (Paris: Georges Courville, 1936), chap. 2.

40 Prioult, *Balzac*, 304.

41 Honoré de Balzac and Horace-Napoléon Raisson, *Code des gens honnêtes, ou L'Art de ne pas être dupe des fripons* (Paris: Barba, 1825); Horace Raisson, *Code pénal: Manuel complet des honnêtes gens, contenant les lois, règles, applications et exemples de l'art de mettre sa fortune, sa bourse et sa réputation à l'abri de toutes les tentatives* (Paris: P. Roret, rev. 3/1829).

42 Raisson, *Code conjugal*, 13–17. Balzac might have written parts of this code; see Honoré de Balzac, *Oeuvres diverses*, ed. Pierre-Georges Castex, 2 vols. (Paris: Gallimard, 1996), 2, 1354–56.

43 Raisson, *Code conjugal*, 105–06. [Art. 212: Les époux se doivent mutuellement fidélité, secours, assistance. / Art. 213: Le mari doit protection à sa femme, la femme obéissance à son mari. / Art. 214: La femme est obligée d'habiter avec le mari, et de le suivre partout où il juge à propos de résider.

44 Ibid., 106–07. [Que la femme soit fidèle à son mari, rien de plus juste; celui-ci d'ailleurs par un légitime retour, a juré aussi devant le maire, de lui garder fidélité: mais qu'elle *suive* son mari comme son ombre, qu'elle lui doive *obéissance*, il y a là de quoi révolter toutes les jeunes mariées du monde. Elles n'ont certes pas tort de crier à la tyrannie, et de se plaindre de ce que "les hommes font les lois."]

45 Jean-Etienne-Marie Portalis, "Exposé des motifs du projet de loi sur le mariage, formant le titre V du Code civil, présenté le 16 ventôse an XI," in *Discours, rapports et travaux inédits sur le Code civil*, ed. Frédéric Portalis (Paris: Joubert, Librairie de la cour de cassation, 1844), 204. [Le mari et la femme doivent incontestablement être fidèles à la foi promise; mais l'infidélité de la femme suppose plus de corruption, et a des effets plus dangereux que

l'infidélité du mari: aussi l'homme a toujours été jugé moins sévèrement que la femme. Toutes les nations éclairées en ce point par l'expérience, et par une sorte d'instinct, se sont accordées à croire que le sexe le plus aimable doit encore, pour le bonheur de l'humanité, être le plus vertueux.]

46 Senancour, *De l'amour*, 1, 117. [En général l'homme est bien plus coupable dans ses égaremens, parce que son infidélité est plus volontaire que celle de la femme, qui est presque toujours une suite de la sienne.]

47 Narcisse-Epaminondas Carré, *Code des femmes: Analyse complète et raisonnée de toutes les dispositions législatives qui règlent les droits et devoirs de la femme dans les différentes positions de la vie* (Paris: J.-P. Roret, 1828).

48 Ibid., iii–iv. [Nous avons donc cru lui rendre un véritable service en choisissant, parmi les dispositions si multipliées de notre législation, celles qui intéressent spécialement les femmes, en les classant dans un ordre méthodique et clair; en les dépouillant, pour les rendre intelligibles, de toute forme scientifique; en les expliquant par le rapprochement des considérations d'utilité ou de justice qui les ont dictées.]

49 Auguste-Charles Guichard, *Le Code des femmes, de leurs droits, privilèges, devoirs et obligations; ou Récits et entretiens dont la simple lecture leur apprend, en peu d'heures et sans nulle fatigue, ce qu'il leur importe le plus de savoir pour être en état de diriger elles-mêmes leurs affaires, de stipuler et défendre leurs intérêts, dans toutes les circonstances de la vie* [1823], 2 vols. (Paris: N. Pichard, rev. 2/1828).

50 Ibid., 1, 277. [C'est surtout son odieux complice que je voudrais faire condamner; car, quant à elle, encore qu'elle soit bien coupable, je serais néanmoins tout disposé à lui pardonner.]

51 Ibid., 1, 277–78. [Oui; mais vous ne pourriez lui faire infliger aucune peine, sans faire condamner en même temps votre femme; et, avant d'intenter une telle action en justice, je vous engage à bien réfléchir à ses conséquences, au fâcheux éclat, au scandale qui résulte presque toujours d'une telle discussion. Je vous exhorte à considérer l'effet moral qu'elle produit dans l'opinion, même à l'égard du mari qui fait accueillir sa plainte! D'ailleurs, la défense de la femme amène presque toujours des récriminations, qui souvent ne tournent pas à l'avantage du plaignant!]

52 François Bruys [chevalier Plante-Amour], *L'Art de connôitre les femmes* (The Hague: Jacques van den Kieboom, 1730); *L'Art de rendre les femmes fidelles, par M**** (Paris: Veuve Laisné, 1713). The word *femme* means both "wife" and "woman," but the context is usually indicative.

53 Bardèche, *Honoré de Balzac*, 14. See Emile Marco de Saint-Hilaire, *L'Art de mettre sa cravate de toutes les manières connues et usitées, enseigné et démontré en seize leçons, précédé de l'histoire complète de la cravate, par le baron Emile de L'Empesé* (Paris: Librairie universelle, 1827), and his *L'Art de payer ses dettes et de satisfaire ses créanciers sans débourser un sou, enseigné en dix leçons* (Paris: Librairie universelle, 2/1827).

54 For the origins of literary physiologies, see Andrée Lhéritier, *Les Physiologies* (Paris: Université de Paris, Institut français de presse, 1958); Catherine Nesci, *La Femme mode d'emploi: Balzac, de la "Physiologie du mariage" à "La Comédie humaine"* (Lexington, Ky.: French Forum, 1992), 35–78; Arlette Michel, Introduction to the *Physiologie du mariage*, in Balzac, *La Comédie humaine*, ed. Castex, 11, 865–901. See also Anthelme Brillat-Savarin, *La Physiologie du goût, ou Méditations de gastronomie transcendante* (Paris: A. Sautelet, 1826).

55 Jean-Gaspard [Johann Kaspar] Lavater, *La Physiognomonie, ou L'art de connaître les hommes d'après les traits de leur physionomie* [1775–78], trans. H. Bacharach (Paris: Delphica, 1979). For works drawing from or influenced by Lavater, see Lhéritier, *Les Physiologies* (1958), 13–51.

56 For the background to the establishment of the social sciences, see Joyce Appleby, Lynn Hunt, and Margaret Jacob, *Telling the Truth about History* (New York: W. W. Norton, 1994), Part One, 15–125.

57 Lhéritier, *Les Physiologies* (1958); Judith Wechsler, *A Human Comedy: Physiognomy and Caricature in 19th Century Paris* (Chicago: University of Chicago Press, 1982), 20–39.

58 Bardèche, *Honoré de Balzac*, 12.

59 *L'Art de rendre les femmes fidelles, par M****.

60 *L'Art de rendre les femmes fidelles*, 2 vols. (Geneva and Paris: Couturier fils, rev. 3/1783), 1, v. [ce ferait un livre à réimprimer; d'abord les femmes l'achèteront pour s'en amuser [. . .] Les jaloux l'achèteront aussi, afin d'en suivre les leçons [. . .] Et les galans pour déconcerter les jaloux.]

61 Ibid., 1, 7 (for the text), and 1, 13, n. 4

(for the "Commentaire"). [D'ailleurs, puisque c'est au mariage que l'homme doit sa naissance, il est obligé de se prêter au mariage pour restituer au monde ce que le monde doit perdre un jour à sa mort [. . .] Je connais à Paris une famille où il y a eu six générations de bâtards sans interruption, & beaucoup de gens ont la modestie de croire que le monde ne perdra rien à leur mort.]

62   Ibid., 1, "Injustice des lois envers les femmes," 22–26. [N'est-il pas insensé d'exiger que nos femmes soient belles, vigoureuses, & remplies de désirs, & non seulement chastes mais encore fidelles à des maris qui ne le sont pas? Si nous voulons qu'elles ne manquent pas à leurs devoirs, observons les lois, non pas celles que notre injustice & notre tyrannie ont faites contre ce sexe charmant, mais celles que les femmes les plus sages ont faites lorsqu'elles en ont eu le pouvoir.]

63   Ibid., "Mauvaise éducation des demoiselles," 1, 40. [Les femmes étant dressées dès l'enfance à l'art de plaire & aux soins d'amour, leur grâce, leur parure, leur langage, tout ce qui les environne, toute leur vie & toute leur instruction ne tendant qu'à ce but. [. . .] Si on la marie à un homme qu'elle n'aime pas, croit-on qu'elle puisse consentir à ne jamais rien aimer, elle qui n'a jamais parlé que d'amour?]

64   *L'Art de rendre les femmes fidèles et ne pas être trompé par elles: A l'usage des maris et des amans. Enseigné en cinq leçons et orné d'une gravure, par Lami* [J-M. Mosès] (Paris: Librairie française et étrangère, 1828). Persius Flaccus (A.D. 34–62) was a satiric Roman poet. [O Janus, que vous étiez heureux d'avoir des yeux par devant et par derrière! On n'avait garde de vous faire les cornes ou les oreilles d'âne, ni de tuer la langue, lorsque vous paraissez. – Perse.]

65   Ibid., "Avis Très-important." [Les dangers continuels auxquels sont exposés les maris et les amans, s'étant manifestés à nous de nouveau et avec des circonstances de plus en plus effrayantes, durant la publication de cet ouvrage, nous éprouvons le besoin de recommander à ces êtres intéressans l'achat le plus prompt de ce petit livre, quelque soit le prix. Seul il pourra les garantir de ce que je ne leur souhaite pas.]

66   Ibid., "Des diverses manières d'être de la femme pendant le mariage," "Des précautions à prendre et les dangers à éviter auprès de sa femme," "Des moyens à employer pour tirer avantage des qualités et des défauts de sa femme," "D'un petit cours de morale et

d'hygiène indispensable à tout mari qui veut rendre sa femme fidèle," "Moyens particuliers à employer par les amans pour rendre leurs maîtresses fidèles."

67   *L'Art de rendre les femmes fidelles*, rev. 3/1783, "Erreurs des philosophes modernes," 1, 27. [Mais il n'est pas vrai que l'infidélité des femmes soit indifférente sous le point de vue politique car elle nuit à la force & à la vertu de l'espèce humaine.]

68   *L'Art de rendre les femmes fidèles*, 1828, 142. [L'infidélité de la femme est encore moins indifférente pour les enfans qu'elle a eus de son mari, lesquels se trouvent frustrés de leurs intérêts patrimoniaux. Dans les états où les enfans étaient élevés aux frais du trésor public et où tous les biens étaient communs, à Sparte par exemple, l'infidélité n'entraînait pas à cet égard les mêmes inconvéniens.]

69   Alexandre Dumas, "Le Cocuage, l'adultère et le code civil," *Mes Mémoires* [1852–55], ed. Pierre Josserand, 5 vols. (Paris: Gallimard, 1954–68), 4, CC, 304–05.

70   Adeline Daumard, *La Bourgeoisie parisienne de 1815 à 1848* (Paris: SEVPEN, 1963), 335. [Le thème de l'adultère dans la littérature ou au théâtre est trop vieux pour avoir la moindre signification historique.]

71   *L'Art de rendre les femmes fidelles*, 1713, 43–45; rev. 3/1783, 1, 116–17; quoted from 1828, 101. [trop libres dans les discours de galanterie, et savantes à parler des détours d'une intrigue amoureuse; elles se font bientôt choisir pour confidentes, et donnent bien souvent des leçons à une femme, qui ne tendent qu'à duper le mari.]

72   "Comment un mari doit s'y prendre pour savoir ce qui se passe chez lui pendant son absence," *L'Art de rendre les femmes fidèles*, 1828, 97–98; see also 1713, 41–42; rev. 3/1783, 1, 114–15. [Outre ces diverses précautions, n'oubliez pas de mettre les valets et domestiques dans vos intérêts: c'est par eux que sont conduites presque toutes les intrigues des femmes, ou du moins ils en ont toujours quelque connaissance, et jamais une femme n'osera s'embarquer en des affaires amoureuses, lorsqu'elle aura sujet de s'en défier. Il n'est rien de si facile à un mari que de se les rendre favorables: quelques gratifications dont il reconnaîtra leur zèle; le congé qu'il leur présentera, lorsqu'ils broncheront, et qu'il les forcera d'accepter à la récidive, le feront aimer et craindre. Apprenez à votre femme la confiance que vous avez en eux, qu'elle sache que vous les récompensez, et qu'elle croie, s'il se peut, que la récompense est encore plus grande

que vous ne dites, afin de lui ôter tout espoir de les gagner.]

73   Chabot, *Grammaire conjugale*, xii. [Enfin j'apprends aux maris les moyens d'être les maîtres dans le ménage, de commander et de s'amuser.]

74   This passage was omitted from the English translation. [*Physiologie du mariage*, in Balzac, *La Comédie humaine*, ed. Castex, 11, 903: Il a en quelque sorte gravé sur le frontispice de son livre la prudente inscription mise sur la porte de quelques établissements: *Les dames n'entrent pas ici.*]

75   On the growth of separate gender spheres, see Maurice Agulhon, *Le Cercle dans la France bourgeoise: 1810–1848, étude d'une mutation de sociabilité* (Paris: A. Colin, Ecole des hautes études en sciences sociales, 1977), 52–53.

76   See, for example, Raisson, *Code conjugal*.

77   The second part of Balzac's *Physiology of Marriage* begins with the same epigraph (121). [*La Comédie humaine*, ed. Castex, 11, 1009: L'être ou ne pas l'être, voilà la question.]

78   Raisson, *Code conjugal*, 217–18. [Ce petit livre toutefois nous semblerait incomplet, si nous ne disions un mot d'un sujet grave et délicat, que plus d'un lecteur a dû s'étonner de ne pas voir encore abordé dans ce code conjugal. / *To be or not to be*, voilà pour beaucoup de maris le point capital; et les désolantes colonnes de la *Gazette des tribunaux* attestent chaque jour que les inquiétudes qui germent à la fois dans tant de têtes sensées, ne sont pas tout-à-fait imaginaires.]

79   Balzac, "Introduction," *Physiology of Marriage*, 1; translation with minor changes. The introduction is dated 15 December 1829. [*La Comédie humaine*, ed. Castex, 11, 904: En effet, à l'époque où, beaucoup plus jeune, il étudia le Droit français, le mot ADULTERE lui causa de singulières impressions. Immense dans le Code, jamais ce mot n'apparaissait à son imagination sans traîner à sa suite un lugubre cortège. Les Larmes, la Honte, la Haine, la Terreur, des Crimes secrets, de sanglantes Guerres, des Familles sans chef, le Malheur se personnifiaient devant lui et se dressaient soudain quand il lisait le mot sacramentel: – ADULTERE!]

80   Chabot, *Grammaire conjugal*, 49–50. [la dissimulation, la pénitence, ou la prison à domicile.]

81   Ibid., 32. [Des qu'une querelle s'est élevée et que le mari a employé la force pour réduire sa femme au silence, peut-il espérer de

vivre désormais avec elle en bonne intelligence? – Non. – Peut-il espérer qu'elle lui restera fidèle? – Non. – Peut-il espérer qu'elle ne lui en repassera pas? – Non. – Qu'il se rappelle que la vengeance est le plaisir des Dieux, et il peut se dire *à soi-même: 'Je le suis!* . . . je le suis!' Et quand il l'est, qu'il ne s'avise pas de devenir jaloux! . . . ce ne sert rien du tout.]

82   Ibid., 45. [*Madame vous resterez quinze jours dans votre appartement*, et je vous défends d'y recevoir personne. [. . .] Enfermez-la dans votre chambre à coucher; tirez la clef, mettez-la dans votre poche, votre mouchoir par dessus; et vous êtes sûr que, si son coeur n'est pas tout-à-fait gâté, cette correction terrible opérera un changement heureux et pour vous et pour elle.]

83   Ibid., 53.

84   Genlis, *Manuel de la jeune femme*, 38–40.

85   Balzac, "Eleventh Meditation: Education in Married Life," *Physiology of Marriage*, 130–37 [Méditation XI: De l'instruction en ménage, 1017–23].

86   For Old Regime attitudes, see Robert-Joseph Pothier, *Oeuvres complètes de Pothier*, ed. Saint-Albin Berville, 26 vols. (Paris: Thomine & Fortic, 1821–24), 10: *Traité du contrat de mariage, de la puissance du mari*, 114. The entry "Mariage" in Diderot's *Encyclopédie* also states that, because extended families lived together, cousins were like siblings; see Denis Diderot and D'Alembert, *Encyclopédie, ou Dictionnaire raisonné des sciences, des arts et des métiers, par une société des gens de lettres*, 17 vols. (Paris: Briasson, 1751–65), 10, 105.

87   For the changes wrought by the Civil Code, see Portalis, "Exposé des motifs du projet de loi sur le mariage," 176–77.

88   Raisson, "Titre cinquième: Ecueils. Chapitre premier. Le petit cousin," *Code conjugal*, 79–82.

89   Ibid., 79. [Le petit cousin est de l'âge de la mariée; ils ont été élevés ensemble. Dans leurs jeux enfantins, ils étaient toujours d'un parfait accord. Ils se tutoyaient.]

90   Ibid., 80. [Il n'y a pas de parti mixte à prendre avec un petit cousin; il faut lui fermer la porte, ou le recevoir cordialement, comme un ami, un parent. Le premier moyen est brutal; le second paraît dangereux.]

91   Vicomte de S***, *Le Conjugalisme*, 160. [épier à chaque instant les familiarités du petit cousin.]

92   Balzac, "Twenty-Fifth Meditation: On Relations and Other Allies," *Physiology of*

Marriage, 287. [Méditation XXV: Des alliés, 1144: je ne sache pas qu'il fasse partie de leur famille, à moins d'être un cousin.]

93 Raisson, *Code conjugal*, 87–88. [Les amies de pension ont plus désuni de ménages que les galens. [. . .] On ne peut empêcher une jeune femme de voir ses amies de pension: tout ce que le mari peut faire, c'est de la quitter le moins possible pendant ces visites, qui bientôt deviendront plus rares.]

94 Ibid., 96.

95 Ibid., 134. He attributed the statement to Julie de l'Espinasse (1732–76), a celebrated eighteenth-century woman of letters who held a Salon attended by many authors of the *Encyclopédie*. [Une jeune femme ne peut sans danger avoir pour ami que son père ou son mari.]

96 Vicomtesse de G***, *L'Art de se faire aimer de son mari*, 74–76. [A bien prendre, une jeune femme doit se lier avec le moins de personnes possible. [. . .] Tout est préférable à la société des femmes: et je suis de l'avis de certain mari qui disait, dans sa franchise un peu singulière, j'aimerais mieux trouver chez une femme un grenadier, que d'y voir une personne de son sexe.]

97 Ibid., 76. [L'on passe en revue toutes les actions du voisinage.]

98 On Gresset, see chapter 1, n. 25 above, where I also give details of the verse's being cited during an adultery trial by the wife's lawyer. The verse is here quoted from "Des Calamités conjugales," chapter XIII of vicomte de S***, *Le Conjugalisme*, 272. [La plainte est pour le fat, le bruit est pour le sot; / L'honnête homme trompé s'éloigne et ne dit mot.]

99 Raisson, *Code galant*, 173–74. [Combien un mari sage doit applaudir à ces paroles de Montaigne: "C'est folie de vouloir s'éclaircir d'un mal auquel il n'y a point de remède, auquel la honte s'augmente et se publie surtout par la jalousie, duquel la vengeance blesse plus nos enfans qu'elle ne nous guérit."]

100 Guichard, *Le Code des femmes*, 1, 276–78.

101 Vicomte de S***, *Le Conjugalisme*, 162–63. For similar arguments, see Louis-Marie Prudhomme [P. L. P.], *Idées du génie et de l'héroïsme des femmes: De la conduite des maris. Des écueils de la beauté et des passions*, 2 vols. (Paris: Achille Desauges, 1826), 1, 117. [Croyez-moi, malgré la satire de Boileau, et tous les détracteurs du beau sexe, la plupart des femmes qui se dérangent, qui cèdent à des amans, ont longtemps lutté au sein de leurs larmes solitaires, ont longtemps déploré l'inconstance d'un mari, qui, volage, joueur, prodigue, entretenu scandaleux de quelque éhontée Laïs, transfuge du lit nuptial, les accablait de silence et de dédains, et ne jouait plus désormais auprès d'elle que le vil rôle d'un affreux eunuque, qui garde, en tyran, un trésor auquel il ne lui est pas permis de toucher. Oui, soyez fidèle, tendre, empressé, donnez le premier l'exemple de l'ordre et des vertus, et vous aurez des épouses vertueuses. Le vice a sa contagion; il est difficile qu'une femme, telle bien née qu'elle soit, conserve sa candeur, son honnêteté avec un mari qui revient chaque soir à la maison, saturé des odeurs épidémiques du libertinage.]

102 Balzac, "First Meditation: The Subject," *Physiology of Marriage*, 114 [Méditation I: Le Sujet, 914: Que la fidélité est impossible, au moins à l'homme.]

103 Vicomtesse de G***, *L'Art de se faire aimer de son mari*, 29–31. [Souvent un homme devient volage, et la bizarrerie de l'esprit humain est telle qu'une épouse jeune, belle et douée de toutes les qualités qui font le charme de la vie, est délaissée pour un autre objet d'un mérite bien inférieur; mais tel est le propre de l'inconstance, on ne doit pas s'en étonner. / La position d'une femme devient alors embarrassante; qu'elle se garde surtout d'irriter son mari par des procédés injurieux; elle ne réussirait qu'à l'exaspérer; qu'au contraire, elle redouble de soins et de prévenances; qu'elle feigne une ignorance profonde sur ses infidélités; qu'une larme s'échappe furtivement de sa paupière, et qu'à l'approche de son mari elle s'empresse de l'essuyer; quelqu'endurci que soit un homme, il ne peut résister à ce spectacle, et bientôt, revenant à lui-même, il sait réparer, par un redoublement d'amitié et d'égards, les torts graves qu'il vient d'avoir. Je sais qu'il en coûte beaucoup de dévorer ses chagrins; mais à quoi servirait l'éclat; une femme prudente doit surtout éviter de compromettre le nom qu'elle porte en affichant aux yeux d'un public toujours malveillant et caustique, les erreurs d'un mari inconsistant.]

104 Ibid., 44. [L'indulgence, je le répète, est le seul moyen à employer pour ramener un époux infidèle.]

105 Vicomte de S***, *Le Conjugalisme*, 230. [Variez aussi votre parure, l'esprit humain aime beaucoup la diversité; soyez tour à tour folâtres, pensives, mélancoliques et étourdies; ne manquez pas de cultiver votre esprit, de l'orner de lectures, de savoir jouer d'un instrument; caméléons séduisans . . .]

106 Ibid., 234. [Ce n'est qu'à votre peu d'art, qu'il faut imputer son inconstance.]

107 Raisson, *Code conjugal*, 172. [Femmes que l'on n'aime plus, cachez vos larmes; elles ne ramèneront jamais un mari à vos pieds. Ne redoublez point d'efforts pour lui plaire; ne cherchez pas à faire briller vos talens, à en acquérir de nouveaux. Ne tentez pas de montrer de l'esprit, de la grâce! Tous ces soins seraient inutiles! [. . .] L'amour éteint ne renaît plus; et si parfois l'amour volage revient près de celle qu'il a trahie, c'est plutôt lorsqu'elle paraît consolée de son absence que lorsqu'elle gémit d'un cruel abandon.]

108 Ibid., 115. [Il est un point dans le mariage sur lequel on n'insiste pas assez; c'est que l'infidélité des maris, cette source permanente de trouble, de querelles et de réciprocités, est la plupart du temps le résultat du peu de peine que les femmes prennent pour leur plaire.]

109 Vicomtesse de G***, *L'Art de se faire aimer de son mari*, 125; see also 77–102. [Les dangers de liaisons et les suites funestes et irréparables de l'infidélité conjugale.]

110 Ibid., 77–78. [Pas de repos pour la femme adultère, elle se voit frappée d'une sorte de réprobation; celui qu'elle a préféré à son époux la délaisse bientôt pour une autre, et la paie par le mépris du sacrifice qu'elle a fait de son honneur. Sort funeste, elle vit errante, le chagrin la consume; personne à qui elle puisse confier des peines dont l'aveu la couvrait de honte; effet terrible d'une seule faute, la mort seule peut mettre un terme à ses maux.]

111 "Comment un mari doit s'y prendre pour savoir ce qui se passe chez lui pendant son absence," *L'Art de rendre les femmes fidèles*, 1828, 97–98; see also 1713, 41–42; rev. 3/1783, 1, 114–15.

112 Vicomtesse de G***, *L'Art de se faire aimer de son mari*, 99. [La malheureuse Adèle embrasse ses genoux, il la regarde avec mépris et sort sans dire un mot.]

113 Ibid., 100–101. [Tout est oublié, lui dit Dupont en l'embrassant, tu as été plus faible que coupable; mais un instant plus tard . . . Souviens-toi, mon Adèle, que la société est remplie d'êtres vicieux pour qui le spectacle de la vertu est un supplice continuel, et dont la seule occupation est de tendre des pièges aux êtres des deux sexes assez faibles pour se laisser guider par leurs perfides conseils.]

114 Ibid., 101–02. [elle n'oubliait jamais, au nombre des conseils que leur donnait sa prudence maternelle, de mettre sous leurs yeux les suites funestes des liaisons dangereuses.]

115 Chabot, "Ce que la femme doit étudier," *Grammaire conjugale*, 56. [1. Nous lui recommandons d'avoir toujours de la modestie; 2. D'obéir ponctuellement à son mari; 3. De l'aimer constamment; 4. De lui rester fidèle; 5. De conserver ses principes d'honnêteté; 6. De fuir la coquetterie; 7. D'être douce, aimable et prévenante; 8. De s'habiller décemment; 9. De prendre soin de son ménage; 10. D'élever ses enfants dans de bons principes; 11. D'étudier *Grammaire conjugale*; 12. Et enfin de penser constamment à demeurer vertueuse.]

116 Marcus, "Introduction to the 1997 Edition," in Balzac, *Physiology of Marriage*, vii–xxi; Arlette Michel, Introduction to *Physiologie du mariage*, in Balzac, *La Comédie humaine*, ed. Castex, 11, 865–901.

117 Ibid., 865.

118 Balzac reviewed it in the *Mercure de France au XIXe siècle* 28 (Feb. 1830): 185–88, and in *Le Feuilleton des journaux politiques*, no. 3, 17 March 1830; they are reprinted in Balzac, *Oeuvres diverses*, ed. Castex, 2, 302–04 and 673–75.

119 Balzac, "Fourth Meditation: The Virtuous Woman," *Physiology of Marriage*, 38–52. [Méditation IV: De la femme vertueuse, 11, 936–48.]

120 See Nesci, *La Femme mode d'emploi*; earlier studies include Prioult, *Balzac*, and Bardèche, *Honoré de Balzac*.

121 Marie-Henriette Faillie has, however, done an admirable job in correlating references to the Code in Balzac's work; see her *La Femme et le Code civil dans "la Comédie humaine" d'Honoré de Balzac* (Paris: Didier, 1968).

122 Balzac, "Fifth Meditation: The Fore-Ordained," *Physiology of Marriage*, 63. [Méditation V: Des Prédestinés, 11, 958: Un homme ne peut pas se marier sans avoir étudié l'anatomie et disséqué une femme au moins.]

123 Ibid., "Twentieth Meditation: An Essay on 'Policy,'" 231; "Twelfth Meditation: The Hygiene of Marriage," 138; "Twenty-Fifth Meditation: On Relations and Other Allies," 288. [Méditation XX: Essai sur la police, 1100; Méditation XII: Hygiène du mariage, 1023; Méditation XXV: Des Alliés, 1147.]

124 Ibid., "Twelfth Meditation: The Hygiene of Marriage," 145; "Thirteenth Meditation: Personal Means," 146; "Eleventh Meditation: Education in Married Life," 131. [Méditation XII: Hygiène du mariage, 1029–30; Méditation XIII: Des Moyens personnels, 1030–31; Méditation XI: De l'instruction en ménage, 1018: L'ignorance: c'est par elle seule que se maintient le despotisme.]

125 Ibid., "Introduction," 10. [Introduc-

tion, 901: de recueillir les choses que tout le monde pense et que personne n'exprime.]

126   This is the main thesis of Alan B. Spitzer, *The French Generation of 1820* (Princeton: Princeton University Press, 1987).

127   Balzac, "Eighth Meditation: The First Symptoms," *Physiology of Marriage*, 96. [Méditation VIII: Des Premiers Symptômes, 989: La conspiration ourdie contre vous par notre million de célibataires affamés semble être unanime dans sa marche.]

128   Ibid., "Fourth Meditation: The Virtuous Woman," 47. [Méditation IV: De la femme vertueuse, 944: Il est impossible qu'ils ne soient pas, un jour, victorieux dans cette lutte!]

129   Ibid., "Twenty-Fifth Meditation: On Relations and Other Allies," 297–98. [Méditation XXV: Des Alliés, 1155: Le mariage est un véritable duel où pour triompher de son adversaire il faut une attention de tous les moments; car si vous avez le malheur de détourner la tête, l'épée du célibat vous perce de part en part.]

130   Ibid., "Twenty-Fifth Meditation: On Relations and Other Allies," 295. [Méditation XXV: Des alliés, 1153: Aussi un mari doit-il se défier de toutes les amies de sa femme.]

131   Eve Kosofsky Sedgwick, *Between Men: English Literature and Male Homosocial Desire* (New York: Columbia University Press, 1985).

132   Balzac, "Fourth Meditation: The Virtuous Woman," *Physiology of Marriage*, 48. [Méditation IV: De la femme vertueuse, 945: aussi fatigante pour eux que dangereuse pour la Société.]

133   Ibid. [L'âge moyen auquel l'homme se marie est celui de trente ans; l'âge moyen auquel ses passions, ses désirs les plus violents de jouissances génésiques se développent, est celui de vingt ans. Or, pendant les dix plus belles années de sa vie, pendant la verte saison où sa beauté, sa jeunesse et son esprit le rendent plus menaçant pour les maris qu'à toute autre époque de son existence, il reste sans trouver à satisfaire *légalement* cet irrésistible besoin d'aimer qui ébranle son être tout entier.]

134   Ibid., "Fourth Meditation: The Virtuous Woman," 47. [Méditation IV: De la femme vertueuse, 945.]

135   Ibid., "Twenty-Fifth Meditation: On Relations and Other Allies," 300. [Méditation XXV: Des alliés, 1157: Cependant un mari, pris dans ce piège, n'aura jamais rien à objecter à sa sévère moitié quand, s'apercevant d'une faute

commise par sa soubrette, elle la renverra dans son pays avec un enfant et une dot.]

136   Chabot, *Grammaire conjugale*, 31. [la femme doit obéissance à son mari. En vain on met le code civil entre les mains du beau sexe; en vain on le force à l'étudier: rien ne peut l'engager à suivre cet article à la lettre.]

137   Marcus, "Introduction," in Balzac, *Physiology of Marriage*, xx.

138   Spitzer, *The French Generation of 1820*; Sedgwick, *Between Men*.

3   When Seeing is Believing

1   [Les Trois Manières de voir. Manière parisienne: Me fâcher . . . on riroit . . . Le parti le plus sage est de se résigner et de prendre courage. Manière anglaise: Sachons mettre à profit chaque infidélité. Demandons en justice une ample indemnité. Manière méridionale: Ah! Monstres, redoutez ma fureur vengeresse, Vous périrez tous deux, perfide et toi traîtresse.]

2   The standard texts on the history of caricature are E. H. Gombrich and Ernst Kris, *Caricature* (Harmondsworth: Penguin, 1940), and Werner Hofmann, *Caricature from Leonardo to Picasso*, trans. M. H. L. (London: John Calder, 1957). On French caricature, the earliest studies include Champfleury [Jules Husson], *Histoire de la caricature moderne* (Paris: Dentu, 1871), and John Grand-Carteret, *Les Moeurs et la caricature en France* (Paris: Librairie illustrée, 1888). Beatrice Farwell has pioneered the study of popular lithography (including caricature) in art history with her series *French Popular Lithographic Imagery, 1815–1870*, 12 vols. (Chicago: University of Chicago Press, 1981–97). Her exhibition catalogues are also valuable research tools, especially *The Charged Image: French Lithographic Caricature 1816–1848* (Santa Barbara, Calif.: Santa Barbara Museum of Art, 1989). Another "pioneer" is Judith Wechsler, *A Human Comedy: Physiognomy and Caricature in 19th Century Paris* (Chicago: University of Chicago, 1982). James Cuno's dissertation, and several articles proceeding from it, have been influential in the study of French caricature; see his *Charles Philipon and La Maison Aubert: The Business, Politics and Public of Caricature in Paris, 1820–1840* (Ph.D. diss., Harvard University: Cambridge, Mass., 1985). There have recently been a number of more special-

ized studies; see Los Angeles: Grunewald Center for the Graphic Arts, University of California, *French Caricature and the French Revolution, 1789–1799* (exh. cat., 1988), esp. Cuno's "Introduction," 3–22; and Michel Melot, "Caricature and the Revolution: The Situation in France in 1789," 25–32. The standard text on political caricature is Robert Justin Goldstein, *Censorship of Political Caricature in Nineteenth-Century France* (Kent, Ohio: Kent State University Press, 1989).

3 See Melot, "Caricature and the Revolution" in Los Angeles: Grunewald Center, *French Caricature and the French Revolution*, 25–32.

4 Ibid., 26.

5 More research is needed on eighteenth-century prints; the Bibliothèque nationale inventory goes only to the letter 'M' so it is difficult even to know what exists. Some helpful texts on this theme include: Victor I. Carlson and John W. Ittmann, eds., *Regency to Empire: French Printmaking 1715–1814* (exh. cat., Baltimore Museum of Art and Minneapolis Institute of Arts, 1984); Emile Dacier, *La Gravure en France au XVIIIe siècle: La Gravure de genre et de mœurs* (Paris and Brussels: Librairie nationale d'art et d'histoire, 1925); Gérôme Doucet, *Peintres et graveurs libertins du XVIII siècle* (Paris: Albert Méricart [1913]); and Paris: Musée du Louvre, *Graveurs français de la seconde moitié du XVIIIe siècle* (exh. cat., 1985). On the subject of domestic genre in general, see Richard Rand, ed., *Intimate Encounters: Love and Domesticity in Eighteenth-Century France* (exh. cat., Hood Museum of Art, Dartmouth College; Princeton: Princeton University Press, 1997), and Louis Hautecoeur, *Peintres de la vie familiale: Évolution d'un thème* (exh. cat., Paris: Galerie Charpentier, 1945). On what were euphemistically called *sujets galants*, see Philip Stewart, *Engraven Desire: Eros, Image, and Text in the French Eighteenth Century* (Durham, N.C.: Duke University Press, 1992), and Jules Gay, *Iconographie des estampes à sujets galants et des portraits de femmes célébres par leur beauté, indiquant les sujets, les peintres, les graveurs de ces estampes, leur valeur et leur prix dans les ventes, les condamnations et prohibitions dont certaines d'entre elles ont été l'objet. Par M. le c. d'I**** (Geneva: J. Gay et fils, 1868).

6 See, for example, Adeline Daumard, *La Bourgeoisie parisienne de 1815 à 1848* (Paris: SEVPEN, 1963), 335.

7 Doucet, *Peintres et graveurs libertins*, 33.

8 On early lithography, see W. McAllister Johnson, *French Lithography: the Restoration Salons 1817–1824* (exh. cat., Kingston, Ontario: Agnes Etherington Art Centre, University of Toronto, 1977), and Michael Twyman, *Lithography 1800–1850* (Oxford: Oxford University Press, 1970). On its use in caricature, see Goldstein, *Censorship of Political Caricature*, and Cuno, *Charles Philipon and La Maison Aubert.*

9 Joseph-Marie Pain and C. de Beauregard, *Nouveau tableaux de Paris, ou Observations sur les mœurs et usages des Parisiens au commencement du XIXe siècle*, 2 vols. (Paris: Pillet aîné, 1828), 1, 290.

10 See Pierre-Louis Duchartre and René Saulnier, *L'Imagerie populaire: Les images de toutes les provinces françaises du XVe siècle au second Empire* (Paris: Librairie de France, 1926); Nicole Garnier, *Musée national des arts et traditions populaire: L'Imagerie populaire française: Gravures en taille-douce et en taille d'épargne*, 2 vols. (Paris: RMN, 1990). There were also cheap stenciled versions of "high-art" engravings; see Pierre-Louis Duchartre and René Saulnier, *L'Imagerie parisienne: L'Imagerie de la rue Saint-Jacques* (Paris: Gründ, 1944).

11 The best history of the trade and function of prints is Pierre Casselle, *La Commerce des estampes à Paris dans la seconde moitié du 18ème siècle*" (thèse, Paris: Ecole nationale des chartes, 1976).

12 On charivari, see Henri Rey-Flaud: *Le Charivari. Les Rituels fondamentaux de la sexualité* (Paris: Payot, 1985); Jacques Le Goff and Jean-Claude Schmitt, eds., *Colloque sur le charivari: Actes de la table ronde organisée à Paris (25–27 avril 1977 par l'Ecole des hautes études en sciences sociales et le Centre national de la recherche scientifique)* (Paris: Mouton, 1981); Natalie Zemon Davis, "The Reasons of Misrule," in her *Society and Culture in Early Modern France* (Stanford, Calif.: Stanford University Press, 1975), 97–123.

13 For a thorough history of the changing censorship laws with regard to visual imagery, see Goldstein, *Censorship of Political Caricature.*

14 On the early history of *Le Nain jaune*, see Goldstein, ibid., 101–04. While *Le Nain jaune* included caricatures as a supplement, the first fully illustrated French periodical has been identified as *La Renommée*, established on 15 June 1819; see Remi Blachon, *La Gravure sur bois aux XIXe siècle: L'Age du bois debout* (Paris: Editions de l'amateur, 2001), 88.

15   Lynn Hunt, *The Family Romance of the French Revolution* (Berkeley and Los Angeles: University of California Press, 1992); Alan B. Spitzer, *The French Generation of 1820* (Princeton: Princeton University Press, 1987); Honoré de Balzac, "La Fille aux yeux d'or," in *La Comédie humaine*, ed. Pierre-Georges Castex, 12 vols. (Paris: Gallimard, 1976–81), 5, 1039–1109; quote on 1039. [qui n'a que deux âges, ou la jeunesse ou la caducité.]

16   For brief biographies of the major caricaturists, see Farwell, *The Charged Image*; minor figures are included in *Dictionnaire des illustrateurs* (Neuchâtel: Ides & Calendes, 1989).

17   Honoré Daumier published his earliest lithographs in 1830; his best-known images on these themes date from the 1840s. Gavarni [Sulpice-Guillaume Chevalier] adopted his pseudonym in 1829; his prints on these themes were also produced later, with his well-known *Lorette* series introduced in 1841.

18   On Philipon, see Cuno, *Charles Philipon and La Maison Aubert*, and his "Charles Philipon, La Maison Aubert, and the Business of Caricature in Paris, 1829–41," *Art Journal*, 43/4 (Winter 1983), 347–54.

19   Eve Kosofsky Sedgwick, *Between Men: English Literature and Male Homosocial Desire* (New York: Columbia University Press, 1985).

20   Michel Melot has identified the early audience for caricature as the enlightened bourgeoisie, in particular the intellectual middle classes; see his "Caricature and the Revolution," in Los Angeles: Grunewald Center, *French Caricature and the French Revolution*, 28–29.

21   Casselle, *La Commerce des estampes à Paris*, 54–56.

22   Goldstein, *Censorship of Political Caricature*, vii–viii.

23   Renate Bridenthal and Claudia Koonz, eds., *Becoming Visible: Women in European History* (Boston: Houghton Mifflin, 1977).

24   For a discussion of such themes, see Alison Stewart, *Unequal Lovers: A Study of Unequal Couples in Northern Art* (New York: Abaris, 1979).

25   On "La Dispute pour la culotte," see Laure Beaumont-Maillet, *La Guerre des sexes, XVe–XIXe siècles: Les Albums du Cabinet des estampes de la Bibliothèque nationale* (Paris: Albin Michel, 1984), 14–23.

26   Natalie Zemon Davis, "Women on Top," in her *Society and Culture in Early Modern France*, 124–51.

27   The plays of Molière are a good exam-ple of this; for early examples of novels on the same theme, see Joan DeJean, *Tender Geographies: Women and the Origins of the Novel in France* (New York: Columbia University Press, 1991).

28   The attack on paternal authority is discussed at length by Hunt, *Family Romance*, 16–52; Carol Duncan, "Fallen Fathers: Images of Authority in Pre-Revolutionary French Art," in her *The Aesthetics of Power: Essays in Critical Art History* (Cambridge: Cambridge University Press, 1993), 27–56; Jean Delumeau and Daniel Roche, eds., *Histoire des pères et de la paternité* (Paris: Larousse-HER, rev. 2000), 241–327.

29   The first French census was completed in 1806 but is unreliable. It is generally accepted that only after 1851 are there any reliable statistics; see Charles H. Pouthas, *La Population française pendant la première moitié du XIXe siècle* (Paris: PUF, 1956), 17–18, and J. Dupâquier, ed., *Marriage and Remarriage in Populations of the Past* (London: Academic Press, 1981), 178–87.

30   The first detailed and reliable statistical information on marriage dates from 1861. Even so, Etienne Van de Walle notes that censuses often shifted women aged 15–19 into the 20–24 category; see his *The Female Population of France in the Nineteenth Century* (Princeton: Princeton University Press, 1974), 99. See also Claude Lévy and Louis Henry, "Ducs et pairs sous l'ancien régime: Caractéristiques démographiques d'une caste," *Population: Revue de l'Institut national d'études démographiques*, 15 (Oct.–Dec. 1960), 807–30; the authors state that, even with incomplete statistics for the period 1650–1799, it can be shown that 50–80 per cent of women in the upper caste were married before age 20, that in the reigning families females were younger at first marriage than in the population as a whole (which married at 24–36) and that French aristocrats married even younger than their European peers. Gérard Duplessis-Le Guélinel also states that women from the upper classes married most often before they were 20; see his *Les Mariages en France*, Cahiers de la Fondation nationale des sciences politiques, 53 (Paris: Armand Colin, 1954), 21–23. In the lower classes and in rural communities, women were often older at first marriage; see Jean-Louis Flandrin, *Familles: Parenté, maison, sexualité dans l'ancienne société*. (Paris: Seuil, rev. 1984), 180–84.

31   See Duplessis-Le Guélinel, *Mariages en France*, 21–23. Daumard, *La Bourgeoisie parisienne*, 328, states that in rich families men

married at the earliest between 25 and 30;. Balzac also noted that men (by whom he meant propertied men) did not marry until at least 30; see Honoré de Balzac, "Fourth Meditation: The Virtuous Woman," in *The Physiology of Marriage*, ed. Sharon Marcus (Baltimore: Johns Hopkins Press, 1997), 48. [Méditation IV: De la femme vertueuse, in *La Comédie humaine*, ed. Castex, 11, 945.]

32 See Dupâquier, *Marriage and Remarriage*, in which several essays make the point that only 10–20 per cent of widows remarried while 50–75 per cent of widowers did; all mention widespread hostility by young men towards this practice.

33 Guillaume-Tell Doin and Edouard Charton, *Lettres sur Paris* (Paris: Crapelet, 1830), 91. See also Balzac, "Fourth Meditation: The Virtuous Woman," *Physiology of Marriage*, 47. [Méditation IV: De la femme vertueuse, in *La Comédie humaine*, ed. Castex, 11, 945.]

34 Although this print is signed Boucher, Baudouin is generally accepted as the artist; for the description, see Bibliothèque nationale de France, Département des estampes, *Inventaire du fonds français: Graveurs du XVIIIe siècle, par Marcel Roux* (Paris: Bibliothèque nationale, 1930–), 2: *Baquoy-Bizac*, 246. [En revenant du palais, Siguret trouve sa femme couchée et endormie dans les bras de l'abbé de Bois-Robert.]

35 On *lettres de cachet*, see Arlette Farge and Michel Foucault, eds., *Le Désordre des familles: Lettres de cachet des archives de la Bastille* (Paris: Gallimard, 1982).

36 Legend has it that this was one of four Venus pictures that Boucher painted for the boudoir of Madame de Pompadour at the Hôtel de l'arsenal in Paris, removed because Louis XVI found them indecent; whatever really happened, they were bought by the 4th Marquess of Hertford and are now in the Wallace Collection, London. See Alexandre Ananoff, *François Boucher*, 2 vols. (Lausanne and Paris: La Bibliothèque des arts, 1976), 2, 121; John Ingamells, *The Wallace Collection: Catalogue of Pictures*, 4 vols., 3: *French before 1815* (London: Wallace Collection, 1989), 42–45.

37 On the Le Mire engraving, see Ananoff, *Boucher*, 2, no. 430 (figure 1236) and commentary.

38 Tony Tanner, *Adultery in the Novel: Contract and Transgression* (Baltimore: Johns Hopkins University Press, 1979), 3–24.

39 On the campaign for a new-model fatherhood, see Jean-Claude Bonnet, "De la famille à la patrie," in Delumeau and Roche, eds., *Histoire des pères*, 245–67; Hunt, *Family Romance*, 21–26. On the campaign for motherhood, see Carol Duncan, "Happy Mothers and Other New Ideas in French Art," in her *The Aesthetics of Power*, 3–26, and Londa Schiebinger, "Why Mammals are Called Mammals: Gender Politics in Eighteenth-Century Natural History," *American Historical Review*, 98/2 (April 1993), 382–41.

40 See Delumeau and Roche, eds., *Histoire des pères*, 246.

41 On this type of image, see Beaumont-Maillet, *La Guerre des Sexes*, 70–77; Roger Chartier, "The World Turned Upside-Down," in his *Cultural History: Between Practices and Representations*, trans. Lydia G. Cochrane (Ithaca, N.Y.: Cornell University Press, 1988), 115–26. Many examples are reproduced by Frédérick Tristan, *Le Monde à l'envers* (Paris: Hachette, 1980).

42 See "The Rise and Fall of the Good Father," in Hunt, *Family Romance*, 17–52; Duncan, "Fallen Fathers."

43 See Honoré Daumier, *Lib Women (Bluestockings and Socialist Women)* [1844-49], ed. Jacqueline Armingeat, trans. Howard Brabyn (Paris and New York: Leon Amiel, 1974).

44 Philippe Ariès, *Centuries of Childhood* [1960], trans. Robert Baldick (New York: Knopf, 1962), 365–407. For a fascinating account of this campaign, see Schiebinger, "Why Mammals Are Called Mammals."

45 Duncan, "Happy Mothers"; see also Schiebinger, "Why Mammals are Called Mammals."

46 Diderot made these comments in his appreciation of Greuze's *La Mère bien-aimée* in the Salon of 1765; see Denis Diderot, *Salons*, ed. Jean Seznec, 3 vols. (Oxford: Clarendon Press, 1979), 2, 155. [Entretiens ta famille dans l'aisance; fais des enfans à ta femme; fais-lui-en tant que tu pourras; n'en fais qu'à elle, et sois sûr d'être bien chez toi.]

47 On "The Bad Mother," see Michel Melot, "La Mauvaise Mère: Etude d'un thème romantique dans l'estampe et la littérature," *Gazette des beaux-arts* (March 1972), 167–76.

48 Emile Dacier, *La Gravure en France*, 49, ascribes the shifting imagery to more moral subjects to the loss of audience for the more licentious themes.

49 On Boilly and the Société républicaine des arts, see A. Détournelle, ed., *Aux armes et aux arts!: Peinture, sculpture, architecture,*

gravure. Journal de la Société républicaine des arts [1794], Première partie, du premier Ventôse au premier Prairial: "Séance du 3 Floréal. Le Citoyen Bousquet, Président," 380; "Séance du 9 Floréal. Bosquet, Président," 382–83. See also Henry Harrisse, *L. L. Boilly, peintre, dessinateur et lithographe: Sa vie et son oeuvre 1761–1845* (Paris: Société de propagation des livres d'art, 1898), 13–15; Dacier, *La Gravure en France*, 50; Susan L. Siegfried, *The Art of Louis-Léopold Boilly: Modern Life in Napoleonic France* (New Haven: Yale University Press, 1995), 29–34.

50   Löys Delteil, *Manuel de l'amateur d'estampes du XVIIIe siècle* (Paris: Dorbon-aîné, 1910), 253. [Ca ira, Les Dangers de l'inexpérience; Ca a été, Le Levé des époux.]

51   Ibid., 253. Boilly's *Une Sainte Famille* was no. 41 in the Salon of 1795; see *Explication des ouvrages de peinture [. . .] exposés dans le grand sallon du museum, au Louvre [. . .] au mois vendémiaire, an quatrième de la République Française* (Paris: Veuve Herissant [1795]).

52   On Debucourt, see Maurice Fenaille, *L'Oeuvre gravé de P.-L. Debucourt (1755–1832)* (Paris: Damascène Morgand, 1899).

53   Joseph-Alexandre de Ségur, *Les Femmes, leur condition et leur influence dans l'ordre sociale chez les différens peuples anciens et modernes*, 4 vols. (Paris: Thiérot & Belin, 1825), 4, 256. There were thirteen editions between 1803 and 1836; the fourth volume, *De la condition et de l'influence des femmes sous l'Empire et depuis la Restauration by M. S. R.*, was added in 1825. On hypocrisy, see also Balzac, "Fourth Meditation: The Virtuous Woman," *Physiology of Marriage*, 38–52 [Méditation IV, De la femme vertueuse, in *La Comédie humaine*, ed. Castex, 11, 936–48]; Anne Martin-Fugier, "Des deux cours de la Restauration," *La Vie élégante ou la formation du tout-Paris 1815–1848* (Paris: Fayard, 1990), 27–63. A "sanitized" study that nevertheless includes a wealth of bibliographical information is A. D. Toledano, *La Vie de famille sous la Restauration et la monarchie de Juillet* (Paris: Alvin Michel, 1943). [Cette sévérité des moeurs qui fut la règle de sa conduite dans les jours de la prospérité comme dans ceux de la disgrâce était sans doute une étrange nouveauté.]

54   Doin and Charton, *Lettres sur Paris*, 93. On dowries, see Duplessis-Le Guélinel, *Mariages en France*, 24–26, and Florence Laroche-Gisserot, "Pratiques de la dot en

France au XIXe siècle," *Annales ESC* (Nov.–Dec. 1988), 6, 1433–52.

55   For a thorough discussion of the eighteenth-century trade in prints, see Casselle, *La Commerce des estampes à Paris*; for a discussion of English print dealers in Paris, see Mary Pedley, "Gentlemen Abroad: Jeffreys and Sayer in Paris," *The Map Collector*, no. 37 (Dec. 1986), 20–23.

4   *For Money or For Love*

1   Stendhal, *The Red and the Black: A Chronicle of the Nineteenth Century* [1830], trans. Lloyd C. Parks (New York: Signet, New American Library, 1970), Book II, chap. IV, 258. [*Le Rouge et le noir: Chronique du XIXe siècle*, ed. Béatrice Didier (Paris: Gallimard, 1972), 298–99: Pourvu qu'on ne plaisantât ni de Dieu, ni des prêtres, ni du roi, ni des gens en place, ni des artistes protégés par la cour, ni de tout ce qui est établi; pourvu qu'on ne dît du bien ni de Béranger, ni des journaux de l'opposition, ni de Voltaire, ni de Rousseau, ni de tout ce qui se permet un peu de franc-parler; pourvu surtout qu'on ne parlât jamais politique, on pouvait librement raisonner de tout.]

2   George Sand, *Indiana* [1832], trans. George Burnham Ives (Chicago: Academy Chicago, 1978), preface to 1832 edition, unpaginated. *Indiana*, ed. Béatrice Didier (Paris: Gallimard, 1984). [le triomphe de la vertu ne se voit plus qu'aux théâtres du boulevard.]

3   Scribe with Mélesville [Anne-Honoré-Joseph Duveyrier], *La Demoiselle à marier* (1826); Louis-Benoît Picard and Edouard-Joseph-Ennemond Mazères, *Heritage et mariage* (1826); Scribe with Antoine-François Varner, *Le Mariage de raison* (1826); Eugène Scribe, *Le Mariage d'argent* (1827), *Malvina, ou Un Mariage d'inclination* (1828); Léon Brunswick, Dartois and Lhérie [Armand d'Artois and Léon Lévy], *Les Suites d'un mariage de raison* (1829).

4   Pierre de Chamblain de Marivaux, *Les Fausses Confidences* (1737); Voltaire, *Nanine, ou Le Préjugé vaincu* (1749); and Denis Diderot, *Le Père de famille* (1758). See André Burguière, "La Famille et l'état: Débats et attentes de la société française à la veille de la Révolution," in Irène Théry and Christian Biet, eds., *La Famille, la loi, l'état: De la Révolution au Code civil* (Paris: Imprimerie nationale,

1989), 150; he erroneously gives the Diderot title as *Le Fils de famille*.

5 See Robert M. Isherwood, *Farce and Fantasy: Popular Entertainment in Eighteenth-Century Paris* (Oxford: Oxford University Press, 1986); F. W. J. Hemmings, *Theatre and State in France, 1760–1905* (Cambridge: Cambridge University Press, 1994).

6 See Patrick Barbier, *Opera in Paris 1800–1850: A Lively History*, trans. Robert Luoma (Portland, Oregon: Amadeus, 1995), 65–104; see also Jane Fulcher, *The Nation's Image: French Grand Opera as Politics and Politicized Art* (Canbridge: Cambridge University Press, 1987). The opera *The Marriage of Figaro* (music by Mozart, libretto by Lorenzo da Ponte) was first performed in Vienna in 1786; the opera *The Barber of Seville* (music by Rossini, libretto by Sterbini) in Rome in 1816. Barbier points out that since the librettos were in Italian, French audiences could not closely follow the plots. The major opera of the period was Auber's *La Muette de Portici* (1828), the plot of which is unrelated to this study.

7 Patrick Berthier, *Le Théâtre au XIXe siècle* (Paris: PUF, 1986), 10–13.

8 On the abolition of censorship, see "13–19 janvier 1791: Décret rélatif aux spectacles," in J.-B. Duvergier, *Collection complète des lois, décrets, ordonnances, règlements et avis du Conseil d'état*, 91 vols. (Paris: Guyot & Scribe, 1824–91), 2: *(1790–1791)*, 151. On the history of censorship in France, see Victor Hallays-Dabot, *Histoire de la censure théâtrale en France* [1862] (Geneva: Slatkine, 1970); Claude Gével and Jean Rabot, "La Censure théâtrale sous la Restauration," *La Revue de Paris*, 6 (Nov.–Dec. 1913), 339–62; and Odile Krakovitch, *Les Pièces de théâtre soumises à la censure (1800–1830): Inventaire* (Paris: Archives nationales, 1982).

9 "8 juin 1806: Décret concernant les théâtres," in Duvergier, *Collection complète des lois*, 15: *(1804–1806)*, 372, art. 14; Berthier, *Le Théâtre au XIXe siècle*, 6. [Aucune pièce ne pourra être jouée sans l'autorisation du ministre de la police.]

10 "25 avril 1807: Arrêté portant règlement pour les théâtres de la capitale et des départmens en exécution du décret du 8 juin 1806," in Duvergier, *Collection complète des lois*, 16: *(1806–1809)*, 119–23. For a list of the licensed theaters and their specializations, see "29 juillet 1807: Décret sur les théâtres," in ibid., 143–44. There were four principal theaters, each of which had its own specialty:

the Théâtre-Français, the Odéon (called the Théâtre de l'Impératrice), the Opéra (called the Académie royale de musique), the Opéra-Comique, (called the Théâtre de l'Empereur) and its annex, the Opéra-Bouffe. Of the four "secondary" theaters, the Vaudeville and the Variétés were the only ones authorized to play vaudevilles, and the Gaîté and the Ambigu-Comique were the only ones authorized to play melodramas. In 1809 the Théâtre de la Porte-Saint-Martin was licensed, bringing the number to nine. At the Restoration that number was increased to fifteen; the new theaters were the Cirque olympique, the Théâtre de Monsieur Comte, the Gymnase dramatique (sometimes called the Théâtre de Madame), the Porte-Saint-Martin, the Nouveautés, and the Jeunes Artistes; see Berthier, *Le Théâtre au XIXe siècle*, 6–7.

11 All theaters were subject to strict censorship; see Krakovitch, *Les Pièces de théâtre*, 18–19; Marie-Pierre Le Hir, *Le Romantisme aux enchères: Ducange, Pixérécourt, Hugo* (Amsterdam: John Benjamins, 1992), 7.

12 The daily police report had sections entitled *Ouvriers, Surveillance générale, Théâtres, Evénements, Bulletin de la Halle, Arrestations, Bourse*; for examples, see Archives nationales, Paris, F7 3868/9/70/71: Police générale. Rapports de la Préfecture de police, 1825–27, and F7 3877/8/9/80/81: Police générale. Bulletins de Paris, 1823–27; see also Hallays-Dabot, *Histoire de la censure théâtrale*, 244–88; Krakovitch, *Les Pièces de théâtre*, 35–37.

13 Hallays-Dabot, *Histoire de la censure théâtrale*, 244–88; Krakovitch, *Les Pièces de théâtre*, 32; Charles-Marc Des Granges, *La Comédie et les moeurs sous la Restauration et la monarchie de Juillet (1815–1848)* (Paris: Albert Fontemoing, 1904), 41–46.

14 Krakovitch, *Les Pièces de théâtre*, 15–30; Des Granges, *La Comédie et les moeurs*, 41–46.

15 Krakovitch, *Les Pièces de théâtre*, 30. See also the epigraph from Stendhal at the opening of this chapter.

16 Sheryl Kroen, "Tartufferie," *Politics and Theater: The Crisis of Legitimacy in Restoration France, 1815–1830* (Berkeley and Los Angeles: University of California Press, 2000), 229–84.

17 See E. J. H. Greene, *Menander to Marivaux: The History of a Comic Structure* (Edmonton: University of Alberta Press, 1977), 116–17.

18 The first play that openly treated this subject after the Restoration was *La Mère et la fille* by Edouard-Joseph-Ennemond Mazères and Adolphe-Joseph-Simonis Empis, which opened in October 1830.

19 Jean-Marie Thomasseau, "Le Mélodrame et la censure sous le premier Empire et la Restauration," *Revue des sciences humaines*, 162 (April–June 1976), 179.

20 On Beaumarchais, see William D. Howarth, *Beaumarchais and the Theatre* (London: Routledge, 1995); Pierre-Augustin Caron de Beaumarchais, *Théâtre: Le Barbier de Séville, Le Mariage de Figaro, La Mère coupable*, ed. René Pomeau (Paris: Flammarion, 1965).

21 See Greene, *Menander to Marivaux*, 2.

22 See Beaumarchais, "Un Mot sur 'La Mère coupable,'" in his *Théâtre*, ed. Pomeau, 247–51. Darius Milhaud, *La Mère coupable* (libretto by Madeleine Milhaud after Beaumarchais) was first performed in Geneva on June 13, 1965.

23 There has been very little modern scholarship on Delavigne, author of *Les Messéniennes* (1818), *Les Vêpres siciliennes* (1819), and *Le Paria* (1821). See Binita Mehta, "Jean-François-Casimir Delavigne," in Barbara T. Cooper, ed., *French Dramatists 1789–1914: Dictionary of Literary Biography*, 192 (Detroit: Gale Research, 1998), 65–70. See also Alexandre Dumas, *Mes Mémoires* [1852–55], ed. Pierre Josserand, 5 vols. (Paris: Gallimard, 1954–68), 1, 258–69.

24 Dumas, *Mes Mémoires*, ed. Josserand, 1, chap. LVIII, 448.

25 Casimir Delavigne, *L'Ecole des vieillards, comédie en cinq actes et en vers* (Paris: J.-N. Barba, 1823).

26 Dumas, *Mes Mémoires*, ed. Josserand, 2, 268; Alphonse de Lamartine, *Lettre de M. Alphonse de Lamartine à M. Casimir Delavigne, qui lui avait envoyé son Ecole des vieillards* (Paris: Urbain Cavel, 1824). The letter is dated February 9, 1824. [*L'Ecole des vieillards* eut un immense succès.]

27 Comtesse Dash, *Mémoires des autres*, 6 vols. (Paris: Librairie illustrée, 1896–97), 2: *Souvenirs anecdotiques sur la Restauration*, 25. [Cette comédie de *l'Ecole des vieillards* faisait courir tout Paris.]

28 Delavigne, *L'Ecole des vieillards*, Act II, scene iii. [Très-galant, beau danseur, tirant fort bien l'épée.]

29 Ibid., Act IV, scene vi. My translation talents do not include reproducing the alexandrine verse form. [Ah! vous croyez, messieurs, qu'on peut impunément, / Masquant ses vils desseins d'un air de badinage, / Attenter à la paix, au bonheur d'un ménage! / On se croyait léger, on devient criminel: / La mort d'un honnête homme est un poids éternel.]

30 Ibid., Act V, scene v. [Dans ce monde enchanteur le piège a trop de charmes.]

31 Ibid., Act V, scene vii. [Tout sera pour le mieux.]

32 Ibid., Act V, scene vii. [Epouser aussi tard femme jeune et jolie, / Cela peut réussir, mais ce n'est pas commun. / Tu fus heureux, d'accord; sur mille on en trouve un.]

33 [Théophile-Marion] Dumersan and [Henri] Dupin, *L'Ecole des béquillards, ou Il faut des époux assortis* (Paris: J.-N. Barba, 1824) opened on 6 January 1824 at the Théâtre des Variétés; Francis, Dartois and Gabriel, *L'Ecole des ganaches: Parodie de l'Ecole des vieillards* (Paris: Huet, 1824) on 8 January 1824 at the Théâtre du Vaudeville. Jacinthe Leclère, *Cadet Buteux à l'Ecole des vieillards: Pot-pourri en 5 actes précédé d'un prologue* (Paris: Duvernois, 1824) was published as a parody but not produced as a play. See also Molière, *L'Ecole des maris* (1661).

34 The fortunes of *The School for Old Men* were chronicled in the column "Boîte," *La Pandore*, 9, 16, 19, and 21 Dec. 1823, and in "Intérieur, Paris, 8 décembre," *Le Constitutionnel*, 9 Dec. 1823.

35 "Boîte," *La Pandore*, 21 Dec. 1823.

36 "Théâtre-Français," *Le Journal des débats*, 3 Jan. 1824. [elle se trouve dans les mains de tous les amateurs, de tous les critiques, de tous les rivaux, de tous les jaloux.]

37 For subsequent productions of the play, see "Boîte," *La Pandore*, 23, 29, and 30 Jan. 1824.

38 "Nouvelles des théâtres," *Le Constitutionnel*, 22 Dec. 1823. He was called "notre jeune Molière, écrivain national" in "Premier Théâtre-Français," *La Pandore*, 10 Dec. 1823. [le poète de notre époque, le Molière de notre temps.]

39 For the comparison with Corneille, see H. J., "Théâtre-Français," *La Quotidienne*, 8 Dec. 1823, and "Théâtre-Français," *Le Journal de Paris*, 7 Dec. 1823.

40 For information on performances, see A. Joannidès, *La Comédie-française de 1680 à 1900: Dictionnaire général des pièces et des auteurs* (Paris: Plon, 1901).

41 C., "Théâtre-Français," *Le Journal des débats*, 3 Jan. 1824. [Si la pièce, comme on a affecté de le dire, n'avoit d'autre mérite que celui du style, ce mérite, tout grand qu'il est aux

yeux du véritable connoisseur, suffiroit-il pour expliquer la vogue populaire de *l'Ecole des vieillards*?]

42 This play has received far less critical attention from scholars today than from previous generations. Des Granges, *La Comédie et les moeurs*, 191–94, proposed that the play succeeded because the bourgeois protagonist, Danville, was presented in a sympathetic light; Louis Allard said essentially the same thing in his *La Comédie de moeurs en France au dix-neuvième siècle*, 2 vols. (Paris: Hachette, 1933), 2: *1815–1830*, 363–77, and Berthier repeated this in *Le Théâtre au XIXe siècle*, 77.

43 [Charles-Guillaume Etienne], "Lettres sur le théâtre: No. XVI," *Le Mercure du dix-neuvième siècle*, 13 Dec. 1823, 473; a revised version of his review, in which this quotation remained unchanged, was published as "Examen critique de l'Ecole des vieillards," in the 1826 edition of the play, reprinted in Casimir Delavigne, *Théâtre de M. C. Delavigne, de l'Académie française*, 4 vols. (Paris: Ladvocat, 1825–34), 1, 163–75. [L'auteur a eu pour but de peindre le danger des unions mal-assorties; son vieillard a eu le tort d'épouser, à soixante ans, une femme qui n'en a que vingt.]

44 "Théâtre-Français," *Le Journal de Paris*, 7 Dec. 1823. [Jeunes femmes et vieux maris / feront *toujours* mauvais ménage.]

45 Delavigne, *L'Ecole des vieillards*, Act IV, scene iii. [dans son indulgence un vieillard est sévère. / Ses conseils sont fort bons, d'accord! mais... absolus. / On est moins tolérant pour des goûts qu'on n'a plus. / Au même âge on s'entend, l'un l'autre on se pardonne: / Dans cet échange égal on reçoit ce qu'on donne.]

46 Honoré de Balzac, "La Fille aux yeux d'or," in *La Comédie humaine*, ed. Pierre-Georges Castex, 12 vols. (Paris: Gallimard, 1976–81), 5, 1039–1109; quotation on 1039. [qui n'a que deux âges, ou la jeunesse ou la caducité.]

47 "Théâtre-Français," *Le Drapeau blanc*, 8 Dec. 1823. Similar opinions were expressed in *Le Courrier français*, 8 Dec. 1823; "Spectacles," *Le Moniteur universel*, 8 Dec. 1823; "Premier Théâtre-Français," *La Gazette de Paris*, 8 Dec. 1823. [il a su, dédaignant le secours facile des équivoques, placer le beau rôle du côté des bonnes moeurs.]

48 C., "Théâtre-Français," *Le Journal des débats*, 10 Dec. 1823. [J'ai entendu blâmer M. Delavigne d'avoir donné un titre éminent de notre ordre social à un personnage coupable. Je

partage cette opinion, non qu'un jeune duc ne puisse, comme tout autre jeune homme, se laisser emporter à une passion coupable, mais le titre n'étoit point nécessaire au plan de l'auteur, et, dans le moment ou la société ébranlée par de si longues et de si terribles convulsions, cherche et commence à se replacer sur les bases de nos nouvelles institutions, les supériorités politiques qu'elles ont consacrées ont besoin d'être entourées de respect, et ne peuvent être trop soigneusement mises à l'abri des atteintes toujours dangereuses pour les jeunes existences. [...] Or, rien n'exige que le neveu d'un ministre, qu'un protecteur tout puissant soit un duc. Je pense donc qu'il eût été mieux de ne point qualifier le séducteur. Mais une considération très importante atténue le tort reproché a M. Delavigne: son duc est coupable, mais il n'est point avili.]

49 [Charles-Guillaume Etienne], "Lettres sur le théâtre: No. XVII," *Le Mercure du dix-neuvième siècle*, 3 Jan. 1824, 616. This was excised from his "Examen critique de l'Ecole des vieillards" (see n. 43 above). [Il est en effet assez singulier qu'on ait permis à l'auteur de *l'Ecole des vieillards*, de faire un duc de son séducteur.]

50 Delavigne, *L'Ecole des vieillards*, Act II, scene vii. [Mon appétit s'en va, lorsque je vois siéger / Tout l'ennui des grands airs dans ma salle à manger; / Ma langue est paresseuse à rompre le silence, / S'il faut, au lieu de *vous*, dire *votre excellence*.]

51 Ibid., Act II, scene vii. [Ma maison me convient.]

52 Ibid., Act II, scene vii. [Rien de mieux, j'en conviens, qu'un beau nom bien porté; / A sa juste valeur j'estime la noblesse. / Qu'on reçoive chez soi marquis, duc et duchesse, / C'est bien, si l'on est duc, et je ne le suis pas!]

53 Scribe's and Varner's *Le Mariage de raison, comédie-vaudeville en deux actes* opened at the Théâtre du Gymnase dramatique (Théâtre de Madame) on October 10, 1826.

54 "Premier Théâtre-Français," *La Pandore*, 12 Jan. 1824. [Les personnes qui critiquent aujourd'hui avec le plus de persévérance ce qu'elles ont loué pendant quelques jours avec tant de ferveur ont dit que l'auteur de *l'Ecole des vieillards* avait su, sans avilir, sans rendre ridicule, le personnage principal de sa pièce, montrer le danger des unions mal-assorties, et faire naître une indignation éminemment morale contre ces hommes qui se font un jeu d'attenter à la paix des ménages; ils pensaient alors et nous continuons à dire, que cette double leçon est une conception originale,

un projet hardi exécuté avec un talent supérieur.]

55 Allard, *La Comédie de moeurs*, 2, 364-65.

56 Théophile Gautier, "Scribe," *La Presse*, 23 Nov. 1840, reprinted in his *Les Maîtres du théâtre français de Rotrou à Dumas fils*, ed. Amédée Gritsch (Paris: Payot, 1929), 245-59; see also Gustave Planche, "Eugène Scribe," *Portraits littéraires* [1836], 2 vols. (Paris: Charpentier, 3/1853), 1, 291-305; Alexandre Dumas, "Dix Ans de la vie d'une femme ou la moralité de M. Scribe," in his *Souvenirs dramatiques*, 2 vols. (Paris: Michel Lévy frères, 1868), 2, 229-64. [honnêtes bourgeois plus ou moins père de famille, qui, sans se préoccuper d'art, de style, de poétique, vont se délasser le soir au théâtre des travaux de la journée.]

57 On Scribe's career, see Jean-Claude Yon, *Eugène Scribe: La Fortune et la liberté* (Paris: A.-G. Nizet, 2000); Neil Cole Arvin, *Eugène Scribe and the French Theatre 1815-1860* (Cambridge, Mass.: Harvard University Press, 1924), esp. 14-16; Douglas Cardwell, "Eugene Scribe (24 December 1791-20 February 1861)," in Cooper, ed., *French Dramatists 1789-1914*, 358-72; Karen Pendle, *Eugene Scribe and French Opera in the 19th Century* (Ann Arbor: UMI, 1979). See also Berthier, *Le Théâtre au XIXe siècle*, 90. Scribe's opera librettos include those for Auber's *La Muette de Portici* (1828), Halévy's *Manon Lescaut* (1830), and for Meyerbeer's *Robert le Diable* (1831) and *Les Huguenots* (1836).

58 Eugène Scribe, *Le Mariage de raison, comédie-vaudeville en deux actes par MM. Scribe et Varner* (Paris: Pollet, 1826).

59 Ibid., Act I, scene x. [Un an après, nous plaidions en séparation, et j'étais le plus malheureux des hommes. Voilà, monsieur, voilà comment, la plupart du temps, commencent et finissent les mariages d'inclination.]

60 Ibid., Act I, scene x. [J'épousai votre mère, que j'appréciais, que j'estimais, mais que je n'adorais pas.]

61 Ibid., Act I, scene x. [L'amour est venu plus tard, vous le savez; non cet amour qui tient du délire des sens, ou de l'imagination, mais cet amour véritable, cimenté par le temps, par notre bonheur mutuel, par toutes les vertus que je découvrais en elle. Cette félicité de tous les instants, cette paix intérieur du ménage, vous en avez été témoin: que ce souvenir-là vous guide; pensez à votre mère, et choisissez.]

62 Ibid., Act I, scene x. [quand cette pre-

mière ardeur sera évaporée, que votre amour pour elle sera dissipé, il ne vous restera plus rien, que le sentiment de votre faute et le regret de l'avoir commise.]

63 Ibid., Act I, scene xi. [Une pareille union est impossible. [...] Il est des convenances qu'on doit respecter, et la société se venge sur ceux qui osent les braver. Si mon fils épousait la femme de chambre de sa mère, dans ce monde où il voudrait t'introduire l'opinion te repousserait, lui-même s'en apercevrait. C'est dans toi qu'il serait humilié, et bientôt il ne t'aimerait plus; car l'amour-propre est malheureusement le premier mobile de l'amour. Alors, dédaignée par le monde, abandonnée par ton mari, il ne te resterait que moi, ma fille, que moi, qui suis bien vieux, et qui ne te consolerais pas longtemps.]

64 Ibid., Act II, scene viii. [Mais les amoureux, vois-tu bien, ça n'est que pour durer un instant; les maris, ça dure toujours. Il faut donc, en fait d'ça, choisir du bon et du solide, parce qu'une fois pris, on ne peut plus en changer, et c'est ce que j'ai fait. [...] Et chez toi, dans ton intérieur, en voyant combien il te rend heureuse, tu feras comme moi; cet amour que tu n'avais pas, viendra peu à peu, peu à peu.]

65 Ibid., Act II, scene vii. [C'est que personne ne t'a jamais aimée comme je t'aime. Et quels sont ces devoirs qu'on t'a imposés malgré toi, malgré ton coeur? Sont-ils plus sacrés que les promesses que tu m'as faites? Oui, Suzette, c'est moi qui ai reçu tes serments; c'est moi qui suis ton amant, ton mari. Viens, fuyons; suis-moi si tu m'aimes.]

66 Ibid., Act II, scene xi. [Ah! quel bonheur d'être marié!]

67 "Théâtre de Madame: Première Représentation du *Mariage de raison*, comédie-vaudeville en deux actes, de MM. Scribe et Varner," *La Pandore*, 11 Oct. 1826. [C'est là ce qu'on appelle *le Mariage de raison*, et ce qu'on devrait plutôt appeler *le Mariage extravagant*; car, pourquoi punir cette malheureuse fille, à laquelle on n'a pas un seul reproche à faire des torts d'un étourdi?]

68 "Théâtre de Madame: *Le Mariage de raison*, vaudeville en 2 actes de MM. Scribe et Varner," *Le Globe*, 14 Oct. 1826, 144. [les mariages de *raison*, ainsi nommés sans doute parce qu'ils sont ordinairement les plus *déraisonnables* de tous.]

69 Ibid., 144. [Ce caractère est vrai: ne voit-on pas certains gentilshommes, improvisés par un décret impérial, fils, frères et époux de couturières, ne rien redouter autant qu'une mésalliance? fort libéraux, du reste, quand ils

ne sont pas employés. Je connais un baron de 1813, grand partisan de l'égalité, et qui ne veut pour gendres que des comtes ou des marquis; ancien ou nouveau, peu lui importe: si vous n'avez pas de titres, achetez-en. Et ce baron a parfaitement raison: puisqu'on vend des titres, c'est pour qu'on les achète.]

70 "Théâtre de Madame," *Le Figaro*, 14 Dec. 1826. [Partout vous entendrez retentir des noms titrés: *M. le comte, Mme la marquise, M. le baron*. [. . .] Ce n'est pas un tableau de fantaisie: l'original de ces moeurs-là est au faubourg St-Germain.]

71 "Tribunal de première instance (2e chambre)," *Gazette des tribunaux*, 3 Dec. 1826, 125–26. *The School for Husbands* is, of course, Molière's play *L'Ecole des maris* (1661). [Qui n'a vue et revue déjà *le Mariage de raison*? M. Scribe, aux yeux d'excellens juges, s'est élevé, par ce spirituel vaudeville, au rang de moraliste, et a bien mérité de la société entière, en apprenant à notre jeunesse comment elle doit s'engager dans le plus doux des liens. *L'Ecole des maris* et *l'Ecole des vieillards* ont trouvé leur pendant; *le Mariage de raison* est vraiment *l'Ecole des jeune-gens*. Aussi les pères y mènent-ils leurs fils, et toutes les mères leurs filles, comme au plus aimable et au plus efficace des sermons, au risque de troubler le spectacle (comme on l'a vu), par des crises de nerfs et des évanouissemens; on dit même que beaucoup de maris y conduisent leurs moitiés, pour leur prouver qu'elles sont les plus heureuses des femmes, et qu'un mariage d'inclination eût été pour elles un véritable abîme. / Quoiqu'il en soit, il se passe peu de jours sans que le Palais-de-Justice ne donne une éclatante confirmation à la charmante leçon de morale du Gymnase.]

72 "Lettres sur la littérature dramatique," *Le Mercure du dix-neuvième siècle*, 15 (1826), 135. [C'est un des plus grands *désenchanteurs* qui soient au monde; c'est un homme qui ne croit ni aux premiers amours, ni aux sympathies mystérieuses, ni aux passions irrésistibles.]

73 Ibid., 136. [Avant vous, l'amour au théâtre était habitué à triompher des préjugés de fortune ou de naissance; c'était lui qui rétablissait l'égalité que le monde a détruite; et si, dans la société, les oncles et les pères s'opposaient à nos inclinations, au moins le théâtre et les romans nous servaient de champ d'asile. Là, pas de préjugés tyranniques; là, les couturières, quand elles sont jolies, épousent des ducs et pairs; car, aux yeux de la philosophie, il n'y a ni titres ni distinctions. [. . .] vous changez tout; au théâtre ce seront maintenant les pères et les

oncles qui triompheront. Plus d'amours irrésistibles; plus de victoires remportées sur les préjugés. Chacun doit se marier avec son égal.]

74 Ibid., 137. [M. Scribe peint le monde comme il est. Quand les hommes pratiqueront l'égalité, il la mettra sur la scène.]

75 Ibid., 141–42. [la société d'aujourd'hui représentée avec une fidélité ingénieuse dans le plus joli tableau de genre que nous ayons encore vu.]

76 See the censorship report "Théatre de Madame, *Le Mariage de raison*," dated September 28, 1826, in Archives nationales F18 656: Censure. Théâtres, Vaudevilles, 1826. [La pièce est conduite avec tant d'art, qu'on partage la vive amitié qu'elle ressent pour lui et qu'on reste convaincu que ce sont les convenances et les qualités personnelles qui font le bonheur de l'hymen et non les vilités passagères d'un amour irréfléchi et disproportionné. La seconde partie de la leçon n'est pas moins bonne. Elle se trouve dans la bouche de M. de Brémont qui fait sentir à Suzette tous les dangers d'une alliance inconvenante, puisque la fortune et l'éducation ne viennent pas effacer la différence des rangs. [. . .] En somme, la pièce est charmante pour le public, et irréprochable pour la Censure.]

77 L. S., "Théâtre de Madame: Première Représentation du *Mariage de raison*, vaudeville en deux actes, de MM. Scribe et Varner," *Journal des débats*, 12 Oct. 1826. [*Le Mariage de raison* étoit depuis un mois annoncé au Gymnase, qui fondoit sur cette pièce de grandes espérances. Les préventions favorables, répandues sur l'ouvrage nouveau, avoient attiré une foule considérable au théâtre de Madame. L'attente du public n'a point été déçue. Le succès a été complet; il sera durable, parce qu'il est légitime. [. . .] Depuis longtemps aucune pièce n'avoit été accueillie avec un plaisir aussi vif par les habitués du Gymnase.]

78 Eugène Scribe's *Malvina, ou Un Mariage d'inclination: Comédie-vaudeville en deux actes* (Paris: Librairie théâtrale, 1828) opened on December 8, 1828 at the Théâtre de Madame; *Les Suites d'un mariage de raison* (Paris: Barba, 1829) by Léon Brunswick, Dartois, and Lhérie, on May 6, 1829 at the Théâtre des Nouveautés.

79 The reviews made it clear that the plot had been "sanitized" in comparison with the published script; see "Théâtre des Nouveautés, *Les Suites d'un mariage de raison*, par MM. Brunswick et Lhérie," *Le Mercure de France au XIX siècle*, 25 (1829), 287–89. For the censorship report, see Archives nationales F21 970:

Armand d'Artois, L. Lhérie, V. Lhérie, *Les Suites d'un mariage de raison.*

80   "Théâtre: Théâtre des Nouveautés, *La Suite du mariage de raison,*" *Le Globe,* 13 May 1829, 304. [Doutez-vous encore que les mariages d'inclination sont les seuls raisonnables? En voilà une preuve.]

81   Ducange and Dinaux [Victor Ducange, Jacques-Félix Beudin, and Prosper-Parfait Goubaux], *Trente ans, ou La Vie d'un joueur: Mélodrame en trois journées [. . .]; Représenté pour la première fois, à Paris, sur le théâtre de la Porte-Saint-Martin, le 19 juin 1827* (Paris: Barba, 1827). On Ducange, see Le Hir, *Le Romantisme aux enchères;* Le Hir, "La Représentation de la famille dans le mélodrame du début du dix-neuvième siècle de Pixérécourt à Ducange," *Nineteenth-Century French Studies,* 18 (Fall–Winter 1989–90), 15–24; and Le Hir, "Victor Ducange," in Cooper, ed., *French Dramatists 1789–1914,* 88–102.

82   Peter Brooks, *The Melodramatic Imagination: Balzac, Henry James, Melodrama, and the Mode of Excess* (New York: Columbia University Press, 1985), 81. On melodrama, see Jean-Marie Thomasseau, *Le Mélodrame* (Paris: PUF, 1984), and Julia Przybos, *L'Entreprise mélodramatique* (Paris: Corti, 1987).

83   Le Hir, "La Représentation de la famille."

84   "Théâtre de la Porte-Saint-Martin: La Pièce à la mode (Le Joueur)," *La Pandore,* 8 July 1827.

85   Ibid.; and L. S., "Théâtre de la Porte-Saint-Martin: *Trente Ans, ou La Vie d'un joueur,* mélodrame en trois journées, de M. Victor Ducange, pour les débuts de M. Frédérick Lemaître," *Journal des débats,* 24 June 1827.

86   "Boîte," *La Pandore,* 20 June 1827. In the published text there is no rape, but it is possible that there was the suggestion of such an event in the production. [Tout ce que l'art mélodramatique a de combinaisons violentes, tout ce que le vice a de hideux, et le crime d'exécrable est réuni dans cet ouvrage, où sont mis en jeu l'ingratitude filiale, la corruption, le rapt, le vol, le faux, l'assassinat et l'incendie.]

87   "Le Théâtre de la Porte-Saint-Martin: *Trente ans de la vie d'un joueur,* mélodrame en trois actes de M. Victor Ducange (2ème représentation)," *La Pandore,* 21 June 1827. [La foule des vendeurs de billets est considérable, le concours des spectateurs immense, la tranquillité des contrôleurs compromise, le

sabre du gendarme tiré et son cheval agité. Les barrières craquent, les femmes crient, les hommes jurent; on se pousse, on se presse et l'on n'avance pas. Le spectacle de la porte est effrayant, celui de l'intérieur est atroce.]

88   Ducange and Dinaut, *Trente ans,* Act I, scene xiii. [Tu n'as plus ici d'autre maître que moi.]

89   Civil Code article 213: "Le mari doit protection à sa femme, la femme obéissance à son mari."

90   Ducange and Dinaut, *Trente ans,* Act I, scene xv. [Rompre mon mariage! Vous auriez déjà payé ce mot de votre vie . . . si cette Amélie dont je suis maintenant l'époux et le maître ne vous appartenait par un lien qui vous protège encore. Quoi! c'était donc pour devenir mon délateur que vous me poursuiviez? Eh! de quel droit prétendez vous inspecter ma conduite, régler mes actions, enchaîner mes volontés? Je suis libre maintenant, je jouis de ma fortune, la loi m'en rend maître; je suis ici chez moi, et songez que j'ai le droit d'en chasser qui m'outrage.]

91   Ibid., Act I, scene xv. [La destinée du joueur est écrite sur les portes de l'enfer. Fils ingrat! fils déjà parricide! tu seras époux coupable et père dénaturé; et ta vie s'éteindra dans la misère, le sang et le remords!]

92   Ibid., Act II, scene ii. [Nous avons passé quinze années sans connaître un seul jour de repos, bien moins encore de bonheur.]

93   While wife-beating was not condoned by the Civil Code, "moderate correction" (*correction modérée*) was considered a husband's prerogative; see Roderick Phillips, *Putting Asunder: A History of Divorce in Western Society* (Cambridge: Cambridge University Press, 1988), 323–44.

94   Ducange and Dinaux, *Trente ans,* Act II, scene xix. [perfide, épouse adultère!]

95   Ibid., Act III, scene xvii. [Maintenant tu ne me quitteras plus! Je te jure par l'enfer!]

96   For the censors' reports, dated February 23 and March 8, 1827, see Archives nationales F21 975: Procès-verbaux de censure. *Trente ans, ou Trois jours de la vie d'un joueur, 8 mars 1827.* The critics invariably summarized the plot, and from their reviews it is apparent that the ending had been changed to conform to the censor's strictures.

97   Ibid., report of March 8, 1827. [plutôt salutaire que nuisible.]

98   See, for example, L. S., "Théâtre de la Porte-Saint-Martin." *Journal des débats,* 24 June 1827, and "Théâtre de la Porte-Saint-

Martin: *Trente ans ou La Vie d'un jouer*, mélodrame en trois actes de M. Victor Ducange (2e
représentation)," *La Pandore*, 21 June 1827.

99 AN F21 975: report of March 8, 1827.
[Il y a dans ce dénouement une confusion de
suicide et de punition céleste qu'on peut tolérer
à condition que le jeu de la scène ne l'éclaircira
pas davantage. [. . .] le spectateur doit être frappé de son épouvantable fin, comme le lecteur:
sans savoir au juste comment elle a lieu.]

100 See L. S., "Théâtre de la Porte-Saint-
Martin," *Journal des débats*, 24 June 1827.

101 Ibid.

102 Victor Hugo, *Hernani, ou L'Honneur
castillan: Drame par Victor Hugo, représenté
sur le Théâtre-Français le 25 février 1830*
(Paris: Mame & Delaunay-Vallée, 1830).

103 Le Hir, *Le Romantisme aux enchères*.
See also Keith Wren, *Hugo: Hernani and Ruy
Blas* (London: Grant & Cutler, 1982), and
Anne Ubersfeld, *Le Roman d'Hernani* (Paris:
Mercure de France & Comédie-Française,
1985).

104 Krakovitch, *Les Pièces de théâtres*, 30.

105 The censor's report disappeared during the nineteenth century, but excerpts from it
were published; see "Rapport du Comité du
Théâtre-Français sur *Hernani*, drame en cinq
actes et en vers, signé par MM. Brifaut,
Chéron, Laya et Sauvo (Paris, octobre 1829),"
in *Catalogue de la collection de lettres autographes manuscrits du comte de Mirabeau,
documents historiques sur la Ligue, la Fronde,
la Révolution, etc. de feu M. Lucas de
Montigny* (Paris: Laverdet, 1860), 275–76,
#1544 (2–3). The excerpts were also published
by Ubersfeld, *Le Roman d'Hernani* 32–38; she
gives a complete history of the censorship battle. [un tissu d'extravagances, auxquelles l'auteur s'efforce vainement de donner un caractère
d'élévation et qui ne sont que triviales et souvent grossières.]

106 Ibid. [Il est bon que le public voie
jusqu'à quel point d'égarement peut aller
l'esprit humain affranchi de toute règle et de
toute bienséance.]

107 Honoré de Balzac, *Le Feuilleton des
journaux politiques*, 24 March, 7 April 1830,
reprinted in his *Oeuvres diverses*, ed. Pierre-
Georges Castex, 2 vols. (Paris: Gallimard,
1996) 2, 677–90; see 685–86. [un vieillard stu-
pide]

108 Hugo, *Hernani*, Act v, scene vi. [vieil-
lard insensé]. I have taken all French quotations
from Victor Hugo, *Théâtre: Amy
Robsart, Marion de Lorme, Hernani, Le Roi

s'amuse*, ed. Raymond Pouilliart (Paris:
Flammarion, 1979); English translations, with
minor revisions, are taken from, *Three Plays by
Victor Hugo: Hernani, The King Amuses
Himself, Ruy Blas*, trans. C. Crosland and F. L.
Slous (New York: Howard Fertig, 1995).

109 Hugo, *Hernani*, Act i, scene ii. [O
l'insensé vieillard, qui, la tête inclinée, / Pour
achever sa route et finir sa journée, / A besoin
d'une femme, et va, spectre glacé, / Prendre
une jeune fille! ô vieillard insensé! / Pendant
que d'une main il s'attache à la vôtre, / Ne
voit-il pas la mort qui l'épouse de l'autre? / Il
vient dans nos amours se jeter sans frayeur! /
Vieillard! Va-t'en donner mesure au foss-
oyeur!]

110 Ibid., Act iii, scene i. [Oh! mon amour
n'est point comme un jouet de verre / Qui brille
et tremble; oh! non, c'est un amour sévère, /
Profond, solide, sûr, paternel, amical / De bois
de chêne, ainsi que mon fauteuil ducal!]

111 Scribe, *Mariage du raison*, Act ii,
scene viii. [choisir du bon et du solide]

112 Delavigne, *L'Ecole des vieillards*, Act
iii, scene ii. [Que le coeur d'un vieillard, en
proie à cette ivresse, / Cède à tous les transports
d'une aveugle tendresse. / Quand on aime avec
crainte, on aime avec excès. / Jeune, on sent
qu'on doit plaire, on est sûr du succès; / Mais
vieux, mais amoureux au déclin de sa vie, /
Possesseur d'un trésor que chacun nous envie, /
On en devient avare, on le garde des yeux.]

113 Hugo, *Hernani*, Act iii, scene i.
[Ecoute, on n'est pas maître / De soi-même,
amoureux comme je suis de toi, / Et vieux. On
est jaloux, on est méchant, pourquoi? / Parce
que l'on est vieux. Parce que beauté, grâce, /
Jeunesse, dans autrui, tout fait peur, tout men-
ace. / Parce qu'on est jaloux des autres, et hon-
teux / De soi.]

114 Vicomte de S*** [J.-P.-R. Cuisin], *Le
Conjugalisme, ou L'Art de se bien marier:
Conseils aux jeunes gens d'épouser une femme
jeune, belle et riche; aux demoiselles de s'unir à
un joli homme, bien fait et fortuné: Code des
leçons matrimoniales, appuyées de préceptes
moraux, d'anecdotes très curieuses touchant le
lien si important du mariage* (Paris: Mansut,
1823), 167–69.

115 See Graham Robb, *Victor Hugo: A
Biography* (New York: W. W. Norton, 1997),
29.

116 On February 22, 1830, Hugo published a letter-preface to *Poésies de feu Charles
Dovalle* announcing his break with the royalists. Dovalle was a twenty-two-year-old jour-

nalist killed in a duel with someone who was displeased with one of his articles. See Ubersfeld, *Le Roman d'Hernani*, 52.

117   See Lynn Hunt, *The Family Romance of the French Revolution* (Berkeley and Los Angeles: University of California Press, 1992), 17–88; Carol Duncan, "Fallen Fathers: Images of Authority in Pre-Revolutionary French Art," in her *The Aesthetics of Power: Essays in Critical Art History* (Cambridge: Cambridge University Press, 1993), 27–56; and Jean Delumeau and Daniel Roche, eds., *Histoire des pères et de la paternité* (Paris: Larousse-HER, rev. 2000), 241–88.

5   *Happily Ever After . . . Or Not*

1   All English translations, with occasional revisions, from Gustave Flaubert, *Madame Bovary: Patterns of Provincial Life* [1857], trans. Francis Steegmuller (New York: Modern Library, 1957), quotation on Part I, VI, 41; [Gustave Flaubert, *Madame Bovary: Moeurs de province*, ed. Maurice Nadeau (Paris: Gallimard, 1972), Part I, VI, 64: quelque roman [. . .] ce n'étaient qu'amours, amants, amantes, dames persécutées s'évanouissant dans les pavillons solitaires, postillons qu'on tue à tous les relais, chevaux qu'on crève à toutes les pages, forêts sombres, troubles du coeur, serments, sanglots, larmes et baisers, nacelles au claire de lune, rossignols dans les bosquets, *messieurs* braves comme des lions, doux comme des agneaux, vertueux comme on ne l'est pas, toujours bien mis et qui pleurent comme des urnes.]

2   Horace Raisson, *Code conjugal, contenant les lois, règles, applications et exemples de l'art de se bien marier et d'être heureux en ménage* (Paris: J.-P. Roret, 1829), 90. [Le plus dangereux ennemi du bonheur des jeunes femmes, et par contrecoup du repos des maris, c'est l'imagination.]

3   See Marguerite Iknayan, *The Idea of the Novel in France: The Critical Reaction 1815–1848* (Geneva: E. Droz, 1961), 11; and Marc Angenot, "La Littérature populaire française au dix-neuvième siècle," in *The Popular Novel in the Nineteenth Century / La Littérature populaire au dix-neuvième siècle*, special issue of *Canadian Review of Comparative Literature / Revue canadienne de littérature comparée* (Sept. 1982), 310.

4   Koenraad W. Swart, " 'Individualism' in the Mid-Nineteenth Century (1826–1860)," in

Journal of the History of Ideas, 23 (Jan.–March 1962), 77–90.

5   Angenot, "La Littérature populaire française," 314. [Pour la classe lettrée, le roman reste une lecture clandestine.]

6   Iknayan, *The Idea of the Novel in France*, 52.

7   On early women novelists, see Joan DeJean, *Tender Geographies: Women and the Origins of the Novel in France* (New York: Columbia University Press, 1991), esp. 128–29.

8   Angenot, "La Littérature populaire française," 310. For a list ranked by number of citations in the catalogues of the *cabinets de lecture*, 1815–30, see Françoise Parent-Lardeur, *Lire à Paris au temps de Balzac: Les Cabinets de lecture à Paris 1815–1830* (Paris, Ecole des hautes études en sciences sociales, 1981), 172. Genlis ranked first.

9   On Sir Walter Scott's success, see Iknayan, *The Idea of the Novel in France*, 26–27, and passim; on male anxiety over novels, see ibid., 53–54.

10   From 210 novels published in 1820, production rose to more than 400 in 1828; see James Smith Allen, *Popular French Romanticism: Authors, Readers and Books in the 19th Century* (Syracuse, N.Y.: Syracuse University Press, 1981), 131; Parent-Lardeur, *Lire à Paris*, 36.

11   There could, of course, be no "pulp fiction" before advances in technology resulted in cheaper, less permanent pulp paper production. Stendhal labeled this type of work "format in-12" because of its small size; see D. Gruffot Papera [pseudonym for Stendhal], "Sur le rouge et le noir," in Stendhal, *Le Rouge et le noir: Chronique du XIXe siècle* [1830], ed. Béatrice Didier (Paris: Gallimard, 1972), 650. All citations are from this edition.

12   Ibid., 650.

13   Ibid., 658. [L'auteur ne traite nullement Julien comme un héros de roman de *femmes de chambre*, il montre tous ses défauts, tous les mauvais mouvements de son âme.]

14   Honoré de Balzac, "At the Sign of the Cat and Racket," in *The Works of Honoré de Balzac: Novelettes*, (New York: Black's Readers Service, 1925), 589; Honoré de Balzac, "La Maison du Chat-qui-pelote," in *La Comédie humaine*, ed. Pierre-Georges Castex, 12 vols. (Paris: Gallimard, 1976–81), I, 39–94; see 51. All quotations from these editions, translations with occasional revisions.

15   See Marie-Catherine le Jumel de Barneville, comtesse d'Aulnoy (?1650–1705), *Histoire des amours d'Hippolyte, comte de*

Douglas, et de Julie, comtesse de Warwick; Claudine-Alexandrine Guérin, marquise de Tencin (1681–1749), *Mémoires du comte de Comminges.*

16 Angenot, "La Littérature populaire française," 329; see also Parent-Lardeur, *Lire à Paris*, 200; Allen, *Popular French Romanticism*, 173–77; and Martyn Lyons, "New Readers in the Nineteenth Century: Women, Children, Workers," in Guglielmo Cavallo and Roger Chartier, eds., *A History of Reading in the West*, trans. Lydia G. Cochrane (Cambridge: Polity Press, 1999), 313–44.

17 Charles Nodier, "Oeuvres de Madame de Staël," in his *Mélanges de littérature et de critique*, ed. Alexandre Barginet, 2 vols. (Paris: Raymond, 1820), I, 383–84. [Le roman est l'expression des moeurs, des caractères, des événements d'un siècle.]

18 Iknayan, *The Idea of the Novel in France*, 35–36.

19 Nodier, "Louise de Sénancourt, par Mme de T., auteur de Cécile de Renneville et de Marie Bolden," in his *Mélanges*, ed. Barginet, I, 402. [un historien de moeurs]

20 Iknayan, *The Idea of the Novel in France*, 44.

21 Stendhal, *The Red and the Black*, trans. Lloyd C. Parks (New York: Signet, New American Library, 1970), Book II, XIX, 359. English translations from this edition with occasional revisions. [Stendhal, *Le Rouge et le noir*, ed. Didier, 414: Un roman est un miroir qui se promène sur une grande route.]

22 Priscilla P. Clark, *The Battle of the Bourgeois: The Novel in France 1789–1814* (Paris: Didier, 1973), 31, 59, 75. J. S. Wood, "Sondages dans le roman français du point de vue social (1789–1830)," in *Revue d'histoire littéraire de la France*, 54/1 (Jan.–March 1954), 33–48.

23 Ibid., 35–36.

24 "Lettres sur la littérature dramatique," *Le Mercure du dix-neuvième siècle*, 15 (1826), 136.

25 On reading, see James Smith Allen, *In the Public Eye: A History of Reading in Modern France, 1800–1940* (Princeton: Princeton University Press, 1991), 3–23; and Reinhard Wittmann, "Was There a Reading Revolution at the End of the Eighteenth Century?," in Cavallo and Chartier, eds., *A History of Reading in the West*, 284–312.

26 Clark, *The Battle of the Bourgeois*, 51.

27 Tony Tanner, *Adultery in the Novel: Contract and Transgression* (Baltimore: Johns Hopkins University Press, 1979), 3–18. Joan

DeJean has qualified this by pointing out that seventeenth-century French women novelists treated the subject of adultery frankly, although this diminished in the early eighteenth century; see her *Tender Geographies*, 127–58.

28 See "Chivalry v. Marriage," in Denis de Rougemont, *Amour et l'Occident* [1930], trans. Montgomery Belgion as *Love in the Western World* (New York: Harcourt Brace, 1940), 32–35.

29 For a comparative discussion of the phenomenon of adultery in novels of England, France, the United States, and Russia, see Judith Armstrong, *The Novel of Adultery* (London: Macmillan, 1976); Bill Overton, *The Novel of Female Adultery: Love and Gender in Continental European Fiction, 1830–1900* (New York: St. Martin's Press, 1996), 6–7; Naomi Segal, *The Adulteress's Child: Authorship and Desire in the Nineteenth-Century Novel* (Cambridge: Polity Press, 1992); Nicholas White and Naomi Segal, *Scarlet Letters: Fictions of Adultery from Antiquity to the 1990s* (London: Macmillan, 1997); Nicholas White, *The Family in Crisis in Late Nineteenth-Century French Fiction* (Cambridge: Cambridge University Press, 1999).

30 For this reading, see Overton, *The Novel of Female Adultery*, 53.

31 All English translations, with occasional revisions, from George Sand, *Indiana* [1832], trans. George Burnham Ives (Chicago: Academy Chicago, 1978); see chap. 22, 188. See also George Sand, *Indiana*, ed. Béatrice Didier (Paris: Gallimard, 1984), 215. The dauphine is Marie-Thérèse Charlotte, daughter-in-law of Charles X. [La Restauration avait donné une impulsion de vertu aux esprits de cette trempe; et, comme la *conduite* était exigée à la cour, la marquise ne haïssait rien tant que le scandale qui perd et qui ruine. Sous madame du Barry, elle eût été moins rigide dans ses principes; sous la dauphine, elle devint *collet monté*.]

32 For a study of this phenomenon in literature, see Segal, *The Adulteress's Child.*

33 Claire-Elisabeth-Jeanne Rémusat, *Essai sur l'éducation des femmes* (Paris: Ladvocat, 1824), 62. [Des romans licencieux échauffaient leur imagination, excitaient leur esprit, énervaient leur coeur.]

34 Etienne Bonnot de Condillac, "Des Vices & des avantages de l'imagination," *Essai sur l'origine des connaissances humaines* [1755], ed. Michèle Crampe-Casnabet (Paris: Alive, 1998), chap. IX, 86–93, quotation on 90.

[Cette explication peut faire connaître combien la lecture des romans est dangereuse pour les jeunes personnes du sexe dont le cerveau est fort tendre. Leur esprit, que l'éducation occupe ordinairement trop peu, saisit avec avidité des fictions qui flattent des passions naturelles à leur âge; elles y trouvent des matériaux pour les plus beaux châteaux en Espagne. / Elles les mettent en oeuvre avec d'autant plus de plaisir, que l'envie de plaire et les galanteries qu'on leur fait sans cesse les entretiennent dans ce goût. Alors il ne faut peut-être qu'un léger chagrin pour tourner la tête à une jeune fille, lui persuader qu'elle est Angélique ou telle autre héroïne qui lui a plu, et lui faire prendre pour les Médors tous les hommes qui l'approchent.]

35 M. de La Rochefoucauld, duc de Doudeauville, *Le Guide de la famille* (Paris: Garnier frères, 1847), 44. [Les romans sont une lecture que tu dois éviter: ils font croire à un bonheur qui n'existe pas et en affaiblissant les forces morales, ils mettent l'âme et l'esprit en dehors de la réalité.]

36 Balzac, "At the Sign of the Cat and Racket," in *Novelettes*, 601; ["La Maison du Chat-qui-pelote," in *La Comédie humaine*, ed. Castex, 1, 69: Sa conduite envers Augustine ne se voit que dans les romans.]

37 Flaubert, *Madame Bovary*, trans. Steegmuller, Part III, chap. VII, 358. [ed. Nadeau, 406: Je vais m'endormir, et tout sera fini!]

38 Ibid., 362–63. [ed. Nadeau, 410: Elle ne tarda pas à vomir du sang. Ses lèvres se serrèrent davantage. Elle avait les membres crispés, le corps couvert de taches brunes, et son pouls glissait sous les doigts comme un fil tendu, comme une corde de harpe près de se rompre. / Puis elle se mettait à crier horriblement.]

39 English translations, with occasional revisions, from Honoré de Balzac, *The Physiology of Marriage* [1829], ed. Sharon Marcus (Baltimore: Johns Hopkins University Press, 1997); see "Eleventh Meditation: Education in Married Life," 131. [*Physiologie du mariage*, in *La Comédie humaine*, ed. Castex: Méditation XI: De l'Instruction en ménage, 11, 1017: Arrière la civilisation! arrière la pensée! . . . voilà votre cri. Vous devez avoir horreur de l'instruction chez les femmes, par cette raison, si bien sentie en Espagne, qu'il est plus facile de gouverner un peuple d'idiots qu'un peuple de savants.]

40 Ibid., 134. [Méditation XI, 1020: les moyens de si bien consumer le temps de votre

femme, que toute espèce de lecture lui sera interdite.]

41 Ibid., 132–33. Jean-Jacques is, of course, Rousseau. [Méditation XI, 1019: Laisser une femme libre de lire les livres que la nature de son esprit la porte à choisir! . . . Mais c'est introduire l'étincelle dans une sainte-barbe; c'est pis que cela, c'est apprendre à votre femme à se passer de vous, à vivre dans un monde imaginaire, dans un paradis. Car que lisent les femmes? Des ouvrages passionnés, les *Confessions* de Jean-Jacques, des romans, et toutes ces compositions qui agissent le plus puissamment sur leur sensibilité.]

42 Ibid., 133–34. [Méditation XI, 1019–20: Aussi, en lisant des drames et des romans, la femme, créature encore plus susceptible que nous de s'exalter, doit-elle éprouver d'enivrantes extases. Elle se crée une existence idéale auprès de laquelle tout pâlit; elle ne tarde pas à tenter de réaliser cette vie voluptueuse, à essayer d'en transporter la magie en elle. Involontairement, elle passe de l'esprit à la lettre, et de l'âme aux sens.]

43 Ibid., 134. [Méditation XI, 1020: Bien des maris se trouveront embarrassés pour empêcher leurs femmes de lire, il y en a même certains qui prétendront que la lecture a cet avantage qu'ils savent au moins ce que font les leurs quand elles lisent.]

44 For examples of lists of forbidden books, see Alexandre-Nicolas Pigoreau, "Notes des ouvrages à supprimer des cabinets de lecture," *La Petite Bibliographie biographico-romancière: Onzième supplément* (Paris: Pigoreau, 1825), xi–xii. See also Félicité de Choiseul-Meuse, *Julie, ou J'ai sauvé ma rose*, 2 vols. (Hamburg and Paris: Léopold Collin, 1807); this novel was also published with the author identified as Madame Guyot or Madame de C***. It carried the epigraph "La mère en défendre la lecture à sa fille," was reprinted numerous times, placed on the Roman Catholic index of forbidden books in 1825, ordered destroyed in 1827, and translated into English in 1840.

45 For examples from the conduct manuals, see [E. Charles Chabot], *Grammaire conjugale, ou Principes généraux à l'aide desquels on peut dresser la femme, la faire marcher au doigt et à l'oeil, et la rendre aussi douce qu'un mouton. Par un petit-cousin des Lovelaces* (Paris: J. Bréauté, 1827), 53; Balzac, *Physiology of Marriage*, "Eleventh Meditation: Education in Married Life," 135–36 [Méditation XI: De l'Instruction en ménage, 1020–21];

Madame la comtesse de G*** [Caroline Félicité-Stéphanie Du Crest, comtesse de Genlis], *Manuel de la jeune femme: Guide complet de la maîtresse de maison* (Paris: Charles-Bechet, 1829), 38–40.

46 Tanner, *Adultery in the Novel*, 14, 17–18.

47 For titles, see n. 29 above.

48 DeJean, *Tender Geographies*, 127–58, traces this back to the earliest novels written by women.

49 See Swart, "'Individualism'."

50 For a discussion of gender, details, and "universality," see Naomi Schor, *Reading in Detail* (New York: Methuen, 1987).

51 Sand, *Indiana*, "Preface to the Edition of 1832," unpaginated. ["Préface de l'édition de 1832," 40: Indiana, si vous voulez absolument expliquer tout dans ce livre, c'est un type; c'est la femme, l'être faible chargé de représenter *les passions* comprimées, ou, si vous l'aimez mieux, supprimées par *les lois*; c'est la volonté aux prises avec la nécessité; c'est l'amour heurtant son front aveugle à tous les obstacles de la civilisation.]

52 See Gérard Duplessis-Le Guélinal, *Les Mariages en France*, Cahiers de la Fondation nationale des sciences politiques, 53 (Paris: Armand Colin, 1954), 22.

53 On the circumstances surrounding the scandal of *Madame Bovary*, see Dominick La Capra, *Madame Bovary on Trial* (Ithaca, N.Y.: Cornell University Press, 1982).

54 Sand, *Indiana*, "Preface to the Edition of 1842," unpaginated. ["Préface de l'édition de 1842," 47: Je n'avais point à faire un traité de jurisprudence, mais à guerroyer contre l'opinion; car c'est elle qui retarde ou prépare les améliorations sociales.]

55 Ibid. [46–47: J'ai écrit *Indiana* avec le sentiment non raisonné, il est vrai, mais profond et légitime, de l'injustice et de la barbarie des lois qui régissent encore l'existence de la femme dans le mariage, dans la famille et la société.]

56 George Sand, *Correspondance*, ed. Georges Lubin, 25 vols. (Paris: Classiques Garnier, 1964–1991), 20, no. 12733, 46–47.

57 For a discussion of the work of these later women novelists, see Overton, *The Novel of Female Adultery*, 117–19.

58 Sand, *Indiana*, "Preface to the Edition of 1842," unpaginated. ["Préface de l'édition de 1842," 44: le moyen de concilier le bonheur et la dignité des individus opprimés par cette même société, sans modifier la société elle-même.]

59 For a statistical survey of the catalogues of the *cabinets de lecture* between 1815 and 1830, see Parent-Lardeur, *Lire à Paris*, 172.

60 Madame la comtesse de Genlis [Caroline-Félicité-Stéphanie Du Crest, comtesse de Genlis], *Les Parvenus, ou Les Aventures de Julien Delmours, écrites par lui-même*, 2 vols. (Paris: Ladvocat, 1819), trans. as *The New Aera; or, Adventures of Julien Delmour, Related by Himself*, 4 vols. (London: Henry Colburn, 1819). All citations from these editions, English translations with occasional revisions.

61 Alain-René Lesage, *L'Histoire de Gil Blas de Santillane* (1715–35).

62 The preface was omitted from the English edition. Genlis, *Les Parvenus*, "Préface," 1, i. [le naturel, la vérité d'observations et de peintures de moeurs.]

63 Clark, *The Battle of the Bourgeois*, 31.

64 See Gabriel de Broglie, *Madame de Genlis* (Paris: Perrin, 1985), 422.

65 Eugène Scribe, with Antoine-François Varner, *Le Mariage de raison, comédie-vaudeville en deux actes par MM. Scribe et Varner: Paris, Théâtre de Madame, 10 octobre 1826* (Paris: Pollet, 1826), Act II, scene xi. [Ah! quel bonheur d'être marié!]

66 See, for example, Chabot, *Grammaire conjugale*, 53.

67 Genlis, *The New Aera*, 2, 26. [*Les Parvenus*, 1, 260: Le mariage n'a de bon que la quinzaine qui le précède et les deux mois qui le suivent.]

68 Ibid., 2, 27. [1, 261: insouciant, léger, dissipateur et incapable de partager un grand attachement.]

69 Ibid., 2, 27. [1, 261: Je connois mes devoirs et n'y manquerai point; mais je saurai prendre mon parti, et je n'aurai pas la sottise de m'affliger des torts d'un mari qui ne me fait pas même l'honneur de me les cacher.]

70 Ibid., 2, 49. [1, 279: que le destin est bizarre, et que les convenances sociales sont tyranniques! Sans ces cruelles convenances, il m'eût été permis de me nommer un beau-frère, pour le bonheur de ma soeur et pour le mien.]

71 Lynn Hunt, *The Family Romance of the French Revolution* (Berkeley and Los Angeles: University of California Press, 1992), 193–204.

72 Genlis, *The New Aera*, 2, 50. [*Les Parvenus*, 1, 280: Par exemple: un banquier, dont le père étoit *porte-balle*, marie sa fille à un grand seigneur; une fille de grande naissance épouse un roturier millionnaire, et le monde approuve ces alliances; mais, si un homme de la

cour connaissoit un roturier sans fortune, jeune, aimable, bien élevé, instruit, spirituel, sensible et vertueux, s'il osoit lui donner sa fille, après avoir mis à l'épreuve leur inclination mutuelle, il seroit universellement accusé d'avoir fait une action pleine de bassesse. Ainsi donc, on ne s'abaisse point en livrant sa fille pour de l'argent ou en la sacrifiant à des vues ambitieuses, et on déroge en la donnant à celui dont on estime le plus les moeurs, les principes, l'esprit et le caractère!]

73 Ibid., 2, 50. [1, 280: Voilà un odieux préjugé! Enfin, continua-t-il, mon cher Julien, il faut se résigner aux maux sans remède!]

74 Natalie Zemon Davis, "Women on Top," in her *Society and Culture in Early Modern France* (Stanford, Calif.: Stanford University Press, 1975), 124–51.

75 Genlis, *The New Aera*, 4, 178. [*Les Parvenus*, 2, 396–97: Dieu, qui lit au fond des coeurs, n'a-t-il pas vu dans le mien une passion adultère, et la plus violente qui fut jamais! Je nourrissois en secret ce penchant criminel [. . .] je l'ai nourri, il a rempli mon coeur et mon imagination.]

76 Genlis, *Les Parvenus*. ["Préface," 1, v: offre aux jeunes gens de toutes les classes des faits historiques, des tableaux frappans et des fictions dont le but principal est de leur faire sentir l'utilité de la vertu et de l'amour du travail.]

77 Genlis, *The New Aera*, 4, 232. [*Les Parvenus*, 2, 444: les amis de la vérité trouver dans cet ouvrage [. . .] le courage de défendre et de soutenir sans crainte et sans ménagement les principes sacrés de la morale.]

78 For a discussion of Balzac and melodrama, see Peter Brooks, *The Melodramatic Imagination: Balzac, Henry James, Melodrama, and the Mode of Excess* (New York: Columbia University Press, 1985), esp. 110–52; for his definition of melodrama, see 11–15.

79 On the simultaneous creation of *Physiologie du mariage* and *Scènes de la vie privée*, see Bernard Guyon, *La Pensée politique et sociale de Balzac* (Paris: Armand Colin, rev. 2/1967), 274–75.

80 Balzac, "Préface de la première édition, *Scènes de la vie privée*" [1830], in *La Comédie humaine*, ed. Castex, 1, 1172–75, quotations on 1173. [le tableau vrai de moeurs que les familles ensevelissent aujourd'hui dans l'ombre et que l'observateur a quelquefois de la peine à deviner.]

81 Ibid. [peindre avec fidélité les événements, dont un mariage est suivi ou précédé.]

82 Ibid. [Cet ouvrage a donc été composé

en haine des sots livres que des esprits mesquins ont présentés aux femmes jusqu'à ce jour.]

83 Guyon, *La Pensée politique et sociale de Balzac*, 330. [six leçons sur les dangers du mariage.]

84 "La Vendetta," "Gobseck" [Les Dangers de l'inconduite], "Le Bal de Sceaux, ou Le Pair de France," "La Maison du chat-qui-pelote" [Gloire et malheur], "Un Double Famille" [La Femme vertueuse], "La Paix du ménage."

85 On Balzac's similarities with popular fiction, see Wood, "Sondages dans le roman français"; on the melodramatic aspects of his work, see Brooks, *The Melodramatic Imagination*, 110–52.

86 On the relation of "La Maison du Chat-qui-pelote" to Balzac's family history, see Anne-Marie Meininger's "Introduction," in Balzac, *La Comédie humaine*, ed. Castex, 1, 25–38.

87 All English translations, with occasional revisions, from Honoré de Balzac, "At the Sign of the Cat and Racket," in *The Works of Balzac: Novelettes* (New York: Black's Readers Service Co., 1925), 580–618, quotation on 608. [Balzac, "La Maison du Chat-qui-pelote," in *La Comédie humaine*, ed. Castex, 1, 39–94; quotation on 79: pénétrée d'attendrissement, en reconnaissant [. . .] le bonheur égal, sans exaltation, il est vrai, mais aussi sans orages, que goûtait ce couple convenablement assorti.]

88 Ibid., 608. [79: Insensiblement amené à estimer, à chérir Virginie, le temps que le bonheur mit à éclore fut, pour Joseph Lebas et pour sa femme, un gage de durée.]

89 Ibid., 615. [89: Ma chère, reprit la grande dame d'une voix grave, le bonheur conjugal a été de tout temps une spéculation, une affaire qui demande une attention particulière. Si vous continuez à parler passion quand je vous parle mariage, nous ne nous entendrons bientôt plus.]

90 Balzac did not discard this structure until the third edition of *Scènes de la vie privée* (1835); see *La Comédie humaine*, ed. Castex, 1, 1537–38.

91 English translation from "The Vendetta," in Balzac, *Novelettes* 128–73, quotation on 172. See also "La Vendetta," in *La Comédie humaine*, ed. Castex, 1, 1035–1102. [1099: et puis un bonheur aussi grand que le mien devait se payer.]

92 Félix Davin, "Introduction," in Honoré de Balzac, *Etudes de moeurs au XIXe siècle*, 9 vols. (Paris: Mme Charles Béchet, 1834–37), vol. 1: *Scènes de la vie privée* (1835), 1–32,

quotation on 19; reprinted in *La Comédie humaine*, ed. Castex, 1, 1143–75. Davin's article was "inspired, corrected, and augmented" by Balzac himself; see Anne-Marie Meininger's introduction, in ibid., 1, 1143–44. [La fille est coupable de désobéissance, quoique la loi soit pour elle.]

93 Davin, in ibid., 1, 1162. [Ici l'auteur a montré qu'un enfant avait tort de se marier en faisant des actes respectueux prescrits par le Code. Il est d'accord avec les moeurs contre un article de loi rarement appliqué.]

94 Civil Code article 151: "The children of the family, having reached the age of majority fixed by article 148, are required, before contracting marriage, to make a respectful and formal request for advice from their father and mother, or their grandmother and grandfather if their mother and father are deceased or if, for some reason, they cannot express their will. / If this respectful act does not obtain the consent, the marriage may be celebrated one month later." [Les enfants de famille ayant atteint la majorité fixée par l'article 148 sont tenus, avant de contracter mariage, de demander, par acte respectueux et formel, le conseil de leur père et mère ou celui de leurs aïeuls et aïeules lorsque leur père et mère sont décédés ou dans l'impossibilité de manifester leur volonté. / Il pourra être, à défaut de consentement sur l'acte respectueux, passé outre, un mois après, à la célébration du mariage.]

95 Honoré de Balzac, "The Sceaux Ball," in *Novelettes*, 227–65; see also "Le Bal de Sceaux," in Balzac, *La Comédie humaine*, ed. Castex, 1, 109–65.

96 English translations from Honoré de Balzac, "A Double Family," in *La Comédie humaine*, trans. William Walton, 53 vols. (Philadelphia: George Barrie & Son, 1897), 22: *The Human Comedy: Private Life*, 5–114; see 98–100. ["Une Double Famille," in *La Comédie humaine*, ed. Castex, 2, 17–130. See 74–75: qu'avez-vous à me reprocher? Vous ai-je trompé, n'ai-je pas été une épouse vertueuse et sage? Mon coeur n'a conservé que votre image, mes oreilles n'ont entendu que votre voix. A quel devoir ai-je manqué, que vous ai-je refusé? – Le bonheur, répondit le comte d'une voix ferme. [. . .] – Ne vous ai-je donc point aimé? demanda-t-elle. – Non, madame.
– Qu'est-ce donc que l'amour? demanda involontairement la comtesse. – L'amour, ma chère, répondit Granville avec une sorte de surprise ironique, vous n'êtes pas en état de le comprendre. [. . .] Se plier à nos caprices, les deviner, trouver des plaisirs dans une douleur, nous sacrifier l'opinion du monde, l'amour-propre, la religion même, et ne regarder ces offrandes que comme des grains d'encens brûlés en l'honneur de l'idole, voilà l'amour . . . – L'amour des filles de l'Opéra, dit la comtesse avec horreur. De tels feux doivent être peu durables, et ne vous laisser bientôt que des cendres ou des charbons, des regrets ou du désespoir. Une épouse, monsieur, doit vous offrir, à mon sens, une amitié vraie, une chaleur égale.]

97 Ibid., 22, 108. [2, 80: doué de tous les vices possibles.]

98 Etienne de Senancour, *De l'amour, selon les lois primordiales et selon les convenances des sociétés modernes* [1806], 2 vols. (Paris: Vieilh de Boisjoslin, rev. 3/1829), 2, 213–14. This work had been republished five times by 1925. [Pour que cette union soit troublée amèrement, il suffira que l'un des deux époux se voie saisi d'une passion nouvelle qu'il croira indomptable.]

99 Balzac, "A Double Family," 22, 114. ["Une Double Famille," 2, 84: Le défaut d'union entre deux époux, par quelque cause qu'il soit produit, amène d'effroyables malheurs.]

100 Balzac, "Gobseck," in *Novelettes*, 265–306. ["Gobseck," in *La Comédie humaine*, ed. Castex, 1, 961–1013.]

101 Balzac, "Domestic Peace," in *Selected Short Stories*, trans. Sylvia Raphael (Harmondsworth: Penguin, 1977), 26–62. ["La Paix du ménage," in *La Comédie humaine*, ed. Castex, 2, 95–130.] See also Davin [1835], in *La Comédie humaine*, ed. Castex, 1, 1163, and Anne-Marie Meininger's introduction to "La Paix du ménage," in ibid., 2, 87–93.

102 Davin [1835], in *La Comédie humaine*, ed. Castex, 1, 1163. [La Paix du ménage est un joli croquis, une vue de l'empire, un conseil donné aux femmes d'être indulgentes pour les erreurs de leurs maris.]

103 Balzac, "At the Sign of the Cat and Racket," 601. ["La Maison du Chat-qui-pelote," 1, 65: A cette singulière époque, le commerce et la finance avaient plus que jamais la folle manie de s'allier aux grands seigneurs.]

104 Ibid. [Ses axiomes favoris étaient que, pour trouver le bonheur, une femme devait épouser un homme de sa classe.]

105 Balzac, "A Double Family," 114. ["Une Double Famille," 2, 84: nous sommes, tôt ou tard, punis de n'avoir pas obéi aux lois sociales.]

106 Balzac, "At the Sign of the Cat and Racket," 606. ["La Maison du Chat-qui-pelote, 1, 77: il est des mésalliances d'esprit

aussi bien que des mésalliances de moeurs et de rang.]

107   Stendhal, *The Red and the Black*, 359; *Le Rouge et le noir*, 414. [Chronique du xixe siècle. [...] Un roman est un miroir qui se promène sur une grande route.]

108   Stendhal, "Avertissement de l'éditeur," *Le Rouge et le noir*, 19. On the chronology and circumstances of its production, see Béatrice Didier, "Postface," in ibid., 577–606, and Donald M. Frame, "Afterward," in Stendhal, *The Red and the Black*, 521–32. [Nous avons lieu de croire que les feuilles suivantes furent écrites en 1827.]

109   For accounts of the trial, see "Justice criminelle: Cour d'assises de l'Isère (Grenoble)," *Gazette des tribunaux*, 28, 29, 30, 31 Dec. 1827. The articles are reprinted in Stendhal, *Le Rouge et le noir*, ed. Didier, 623–46. On Berthet, see also René Fonvieille, *La Véritable Julien Sorel* (Paris: Arthaud, 1971).

110   On the relative ages of the protagonists, see Stendhal, *The Red and the Black*, for Madame de Rênal: Book I, chap. vii, 47, and i, vii, 51; for Julien Sorel: i, vi, 38; and for Monsieur de Rênal, i, i, 14. [*Le Rouge et le noir*, for Madame de Rênal: 63 and 69; for Julien Sorel: 52; and for Monsieur de Rênal: 24: quarante-huit ou cinquante ans]

111   Ibid., i, vii, 52. [60.]

112   Ibid., i, xix, 121. [142: vos paroles ne peuvent ôter la fièvre à notre Stanislas.]

113   Ibid., i, xix, 121. [143: Le ciel me punit, aux yeux de Dieu, je suis coupable de meurtre. [...] Idées romanesques que tout cela! Julien, faites appeler le médecin à la pointe du jour.]

114   Ibid., i, ix.

115   Ibid., i, xi, 74. [92: Ne serait-ce pas, se dit-il, une façon de se moquer de cet être, si comblé de tous les avantages de la fortune, que de prendre possession de la main de sa femme, précisément en sa présence? Oui, je le ferai, moi, pour qui il a témoigné tant de mépris.]

116   Eve Kosofsky Sedgwick, *Between Men: English Literature and Male Homosocial Desire* (New York: Columbia University Press, 1985), 1–20.

117   "Tribunal de Rouen," *Gazette des tribunaux*, 20 Jan. 1827, 326; "Chronique judiciare," *GT*, 30 Jan. 1827, 362.

118   Stendhal, *The Red and the Black*, i, xix, 126. [149: Dès le même soir M. de Rênal reçut de la ville, avec son journal, une longue lettre anonyme qui lui apprenait dans le plus grand détail ce qui se passait chez lui.]

119   Ibid., i, xx, 130. [153: Madame,

Toutes vos petites menées sont connues; mais les personnes qui ont intérêt à les réprimer sont averties.]

120   Ibid., i, xxi, 134. Rênal refers to article 324 of the Penal Code, which states "The murder committed by the husband of his wife, as well as of her accomplice, at the moment when he catches them *in flagrante delicto* in the conjugal dwelling is excusable." [le meurtre commis par l'époux sur son épouse, ainsi que sur le complice, à l'instant où il les surprend en flagrant délit dans la maison conjugale, est excusable.] [157: je n'ai point de fille, et la façon dont je vais punir la mère ne nuira point à l'établissement de mes enfants; je puis surprendre ce petit paysan avec ma femme, et les tuer tous les deux; dans ce cas, le tragique de l'aventure en ôtera peut-être le ridicule. Cette idée lui sourit; il la suivit dans tous ses détails. Le Code pénal est pour moi et, quoi qu'il arrive, notre congrégation et mes amis du jury me sauveront.]

121   See A. Bedel, *Nouveau Traité de l'adultère et des enfans adultérins, selon les lois civiles et pénales* (Paris: Warée fils aîné, F. Bernard, 1826), 108. Bedel compared the Penal Code with standard Old Regime law, pointing out and analyzing the differences.

122   Stendhal, *The Red and the Black*, i, xxi, 135. [158: Un homme bien né, qui tient son rang comme moi, est haï de tous les plébéiens. Je me verrai dans ces affreux journaux de Paris; ô mon Dieu! quel abîme! voir l'antique nom de Rênal plongé dans la fange du ridicule ... Si je voyage jamais, il faudra changer de nom; quoi! quitter ce nom qui fait ma gloire et ma force. Quel comble de misère!]

123   Ibid., i, xvi, 100. [120: Le rang de sa maîtresse semblait l'élever au-dessus de lui-même.]

124   Ibid., i, xix, 121. [143: Mais comment ai-je pu inspirer un tel amour, moi, si pauvre, si mal élevé, si ignorant, quelquefois si grossier dans mes façons?]

125   Ibid., i, xix, 124. [147: Elle a beau être noble, et moi le fils d'un ouvrier, elle m'aime ... Je ne suis pas auprès d'elle un valet de chambre chargé des fonctions d'amant.]

126   Ibid., i, xxi, 135. [158: Si je ne tue pas ma femme, et que je la chasse avec ignominie, elle a sa tante à Besançon, qui lui donnera de la main à la main toute sa fortune. Ma femme ira vivre à Paris avec Julien; on le saura à Verrières, et je serai encore pris pour dupe.]

127   Ibid., i, xxi, 135. [158: Quoi, diront-ils, il n'a pas su même se venger de sa femme!]

128   Ibid., i, viii, 57. [74.]

129 Ibid., I, XXI, 136. [159: Elle se figurait sans cesse son mari tuant Julien à la chasse, comme par accident, et ensuite le soir lui faisant manger son coeur.]

130 Ibid., I, XXI, 142. [167: Il eût été sans pitié pour moi, se dit-elle!]

131 Ibid., I, XXI, 142. [167: Une odalisque du sérail peut à toute force aimer le sultan; il est tout-puissant, elle n'a aucun espoir de lui dérober son autorité par une suite de petites finesses. La vengeance du maître est terrible, sanglante, mais militaire, généreuse: un coup de poignard finit tout. C'est a coups de mépris public qu'un mari tue sa femme au XIXe siècle; c'est en lui fermant tous les salons.]

132 Overton, *The Novel of Female Adultery*, 5. Overton defines a "novel of adultery" as one where the adulterous liaison is central to its concerns, and by that criterion disqualifies *The Red and the Black*.

133 Translations, with occasional revisions, are taken from George Sand, *Indiana* [1832], trans. George Burnham Ives (Chicago: Academy Chicago Publishers, 1978); see also George Sand, *Indiana*, ed. Béatrice Didier (Paris: Gallimard, 1984).

134 Sand, *Indiana*, trans. Ives, XX, 193. [ed. Didier, XX, 219: la chaîne sous laquelle s'est brisée ma vie et flétrie ma jeunesse.]

135 Ibid., XXVI, 251. [271: Il avait pris une femme comme il eût pris une gouvernante.]

136 Ibid., "Preface to the edition of 1832," unpaginated. ["Préface de l'édition de 1832," 41: Raymon, répondra l'auteur, c'est la fausse raison, la fausse morale par qui la société est gouvernée.]

137 Ibid. [37: l'écrivain n'a presque rien créé. Si, dans le cours de sa tâche, il lui est arrivé d'exprimer des plaintes arrachées à ses personnages par le malaise social dont ils sont atteints; s'il n'a pas craint de répéter leurs aspirations vers une existence meilleure, qu'on s'en prenne à la société pour ses inégalités, à la destinée pour ses caprices! L'écrivain n'est qu'un miroir qui les reflète, une machine qui les décalque, et qui n'a rien à se faire pardonner si ses empreintes sont exactes, si son reflet est fidèle.]

138 Ibid. [41: un historien qui passe brutalement au milieu des faits, coudoyant à droite et à gauche sans plus d'égard pour un camp que pour l'autre.]

139 For the first edition, see George Sand, *Indiana*, 2 vols. (Paris: J.-P. Roret & H. Dupuy, 1832). [I, Part II, chap. XIV, 268: Vous voyez que je vous raconte une histoire extrêmement

vraisemblable et que confirme l'expérience de tous les jours.]

140 Ibid. [2, Part III, chap. VII, 134: un historien du coeur [. . .] les besoins, les désirs et les passions humaines aux prises avec les nécessités de la vie légale.]

141 Sand, *Indiana*, (trans. Ives), "Introduction" (1852), unpaginated [ed. Didier, "Notice" (1852), 35: On voulut y voir un plaidoyer bien prémédité contre le mariage. Je n'en cherchais pas si long.]

142 Ibid., XXV, 243. [264: Ces réflexions positives lui montraient à nu la sécheresse de coeur qui préside aux unions de convenance, et l'espoir d'avoir un jour une compagne digne de son amour n'entrait que par hasard dans les chances de son bonheur.]

143 Ibid., XXI, 206. [232: Je sais que je suis l'esclave et vous le seigneur. La loi de ce pays vous a fait mon maître. Vous pouvez liez mon corps, garrotter mes mains, gouverner mes actions. Vous avez le droit du plus fort, et la société vous le confirme.]

144 Ibid., XXIII, 224. [249: Vous vous croyez les maîtres du monde; je crois que vous n'en êtes que les tyrans. Vous pensez que Dieu vous protège et vous autorise à usurper l'empire de la terre; moi, je pense qu'il le souffre pour un peu de temps, et qu'un jour viendra où, comme des grains de sable, son souffle vous dispersera.]

145 Ibid., XXIII, 225. [249: toute votre morale, tous vos principes, ce sont les intérêts de votre société que vous avez érigés en lois et que vous prétendez faire émaner de Dieu même.]

146 Ibid., "Preface to the 1832 Edition," unpaginated. ["Préface de l'édition de 1832," 39: vous trouverez mauvais que je n'aie pas jeté dans la misère et l'abandon l'être qui, pendant deux volumes, a transgressé les lois humaines. Ici, l'auteur vous répondra qu'avant d'être moral, il a voulu être vrai.]

147 George Sand, "Lettre XII, à M. Nisard," *Lettres d'un voyageur* (Paris: Michel Lévy, 1869), 336; the letter was written in 1836 to the *Revue de Paris*, where Nisard had published an article on Sand.

148 Sand, *Indiana*, trans. Ives, XI, 107. [ed. Didier, XI, 142: J'aime mon cousin comme un frère.]

149 Ibid., XXX, 301. [318.]

150 Stendhal, *The Red and the Black*, I, XIX, 123. [145: t'aimerai-je comme un frère? Est-il en mon pouvoir de t'aimer comme un frère?]

151 Sand, *Indiana*, trans. Ives, XIX, 283. [ed. Didier, 301: de tuteur et de père.]

152 Ibid., "Preface to the Edition of 1842," unpaginated. [ed. Didier, "Préface de l'édition de 1842," 42: une série de romans basés à peu près tous sur la même donnée: le rapport mal établi entre les sexes, par le fait de la société.]

153 Ibid., "Conclusion," 326 (my revised translation). ["Conclusion," 342: vous êtes jeune, répondit-il; pour vous, conscience naïve et pure que n'a pas salie le monde, notre bonheur signe notre vertu; pour le monde, il fait notre crime.]

154 Ibid., XXVI, 252. [272: Aussi toutes les réflexions d'Indiana, toutes ses démarches, toutes ses douleurs, se rapportaient à cette grande et terrible lutte de la nature contre la civilisation.]

155 Ibid., XXVI, 252. [272: Mais peut-être ce besoin de bonheur qui nous dévore, cette haine de l'injustice, cette soif de liberté qui ne s'éteignent qu'avec la vie, sont-ils les facultés constituantes de l'*égotisme*, qualification par laquelle les Anglais désignent l'amour de soi, considéré comme un droit de l'homme et non comme un vice.]

6 Many Ways to Ride a Horse

1 Jürgen N. Schultze, *Art of Nineteenth-Century Europe*, trans. Barbara Forryan (New York: Harry N. Abrams, 1979), 52.

2 Paris: Grand Palais; Detroit Institute of Arts; New York: Metropolitan Museum of Art, *French Painting 1774–1830: The Age of Revolution* (exh. cat., 1974–75), 653.

3 There are seven paintings and eight drawings or prints of *Paolo and Francesca*; see Patricia Condon, *Ingres. In Pursuit of Perfection: The Art of J.-A.-D. Ingres* (exh. cat., Louisville, Ky.: J. B. Speed Art Museum, 1983), 70–77, 170–75. There are four paintings and five drawings or prints of *Antiochus and Stratonice*; ibid, 60–63.

4 See, for example, Tintoretto, *Joseph and Potiphar's Wife*, 1555 (Prado, Madrid).

5 See, for example, Titian, *Lucretia*, 1515 (Kunsthistorisches Museum, Vienna); Veronese, *Lucretia*, 1580–83 (Kunsthistorisches Museum, Vienna); Rembrandt, *Lucretia*, 1664 (National Gallery of Art, Washington, D.C.); Gavin Hamilton, *Brutus Swearing to Avenge Lucretia's Death*, c. 1763 (Drury Lane Theatre, London).

6 The only nineteenth-century French painting of this theme that I have located is Emile Signol's *Christ and the Woman Taken in Adultery*, 1842 (Detroit Institute of Arts).

7 See Victor Hugo, "Mazeppa," *Poésie*, ed. Bernard Leuillot, 3 vols. (Paris: Seuil, 1972), 1, 250–52; for *Les Orientales*, see 206–64.

8 For Byron's "Mazeppa" [1818], see *Byron: Poetical Works*, ed. Frederick Page (Oxford: Oxford University Press, 1970), 341–48.

9 Léopold and Cuvelier [Léopold A. Chandenson and Jean Cuvelier de Trie], *Mazeppa, ou Le Cheval tartare, mimodrame en trois actes, tiré de lord Byron, par MM. Léopold et Cuvelier, mis en scène par M. Franconi jeune, musique de M. Sergent, représenté pour la première fois au Cirque de MM. Franconi, directeurs privilégiés du roi* (Paris: Chez Bezou, 1825). It was first performed at the Théâtre du Cirque olympique in Paris on January 11, 1825. Information on the various print editions was published by Jean-Pierre Mouilleseaux, in *Mazeppa: Variations sur un thème romantique* (exh. cat., Rouen: Musée des beaux-arts, 1978).

10 Hubert F. Babinski, *The Mazeppa Legend in European Romanticism* (New York: Columbia University Press, 1974), an indispensable reference book, was the first to catalogue all the occurrences of the theme; the study focuses on Eastern Europe, however, labeling Western manifestations merely as products of "the European imagination"; see 18. Mouilleseaux, in *Mazeppa*, also catalogued most of the Western works of art and literature inspired by the Mazeppa theme. Neither Mouilleseaux nor Babinski offered any interpretations.

11 Biographical information on Mazeppa [or Mazepa] is extremely polarized, depending on whether the historian's allegiances are with the Ukraine or with Russia. For a pro-Ukraine, pro-Mazeppa account, see Elie Borschak and René Martel, *Vie de Mazeppa* (Paris: Calmann-Lévy, 1931), or Clarence A. Manning, *Hetman of Ukraine: Ivan Mazeppa* (New York: Bookman, 1957). For a pro-Russia, anti-Mazeppa account, see Evgenii Anisimov, *The Reforms of Peter the Great: Progress through Coercion in Russia*, trans. John T. Alexander (New York: Armonk; and London: M. E. Sharpe, 1993), 111–17.

12 See Jan Chrysostome [Chryzostom] Pasek, *Les Mémoires de Jean Chrysostome Pasek, gentilhomme polonais 1656–1688,*

trans. and ed. Paul Cazin (Paris: Les Belles-let-tres, n.d.); for the story of Mazeppa's alleged affair and punishment, see 188–89. Note that the dates given by Cazin for Pasek's years of birth and death have been revised by later scholarship.

13 Manning, *Hetman of the Ukraine,* 227.

14 Anisimov, *The Reforms of Peter the Great,* 111.

15 Voltaire, *Histoire de Charles XII, roi de Suède* [1731] (Amsterdam: Libraires associés, 1805), 168.

16 Biographical discussion of Byron is based on Leslie A. Marchand, *Byron: A Biography,* 3 vols. (New York: Alfred A. Knopf, 1957); for "Mazeppa," see 2, 754. A complete list of editions of Byron's works in France is given by Edmond Estève, *Byron et le romantisme française: Essai sur la fortune et l'influence de l'oeuvre de Byron en France de 1812 à 1850* (Paris: Boivin, 1929), 525–33. "Mazeppa" was first published in English in France as part of *The Works of the Right Honourable Lord Byron* (Paris: Galignani, 1818). The first French translation of "Mazeppa" was by Amédée Pichot and Eusèbe de Salle in their *Oeuvres de lord Byron,* 10 vols. (Paris: Ladvocat, 1819–21); "Mazeppa" is in vol. 2. For additional information about Byron in France, see also Paris: Maison Renan-Scheffer, Musée de la vie romantique, *Lord Byron: une vie romantique 1788–1824* (exh. cat., 1988).

17 For Byron's behavior and the rumors surrounding his separation from his wife, spread by the Poet Laureate Robert Southey, see Marchand, *Byron: A Biography,* 2, 563–608. Jane Clairmont was the legal, although not the blood, sister of Mary Shelley; ibid., 2, 752–53.

18 See Iris Origo, *The Last Attachment: The Story of Byron and Teresa Guiccioli as Told in Their Unpublished Letters and Other Family Papers* (New York: Charles Scribner's Sons, 1949). Byron had met the contessa Guiccioli before he wrote "Mazeppa," but their passionate affair did not begin until several months later. He wrote "I have fallen in love with a Romagnuola Countess from Ravenna – who is nineteen years old & has a Count of fifty whom she seems disposed to qualify the first year of marriage being just over. – I knew her a little last year at her starting, but they always wait a year – at least generally"; letter to John Cam Hobhouse, April 6, 1819, in George Gordon, Lord Byron, *Byron's Letters and Journals,* ed. Leslie A. Marchand, 12 vols.

(Cambridge, Mass.: Harvard University Press, 1973–82), 6: *(1818–1819),* 106–08. For brief biographies of conte and contessa Guiccioli, see 6, 276–78. See also Marchand, *Byron: A Biography,* 2, 773–74, 754.

19 On Byron's fears of the count, see his letters to Douglas Kinnaird, July 20, 1820, in *Byron's Letters,* ed. Marchand, 7: *(1820),* 136–37, and to the countess, July 23, 1820, in ibid., 139–40.

20 See Alan Spitzer, *The French Generation of 1820* (Princeton: Princeton University Press, 1987).

21 See Estève, *Byron et le romantisme française,* 32.

22 See the following poems in *Byron: Poetical Works,* ed. Page: "Ode to Napoleon Buonaparte," 73–75; "On Napoleon's Escape from Elba," 84; "Ode from the French," 84–85; "On the Star of 'The Legion of Honour,' " 85–86; "Napoleon's Farewell," 86. All citations of Byron's poetry are from this edition.

23 See, for example, "Memoir of the Right Honorable Lord Byron," in *Lord Byron's Works,* 12 vols. (Paris: Louis & Baudry, 1820–24), 1, xii, and Amédée Pichot, "Essai sur le génie et le caractère de lord Byron," in *Oeuvres de lord Byron [. . .], précédée d'une notice sur lord Byron par Charles Nodier,* trans. Pichot, 8 vols. (Paris: Ladvocat, rev. 4/1822–25), 1, lxxii.

24 W. C., "Critical Remarks on New Publications: Mazeppa, a Poem by Lord Byron," *The New Monthly Magazine,* 12 (1 Aug. 1819), 67.

25 Pichot, "Essai sur le génie et le caractère de lord Byron," in *Oeuvres de lord Byron,* 1, iv. These English interpretations of Byron's "Mazeppa" are not mentioned in Marchand, Babinski, or Mouilleseaux, nor in William H. Marshall, "A Reading of Byron's 'Mazeppa,' " *Modern Language Notes,* 76 (Feb. 1961), 120–24. [Quelques-uns de ces hommes aujourd'hui si communs en Angleterre, qui cherchent partout de criminelles intentions, se sont écriés que lord Byron a voulu consacrer l'adultère et l'inceste.]

26 Pichot, "Essai sur le génie et le caractère de lord Byron," in *Oeuvres de lord Byron,* 1, iv. [Lord Byron a tellement identifié son caractère avec ses écrits, dont une grand partie est comme un miroir où se réfléchissent tous les mouvements de son âme, que le critique doit bien se pénétrer du sentiment de son impartialité avant de condamner dans ses jugements l'homme avec le poète.]

27   Babinski, *The Mazeppa Legend*, 22.

28   A. de V. [Alfred de Vigny], "Littérature anglaise: Oeuvres complètes de lord Byron," *Conservateur littéraire*, 3 (Dec. 1820), 214–15. [*Mazeppa* est un effort extraordinaire d'une imagination bien riche; car quel autre que lord Byron aurait osé composer un poëme avec le simple récit d'un homme emporté par un cheval sauvage? Quel autre aurait pu réussir?]

29   My quotations are from the English version of "Mazeppa" in *Byron: Poetical Works*, ed. Page, 341–48, as it is impossible to know who read which of the English and French versions available in France during the 1820s. The plot line remained the same, however, in all the editions, and, in any case, most of the artists cited here read English.

30   "Mazeppa," in Pierre Larousse, *Grand Dictionnaire universel du XIXe siècle*, 17 vols. (Paris: Librairie classique Larousse et Boyer, 1866–90). [Dans leurs âpres imaginations, je les ai souvent entendus dire que la France, liée à sa révolution, rassemble à *Mazeppa* emporté loin de toutes les routes frayées par le cheval que sa main ne peut régir. [. . .] Cela est vrai peut-être; seulement, il fallait ajouter qu'au moment où tout semble perdu, c'est alors qu'il se relève au bruit des acclamations de ceux qui l'ont fait roi.]

31   Plato, "Phaedrus," *The Dialogues of Plato*, trans. B. Jowett, 2 vols. (New York: Random House, 1937), 1, 250–51, 257–58.

32   See "Cheval," in Jean Chevalier and Alain Gheerbrant, *Dictionnaire des symboles, mythes, rêves, coutumes, gestes, formes, figures, couleurs, nombres* (Paris: Robert Laffont, rev. 1982). The authors point out that Christ, Buddha, and Muhammad all are depicted riding white horses. On equestrian imagery, see also Walter Liedtke, *The Royal Horse and Rider: Painting, Sculpture and Horsemanship 1500–1800* (New York: Abaris Books and Metropolitan Museum of Art, 1989).

33   See Roger Chartier, "The World Turned Upside-Down," in his *Cultural History: Between Practices and Representations*, trans. Lydia G. Cochrane (Ithaca, N.Y.: Cornell University Press, 1988), 115–26; Natalie Zemon Davis, "Women on Top," in her *Society and Culture in Early Modern France* (Stanford, Calif.: Stanford University Press, 1975), 124–51; Frédérick Tristan, *Le Monde à l'envers* (Paris: Hachette, 1980).

34   Ruth Mellinkoff, "Riding Backwards: Theme of Humiliation and Symbol of Evil," *Viator: Medieval and Renaissance Studies*, 4 (1973), 153–76.

35   See Henri Rey-Filaud, *Le Charivari: Les Rituels fondamentaux de la sexualité* (Paris: Payot, 1985), 145–47; Jacques Le Goff and Jean-Claude Schmitt, eds., *Colloque sur le Charivari: Actes de la table ronde organisée à Paris (25–27 avril 1977 par l'Ecole des hautes études en sciences sociales et le Centre national de la recherche scientifique)* (Paris: Mouton, 1981); Davis, "The Reasons of Misrule," in her *Society and Culture in Early Modern France*, 97–123.

36   See Morton W. Bloomfield, *The Seven Deadly Sins: An Introduction to the History of a Religious Concept with Special Reference to Medieval English Literature* (East Lansing: Michigan State University Press, 1967), 131–32.

37   See Pauline Schmitt-Pantel, "L'Ane, l'adultère et la cité," in Le Goff and Schmitt, eds., *Colloque sur le Charivari*, 117–22. Schmitt-Pantel describes the ritual "feminization" of the bachelor adulterer as including the shaving of his body and the wearing of a woman's cap.

38   Cesare Ripa, *Baroque and Rococo Pictorial Imagery: The 1758–60 Hertel Edition of Ripa's Iconolgia*, ed. Edward A. Maser (New York: Dover, 1971), pl. 46. Among French editions, see "Adultère," in Jean-Baptiste Boudard, *Iconologie tirée de divers auteurs, ouvrage utile aux gens de lettres, aux poëtes, aux artistes, et généralement à tous les amateurs des beaux-arts*, 2 vols. (Parma and Paris: Tilliard, 1759), 1, 12, and "Adultère," in Eugéne Droulers, *Dictionnaire des attributs, allégories, emblèmes et symboles* (Turnhout, Belgium: Brépols, n.d.).

39   "Adultère," in Boudard, *Iconologie*, 1, 12. [Ce vice énorme est figuré par un homme replet, dans un déshabillé voluptueux, & couché mollement sur des coussins; ses attributs sont une lamproie accouplée avec un serpent & un anneau conjugal qui est rompu.]

40   Estève, *Byron et le romantisme française*, 193. I am not the first to note Géricault's identification with Mazeppa; Dénise Aimé-Azam titled her biography *Mazeppa, Géricault et son temps* (Paris: Plon, 1956), republished as *La Passion de Géricault* (Paris: Fayard, 1970). The film *Mazeppa* (1993) by Bartabas with text by Homéric also recounts the biography of Géricault through the story of Mazeppa. See also J. V. L., "Littérature étrangère. Mazeppa: A Poem by Lord Byron,"

Lycée français, ou Mélanges de littérature et de critique, 1 (1819), 161.

41 The lithographs are reproduced in Löys Delteil, *Le Peintre-Graveur illustré*, 18: *Géricault* [1924] (New York: Da Capo, 1969); see no. 94.

42 Her identity was unknown until Lorenz Eitner identified her in his *Géricault* (exh. cat., Los Angeles County Museum of Art, 1971). On the affair, see Michel Le Pesant, "Documents inédits sur Géricault," *Revue de l'art*, 31 (1976), 73–81.

43 Henry Houssaye in *La Revue des deux-mondes* (Nov. 1879), quoted in Pierre Courthion, ed., *Géricault raconté par lui-même et par ses amis* (Geneva: P. Cailler, 1947), 172. [Cette liaison qui eut une influence fatale sur toute la vie de Géricault, explique son existence fantasque, inquiète, tourmentée, pleine d'angoisses et de douleurs.]

44 Robert Viscusi, "Coining," *Differentia: Review of Italian Thought*, 2 (Spring 1988), 9–42.

45 Eitner, *Géricault*, cat. no. 34.

46 Ibid. See also "Centaurs and Nymphs," in Lorenz Eitner, *Géricault: His Life and Work* (London: Orbis, 1983), 102–10.

47 Undated letter to Pierre-Joseph Dedreux-Dorcy from Italy, published in Charles Clément, *Géricault: Etude biographique et critique avec le catalogue raisonné de l'oeuvre du maître* (Paris: Didier, 1868), 89. [des embarras terribles où je me suis jeté imprudemment.]

48 On Géricault's "Centauromachie," see Germain Bazin, *Théodore Géricault: Etude critique, documents et catalogue raisonné*, 7 vols. (Paris: Bibliothèque des arts, 1987–97), 4: *Le Voyage en Italie*, 26; Bazin identifies them all as either Nessus abducting Deianira or the abduction of a female lapith at the banquet of Pirithos.

49 Racine treated the theme in his tragedy *Phèdre* (1677) and Guérin, Géricault's teacher, painted *Phaedra and Hippolytus* in 1802 (Figure 78 above). There were other paintings of the death of Hippolytus in the Salon during these years: Jacques-Charles Bordier du Bignon showed *Le Combat d'Hippolite contre le monstre* (no. 128) and *La Mort d'Hippolite* (no. 129) in the Salon of 1814; Alexandre-Charles Guillemot showed *La Mort d'Hypolite, suivant le récit de Théramène* (no. 654) in the Salon of 1822. See the corresponding Salon catalogues: Paris: Musée royal des arts, *Explication des ouvrages de peinture*.

50 Le Pesant, "Documents inédits sur Géricault," 76–77. Géricault's will of November 30, 1823 left everything to his father, and his father's will of December 2, 1823 bequeathed everything to Georges Hippolyte. After Géricault died on January 26, 1824, however, his father was persuaded by a nephew to remake his will, which he did on July 24, 1824, leaving Géricault's son a few farms and dividing the rest among cousins, nieces, and nephews.

51 Lorenz Eitner has also linked the painting's subject to Géricault's personal life; see his *Géricault's Raft of the Medusa* (London: Phaidon, 1972), 13.

52 Eitner, *Géricault: His Life and Work*, 214–37.

53 See Paris: Grand Palais, *Géricault*, 1991, cat. no. 291.

54 Alfred de Musset, *Confession of a Child of the Century* [1836] (New York: Current Literature Publishing Company, 1910), 84 (with minor revisions); Alfred de Musset, *La Confession d'un enfant du siècle* (Paris: A. Colin, 1962), Part 2, chap. 2, 77. [Ils s'attachent sur la débauche comme Mazeppa sur sa bête sauvage; ils s'y garrottent, ils se font centaures; et ils ne voient ni la route de sang que les lambeaux de leur chair tracent sur les arbres, ni les yeux des loups qui se teignent de pourpre à leur suite, ni le désert, ni les corbeaux.]

55 See Philippe Grunchec, *Géricault: Dessins et aquarelles de chevaux* (Paris: Edita, Bibliothèque des arts, 1982).

56 See Alfred Robaut, *L'Oeuvre complet de Eugène Delacroix* [1885] (New York: Da Capo, 1969), nos. 1493–94 and 262.

57 On the Cairo *Mazeppa*, see Lee Johnson, "Mazeppa in Giza: A Riddle Solved," *Burlington Magazine*, 125 (Aug. 1983), 491–94, where the picture is dated to 1824 on the basis of style and repeated mentions of such a theme in Delacroix's journal entries from March to May 1824. Robaut had dated it 1828 (no. 262), possibly because of the Vernet and Delacroix paintings in the Salon of 1827–28. The "riddle" is the mention in the literature of a *Mazeppa* belonging to David d'Angers, identified by Johnson as the Cairo picture. Johnson's discussion includes all the surviving Delacroix Mazeppas, the two pencil drawings, the copy after Géricault, and the watercolor.

58 George Heard Hamilton, "Eugène Delacroix and Lord Byron," *Gazette des beaux-arts*, ser. 6/23 (Feb. 1943), 99–110, and ser. 6/26 (July–Dec. 1944), 365–86.

59   Robaut, *L'Oeuvre complet de Eugène Delacroix,* no. 1493. [un beau prétexte à un grand développement de lignes, à de fiers mouvements, à un rare déploiement d'énergie, en même temps que de précieux contrastes pittoresques.]

60   Johnson, "Mazeppa in Giza," 492.

61   Information on Soulier is drawn from Eugène Delacroix, *Journal 1822–1863,* ed. André Joubin (Paris: Plon, 1980), 26, n. 5, and from Raymond Escholier, *Delacroix et les femmes* (Paris: Fayard, 1963), 43–50.

62   Escholier, 43–50.

63   See the entries in Delacroix, *Journal,* ed. Joubin, 27 Oct. 1822 to 23 Dec. 1823.

64   Ibid., 27 Oct. 1822. [Le premier moment a été tout au bonheur de le revoir. J'ai senti ensuite un serrement pénible. [. . .] j'espère que mon tort envers lui n'influera pas sur ses relations avec . . . Dieu veuille qu'il l'ignore toujours! Et pourquoi dans ce moment même, sens-je quelque chose comme de la vanité satisfaite? Oh! s'il apprenait quelque chose, il serait désolé.]

65   See Lee Johnson, *The Paintings of Eugène Delacroix,* 2 vols. (Oxford: Clarendon Press, 1981), 1, 97–98; 2, pl. 97. Johnson dated it *c.* 1825 while giving as its sources works published in 1822 and 1824. As there is no firm evidence of the later date, I think that it is more likely that it was actually painted 1822–24.

66   Delacroix, *Journal,* ed. Joubin, 10 Nov. 1823. [Dis que ton coeur est assez vaste pour deux amis: car l'un ni l'autre n'est amant. Alors, je ne serai pas jaloux, alors, je crois que je ne me regarderai pas comme coupable en te possédant.]

67   Johnson did so in 1983; see his "Mazeppa in Giza."

68   Punishment for adultery was specified in Penal Code articles 324 and 337–38.

69   Unfortunately there is little recent scholarship on Vernet; see Rome: Académie de France à Rome; Paris: Ecole nationale supérieure des beaux-arts, *Horace Vernet (1789–1863)* (exh. cat., 1980).

70   See "Horace Vernet," in Paris: Grand Palais, *French Painting 1774–1830,* 651–54, and [Victor-Joseph de] Jouy and [Antoine] Jay, *Salon d'Horace Vernet: Analyse historique et pittoresque des quarante-cinq tableaux exposés chez lui en 1822* (Paris: Ponthieu, 1822).

71   See Paris: Galerie Lebrun, *Exposition des ouvrages de peintures exposés au profit des Grecs: Galerie Lebrun, rue du Gros-Chênet* (exh. cat., Paris: Didot, 1826), no. 189. For an account of the exhibition and an appendix

reprinting the catalogue, see Nina Maria Athanassoglou-Kallmyer, *French Images from the Greek War of Independence 1821–1830: Art and Politics under the Restoration* (New Haven: Yale University Press, 1989), 39–40, 156–65. This painting was acquired by the king in 1832, was installed at the National Assembly in Paris, and was destroyed by fire in 1961.

72   Vitet wrote five articles on the exhibition, the first of which appeared on May 23, 1826 on the front page; see L. V. [Louis Vitet], "France. Beaux-arts: Exposition de tableaux au bénéfice des grecs," *Le Globe, Journal littéraire* (23 May 1826), 345–46. [Aussitôt ils formèrent le projet, ils arrêtèrent le plan d'une exposition libre et déjà ils en commençaient les apprêts quand les cris de détresse des malheureux Hellènes se firent entendre. Consacrer au projet du malheur une entreprise fait au profit de l'art, convertir un acte d'indépendance en une oeuvre de charité, tel fut le voeu spontané de tous les artistes, et l'exposition s'est ouverte au bénéfice des grecs.]

73   See Paris: Galerie Lebrun, *Exposition des ouvrages de peintures,* cat. no. 44. Vitet also quoted the catalogue legend, in *Le Globe* (1 June 1826), 372. [Le Doge de Venise, Marino Faliero ayant, à l'âge de plus de quatre-vingts ans, conspiré contre la république, avait été condamné à mort par le Senat.]

74   See Paris: Galerie Lebrun, *Expositions des ouvrages de peinture,* cat. no. 189: "Mazeppa, sujet tiré d'une nouvelle de lord Byron."

75   Vernet sent several paintings to the Salon, including both versions of *Mazeppa;* they were listed in the catalogue as "1031: Plusieurs tableaux"; see Paris: Musée royal des arts, *Explication des ouvrages de peinture [. . .] exposés [. . .] le 4 novembre 1827* (Paris: Mme Veuve Ballard, 1827). I have identified the paintings through the reviews.

76   Auguste Jal, *Esquisses, croquis, pochades, ou Tout ce qu'on voudra sur le Salon de 1827* (Paris: Ambroise Dupont, 1828), 339. [Cet ouvrage eut du succès même avant que d'être achevé, car M. Horace n'est pas moins heureux que le poëte dont on a dit 'On récite déjà les vers qu'il fait encore.']

77   Ibid., 343. [Trop polis; note that the word *poli* means both "polished" and "polite."] Antoine-Nicolas Béraud, *Annales de l'Ecole française des beaux-arts: Recueil de gravures [. . . Salon de 1827]* (Paris: Pillet-aîné, 1828), 68. [mentir à leur nature sauvage.]

78 Jal, *Esquisses*, 343. [c'est moins une académie.]

79 Several examples of Mazeppa-inspired objects are reproduced in Mouilleseaux, *Mazeppa*.

80 He is quoted in Aug. Deloye, *Notice des tableaux exposés dans les galeries du Museum-Calvet à Avignon* (Avignon: Seguin frères, 1879), 118. [une de ses moins mauvaises productions.]

81 There are two identical versions of this painting, both in the Musée Calvet, Avignon, and a sketch for it in the Kunsthalle, Bremen. When the painting was slightly damaged, Vernet repaired it, but the museum commissioned him to paint a replica and now owns both paintings. See Avignon: Musée Calvet, *Notice des tableaux exposés au profit des pauvres dans la galerie Vernet au Muséum Calvet* (exh. cat., Avignon: Guichard aîné, 1826); Joseph Girard, "Les Souvenirs des Vernet au Musée Calvet: Conférence faite pendant le séance de l'Académie de Vaucluse au Musée Calvet le 12 mai 1927 pour la commémoration du centenaire de la galerie Vernet," *Mémoires de l'Académie de Vaucluse*, 2nd ser., 27 (1927), 49–61; Joseph Girard, *Catalogue des tableaux exposés dans les galeries du Musée-Calvet d'Avignon* (Avignon: Seguin, 1909), nos. 417–18; Paris: Grand Palais, *French Painting 1774–1830*, no. 187.

82 Jal, *Esquisses*, 341. [Tous les dangers dont la route de Mazeppa est semée, les torrens, les arbres renversés, l'épaisseur des bois et la nuit qui, laissant le coursier sans direction, va le livrer peut-être aux loups; tous ces dangers sont d'une excellente invention.]

83 For a similar reaction, see [Armand-Denis Vergnaud], *Examen du Salon de 1827: Seconde Partie, novembre et décembre* (Paris: Roret, 1828), 31.

84 For a summary of the literature on this painting, see Paris: Grand Palais, *French Painting 1774–1830*, 652–54. [Le produit de cette lithographie est destiné à secourir les familles victimes des mémorables événements de juillet 1830.]

85 Avignon: Musée Calvet, *Notice des tableaux*; Girard, "Les Souvenirs des Vernets au Musée Calvet," 49–61. [au profit des pauvres].

86 Paris: Musée royal des arts, *Explication des ouvrages de peinture [. . .] le 4 novembre 1827, Ier supplément*, no. 1435. See also Aristide Marie, *Le Peintre poète Louis Boulanger* (Paris: H. Floury, 1925), 24–28.

87 Hugo, "Mazeppa," in *Poésie*, ed. Leuillot, 1, 250–52.

88 Charles Baudelaire, "Salon of 1845," *Art in Paris 1845–1862*, trans. and ed. Jonathan Mayne (Oxford: Phaidon, 1981), 13 (with revisions); Baudelaire, "Salon de 1845," *Écrits sur l'art*, ed. Yves Florenne, 2 vols. (Paris: Gallimard, 1971), 1, 75. [Voilà les dernières ruines de l'ancien romantisme – voilà ce que c'est que de venir dans un temps où il as reçu de croire que l'inspiration suffit et remplace le reste; – voilà l'abîme où mène la course désordonnée de Mazeppa. – C'est M. Victor Hugo qui a perdu M. Boulanger – après en avoir perdu tant d'autres – c'est le poëte qui a fait tomber le peintre dans la fosse.]

89 Pétrus Borel, "Des Artistes penseurs et des artistes creux," *L'Artiste*, 1st ser., 5 (1833), 253–59; quotation on 258. [Car Louis Boulanger non-seulement est un homme de pensée, un peintre de conviction, mais il possède ce qui peut tout racheter, une prodigieuse imagination. [. . .] Quelle science, quelle énergie, quel mouvement, quelle cohue, quelle terreur, quel effroi! [. . .] Ses compositions sont toujours empreintes de gravité, de tristesse, de rêverie, qui charment, qui séduisent; elles sont toujours expressives et largement poétiques. [. . .] Dès son premier essor, dès son tableau de *Mazeppa*, Boulanger décela toutes ses éminentes qualités.]

90 See Paris: Musée royal des arts, *Explication des ouvrages de peinture [. . .] le 4 november 1827, Ier supplément*, no. 1435. [Mazeppa est attaché sur un cheval indompté, par l'ordre du comte Palatin, qu'il a outragé. (Lord Byron, Mazeppa, strophe 10); *recte* stanza 9.]

91 Schmitt-Pantel, "L'Ane, l'adultère et la cité," 117–22.

92 See Eve Kosofsky Sedgwick, *Between Men: English Literature and Male Homosocial Desire* (New York: Columbia University Press, 1985), 1–20.

93 E.-J. Delécluze, "Beaux-arts: Troisième Lettre au rédacteur du *Lycée français*, sur l'exposition des ouvrages de peinture, sculpture, architecture et gravure des artistes vivans," *Lycée français, ou Mélanges de littérature et de critique par une société de gens de lettres*, 1 (10 Sept. 1819), 361–71.

94 See chapter 3, n. 15.

95 Quotations from Hugo's "Mazeppa" are from his *Poésie*, ed. Leuillot, 1, 250–52. For Hugo's epigraph, see *Byron: Poetical Works*, ed. Page, "Mazeppa," 344, line 375.

96 Hugo, "Mazeppa," *Poésie*, ed. Leuillot, 1, 250–52, lines 103–08; my translation. [Ainsi, lorsqu'un mortel, sur qui son dieu

s'étale, / S'est vu lier vivant sur ta croupe fatale, / Génie, ardent coursier, / En vain il lutte, hélas! tu bondis, tu l'emportes / Hors du monde réel dont tu brises les portes / Avec tes pieds d'acier!]

97 Translation from Babinski, *The Mazeppa Legend*, with revisions, 72; Hugo, "Mazeppa," *Poésie*, ed. Leuillot, 1, 250–52, lines 133–38. [Il crie épouvanté, tu poursuis implacable. / Pâle, épuisé, béant, sous ton vol qui l'accable / Il ploie avec effroi; / Chaque pas que tu fais semble creuser sa tombe. / Enfin le terme arrive . . . il court, il vole, il tombe, / Et se relève roi!]

98 "L-x" [Pierre Leroux], "Littérature: Du style symbolique," *Le Globe: Recueil philosophique, politique et littéraire*, 8 April. 1829, 223. [Ainsi s'opère la fusion de l'idée morale dans l'image physique; l'assimilation est parfaite. Le génie, ses tourments intérieurs, les blasphèmes qui le poursuivent d'abord, les adorations qui succèdent aux blasphèmes, toutes ces pures conceptions de l'intelligence, sont devenus visibles. Nous avons un symbole, et non pas une comparaison.]

99 See n. 9 above; Estève, *Byron et le romantisme française*, gives the date incorrectly as 1826.

100 Klaus Berger, *Géricault et son oeuvre*, trans. Maurice Beerblock (Paris: Bernard Grasset, 1952), 8.

101 John Howard Payne, *Mazeppa, or The Wild Horse of Tartary*, in *Trial without Jury and Other Plays by John Howard Payne*, ed. Codman Hislop and W. R. Richardson (Princeton: Princeton University Press, 1940), 163–204. According to the editors, it was never performed. Henry M. Milner, *Mazeppa: A Romantic Drama in Three Acts, Dramatised from Lord Byron's Poem* (London: John Cumberland [?1831]). Milner's version premièred at the Royal Adelphi Theatre in London on April 4, 1831, and later played in New York at the Bowery Theatre, July 22, 1833. On these two plays, see the introductory remarks in Milner, *Mazeppa*, 5–8, and the preface to Payne, *Trial without Jury*, 165.

102 Léopold and Cuvelier, *Mazeppa*, 44. [vive Mazeppa]

103 Ibid., 62. [ce n'est plus cet obscur Casimir, indigne de ton amour, c'est Mazeppa, prince des Tartares. Viens, suis-moi, au milieu de mon camp, pour y être proclamée et mon épouse et souveraine.]

104 Ibid., 63. [Mazeppa, sauve mon père, et que Olinska soit le gage de la paix.]

105 All the critics mentioned the production's popularity whether they approved or not. See, for example, "Cirque olympique: *Mazeppa, ou le cheval tartare*, mimodrame en trois actes de MM. Cuvelier et Léopold, mis en scène par M. Franconi jeune," *Journal de Paris et des départements, politique, commercial et littéraire*, 13 Jan. 1825, 1; "Cirque olympique: Première Représentation de *Mazeppa, ou le cheval tartare*, mimodrame en trois actes," *La Pandore: Journal des spectacles, des moeurs, des arts, des lettres et des modes*, 13 Jan. 1825, 3; F., "Cirque olympique: Première Représentation de *Mazeppa, ou le cheval tartare*, mimodrame, imité de lord Byron," *La Quotidienne*, 16 Jan. 1825.

106 Richard Westall, [*Illustrations of Lord Byron's Poetry*] (London: John Murray, 1819); the engraver was Charles Heath. See Anthony Burton and John Murdoch, *Byron* (exh. cat., London: Victoria and Albert Museum, 1974), no. S63. See also George Cruikshank, *Forty Illustrations of Lord Byron* (London: J. Robins & Co., 1825).

107 Thomas Barker [Barker of Bath] did a painting of *The Discovery of Mazeppa* either in the late 1820s or in the early 1830s, bypassing the theme of the wild ride altogether; it is listed in London: Tate Gallery, *The Romantic Movement* (exh. cat., Arts Council of Great Britain, 1959), 63, no. 11. Other English artists who painted the Mazeppa theme include Richard Barrett Davies, *Portrait of Mazeppa* (exh. Royal Academy, London, 1820); Thomas Foster, *Mazeppa* (exh. Royal Academy, 1822); Thomas Woodward, *Mazeppa* (exh. Royal Academy, 1828).

108 Roger Fulford, *Trial of Queen Caroline* (London: B. T. Batsford, 1967), gives a complete account of the event. Some recent interpretations include Anna Clark, "Queen Caroline and the Sexual Politics of Popular Culture in London, 1820," *Representations*, 31/2 (Summer 1990), 47–68, and Thomas W. Laqueur, "The Queen Caroline Affair: Politics as Art in the Reign of George IV," *Journal of Modern History*, 54/3 (Sept. 1982), 417–66. See also Joanna Richardson, *The Disastrous Marriage: A Study of George IV and Caroline of Brunswick* (London: Cape, 1960). All relevant contemporaneous documents are anthologized by E. A. Smith, *A Queen on Trial: The Affair of Queen Caroline* (Dover, N.H.: Alan Sutton, 1993). For contemporaneous cartoons commenting on the affair, see London: British Museum, *Catalogue of Political and Personal Satires Preserved in the Department of Prints and Drawings of the British Museum*, 11 vols.

(London: British Museum, 1870–1954; reprint 1978), 10: *1820–27*, and, for the accompanying illustrations: *English Cartoons and Satirical Prints, 1320–1832 in the British Museum* (Cambridge: Chadwyck-Healy Ltd, 1978). See also George Cruickshank's engravings for *The Attorney-General's Charges against the Late Queen, Brought Forward in the House of Peers, on Saturday, August 19, 1820, Illustrated with Fifty Coloured Engravings* (London: G. Humphrey, n.d.).

109 See Byron's letter to Francis Hodgson, Oct. 22, 1820, in *Byron's Letters*, ed. Marchand, 7: *(1820)*, 253.

110 There are numerous references to and comments on the trial in his letters of 1820–21. See ibid., 7: *(1820)*, esp. 149, 153–54, 158–59, 208, 253, and 8: *(1821)*, 147–48.

111 See Byron's letter to Francis Hodgson, Oct. 22, 1820, in ibid., 7: *(1820)*, 253.

112 See Byron's letter to Thomas Moore, Oct. 17, 1820, in ibid., 7: *(1820)*, 206–07.

113 Sixteen lithographs on this subject, some of them English editions, were registered in the *Bibliographie de la France* during 1820, beginning in August.

114 Fulford, *The Trial of Queen Caroline*, 242–43.

115 See Fulford's appendix, "A Bill to deprive her Majesty Caroline Amelia Elizabeth of the Prerogatives, Rights, Privileges, and Pretensions of Queen Consort of the Realm, and to dissolve the Marriage between his Majesty and the said Queen", ibid., 244–45.

116 See Byron's letter to John Murray, Jan. 2, 1817, in *Byron's Letters*, ed. Marchand, 5: *(1816–1817)*, 155.

7 The Marriage of Contradiction

1 Honoré de Balzac, "At the Sign of the Cat and Racket," in *The Works of Balzac: Novelettes* (New York: Black's Readers Service Co., 1925), 615; "La Maison du Chat-qui-pelote," in *La Comédie humaine*, ed. Pierre-Georges Castex, 12 vols. (Paris: Gallimard, 1976–81), I, 89. [Si vous continuez à parler passion quand je vous parle mariage, nous ne nous entendrons bientôt plus.]

2 Christopher Lasch, *Haven in a Heartless World: The Family Besieged* (New York: Basic Books, 1977).

3 Alan B. Spitzer, *The French Generation of 1820* (Princeton: Princeton University Press, 1987).

4 Carol Duncan, "Fallen Fathers: Images of Authority in Pre-Revolutionary French Art," in her *The Aesthetics of Power: Essays in Critical Art History* (Cambridge: Cambridge University Press, 1993), 27–56; Lynn Hunt, *The Family Romance of the French Revolution* (Berkeley and Los Angeles: University of California Press, 1992).

5 See chapter 3, n. 15.

6 Caroline-Stéphanie-Félicité Du Crest, comtesse de Genlis, *Les Parvenus, ou Les Aventures de Julien Delmours, écrites par lui-même*, 2 vols. (Paris: Ladvocat, 1819), I, 279; trans. as *The New Aera; or, Adventures of Julien Delmour, Related by Himself*, 4 vols. (London: Henry Colburn, 1819), 2, 49.

7 "Police correctionnelle de Paris (6e chambre)," *Gazette des tribunaux*, 7 May 1827, 787. [M. *le président*: Vous aviez une coupable liaison avec Tendre. *La femme*: [. . .] Il m'a retirée de la misère et nous avons vécu ensemble.]

8 "Justice criminelle: Police correctionnelle de Paris," *GT*, 14 June 1827, 953–54.

9 See Joan DeJean, *Tender Geographies: Women and the Origins of the Novel in France* (New York: Columbia University Press, 1991), 159–99.

10 See Eve Kosofsky Sedgwick, *Between Men: English Literature and Male Homosocial Desire* (New York: Columbia University Press, 1985).

11 George Sand, *Indiana* [1832], trans. George Burnham Ives (Chicago: Academy Chicago, 1978), "Preface to the Edition of 1842," unpaginated; *Indiana*, ed. Béatrice Didier (Paris: Gallimard, 1984), "Préface de l'édition de 1842," 42.

12 See *Code civil annoté par Ed. Fuzier-Herman*, ed. René Demogue, 5 vols. (Paris: Librairie du Recueil Sirey [1935–40]), I, 335; the complete annotation is included under Titre VI, "Du Divorce," I, 245–370. See also Jean-Louis Halpérin, *Histoire du droit privé français depuis 1804* (Paris: PUF, 1996), 210.

13 Wesley D. Camp, *Marriage and the Family in France since the Revolution: An Essay in the History of Population* (New York: Bookman, 1961), 72; Francis Ronsin, *Les Divorciaires: Affrontements politiques et conceptions du mariage dans la France du XIXe siècle* (Paris: Aubier, 1992), 27–145.

14 See "27–29 juillet 1884: Loi qui rétablit le divorce," in J.-B. Duvergier, *Collection complète des lois, décrets, ordonnances, règlements et avis du Conseil d'état*, 91 vols. (Paris: Guyot & Scribe, 1824–91), 84: *(1884)*, 231–38.

15   See "Loi No. 75–617, 11 juillet 1975," at www.senat.fr/lc/lc11/lc113.html. For a résumé of French divorce and family law, see www.justice.gouv.fr/presse/confo91001b.html. The law of 1975 revised articles 229 and 237–46 of the Civil Code. See also Halpérin, *Histoire du droit privé.*

16   See *Code civil annoté par Ed. Fuzier-Herman,* 1, 335; Halpérin, *Histoire du droit privé,* 210; and Louis Delzons, "La Législation pénale de l'adultère," *Revue politique et littéraire, Revue bleue,* ser. 5/1 (12 March 1904), 338–42.

17   See Emmanuel de Waresquiel and Benoît Yvert, *Histoire de la Restauration, 1814–1830: Naissance de la France moderne* (Paris: Librairie académique Perrin, 1996); Marie-Claude Chaudonneret, *L'Etat et les artistes: De la Restauration à la monarchie de Juillet, 1855–1833* (Paris: Flammarion, 1999); and Sheryl Kroen, *Politics and Theater: The Crisis of Legitimacy in Restoration France, 1815–1830* (Berkeley and Los Angeles, University of California Press, 2000).

18   Emile Zola, "L'Adultère dans la bourgeoisie," *Le Figaro,* 28 Feb. 1881. [l'adultère est la plaie de la bourgeoisie, comme la prostitution est celle du peuple.]

Select Bibliography

Many works cited in the text, particularly short newspaper articles and works tangential to my main thesis, are omitted from this bibliography, as they are reflected in full in the notes. The list below includes archival sources, inventories, and the principal books and articles I have consulted. Exhibition and museum catalogues are entered under the relevant city or, where applicable, under the name of the editor(s). Anonymous works are entered alphabetically by the first main word of the title (e.g. *L'Art de rendre les femmes fidèles* is under "A").

Archives

Paris, Archives nationales (AN):
    F7 3868/9/70/71: Police générale. Rapports de la Préfecture de police, 1825–27
    F7 3877/8/9/80/81: Police générale. Bulletins de Paris, 1823–27
    F18 592/593/594: Censure. Théâtres, Comédies, 1822–30
    F18 647/648: Censure. Théâtres, Vaudevilles, 1822–24
    F18 656: Censure. Théâtres, Vaudevilles, 1826
    F18 660/661: Censure. Théâtres, Vaudevilles, 1826–29
    F18 665A/B/666B: Censure. Théâtres, Vaudevilles, 1828–29
    F18 1322/26: Censure. Théâtres, Cirque olympique, 1815–26
    F21 966–97: Censure. Théâtres, Procès-verbaux de censure, 1820–29
Rouen, Archives départementales de la Seine-Maritime, 5 Mi 1998: 1804, no. 4: Mariage de Augustin de Cairon et de Adélaïde Haïs Delamotte

Official Publications and Inventories

Archives parlementaires de 1787 à 1860: Recueil complet des débats législatifs et politiques des chambres françaises, ed. Jérôme Mavidal and Emile Laurent, 1st ser.: (1789–99), 96 vols. (Paris: Paul Dupont, 1879–87).
Arrêt rendu par la Cour royale de Rouen le 28 avril 1824, au profit de la dame Hays-Delamotte, épouse du sieur Augustin de Cairon et attaqué en cassation par ce dernier (Paris: Le Normant fils [1825]).
Bibliothèque nationale de France, Département des estampes. *Inventaire du fonds français après 1800, par Jean Adhémar et Jacques Lethève* (Paris: Bibliothèque nationale, 1930–).
———. *Inventaire du fonds français: Graveurs du XVIIIe siècle, par Marcel Roux* (Paris: Bibliothèque nationale, 1930–).

Bonald, Louis-Gabriel-Amboise, vicomte de. Chambre des députés no. 115. *Proposition faite à la chambre des députés, par M. de Bonald, Député du département de l'Averyon. Séance du 26 décembre 1815* (Paris: Hacquert, n.d.).

Code civil annoté par Ed. Fuzier-Herman, ed. René Demogue, 5 vols. (Paris: Librairie du Recueil Sirey [1935–40]).

Code civil: Edition nouvelle, conforme au Bulletin des lois, à laquelle on a ajouté la loi sur l'abolition du divorce et terminée par une table analytique et raisonnée des matières (Paris: Dabo, Tremblay, Feret & Gayet, 1819).

Code d'instruction criminelle (Paris: Firmin-Didot, père et fils, 1824).

Code Napoléon: Edition originale et seule officielle (Paris: Imprimerie impériale, 1807).

Code pénal: Edition collationnée sur l'édition officielle, suivie d'une table analytique et raisonnée des matières (Paris: Firmin-Didot, père et fils, 1824).

Code pénal: Edition conforme au Bulletin des lois (No. 227 bis) (Paris: Chez Bachet, Librairie, 1810).

Compte général de l'administration de la justice criminelle en France, pendant l'année 1825: Présenté au roi, par le garde des sceaux, ministre secrétaire d'état au département de la justice (Paris: Imprimerie royale, 1827) [published annually 1825–58].

Duvergier, J.-B. *Collection complète des lois, décrets, ordonnances, règlements et avis du Conseil d'état*, 91 vols. (Paris: Guyot & Scribe, 1824–91).

[Factum: Cairon]. See: *Arrêt rendu par la Cour royale de Rouen.*

[Factum: Adélaïde Hays-Delamotte de Cairon]. *Aux magistrats composant la Cour royale de Rouen: Madame de Cairon contre Monsieur de Cairon son mari, signé Barthe et Billecocq* (Paris: A. Vovée, 1823).

———. *Observations pour Madame de Cairon sur le dernier mémoire de M. de Cairon* (Paris: Plassan [1825]); excerpts in "Observations de Madame de Cairon sur le dernier mémoire de M. de Cairon," *Gazette des tribunaux*, 15 Nov. 1825, 3–4.

[Factum: Augustin de Cairon]. *Mémoire et consultation pour M. Augustin de Cairon, signé Charles Ledru, Berryer fils, Garnier, Bourguinon, Dupin* (Paris: J. Tastu, 1825).

[Factum: Joseph-François Soubiranne]. *Observations pour François Soubiranne, présentées par lui à l'audience du Tribunal correctionnel, 6e chambre, pour servir de réponse à un mémoire signé Augustin de Cairon* (Paris: A. Boucher, 1825).

[———]. *Du Dernier Procès de l'"Indiscret": Explication* (Paris: A. Belin [1836]).

[———]. *A MM. le président, juges, et substitut de procureur impérial composant la sixième chambre* (Paris: E. Brière [1856]).

Fenet, P.-Antoine. *Recueil complet des travaux préparatoires du Code civil*, 15 vols. (Paris: Ducessois, 1827).

Joannidès, A. *La Comédie-française de 1680 à 1900: Dictionnaire général des pièces et des auteurs* (Paris: Plon, 1901).

Jouanneau, L., C., and Solon, *Discussions du Code civil dans le Conseil d'état, précédées des articles correspondans du texte et du projet*, 2 vols. (Paris: Chez Demonville, An XIII [1805]).

Krakovitch, Odile. *Les Pièces de théâtre soumises à la censure (1800–1830): Inventaire* (Paris: Archives nationales, 1982).

Lazare, Félix, and Louis Lazare. *Dictionnaire administratif et historique des rues et monuments de Paris* [1855], 2 vols. (Paris: reprint, Maisonneuve & Larose, 1994).

Locré, Jean-Guillaume. *Procès-verbaux du Conseil d'état, contenant la discussion du projet de Code civil*, 5 vols. (Paris: Imprimerie de la République, An XII [1803–04]).

———. *La Législation civile, commerciale et criminelle de la France, ou Commentaire et complément des codes français*, 31 vols. (Paris: Treuffel & Würtz, 1827–31).

London: British Museum, *Catalogue of Political and Personal Satires Preserved in the*

Department of Prints and Drawings of the British Museum, 11 vols. (London: British Museum, 1870–1954; reprint 1978). Accompanying illustrations: *English Cartoons and Satirical Prints, 1320–1832 in the British Museum* (Cambridge: Chadwyck-Healy Ltd, 1978).

Palm d'Aelders, Etta. "Adresse des citoyennes françoises à l'Assemblée nationale" (1791), in *Recueil sur les femmes* [n.d.], 2 vols. Bibliothèque historique de la ville de Paris 12807-in-8: 1, 15, 37–40.

Portalis, Jean-Etienne-Marie. "Exposé des motifs du projet de loi sur le mariage, formant le titre v du Code civil, présenté le 16 ventôse an XI" [March 7, 1803] in *Discours, rapports et travaux inédits sur le Code civil,* ed. Frédéric Portalis (Paris: Joubert, Librairie de la cour de cassation, 1844), 162–208.

———. *Corps législatif, Conseil des anciens: Rapport fait par Portalis sur la résolution du 29 prairial dernier, relative au divorce. Séance du 27 thermidor, an V* (Paris: Imprimerie nationale, An v [1797]), 176–77.

Wicks, Charles Beaumont. *The Parisian Stage: Alphabetical Index of Plays and Authors.,* 5 vols. (Birmingham: University of Alabama Press, 1950–79).

Books, Articles, and Catalogues

Agulhon, Maurice. *Le Cercle dans la France bourgeoise: 1810–1848, étude d'une mutation de sociabilité* (Paris: A. Colin, Ecole des hautes études en sciences sociales, 1977).

Aimé-Azam, Dénise. *Mazeppa, Géricault et son temps* (Paris: Plon, 1956); republished as *La Passion de Géricault* (Paris: Fayard, 1970).

Allard, Louis. *La Comédie de moeurs en France au dix-neuvième siècle,* 2 vols. (Paris: Hachette, 1933).

Allen, James Smith. *Popular French Romanticism: Authors, Readers and Books in the 19th Century* (Syracuse, N.Y.: Syracuse University Press, 1981).

———. *In the Public Eye: A History of Reading in Modern France, 1800–1940* (Princeton: Princeton University Press, 1991).

Angenot, Marc. "La Littérature populaire française au dix-neuvième siècle," in *The Popular Novel in the Nineteenth Century / La littérature populaire au dix-neuvième siècle,* special issue of *Canadian Review of Comparative Literature /Revue canadienne de littérature comparée* (Sept. 1982), 307–33.

Anisimov, Evgenii. *The Reforms of Peter the Great: Progress through Coercion in Russia,* trans. John T. Alexander (New York: Armonk; and London: M. E. Sharpe, 1993).

Appleby, Joyce, Lynn Hunt, and Margaret Jacob. *Telling the Truth about History* (New York: W. W. Norton, 1994).

Ariès, Philippe. *Centuries of Childhood* [1960], trans. Robert Baldick (New York: Knopf, 1962).

Ariès, Philippe, and Georges Duby, eds. *Histoire de la vie privée.* 5 vols (Paris: Seuil, 1986); trans. as *A History of Private Life,* 5 vols. (Cambridge, Mass.: Harvard University Press, 1987–91), 4: *From the Fires of Revolution to the Great War,* ed. Michelle Perrot.

Armstrong, Judith. *The Novel of Adultery* (London: Macmillan, 1976).

Arrigon, L.-J. *Les Années romantiques de Balzac* (Paris: Perrin, 1927).

L'Art de rendre les femmes fidelles, par M*** (Paris: Veuve Laisné, 1713).

L'Art de rendre les femmes fidelles, 2 vols. (Geneva and Paris: Couturier fils, rev. 3/1783).

L'Art de rendre les femmes fidèles et de ne pas être trompé par elles: A l'usage des maris et des amans. Enseigné en cinq leçons et orné d'une gravure, par Lami [J.-M. Mosès] (Paris: Librairie française et étrangère, 1828).

Arvin, Neil Cole. *Eugène Scribe and the French Theatre 1815–1860* (Cambridge, Mass.: Harvard University Press, 1924).

Atthanassoglou-Kallmyer, Nina Maria. *French Images from the Greek War of Independence 1821–1830: Art and Politics under the Restoration* (New Haven: Yale University Press, 1989).

———. *Eugène Delacroix: Prints, Politics and Satire 1814–1822* (New Haven: Yale University Press, 1991).

Avignon: Musée Calvet, *Notice des tableaux exposés au profit des pauvres dans la galerie Vernet au Muséum Calvet* (exh. cat., Avignon: Guichard aîné, 1826).

Babinski, Hubert F. *The Mazeppa Legend in European Romanticism* (New York: Columbia University Press, 1974).

Balzac, Honoré de. *La Comédie humaine*, ed. Pierre-Georges Castex, 12 vols. (Paris: Gallimard, 1976–81). English translations: *La Comédie humaine*, trans. William Walton, 53 vols. (Philadelphia: George Barrie & Son, 1897); *Selected Short Stories*, trans. Sylvia Raphael (Harmondsworth: Penguin, 1977); *The Works of Honoré de Balzac: Novelettes* (New York: Black's Readers Service, 1925).

———. *Oeuvres diverses*. ed. Pierre-Georges Castex, 2 vols. (Paris: Gallimard, 1996).

———. *Physiologie du mariage, ou Méditations de philosophie éclectique, sur le bonheur et le malheur conjugal. Publiées par un jeune célibataire* [1829], in *La Comédie humaine*, ed. Pierre-Georges Castex, 12 vols. (Paris: Gallimard, 1976–81, 11, 903–1205; trans. as *The Physiology of Marriage* [1904], ed. Sharon Marcus (Baltimore: Johns Hopkins University Press, 1997).

Balzac, Honoré de, and Horace-Napoléon Raisson. *Code des gens honnêtes, ou L'Art de ne pas être dupe des fripons* (Paris: J.-N. Barba, 1825).

Barbier, Patrick. *Opera in Paris 1800–1850: A Lively History*, trans. Robert Luoma (Portland, Oregon: Amadeus, 1995).

Bardèche, Maurice. *Honoré de Balzac: Physiologie du mariage pré-originale (1826)* (thèse complémentaire pour le doctorat ès lettres, Paris: G. Droz, 1940).

Baudelaire, Charles. *Ecrits sur l'art*, ed. Yves Florenne, 2 vols. (Paris: Gallimard, 1971).

———. *Art in Paris 1845–1862*, trans. and ed. Jonathan Mayne (Oxford: Phaidon, 1981).

Bazin, Germain. *Théodore Géricault: Etude critique, documents et catalogue raisonné*, 7 vols. (Paris: Bibliothèque des arts, 1987–97).

Beaumarchais, Pierre-Augustin Caron de. *Théâtre: Le Barbier de Séville, Le Mariage de Figaro, La Mère coupable*, ed. René Pomeau. (Paris: Flammarion, 1965).

Beaumont-Maillet, Laure. *La Guerre des sexes, XVe–XIXe siècles: Les Albums du Cabinet des estampes de la Bibliothèque nationale* (Paris: Albin Michel, 1984).

Bedel, A. *Nouveau Traité de l'adultère et des enfans adultérins, selon les lois civiles et pénales* (Paris: Warée fils aîné, F. Bernard, 1826).

Béraud, Antoine-Nicolas. *Annales de l'École française des beaux-arts: Recueil de gravures* [. . . . *Salon de 1827*] (Paris: Pillet-aîné, 1828).

Berger, Klaus. *Géricault et son oeuvre*, trans. Maurice Beerblock (Paris: Bernard Grasset, 1952).

Bernardin de Saint-Pierre, Jacques-Henri. "Discours sur cette question: Comment l'éducation des femmes pourrait contribuer à rendre les hommes meilleurs" [1777], in *Oeuvres posthumes de Jacques-Henri Bernardin de Saint-Pierre*, ed. L. Aimé-Martin [Louis-Aimé Martin] (Paris: Lefèvre, 1833), 447–62.

Bernheimer, Charles. *Figures of Ill Repute: Representing Prostitution in Nineteenth-Century France* (Cambridge, Mass.: Harvard University Press, 1989).

Berthier, Patrick. *Le Théâtre au XIXe siècle* (Paris: PUF, 1986).

Bertholet, Denis. *Les Français par eux-mêmes 1815–1885* (Paris: Olivier Orban, 1991).

Bertier de Sauvigny, Guillaume de. *La Restauration* [1955], trans. Lynn M. Case. as *The Bourbon Restoration* (Philadelphia: University of Pennsylvania Press, 1967).

Bertier de Sauvigny, Guillaume de, and Alfred Fierro. *Bibliographie critique des mémoires sur la Restauration écrits ou traduits en français* (Geneva: Droz, 1988).

Blachon, Remi. *La Gravure sur bois aux XIXe siècle: L'Âge du bois debout* (Paris: Editions de l'amateur, 2001).

Bloomfield, Morton W. *The Seven Deadly Sins: An Introduction to the History of a Religious Concept with Special Reference to Medieval English Literature* (East Lansing: Michigan State University Press, 1967).

Bonnet, Jean-Claude. "De la famille à la patrie," in Jean Delumeau and Daniel Roche, eds., *Histoire des pères et de la paternité* (Paris: Larousse-HER, rev. 2000), 245–67.

Bordeaux, Michèle. "Le Maître et l'infidèle: Des Relations personnelles entre mari et femme de l'ancien droit au Code civil." in Irène Théry and Christian Biet, eds., *La Famille, la loi, l'état* (Paris: Imprimerie nationale, 1989), 432–46.

Borel, Pétrus. "Des Artistes penseurs et des artistes creux," *L'Artiste*, 5 (1833), 253–59.

Borschak, Elie, and René Martel. *Vie de Mazeppa* (Paris: Calmann-Lévy, 1931).

Boudard, Jean-Baptiste. *Iconologie tirée de divers auteurs, ouvrage utile aux gens de lettres, aux poëtes, aux artistes, et généralement à tous les amateurs des beaux-arts,* 2 vols. (Parma and Paris: Tilliard, 1759).

Bourdieu, Pierre. *The Field of Cultural Production: Essays on Art and Literature* (New York: Columbia University Press, 1993).

Brillat-Savarin, Anthelme. *La Physiologie du goût, ou Méditations de gastronomie transcendante* (Paris: A. Sautelet, 1826).

Broglie, Gabriel de. *Madame de Genlis* (Paris: Perrin, 1985).

Brooks, Peter. *The Melodramatic Imagination: Balzac, Henry James, Melodrama, and the Mode of Excess* (New York: Columbia University Press, 1985).

Bruys, François [chevalier Plante-Amour]. *L'Art de connoître les femmes* (The Hague: Jacques van den Kieboom, 1730).

———. *L'Art de connoître les femmes, avec des pensées libres sur divers sujets, et une dissertation sur l'adultère par le chevalier Plante-Amour* (Amsterdam: Chez Michel, 1749).

———. *L'Art de connaître les femmes, par le chevalier Plante-Amour* (Paris: Delaunay, 1820).

———. *L'Art de connaître les femmes: 2e édition augmentée d'une dissertation sur l'adultère, par M. G**** (Paris: Les marchands de nouveautés, 2/1821).

Burguière, André. "La Famille et l'état: Débats et attentes de la société française à la veille de la Révolution," in Irène Théry and Christian Biet, eds., *La Famille, la loi, l'état* (Paris: Imprimerie nationale, 1989), 147–56.

Burton, Anthony, and John Murdoch. *Byron* (exh. cat., London: Victoria and Albert Museum, 1974).

Byron, *The Works of the Right Honourable Lord Byron* (Paris: Galignani, 1818).

———. *Oeuvres de lord Byron*, trans. Amédée Pichot and Eusèbe de Salle, 10 vols. (Paris: Ladvocat, 1819–21).

———. *Oeuvres de lord Byron* [. . .] *précédée d'une notice sur lord Byron par Charles Nodier*, 8 vols. (Paris: Ladvocat, rev. 4/1822–25).

———. *Lord Byron's Works*, 12 vols. (Paris: Louis & Baudry, 1820–24).

————. *Byron: Poetical Works*, ed. Frederick Page (Oxford: Oxford University Press, 1970).

————. *Byron's Letters and Journals*, ed. Leslie A. Marchand, 12 vols. (Cambridge, Mass.: Harvard University Press, 1973–82).

Cairon. See [Factum: . . .] under "Official Publications and Inventories."

Camp, Wesley D. *Marriage and the Family in France since the Revolution: An Essay in the History of Population* (New York: Bookman, 1961).

Cardwell, Douglas. "Eugene Scribe (24 December 1791–20 February 1861)," in Barbara T. Cooper, ed., *French Dramatists 1789–1914: Dictionary of Literary Biography*, 192 (Detroit: Gale Research, 1998), 358–72.

Carlson, Victor I., and John W. Ittmann, eds. *Regency to Empire: French Printmaking 1715–1814*, (exh. cat., Baltimore Museum of Art and Minneapolis Institute of Arts, 1984).

Carré, Narcisse-Epaminondas. *Code des femmes: Analyse complète et raisonnée de toutes les dispositions législatives qui règlent les droits et devoirs de la femme dans les différentes positions de la vie* (Paris: J.-P. Roret, 1828).

Casselle, Pierre. *La Commerce des estampes à Paris dans la seconde moitié du 18ème siècle* (thèse, Paris: Ecole nationale des chartes, 1976).

Catalogue de la collection de lettres autographes manuscrits du comte de Mirabeau, documents historiques sur la Ligue, la Fronde, la Révolution, etc. de feu M. Lucas de Montigny (Paris: Laverdet, 1860).

Cavallo, Guglielmo, and Roger Chartier, eds. *A History of Reading in the West*, trans. Lydia G. Cochrane (Cambridge: Polity Press, 1999).

[Chabot, E.-Charles]. *Grammaire conjugale, ou Principes généraux à l'aide desquels on peut dresser la femme, la faire marcher au doigt et à l'oeil, et la rendre aussi douce qu'un mouton. Par un petit-cousin des Lovelaces* (Paris: J. Bréauté, 1827).

Champfleury [Jules Husson], *Histoire de la caricature moderne* (Paris: Dentu, 1871).

Chartier, Roger. *Cultural History: Between Practices and Representations*, trans. Lydia G. Cochrane (Ithaca, N.Y.: Cornell University Press, 1988).

Chartier, Roger, Alain Boureau, and Cécile Dauphin. *Correspondence: Models of Letter-Writing from the Middle Ages to the Nineteenth Century*, trans. Christopher Woodall (Cambridge: Polity Press, 1997).

Chaudonneret, Marie-Claude. *L'Etat et les artistes: De la Restauration à la monarchie de Juillet, 1815–1833* (Paris: Flammarion, 1999).

Chevalier, Jean, and Alain Gheerbrant. *Dictionnaire des symboles, mythes, rêves, coutumes, gestes, formes, figures, couleurs, nombres* (Paris: Robert Laffont, rev. 1982).

Choiseul-Meuse, Félicité de. *Julie, ou J'ai sauvé ma rose*, 2 vols. (Hamburg and Paris: Léopold Collin, 1807).

Clark, Anna. "Queen Caroline and the Sexual Politics of Popular Culture in London, 1820," *Representations*, 31/2 (Summer 1990), 47–68.

Clark, Priscilla P. *The Battle of the Bourgeois: The Novel in France 1789–1814* (Paris: Didier, 1973).

Clayson, Hollis. *Painted Love: Prostitution in French Art of the Impresionist Era* (New Haven: Yale University Press, 1991).

Clément, Charles. *Géricault: Etude biographique et critique avec le catalogue raisonné de l'oeuvre du maître* (Paris: Didier, 1868).

Cohen, Margaret. *The Sentimental Education of the Novel* (Princeton: Princeton University Press, 1999).

Condillac, Etienne Bonnot de. *Essai sur l'origine des connaissances humaines* [1755], ed. Michèle Crampe-Casnabet (Paris: Alive, 1998).

Condon, Patricia. *Ingres. In Pursuit of Perfection: The Art of J.-A.-D. Ingres* (exh. cat., Louisville, Ky.: J. B. Speed Art Museum, 1983).

Condorcet, Antoine Caritat, marquis de. *Oeuvres de Condorcet*, ed. A. Condorcet O'Connor and F. Arago, 12 vols. (Paris: Firmin-Didot frères, 1847–49), 6: *Esquisse d'un tableau historique des progrès de l'esprit humain*; 7: *Sur l'instruction publique*.

Cooper, Barbara T., ed. *French Dramatists 1789–1914: Dictionary of Literary Biography*, 192 (Detroit: Gale Research, 1998).

Corbin, Alain. *Les Filles de noce: Misère sexuelle et prostitution (19e et 20e siècle)* (Paris: Aubier Montaigne, 1978).

Corbin, Alain, Jacqueline Lalouette, and Michèle Riot-Sarcey, eds. *Femmes dans la cité 1815–1871* (Grâne, France: Créaphis [1997]).

Coulon, Henri. *Le Divorce et la séparation de corps*, 3 vols. (Paris: Marchal & Billard, 1890).

———. *Le Divorce et l'adultère: De l'abrogation des lois pénales en matière d'adultère* (Paris: Marchal & Billard, 1892).

Courthion, Pierre, ed. *Géricault raconté par lui-même et par ses amis* (Geneva: P. Cailler, 1947).

Cruikshank, George. *The Attorney-General's Charges against the Late Queen, Brought Forward in the House of Peers, on Saturday, August 19, 1820, Illustrated with Fifty Coloured Engravings* (London: G. Humphrey, n.d.).

———. *Forty Illustrations of Lord Byron* (London: J. Robins & Co., 1825).

Cuisin, J.-P.-R. [vicomte de S***]. *Le Conjugalisme, ou L'Art de se bien marier: Conseils aux jeunes gens d'épouser une femme jeune, belle et riche; aux demoiselles de s'unir à un joli homme, bien fait et fortuné: Code des leçons matrimoniales, appuyées de préceptes moraux, d'anecdotes très curieuses touchant le lien si important du mariage* (Paris: Mansut, 1823).

———. *Le Nouveau Secrétaire universel, ou le code épistolaire, présentant des modèles de lettres d'amour, de mariage, de commerce, d'affaires; placets au roi, aux princes, etc.; un exposé des encres sympathiques de la sténographie, et généralement tout ce qui rentre dans les attributions du cérémonial et du style épistolaires* (Paris: Corbet aîné, 1824).

Cuno, James. "Charles Philipon, La Maison Aubert, and the Business of Caricature in Paris, 1829–41," *Art Journal*, 43/4 (Winter 1983), 347–54.

———. "*Charles Philipon and La Maison Aubert: The Business, Politics and Public of Caricature in Paris, 1820–1840*" (Ph.D. diss., Harvard University: Cambridge, Mass., 1985).

Dacier, Emile. *La Gravure en France au XVIIIe siècle: La Gravure de genre et de moeurs* (Paris and Brussels: Librairie nationale d'art et d'histoire, 1925).

Darrow, Margaret. *Revolution in the House: Family, Class and Inheritance in Southern France, 1775–1825* (Princeton: Princeton University Press, 1989).

Dartois, Léon Brunswick, and Lhérie [Armand d'Artois and Léon Lévy, pseud. Léon Brunswick, V. Lhérie, L. Lhérie], *Les Suites d'un mariage de raison* (Paris: J.-N. Barba, 1829).

Dash, comtesse [Gabrielle-Anne Cisterne de Courtiras, vicomtessse de Pouilloüe de Saint-Mars]. *Mémoires des autres*, 6 vols. (Paris: Librairie illustrée, 1896–97), 2: *Souvenirs anecdotiques sur la Restauration*.

Daumard, Adeline. *La Bourgeoisie parisienne de 1815 à 1848* (Paris: SEVPEN, 1963).

———, ed. *Les Fortunes françaises au XIXe siècle* (Paris: Mouton, 1973).

Daumier, Honoré. *Lib Women (Bluestockings and Socialist Women)* [1844–49], ed.

Jacqueline Armingeat, trans. Howard Brabyn (Paris and New York: Leon Amiel, 1974).

Davin, Félix. "Introduction," in Honoré de Balzac, *Etudes de moeurs au XIXe siècle*, 9 vols. (Paris: Mme Charles Béchet, 1834–37), vol. 1: *Scènes de la vie privée* (1835); reprinted in Balzac, *La Comédie humaine*, ed. Pierre-Georges Castex, 12 vols. (Paris: Gallimard, 1976–81), 1, 1143–75.

Davis, Natalie Zemon. "The Reasons of Misrule" and "Women on Top," in her *Society and Culture in Early Modern France* (Stanford, Calif.: Stanford University Press, 1975), 97–123 and 124–51.

———. *Fiction in the Archives: Pardon Tales and Their Tellers in Sixteenth-Century France* (Stanford, Calif.: Stanford University Press, 1987).

DeJean, Joan. *Tender Geographies: Women and the Origins of the Novel in France* (New York: Columbia University Press, 1991).

Delacroix, Eugène. *Journal 1822–1863*, ed. André Joubin (Paris: Plon, 1980).

Delavigne, Casimir. *L'Ecole des vieillards, comédie en cinq actes et en vers* (Paris: J.-N. Barba, 1823).

———. *Théâtre de M. C. Delavigne, de l'Académie française*, 4 vols. (Paris: Ladvocat, 1825–34).

Delécluze, E.-J. "Beaux-arts: Troisième Lettre au rédacteur du *Lycée français*, sur l'exposition des ouvrages de peinture, sculpture, architecture et gravure des artistes vivans," *Lycée français, ou Mélanges de littérature et de critique par une société de gens de lettres*, 1 (10 Sept. 1819), 361–71.

Deloye, Aug. *Notice des tableaux exposés dans les galeries du Muséum-Calvet à Avignon* (Avignon: Seguin frères, 1879).

Delteil, Löys. *Manuel de l'amateur d'estampes du XVIIIe siècle* (Paris: Dorbon-aîné, 1910).

———. *Le Peintre-graveur illustré* [1924], 31 vols. (New York: Da Capo, 1969).

Delumeau, Jean, and Daniel Roche, eds. *Histoire des pères et de la paternité* (Paris: Larousse-HER, rev. 2000).

Delzons, Louis. "La Législation pénale de l'adultère," *Revue politique et littéraire, Revue bleue*. ser. 5/1 (12 March 1904), 338–42.

Desan, Suzanne. "Reconstituting the Social after the Terror: Family, Property and the Law in Popular Politics," *Past and Present*, 164 (Aug. 1999) 81–121.

———. "War between Brothers and Sisters: Inheritance Law and Gender Politics in Revolutionary France," *French Historical Studies*, 20/4 (Fall 1997), 597–634.

Des Granges, Charles-Marc. *La Comédie et les moeurs sous la Restauration et la monarchie de Juillet (1815–1848)* (Paris: Albert Fontemoing, 1904).

———. *La Presse littéraire sous la Restauration 1815–1830* (Paris: Mercure de France, 1907).

Détournelle, A., ed. *Aux armes et aux arts!: Peinture, sculpture, architecture, gravure. Journal de la Société républicaine des arts* [1794].

Diderot, Denis. *Salons*, ed. Jean Seznec, 3 vols. (Oxford: Clarendon Press, 1979).

Diderot, Denis, and D'Alembert. *Encyclopédie, ou Dictionnaire raisonné des sciences, des arts et des métiers, par une société des gens de lettres*, 17 vols. (Paris: Briasson, 1751–65).

Doin, Guillaume-Tell, and Edouard Charton. *Lettres sur Paris* (Paris: Crapelet, 1830).

Doucet, Gérôme. *Peintres et graveurs libertins du XVIII siècle* (Paris: Albert Méricart [1913]).

Droulers, Eugène. *Dictionnaire des attributs, allégories, emblèmes et symboles* (Turnhout, Belgium: Brépols, n.d.).

Ducange and Dinaux [Victor Ducange, Jacques-Félix Beudin, and Prosper-Parfait Goubaux]. *Trente ans, ou La Vie d'un joueur: Mélodrame en trois journées.* [. . .] *Représenté pour la première fois, à Paris, sur le théâtre de la Porte-Saint-Martin, le 19 juin 1827* (Paris: J.-N. Barba, 1827).

Duchartre, Pierre-Louis, and René Saulnier. *L'Imagerie parisienne: L'Imagerie de la rue Saint-Jacques* (Paris: Gründ, 1944).

———. *L'Imagerie populaire: Les images de toutes les provinces françaises du XVe siècle au second Empire* (Paris: Librairie de France, 1926).

Dumas, Alexandre. *Mes Mémoires* [1852–55], ed. Pierre Josserand, 5 vols. (Paris: Gallimard, 1954–68).

———. *Souvenirs dramatiques.* 2 vols. (Paris: Michel Lévy frères, 1868).

Dumersan, [Théophile-Marion], and [Henri] Dupin. *L'Ecole des béquillards, ou Il faut des époux assortis* (Paris: J.-N. Barba, 1824).

Duncan, Carol. "Happy Mothers and Other New Ideas in French Art" and "Fallen Fathers: Images of Authority in Pre-Revolutionary French Art," in her *The Aesthetics of Power: Essays in Critical Art History* (Cambridge: Cambridge University Press, 1993), 3–26 and 27–56.

Dupâquier, J., ed. *Marriage and Remarriage in Populations of the Past* (London: Academic Press, 1981).

Duplessis-Le Guélinal, Gérard. *Les Mariages en France*, Cahiers de la Fondation nationale des sciences politiques, 53 (Paris: Armand Colin, 1954).

Eitner, Lorenz. *Géricault.* (exh. cat., Los Angeles County Museum of Art, 1971).

———. *Géricault's Raft of the Medusa* (London: Phaidon, 1972).

———. *Géricault: His Life and Work* (London: Orbis, 1983).

Escholier, Raymond. *Delacroix et les femmes* (Paris: Fayard, 1963).

Estève, Edmond. *Byron et le romantisme française: Essai sur la fortune et l'influence de l'oeuvre de Byron en France de 1812 à 1850* (Paris: Boivin, 1929).

Etienne, Charles-Guillaume. "Examen critique de l'Ecole des vieillards," in Casimir Delavigne, *Théâtre de M. C. Delavigne, de l'Académie française*, 4 vols. (Paris: Ladvocat, 1825–34), 1, 163–75.

Faillie, Marie-Henriette. *La Femme et le Code civil dans "la Comédie humaine" d'Honoré de Balzac* (Paris: Didier, 1968).

Farge, Arlette, ed. *Le Miroir des femmes* (Paris: Montalba, 1982).

Farge, Arlette, and Michel Foucault, eds. *Le Désordre des familles: Lettres de cachet des archives de la Bastille* (Paris: Gallimard, 1982).

Farwell, Beatrice. *The Cult of Images: Baudelaire and the Nineteenth-Century Media Explosion* (exh cat., Santa Barbara, Calif.: University of California at Santa Barbara Museum, 1977).

———. *The Charged Image: French Lithographic Caricature 1816–1848* (exh. cat., Santa Barbara, Calif.: Santa Barbara Museum of Art, 1989).

———. *French Popular Lithographic Imagery, 1815–1870*, 12 vols. (Chicago: University of Chicago Press, 1981–97).

Fayet, P. *Observations sur la statistique intellectuelle et morale de la France pendant la période de vingt ans (1828–47)* (Paris: Bureau du correspondant, 1851).

Fenaille, Maurice. *L'Oeuvre gravé de P.-L. Debucourt (1755–1832)* (Paris: Damascène Morgand, 1899).

Fenéon, Félix. "L'Adultère dans le roman contemporain" [1887], in his *Oeuvres plus que complètes*, ed. Joan U. Halperin, 2 vols. (Geneva: Librairie Droz, 1970), 2, 692–95.

Fenet, P.-Antoine. *Pothier analysé dans ses rapports avec le Code civil, et mis en ordre, sous chacun des articles de ce code* (Paris: L'Auteur, Dépôt rue Saint-André des arts, 1826).

Flandrin, Jean-Louis. *Familles: Parenté, maison, sexualité dans l'ancienne société* (Paris: Seuil, rev. 1984).

Flaubert, Gustave. *Madame Bovary: Moeurs de province* [1857], ed. Maurice Nadeau (Paris: Gallimard, 1972), trans. Francis Steegmuller as *Madame Bovary: Patterns of Provincial Life* (New York: Modern Library, 1957).

Fonvieille, René. *Le Véritable Julien Sorel* (Paris: Arthaud, 1971).

Foucault, Michel. *Histoire de la sexualité*, trans. Robert Hurley as *A History of Sexuality*, 3 vols. (New York: Vintage, 1988–90).

Fournel, Jean-François. *Traité de l'adultère considéré dans l'ordre judiciaire* (Paris: Jean-François Bastien, 1778).

Francis, Dartois [Armand d'Artois] and Gabriel [Gabriel de Lurieu]. *L'Ecole des ganaches: Parodie de l'Ecole des vieillards* (Paris: Huet, 1824).

Fuchs, Rachel G. "Seduction, Paternity and the Law in Fin-de-Siècle France," *The Journal of Modern History*, 72/4 (Dec. 2000), 944–89.

Fulcher, Jane. *The Nation's Image: French Grand Opera as Politics and Politicized Art* (Cambridge: Cambridge University Press, 1987).

Fulford, Roger. *The Trial of Queen Caroline* (London: B. T. Batsford, 1967).

G***, Eusèbe. See Girault de Saint-Fargeau, Eusèbe.

G***, Madame la comtesse de. See Genlis, Caroline-Félicité-Stéphanie Du Crest, comtesse de.

G***, vicomtesse de. *L'Art de se faire aimer de son mari: Recueil de préceptes à l'usage des femmes qui ont serré le lien conjugal, et très utiles aux demoiselles qui désirent s'engager sous les lois de l'hymen* (Paris: Librairie française et étrangère, 1823).

Garaud, Marcel, and Romuald Szramkiewicz. *La Révolution française et la famille* (Paris: PUF, 1978).

Garnier, Nicole. *Musée national des arts et traditions populaires: L'Imagerie populaire française: Gravures en taille-douce et en taille d'épargne*, 2 vols. (Paris: RMN, 1990).

Gautier, Théophile. *Les Maîtres du théâtre français de Rotrou à Dumas fils*, ed. Amédée Gritsch (Paris: Payot, 1929).

Gay, Jules. *Iconographie des estampes à sujets galants et des portraits de femmes célèbres par leur beauté, indiquant les sujets, les peintres, les graveurs de ces estampes, leur valeur et leur prix dans les ventes, les condamnations et prohibitions dont certaines d'entre elles ont été l'objet. Par M. le c. d'I*** (Geneva: J. Gay et fils, 1868).

Genlis, Caroline-Félicité-Stéphanie Du Crest, comtesse de. *Adèle et Théodore, ou Lettres sur l'éducation* [1782], 4 vols. (Paris: Lecointe & Durey, 1827).

———. *Les Parvenus, ou Les Aventures de Julien Delmours, écrites par lui-même*, 2 vols. (Paris: Ladvocat, 1819), trans. as *The New Aera; or, Adventures of Julien Delmour, Related by Himself*, 4 vols. (London: Henry Colburn, 1819).

———. [Madame la comtesse de G***]. *Manuel de la jeune femme: Guide complet de la maîtresse de maison* (Paris: Charles Béchet, 1829).

Gével, Claude, and Jean Rabot. "La Censure théâtrale sous la Restauration," *La Revue de Paris*, 6 (Nov.–Dec. 1913), 339–62.

Giesey, Ralph E. "Rules of Inheritance and Strategies of Mobility in Prerevolutionary France," *American Historical Review*, 82/2 (April 1977), 271–89.

Girard, Joseph. *Catalogue des tableaux exposés dans les galeries du Musée-Calvet d'Avignon* (Avignon: Seguin, 1909).

———. "Les Souvenirs des Vernet au Musée Calvet: Conférence faite pendant le séance de l'Académie de Vaucluse au Musée Calvet le 12 mai 1927 pour la commémoration du centenaire de la galerie Vernet," *Mémoires de l'Académie de Vaucluse.* 2nd ser., 27 (1927), 49–61.

Girault de Saint-Fargeau, Eusèbe [Eusèbe G***]. *Revue des romans: Recueil d'analyses raisonnées des productions remarquables des plus célèbres romanciers français et étrangers,* 2 vols. (Paris: Firmin-Didot frères, 1839).

Gleyses, Chantal. *La Femme coupable: Petite Histoire de l'épouse adultère au XIXe siècle* (Paris: Imago, 1994).

Goldstein, Robert Justin. *Censorship of Political Caricature in Nineteenth-Century France* (Kent, Ohio: Kent State University Press, 1989).

Gombrich, E. H., and Ernst Kris. *Caricature* (Harmondsworth: Penguin, 1940).

Grand-Carteret, John. *Les Moeurs et la caricature en France* (Paris: Librairie illustrée, 1888).

Greene, E. J. H. *Menander to Marivaux: The History of a Comic Structure* (Edmonton: University of Alberta Press, 1977).

Grunchec, Philippe. *Géricault: Dessins et aquarelles de chevaux* (Paris: Edita, Bibliothèque des arts, 1982).

Guichard, Auguste-Charles. *Le Code des femmes, de leurs droits, privilèges, devoirs et obligations; ou Récits et entretiens dont la simple lecture leur apprend, en peu d'heures et sans nulle fatigue, ce qu'il leur importe le plus de savoir pour être en état de diriger elles-mêmes leurs affaires, de stipuler et défendre leurs intérêts, dans toutes les circonstances de la vie* [1823], 2 vols. (Paris: N. Pichard, rev. 2/1828).

Guizot, Pauline. *Education domestique, ou Lettres de famille sur l'éducation,* 2 vols. (Paris: Bechet aîné, 1826).

Guyon, Bernard. *La Pensée politique et sociale de Balzac* (Paris: Armand Colin, rev. 2/1967).

Hallays-Dabot, Victor. *Histoire de la censure théâtrale en France* [1862] (Geneva: Slatkine, 1970).

Halpérin, Jean-Louis. *L'Impossible Code civil* (Paris: PUF, 1992).

———. *Histoire du droit privé français depuis 1804* (Paris: PUF, 1996).

Hamilton, George Heard. "Eugène Delacroix and Lord Byron," *Gazette des beaux-arts,* ser. 6/23 (Feb. 1943), 99–110, and ser. 6/26 (July–Dec. 1944), 365–86.

Hanley, Sarah. "Engendering the State: Family Formation and State Building in Early Modern France," *French Historical Studies,* 16/1 (Spring 1989), 4–27.

———. "The Monarchic State in Early Modern France: Marital Regime Government and Male Right," in Adrianna E. Bakos, ed., *Politics, Ideology, and the Law* (Rochester, N.Y.: University of Rochester Press, 1994), 107–26,

———. "Social Sites of Political Practice in France: Lawsuits, Civil Rights, and the Separation of Powers in Domestic and State Government, 1500–1800," *American Historical Review,* 102/1 (Feb. 1997), 27–52.

———. " 'The Jurisprudence of the Arrêts': Marital Union, Civil Society and State Formation in France, 1550–1650," forthcoming in *Law History Review,* 21/1 (2003).

Harrisse, Henry. *L. L. Boilly, peintre, dessinateur et lithographe: Sa vie et son oeuvre 1761–1845* (Paris: Société de propagation des livres d'art, 1898).

Harsin, Jill. *Policing Prostitution in Nineteenth-Century Paris* (Princeton: Princeton University Press, 1985).

Haubre, Gabrielle. "L'Entrée dans le monde: Le Jeune Homme et les femmes (première moitié du XIXe siècle)," in Alain Corbin, Jacqueline Lalouette, and Michèle Riot-Sarcey, eds., *Femmes dans la cité 1815–1871* (Grâne, France: Créaphis [1997]), 261–77.

Hautecoeur, Louis. *Peintres de la vie familiale: Evolution d'un thème* (exh. cat., Paris: Galerie Charpentier, 1945).

Hemmings, F. W. J. *Culture and Society in France, 1789–1848* (Leicester: Leicester University Press, 1987).

——. *Theatre and State in France, 1760–1905* (Cambridge: Cambridge University Press, 1994).

Hofmann, Werner. *Caricature from Leonardo to Picasso*, trans. M. H. L. (London: John Calder, 1957).

Howarth, William D. *Beaumarchais and the Theatre* (London: Routledge, 1995).

Hugo, Victor. *Hernani, ou L'Honneur castillan: Drame par Victor Hugo, représenté sur le Théâtre-Français le 25 février 1830* (Paris: Mame & Delaunay-Vallée, 1830).

——. *Poésie*, ed. Bernard Leuillot, 3 vols. (Paris: Seuil, 1972).

——. *Théâtre: Amy Robsart, Marion de Lorme, Hernani, Le Roi s'amuse*, ed. Raymond Pouilliart (Paris: Flammarion, 1979).

——. *Three Plays by Victor Hugo: Hernani, The King Amuses Himself, Ruy Blas*, trans. C. Crosland and F. L. Slous (New York: Howard Fertig, 1995).

Hunt, Lynn. *The Family Romance of the French Revolution* (Berkeley and Los Angeles: University of California Press, 1992).

Iknayan, Marguerite. *The Idea of the Novel in France: The Critical Reaction 1815–1848* (Geneva: E. Droz, 1961).

Isherwood, Robert M. *Farce and Fantasy: Popular Entertainment in Eighteenth-Century Paris* (Oxford: Oxford University Press, 1986).

Jal, Auguste. *Esquisses, croquis, pochades, ou Tout ce qu'on voudra sur le Salon de 1827* (Paris: Ambroise Dupont, 1828).

Janin, Jules-Gabriel. *Critique dramatique. La Comédie.* Vol. 6 of *Oeuvres diverses.* Ed. Albert de La Fizelière, 12 vols. (Paris: Librairie des bibliophiles, 1876–83).

Jardin, André, and André-Jean Tudesq. *La France des notables*, 2 vols. [1973], trans. Elborg Forster as *Restoration & Reaction 1815–1848* (Cambridge: Cambridge University Press, 1983).

Johnson, Lee. *The Paintings of Eugène Delacroix*, 2 vols. (Oxford: Clarendon Press, 1981).

——. "Mazeppa in Giza: A Riddle Solved," *Burlington Magazine*, 125 (Aug. 1983), 491–94.

Johnson, W. McAllister. *French Lithography: The Restoration Salons 1817–1824* (exh. cat., Kingston, Ontario: Agnes Etherington Art Centre, University of Toronto, 1977).

Jouy [Victor-Joseph de] and [Antoine] Jay. *Salon d'Horace Vernet: Analyse historique et pittoresque des quarante-cinq tableaux exposés chez lui en 1822* (Paris: Ponthieu, 1822).

J. V. L. "Littérature étrangère. Mazeppa: A poem by lord Byron," *Lycée français, ou Mélanges de littérature et de critique*, 1 (1819), 160–67.

Krakovitch, Odile. *Hugo censuré: La Liberté au théâtre au XIXe siècle* (Paris: Calmann-Lévy, 1985).

Kroen, Sheryl. *Politics and Theater: The Crisis of Legitimacy in Restoration France, 1815–1830* (Berkeley and Los Angeles: University of California Press, 2000).

La Capra, Dominick. *Madame Bovary on Trial* (Ithaca, N.Y.: Cornell University Press, 1982).

Lamartine, Alphonse de. *Lettre de M. Alphonse de Lamartine à M. Casimir Delavigne, qui lui avait envoyé son Ecole des vieillards* (Paris: Urbain Cavel, 1824).

Lami. See Mosès.

Laqueur, Thomas W. "The Queen Caroline Affair: Politics as Art in the Reign of George
IV," *Journal of Modern History*, 54/3 (Sept. 1982), 417–66.

La Rochefoucauld, M. de, duc de Doudeauville [La Rochefoucauld-Doudeauville, Louis-
François-Sosthène de]. *Le Guide de la famille* (Paris: Garnier frères, 1847).

Laroche-Gisserot, Florence. "Pratiques de la dot en France au XIXe siècle," *Annales ESC*,
43/6 (Nov.–Dec. 1988), 1433–52.

Larousse, Pierre. *Grand Dictionnaire universel du XIXe siècle*, 17 vols. (Paris: Librairie
classique Larousse et Boyer, 1866–90).

Lascoumes, Pierre, Pierrette Poncela, and Pierre Lenoël. *Au Nom de l'ordre: Une
Histoire politique du code pénal* (Paris: Hachette, 1989).

Lavater, Jean-Gaspard [Johann Kaspar]. *La Physiognomonie, ou L'art de connaître les
hommes d'après les traits de leur physionomie* [1775–78], trans. H. Bacharach (Paris:
Delphica, 1979).

Leclère, Jacinthe. *Cadet Buteux à l'Ecole des vieillards: Pot-pourri en 5 actes précédé
d'un prologue* (Paris: Duvernois, 1824).

Le Goff, Jacques, and Jean-Claude Schmitt, eds. *Colloque sur le charivari: Actes de la
table ronde organisée à Paris (25–27 avril 1977 par l'Ecole des hautes études en
sciences sociales et le Centre national de la recherche scientifique)* (Paris: Mouton,
1981).

Le Hir, Marie-Pierre. "La Représentation de la famille dans le mélodrame du début du
dix-neuvième siècle de Pixérécourt à Ducange," *Nineteenth-Century French Studies*,
18 (Fall–Winter 1989–90), 15–24.

———. *Le Romantisme aux enchères: Ducange, Pixérécourt, Hugo* (Amsterdam: John
Benjamins, 1992).

———. "Victor Ducange," in Barbara T. Cooper, ed., *French Dramatists 1789–1914:
Dictionary of Literary Biography*, 192 (Detroit: Gale Research, 1998), 88–102.

Léopold and Cuvelier [Léopold A. Chandenson and Jean Cuvelier de Trie]. *Mazeppa,
ou Le Cheval tartare, mimodrame en trois actes, tiré de Lord Byron, par MM.
Léopold et Cuvelier, mis en scène par M. Franconi jeune, musique de M. Sergent,
représenté pour la première fois au Cirque de MM. Franconi, directeurs privilégiés du
roi* (Paris: Chez Bezou, 1825).

Le Pesant, Michel. "Documents inédits sur Géricault," *Revue de l'art*, 31 (1976), 73–81.

Leroux, Pierre [L-x]. "Littérature: Du style symbolique," *Le Globe: Recueil
philosophique, politique et littéraire*, 8 April 1829, 220–23.

Le Roux de Lincy, Antoine. *Le Livre des proverbes français, précédé de recherches
historiques sur les proverbes français et leur emploi dans la littérature du moyen âge
et de la renaissance*, 2 vols. (Paris: Adolphe Delahays, rev. 2/1859).

Lévy, Claude, and Louis Henry. "Ducs et pairs sous l'ancien régime: Caractéristiques
démographiques d'une caste," *Population: Revue de l'Institut national d'études démographiques*, 15 (Oct.–Dec. 1960), 807–30.

Levy, Darline Gay, Harriet Branson Applewhite, and Mary Durham Johnson. *Women
in Revolutionary Paris 1789–1795* (Urbana: University of Illinois Press, 1979).

Lhéritier, Andrée. *Les Physiologies* (Paris: Université de Paris, Institut français de presse,
1958).

———. *Les Physiologies 1840–1845: Bibliographie descriptive* (Paris: Service international de microfilms, 1966).

Liedtke, Walter. *The Royal Horse and Rider: Painting, Sculpture and Horsemanship
1500–1800* (New York: Abaris Books and Metropolitan Museum of Art, 1989).

London: British Museum. See under "Official Publications and Inventories."

London: Tate Gallery, *The Romantic Movement* (exh. cat., Arts Council of Great Britain, 1959).

Los Angeles: Grunewald Center for the Graphic Arts, University of California, *French Caricature and the French Revolution 1789–1799* (exh. cat., 1988).

Lucas, Hippolyte. "La Femme adultère," in *Les Français peints par eux-mêmes*, 8 vols. (Paris: L. Curmer, 1840–42), 3, 265–72.

Lynch, Katherine A. *Family, Class, and Ideology in Early Industrial France: Social Policy and the Working-Class Family, 1825–1848* (Madison: University of Wisconsin Press, 1988).

Lyons, Martyn. "New Readers in the Nineteenth Century: Women, Children, Workers," in Guglielmo Cavallo and Roger Chartier, eds., *A History of Reading in the West*, trans Lydia G. Cochrane (Cambridge: Polity Press, 1999), 313–44.

Mainardi, Patricia. "Impertinent Questions," *French Historical Studies*, 19/2 (Fall 1995), 399–414.

———. "Husbands, Wives and Lovers: *Mazeppa*, or Marriage and Its Discontents in Nineteenth-Century France," in Régis Michel, ed., *Géricault*, 2 vols. (Paris: La Documentation française, 1996), 1, 273–92, 312–17.

———. "Why is Caricature Funny?" *Persistence of Vision*, 14 (1997), 8–24.

———. "Mazeppa," *Word & Image*, 16/4 (Oct.–Dec. 2000), 335–51.

Manning, Clarence A. *Hetman of the Ukraine: Ivan Mazeppa* (New York: Bookman, 1957).

Marchand, Leslie A. *Byron: A Biography*, 3 vols. (New York: Alfred A. Knopf, 1957).

———, ed. *Byron's Letters and Journals*, 12 vols. (Cambridge, Mass.: Harvard University Press, 1973–82).

Marie, Aristide. *Le Peintre poète Louis Boulanger* (Paris: H. Floury, 1925).

Marshall, William H. "A Reading of Byron's 'Mazeppa,'" *Modern Language Notes*, 76 (Feb. 1961), 120–24.

Martin-Fugier, Anne. *La Vie élégante ou la formation du tout-Paris 1815–1848* (Paris: Fayard, 1990).

Matlock, Jann. "The Limits of Reformism: The Novel, Censorship and the Politics of Adultery in Nineteenth-Century France." in *Cultural Institutions of the Novel*, ed. Deidre Lynch and William B. Warner (Durham, N.C.: Duke University Press, 1996), 335–68.

Maza, Sarah. *Private Lives and Public Affairs: The Causes Célèbres of Prerevolutionary France* (Berkeley and Los Angeles: University of California Press, 1993).

Mazères, Edouard-Joseph-Ennemond and Adolphe-Joseph-Simonis Empis, *La Mère et la fille*. Paris: Boule [1830].

McBride, Theresa. "Public Authority and Private Lives: Divorce after the French Revolution," *French Historical Studies*, 17/3 (Spring 1992), 747–68.

Mehta, Binita. "Jean-François-Casimir Delavigne," in Barbara T. Cooper, ed., *French Dramatists 1789–1914: Dictionary of Literary Biography*, 192 (Detroit: Gale Research, 1998), 65–70.

Mellinkoff, Ruth. "Riding Backwards: Theme of Humiliation and Symbol of Evil," *Viator: Medieval and Renaissance Studies*, 4 (1973), 153–76.

Melot, Michel. "La Mauvaise Mère: Etude d'un thème romantique dans l'estampe et la littérature," *Gazette des beaux-arts* (March 1972), 167–76.

Mespoulet, Marguerite. *Images et romans: Parenté des estampes et du roman réaliste de 1815 à 1865* (Paris: Belles Lettres, 1939).

Michel, Régis, ed. *Géricault*, 2 vols. (Paris: La Documentation française, 1996).

Milner, Henry M. *Mazeppa: A Romantic Drama in Three Acts, Dramatised from Lord Byron's Poem* (London: John Cumberland [?1831]).

Mosès, J.-M. [Lami]. *L'Art de rendre les femmes fidèles et de ne pas être trompé par elles: A l'usage des maris et des amans. Enseigné en cinq leçons et orné d'une gravure, par Lami* (Paris: Librairie française et étrangère, 1828).

———. *L'Art de se faire aimer des femmes et de se conduire dans le monde, ou Conseils aux hommes* (Paris: rue des filles Saint-Thomas, no. 5 [1822]).

Mouilleseaux, Jean-Pierre. *Mazeppa: Variations sur un thème romantique* (exh. cat., Rouen: Musée des beaux-arts, 1978).

Mulliez, J. "La Volonté d'un homme," in Jean Delumeau and Daniel Roche, eds., *Histoire des pères et de la paternité* (Paris: Larousse-HER, rev. 2000), 289–327.

Musset, Alfred de. *La Confession d'un enfant du siècle* [1836] (Paris: A. Colin, 1962); trans. as *Confession of a Child of the Century* (New York: Current Literature Publishing Company, 1910).

Nesci, Catherine. *La Femme mode d'emploi: Balzac, de la "Physiologie du mariage" à "La Comédie humaine"* (Lexington, Ky.: French Forum, 1992).

Nodier, Charles. *Mélanges de littérature et de critique*, ed. Alexandre Barginet, 2 vols. (Paris: Raymond, 1820).

Origo, Iris. *The Last Attachment: The Story of Byron and Teresa Guiccioli as Told in Their Unpublished Letters and Other Family Papers* (New York: Charles Scribner's Sons, 1949).

Ourliac, Paul, and J. de Malafosse. *Histoire du droit privé*, 3 vols. (Paris: PUF, 1968).

Overton, Bill. *The Novel of Female Adultery: Love and Gender in Continental European Fiction, 1830–1900* (New York: St. Martin's Press, 1996).

P., comte de. *L'Art de se faire aimer de sa femme* (Paris: Delaunay, 1823).

Pain, Joseph-Marie, and C. de Beauregard. *Nouveau tableaux de Paris, ou Observations sur les moeurs et usages des Parisiens au commencement du XIXe siècle*, 2 vols. (Paris: Pillet-aîné, 1828).

Le Palais-Royal, ou les filles en bonne fortune (Paris: Bocquet, 1815).

Parent-Duchâtelet, Alexandre J.-B. *De la prostitution dans la ville de Paris* [1836], ed. Alain Corbin as *La Prostitution à Paris au XIXe siècle* (Paris: Seuil, 1981).

Parent-Lardeur, Françoise. *Lire à Paris au temps de Balzac: Les Cabinets de lecture à Paris 1815–1830* (Paris: Ecole des hautes études en sciences sociales, 1981).

Paris: *Explication des ouvrages de peinture, sculpture, gravure, lithographie et architecture des artistes vivants [. . .]* (Salon exh. cats., 1673–1881).

Paris: Galerie Lebrun, *Exposition des ouvrages de peintures exposés au profit des Grecs: Galerie Lebrun, rue du Gros-Chênet* (exh. cat., Paris: Didot, 1826).

Paris: Grand Palais, *Géricault* (exh. cat., 1991).

Paris: Grand Palais; Detroit Institute of Arts; New York, Metropolitan Museum of Art, *French Painting 1774–1830: The Age of Revolution* (exh. cat., 1974–75).

Paris: Maison Renan-Scheffer, Musée de la vie romantique, *Lord Byron: une vie romantique 1788–1824* (exh. cat., 1988).

Paris: Musée du Louvre, *Graveurs français de la seconde moitié du XVIIIe siècle* (exh. cat., 1985).

Pariset, Madame. *Manuel de la maîtresse de maison, ou Lettres sur l'économie domestique* (Paris: Audot, 1821).

Pasek, Jan Chrysostome [Chryzostom]. *Les Mémoires de Jean Chrysostome Pasek, gentilhomme polonais 1656–1688*, trans. and ed. Paul Cazin (Paris: Les Belles-lettres, n.d.).

Payne, John Howard. *Mazeppa, or The Wild Horse of Tartary*, in *Trial Without Jury and Other Plays by John Howard Payne*, ed. Codman Hislop and W. R. Richardson (Princeton: Princeton University Press, 1940), 163–204.

Pedley, Mary. "Gentlemen Abroad: Jeffreys and Sayer in Paris," *The Map Collector*, no. 37, Dec. 1986, 20–23.

Pendle, Karen. *Eugene Scribe and French Opera in the 19th Century* (Ann Arbor: UMI, 1979).

Phillips, Roderick. *Putting Asunder: A History of Divorce in Western Society* (Cambridge: Cambridge University Press, 1988).

Picard, Louis-Benoît and Edouard-Joseph-Ennemond Mazères. *Héritage et mariage* (Paris: A. Leroux & C. Chantpie, 1826).

Pichot, Amédée. "Essai sur le génie et le caractère de lord Byron," in *Oeuvres de lord Byron [. . .] précédée d'une notice sur lord Byron par Charles Nodier*, trans. Pichot, 8 vols. (Paris: Ladvocat, rev. 4/1822–25), 1, i–cxlix.

Pigoreau, Alexandre-Nicolas. "Notes des ouvrages à supprimer des cabinets de lecture," *La Petite Bibliographie biographico-romancière: Onzième supplément* (Paris: Pigoreau, 1825).

Pius VIII, Pope. "Lettre encyclique de notre saint père le pape Pie VIII à tous les patriarches, primats, archevêques et évêques," *Ami de la religion et du roi*, 61/1566 (12 Aug. 1829).

Planche, Gustave. *Portraits littéraires* [1836], 2 vols. (Paris: Charpentier, 3/1853).

Ponteil, Félix. *Les Institutions de la France de 1814 à 1870* (Paris: PUF, 1966).

Posner, Donald. "The Swinging Women of Watteau and Fragonard," *Art Bulletin*, 64/1 (March 1982), 75–88.

Pothier, Robert-Joseph. *Oeuvres complètes de Pothier*, ed. Saint-Albin Berville, 26 vols. (Paris: Thomine & Fortic, 1821–24), 10: *Traité du contrat de mariage, de la puissance du mari*.

Pouthas, Charles H. *La Population française pendant la première moitié du XIXe siècle* (Paris: PUF, 1956).

Pradel, Eugène de. *L'Art de se faire aimer de son mari, à l'usage des demoiselles à marier* (Paris: Bailleul aîné, 1823).

Prioult, Albert-Pierre. *Balzac avant la "Comédie humaine" (1818–1829): Contribution à l'étude de la genèse de son oeuvre* (Paris: Georges Courville, 1936).

Prudhomme, Louis-Marie. [P. L. P.] *Idées du génie et de l'héroïsme des femmes: De la conduite des maris. Des écueils de la beauté et des passions*, 2 vols. (Paris: Achille Desauges, 1826).

Przybos, Julia. *L'Entreprise mélodramatique* (Paris: Corti, 1987).

Raisson, Horace [-Napoléon]. *Code civil: Manuel complet de la politesse, du ton, des manières de la bonne compagnie, contenant les lois, règles, applications, et exemples de l'art de se présenter et de se conduire dans le monde par l'auteur du Code gourmand* (Paris: J.-P. Roret, rev. 2/1828).

——. *Code de la cravate: Traité complet des formes, de la mise, des couleurs de la cravate; Ouvrage indispensable à tout homme de bon ton* (Paris: Audin, 1828).

——. *Code conjugal, contenant les lois, règles, applications et exemples de l'art de se bien marier et d'être heureux en ménage* (Paris: J.-P. Roret, 1829).

——. *Code des boudoirs, ou Moyens adroits de faire des conquêtes, de devenir bientôt heureux en amour, et d'acquérir un certain aplomb auprès des femmes, par un jurisconsulte de Cythère* (Paris: Bréaute, 1829).

——. *Code galant, ou Art de conter fleurette* (Paris: Charpentier, 1829).

——. *Code pénal: Manuel complet des honnêtes gens, contenant les lois, règles, appli-*

cations et exemples de l'art de mettre sa fortune, sa bourse et sa réputation à l'abri de toutes les tentatives (Paris: J.-P. Roret, rev. 3/1829).

Raisson, Horace, and Honoré de Balzac. *Code des gens honnêtes, ou l'Art de ne pas être dupe des fripons* (Paris: J.-N. Barba, 1825).

Rand, Richard, ed. *Intimate Encounters: Love and Domesticity in Eighteenth-Century France* (exh. cat., Hood Museum of Art, Dartmouth College; Princeton, N.J.: Princeton University Press, 1997).

Rawson, Beryl, ed. *The Family in Ancient Rome: New Perspectives* (Ithaca, N.Y.: Cornell University Press, 1986).

Reddy, William R. "Marriage, Honor, and the Public Sphere in Post-Revolutionary France: *Séparations de corps*, 1815–1848," *Journal of Modern History*, 65/3 (Sept. 1993), 437–72.

———. *The Invisible Code: Honor and Sentiment in Postrevolutionary France, 1814–1848* (Berkeley and Los Angeles: University of California Press, 1997).

Rémusat, Claire-Elisabeth-Jeanne. *Essai sur l'éducation des femmes* (Paris: Ladvocat, 1824).

Rey-Flaud, Henri. *Le Charivari: Les Rituels fondamentaux de la sexualité* (Paris: Payot, 1985).

Richardson, Joanna. *The Disastrous Marriage: A Study of George IV and Caroline of Brunswick* (London: Jonathan Cape, 1960).

———. *The Courtesans: The Demi-monde in Nineteenth-Century France* (Cleveland: World Publishing, 1967).

Ripa, Cesare. *Baroque and Rococo Pictorial Imagery: The 1758–60 Hertel Edition of Ripa's Iconolgia*, ed. Edward A. Maser (New York: Dover, 1971).

Robaut, Alfred. *L'Oeuvre complet de Eugène Delacroix* [1885] (New York: Da Capo, 1969).

Robb, Graham. *Victor Hugo: A Biography* (New York: W. W. Norton, 1997).

Rome: Académie de France à Rome; Paris: Ecole nationale supérieure des beaux-arts. *Horace Vernet (1789–1863)* (Exh. cat., 1980).

Ronsin, Francis. *Le Contrat sentimental: Débats sur le mariage, l'amour, le divorce, de l'Ancien Régime à la Restauration* (Paris: Aubier, 1990).

———. *Les Divorciaires: Affrontements politiques et conceptions du mariage dans la France du XIXe siècle* (Paris: Aubier, 1992).

Rougement, Denis de. *Amour et l'Occident* [1939], trans. Montgomery Belgion as *Love in the Western World* (New York: Harcourt Brace, 1940).

Saint-Hilaire, Emile Marco de. *L'Art de mettre sa cravate de toutes les manières connues et usitées, enseigné et démontré en seize leçons, précédé de l'histoire complète de la cravate, par le baron Emile de L'Empesé* (Paris: Librairie universelle, 1827).

———. *L'Art de payer ses dettes et de satisfaire ses créanciers sans débourser un sou, enseigné en dix leçons* (Paris: Librairie universelle, 2/1827).

Saint-Just, Louis-Antoine-Léon de. "Esprit de la Révolution et de la Constitution de France" [1791], in his *Théorie politique*, ed. Alain Liénard (Paris: Seuil, 1976).

Sand, George. *Indiana*. 2 vols. (Paris: J.-P. Roret & H. Dupuy, 1832); ed. Béatrice Didier (Paris: Gallimard, 1984); trans. George Burnham Ives (Chicago: Academy Chicago, 1978).

———. *Lettres d'un voyageur* (Paris: Michel Lévy, 1869).

———. *Correspondance*, ed. Georges Lubin, 25 vols. (Paris: Classiques Garnier, 1964–91).

S***, vicomte de. See Cuisin, J.-P.-R.

Schiebinger, Londa. "Why Mammals are Called Mammals: Gender Politics in

Eighteenth-Century Natural History," *American Historical Review*, 98/2 (April 1993), 382–41.

Schmitt-Pantel, Pauline. "L'Ane, l'adultère et la cité," in Le Goff and Schmitt, eds., *Colloque sur le charivari* (Paris: Mouton, 1981), 117–22.

Schor, Naomi. *Reading in Detail* (New York: Methuen, 1987).

Schroder, Anne L. "Genre Prints in Eighteenth-Century France: Production, Market, and Audience," in Richard Rand, ed., *Intimate Encounters* (Princeton: Princeton University Press), 69–86.

Schultze, Jürgen N. *Art of Nineteenth-Century Europe*, trans. Barbara Forryan (New York: Harry N. Abrams, 1979).

Scribe, Eugène, with Mélesville [Anne-Honoré-Joseph Duveyrier]. *La Demoiselle à marier, ou La Première Entrevue: Comédie-vaudeville en un acte, par MM. Scribe et Mélesville* (Paris: Pollet, 1826).

———. *Le Mariage d'argent, comédie en cinq actes* (Paris: Didot l'aîné [1827]).

———. *Malvina, ou Un Mariage d'inclination: Comédie-vaudeville en deux actes* (Paris: Librairie théâtrale, 1828).

Scribe, Eugène, with Antoine-François Varner. *Le Mariage de raison, comédie-vaudeville en deux actes par MM. Scribe et Varner: Paris, Théâtre de Madame, 10 octobre 1826* (Paris: Pollet, 1826).

Sedgwick, Eve Kosofsky. *Between Men: English Literature and Male Homosocial Desire* (New York: Columbia University Press, 1985).

Segal, Naomi. *The Adulteress's Child: Authorship and Desire in the Nineteenth-Century Novel* (Cambridge: Polity Press, 1992).

Segalen, Martine. *Amours et mariages de l'ancien France* (Paris: Berger-Levrault, 1981).

Ségur, Joseph-Alexandre. *Les Femmes, leur condition et leur influence dans l'ordre sociale chez les différens peuples anciens et modernes*, 4 vols. (Paris: Thiérot & Belin, 1825).

Senancour, Etienne de. *De l'amour, selon les lois primordiales et selon les convenances des sociétés modernes* [1806], 2 vols. (Paris: Vieilh de Boisjoslin, rev. 3/1829).

Shorter, Edward. *The Making of the Modern Family* (New York: Basic Books, 1975).

Siegfried, Susan L. *The Art of Louis-Léopold Boilly: Modern Life in Napoleonic France* (New Haven: Yale University Press, 1995).

Smith, E. A. *A Queen on Trial: The Affair of Queen Caroline* (Dover, N.H.: Alan Sutton, 1993).

Solomon-Godeau, Abigail. *Male Trouble: A Crisis in Representation* (London: Thames & Hudson, 1997).

Soubiranne. See [Factum: Joseph-François Soubiranne] under "Official Publications and Inventories."

Soubiranne, Joseph-François. *Le Chaos: Réponse au plus grand des Hugolins* (Paris: Tous les librairies, 1853).

Soubiranne de La Motte, P. *A propos de la crise financière: La Barque de L'avenir. Délégations commerciales* (Marseilles: Blanc & Bernard, 1882).

Spitzer, Alan B. *The French Generation of 1820* (Princeton: Princeton University Press, 1987).

Stendhal [Henri Beyle]. *De l'amour* [1822], ed. Henri Martineau (Paris: Garnier frères, 1959).

———. *Le Rouge et le noir: Chronique du XIXe siècle* [1830], ed. Béatrice Didier (Paris: Gallimard, 1972); trans. Lloyd C. Parks as *The Red and the Black* (New York: Signet, New American Library, 1970).

Stewart, Alison. *Unequal Lovers: A Study of Unequal Couples in Northern Art* (New York: Abaris, 1979).

Stewart, Philip. *Engraven Desire: Eros, Image, and Text in the French Eighteenth Century* (Durham, N.C.: Duke University Press, 1992).

Stone, Lawrence. *The Family, Sex and Marriage in England, 1500–1800* (New York: Harper & Row, 1977).

Swart, Koenraad W. "'Individualism' in the Mid-Nineteenth Century (1826–1860)," *Journal of the History of Ideas*, 23 (Jan.–March 1962), 77–90.

Tanner, Tony. *Adultery in the Novel: Contract and Transgression* (Baltimore: Johns Hopkins University Press, 1979).

Théry, Irène, and Christian Biet, eds. *La Famille, la loi, l'état: De la Révolution au Code civil* (Paris: Imprimerie nationale, 1989).

Thibault-Laurent, Gérard. *La Première Introduction du divorce en France sous la Révolution et l'Empire (1792–1816)* (thèse pour le doctorat, Clermont-Ferrand: Imprimerie Moderne, 1938).

Thomasseau, Jean-Marie. "Le Mélodrame et la censure sous le premier Empire et la Restauration," (*Revue des sciences humaines*, 162 (April–June 1976), 171–82.

———. *Le Mélodrame* (Paris: PUF, 1984).

Toledano, A. D. *La Vie de famille sous la Restauration et la monarchie de Juillet* (Paris: Alvin Michel, 1943).

Traer, James F. "The French Family Court," *History*, 59 (June 1974), 211–28.

———. *Marriage and the Family in Eighteenth-Century France* (Ithaca, N.Y.: Cornell University Press, 1980).

Tristan, Frédérick. *Le Monde à l'envers* (Paris: Hachette, 1980).

Twyman, Michael. *Lithography 1800–1850* (Oxford: Oxford University Press, 1970).

Ubersfeld, Anne. *Le Roman d'Hernani* (Paris: Mercure de France & Comédie-Française, 1985).

Van de Walle, Etienne. *The Female Population of France in the Nineteenth Century* (Princeton: Princeton University Press, 1974).

[Vergnaud, Armand-Denis]. *Examen du Salon de 1827: Seconde Partie, novembre et décembre* (Paris: J.-P. Roret, 1828).

Vigny, Alfred de [A. de V.]. "Littérature anglaise: Oeuvres complètes de lord Byron," *Conservateur littéraire*, 3 (Dec. 1820), 212–16.

Viscusi, Robert. "Coining." *Differentia: Review of Italian Thought*, 2 (Spring 1988), 9–42.

Voltaire [François-Marie Arouet]. *Histoire de Charles XII, roi de Suède* [1731] (Amsterdam: Libraires associés, 1805).

———. "L'Education des filles" [1761], in *Oeuvres complètes de Voltaire*, 52 vols. (Paris: Garnier frères, 1877–85), 24: *Mélanges III*, 284–87.

———. "Adultère," *Questions sur l'Encyclopédie, par des amateurs*, 6 vols. (1775), 1, 60–71.

Waller, Margaret. "*Cherchez la Femme*: Male Malady and Narrative Politics in the French Romantic Novel," *PMLA* [Publications of the Modern Language Association of America], 104/2 (March 1989), 141–51.

Waresquiel, Emmanuel de, and Benoît Yvert, *Histoire de la Restauration, 1814–1830: Naissance de la France moderne* (Paris: Librairie académique Perrin, 1996).

W. C. "Critical Remarks on New Publications: Mazeppa, a Poem by Lord Byron," *The New Monthly Magazine*, 12 (1 Aug. 1819), 64–67.

Wechsler, Judith. *A Human Comedy: Physiognomy and Caricature in 19th Century Paris* (Chicago: University of Chicago Press, 1982).

Westall, Richard. [*Illustrations of Lord Byron's Poetry*] (London: John Murray, 1819).

White, Nicholas. *The Family in Crisis in Late Nineteenth-Century French Fiction* (Cambridge: Cambridge University Press, 1999).

White, Nicholas, and Naomi Segal. *Scarlet Letters: Fictions of Adultery from Antiquity to the 1990s* (London: Macmillan, 1997).

Wittmann, Reinhard. "Was There a Reading Revolution at the End of the Eighteenth Century?," in Guglielmo Cavallo and Roger Chartier, eds., *A History of Reading in the West*, trans. Lydia G. Cochrane (Cambridge: Polity Press, 1999), 284–312.

Wood, J. S. "Sondages dans le roman français du point de vue social (1789–1830)," in *Revue d'histoire littéraire de la France*, 54/1 (Jan.–March 1954), 33–48.

Wren, Keith. *Hugo: Hernani and Ruy Blas* (London: Grant & Cutler, 1982).

Yon, Jean-Claude. *Eugène Scribe: La Fortune et la liberté* (Paris: A.-G. Nizet, 2000).

Zola, Emile. "L'Adultère dans la bourgeoisie," *Le Figaro*, 28 Feb. 1881.

Index